# Marriage Licenses of Frederick County Maryland

## 1778-1810

### Second Edition

*Margaret E. Myers*

HERITAGE BOOKS
2007

# HERITAGE BOOKS
*AN IMPRINT OF HERITAGE BOOKS, INC.*

Books, CDs, and more—Worldwide

For our listing of thousands of titles see our website
at
www.HeritageBooks.com

Published 2007 by
HERITAGE BOOKS, INC.
Publishing Division
65 East Main Street
Westminster, Maryland 21157-5026

Copyright © 1994 Margaret E. Myers

Other books by the author:

*Marriage Licenses of Frederick County, Maryland: 1811–1840*

*Marriage Licenses of Frederick County, Maryland: 1841–1865*

*Records of the Evangelical Lutheran Church at Union Chapel, Liberty District, Frederick County, Maryland, 1864–1945, 1946–1947; Woodsboro, Maryland, January 1, 1862–September 4, 1885; Frederick, Frederick County, Maryland, Births and Baptisms October 21, 1848–December 26, 1885*

All rights reserved. No part of this book may be reproduced or transmitted in any form or by any means, electronic or mechanical, including photocopying, recording or by any information storage and retrieval system without written permission from the author, except for the inclusion of brief quotations in a review.

International Standard Book Number: 978-1-58549-097-0

## INTRODUCTION

These entries were taken from the records of marriage licenses held at the courthouse in Frederick, Maryland. The courthouse records contain only the dates of the license, and names of the bride and groom. There are two sections, one for the groom and one for the bride. Each is arranged alphabetically by the first letter of the surname and first letter of the given name. This compilation is based on the male section only. This section was completely alphabetized by male and combined with a copy of the same section rearranged and alphabetized by female. The "female" section of the courthouse records was not used except to resolve a few discrepancies.

The courthouse records themselves were copied some time ago from the original Books, 1, 2, 3 and 4 which are now at the State Archives, Annapolis, Maryland. (These had been presumed lost by this compiler until recently when it was learned that they had been held at the warehouse, until the opening of the new Hall of Records where they are now available for examination.)

All duplicate entries have been retained.

Subsequent volumes will be available in the near future.

This second edition includes entries that were omitted in the first edition. Except for two entries the omissions consisted of all those surnames which began with Wa and up to Welsh, Henry. Errata sheets are available for the first edition on request to the publisher, Family Line Publications, 13405 Collingwood Terrace, Silver Spring, Maryland 20904.

```
Jun 21 1778 ---, Mary A. to Stoker, Michael
Apr  6 1805 Abbott, Margaret to Hampton, John
Oct 23 1790 Abell, John to Thomas, Sarah
Jul 25 1778 Abey, Peter to Heffner, Elizabeth
Jun  5 1780 Able, John to Declve, Magdaline
Jan  1 1791 Abricks, Hermanus to Liggat, Jane
Feb 21 1794 Abricks, West to Peyton, Ann
Dec 24 1802 Abright, Mary to Leatch, Edward
Apr 20 1805 Ackers, Sarah to Condon, James
Apr 23 1807 Adair, Sarah to Bigham, David
Dec 15 1792 Adams, Abraham to Shipley, Rebecca
Apr 14 1798 Adams, Abraham to Albaugh, Mary
Apr 15 1793 Adams, James to Meredith, Lyda
Jan 19 1791 Adams, Joseph to Curran, Biddy
Aug 23 1806 Adams, Magdalena to Fout, William
Jun 18 1791 Adams, Margaret to Albaugh, Abraham
May  5 1800 Adams, Margaret to Staley, John
Jan 28 1786 Adams, Mary to Bare, George
May 20 1802 Adams, Mary to Cress, Jacob
Feb 23 1778 Adams, Mary to Simmons, Thomas
Dec 20 1788 Adams, Mary to Spangler, John
Sep  5 1782 Adams, Mary Ann to Myers, John
May  3 1801 Adams, Robert to Cordell, Lucy
Nov 23 1809 Adams, William to Myers, Catharine
Sep 13 1786 Adamson, Sophia to Doyle, John
Apr 15 1786 Adamson, Susanna to Madera, Nicholas
Aug 14 1779 Addison, Robert to Darlon, Remela
Nov 27 1783 Ader, John to Anst, Sarah
Apr 13 1799 Adkins, Priscilla to Pearl, James
Jul 20 1793 Adkins, William to King, Elizabeth
Nov  6 1790 Adlum, Catherine to Culp, Henry
Dec 13 1805 Adlum, John to Adlum, Margaret
Jun  7 1806 Adlum, John, Jr. to Cooley, Mary
Dec 13 1805 Adlum, Margaret to Adlum, John
Jan  4 1795 Adlum, Mary to Crabb, Thomas
Jan  5 1805 Ahalt, Catherine to Easterday, Conrad
Feb 22 1805 Ahalt, Henry to Beigler, Madelena
Sep 18 1802 Aider, George to Albaugh, Susannah
Apr 17 1781 Aiter, Abraham to Reigh, Elizabeth
Apr 12 1797 Aiter, David to Stoner, Elizabeth
Aug 26 1783 Akin, Elizabeth to Shurr, John
Jun 18 1791 Albaugh, Abraham to Adams, Margaret
Oct 26 1779 Albaugh, Anna to Iser, Philip
Mar 18 1799 Albaugh, Catherine to Smith, Peter
Sep  1 1808 Albaugh, Catherine to Wagner, John
Jan 23 1800 Albaugh, Daniel to Collins, Senah
May 25 1809 Albaugh, David to Myers, Sarah
Mar 16 1782 Albaugh, David to Harter, Mary
Oct  4 1800 Albaugh, Elizabeth to Smith, John
Oct  4 1790 Albaugh, Elizabeth to Smith, Peter
Nov  9 1799 Albaugh, Eve to Creger, Peter
Jun 20 1798 Albaugh, George to Springer, Catharine
Jan 26 1793 Albaugh, John to Smith, Mary
Apr 14 1798 Albaugh, Mary to Adams, Abraham
Feb 12 1785 Albaugh, Mary to Beamer, Adam
```

```
Jun 30 1789 Albaugh, Mary to Etsler, Daniel
Jan  6 1809 Albaugh, Peter to Culler, Barbara
Jun  9 1793 Albaugh, Samuel to Whiteneck, Hannah
Sep  3 1808 Albaugh, Sarah to Curtis, Henry
Dec 28 1808 Albaugh, Sarah to Ridgely, Frederick
Sep 18 1802 Albaugh, Susannah to Aider, George
Mar 19 1803 Albaugh, William to Weaver, Mary
Mar 23 1804 Albaugh, William to Rodrock, Susanna
Mar 24 1801 Albert, Christian to Powell, Elizabeth
Jan  8 1781 Albright, Henry to Swawin, Anna Margaret
Nov 14 1783 Aldridge, John to Lakin, Mary
Feb  4 1809 Aldridge, Rebecca to Conroy, Andrew
Dec 24 1793 Aldridge, Sarah to Sheets, Martin
Feb  4 1791 Aldridge, Thomas to Blackburn, Mary
Aug 11 1787 Aldrige, Ann to Beall, Robert
Oct 12 1778 Ale, Daniel to Keller, Madelene
Jul 10 1793 Alexander, Ann to Holtzman, John
Dec 26 1799 Alexander, Ashton to Thomas, Catharine
Dec 26 1799 Alexander, Ashton to Thomas, Catharine Hanson
May 26 1808 Alexander, Catherine to Long, John
Dec 23 1808 Alexander, Elizabeth to Feet, Henry
Jun 30 1808 Alexander, Elizabeth to Koontz, Jacob
Oct  3 1809 Alexander, Isabella to Wharton, James
Dec 19 1799 Alexander, Jane to Armstrong, Joseph
Dec 23 1803 Alexander, Mary to Weaver, Philip
Mar 16 1809 Alexander, William to Clingan, Nancy
Aug 19 1780 Alfort, John to Ashman, Margaret
Nov 18 1803 Allder, John to Goodley, Polly
Mar 10 1806 Alldridge, John to Beall, Harriet
Sep 15 1802 Allen, James to Philpott, Martha
Jun  8 1778 Allen, Philip to Grimes, Jane
Nov 10 1786 Allen, Elizabeth to Jones, Richard
Jun  4 1809 Allex, Catherine to Crumpvine, Jacob
Jun 15 1797 Allison, George to Zimmerman, Christena
Aug 14 1807 Allison, Mary to Duvall, Samuel
Dec 27 1797 Allison, Mary to Wigley, George
Feb 17 1800 Allison, Sarah to Hoover, John
Jul 29 1809 Allnutt, Susanna H. to Dawson, Thomas
Dec  8 1783 Ambrose, Catharine to Snook, John
Aug  1 1794 Ambrose, John to Lynn, Catharine
May  2 1796 Ambrose, Mary to Swain, Jacob
May  3 1797 Amelong, Frederick M. to Furnival, Louise Sophia
Sep 20 1785 Amelung, Fredericka to Keener, Andrew
Aug  9 1797 Amelung, Sophia Christine Dorothea to Valkmon, Peter
            Adolphus
Apr  8 1797 Amerson, Charles to Crampton, Philipena
Aug 21 1810 Anchors, Samuel to Harrison, Anne
Mar 20 1779 Ancrum, Jacob to Clark, Elizabeth
Apr 25 1808 Anders, Anne to Barnhart, William
Mar 17 1796 Anderson, Ann to Myers, John
Dec  8 1807 Anderson, Anne to Powers, Michael
Sep 17 1803 Anderson, Dorcas to Weiy, David
Jul 23 1810 Anderson, Edward H. (Dr.) to Morris, Catharine
            Precilla
Apr 14 1807 Anderson, Elizabeth to Cromwell, Joseph M.
Feb 17 1802 Anderson, Elizabeth to French, Otho
```

```
Dec 18 1809 Anderson, Francis to Jones, Susanna
Dec 21 1802 Anderson, Harriet to Worthington, William, Jr.
Jan 13 1802 Anderson, Hugh to Boyd, Mary
Apr 10 1797 Anderson, John to Ship, Elizabeth
Jun 12 1779 Anderson, John to Loney, Catharine
Nov 26 1810 Anderson, Jonathan M. to Eater, Ann
Oct  5 1797 Anderson, Lucy to Gantt, Daniel
May 22 1806 Anderson, Mary to Tarman, Aquila
Mar 12 1796 Anderson, Robert to Brashears, Mary
Nov 24 1805 Anderson, Sally to Beatty, Mahlon
Sep 26 1778 Anderson, William to Brashears, Cavey
May 12 1796 Anderson, William to Thomas, Anna
Sep 26 1795 Andrew, Elizabeth to Hamilton, Robert
Oct 26 1802 Andrews, Charles to Mobley, Harriett
Aug 23 1809 Angleberger, George to Devilbiss, Margaret
May 14 1801 Angleberger, Margaret to Heffner, Jacob
Jul 21 1810 Angleberger, Mary to Frushour, John
Apr 25 1797 Angling, Permelia to Foy, Joseph
May 19 1795 Angus, Jemima to Conroy, Edward
Apr 30 1783 Ankrom, Aaron to Marley, Mary
May  4 1803 Annin, Samuel to Cross, Martha
Jan 12 1786 Ansell, Samuel to Graves, Priscilla
Nov 27 1783 Anst, Sarah to Ader, John
Jan  4 1794 Apollo, Lewis Benjamin to Starchberger, Polly
Feb 13 1796 Apollo, Lewis Benjamin to Slicker, Catharine
Mar 28 1807 Applebee, Joseph to Tobery, Elizabeth
Aug  7 1790 Appleby, Elizabeth to Conner, Lawrence
Aug  6 1808 Appler, David to Foacht, Rachel
Apr  7 1807 Appler, Peggy to Creager, George, Esq.
Jun  9 1800 Appold, Lewis Benjamin to Usher, Mary
Mar 28 1778 Archebald, Samuel to Cock, Catharine
Dec 19 1799 Armstrong, Joseph to Alexander, Jane
Nov 30 1803 Armstrong, Nelly to Bess, Michael
Oct 12 1778 Arnold, Ann to Gassaway, Ricahrd
Aug 22 1782 Arnold, Anthony to Leatherman, Francis
Nov 22 1781 Arnold, Catharine to Richards, John
Mar  1 1793 Arnold, David to Pearrie, Eleanor
Sep 27 1802 Arnold, Ephraim to Ensey, Eleanor
May 17 1802 Arnold, John to Morgan, Catharine
Jan 19 1801 Arnold, Jonathan to Sellman, Althea
Mar 23 1799 Arnold, Peter to Perry, Nancy
May  8 1783 Arnold, Rachel to Farver, John
Mar 30 1808 Arnold, Susanna to Ogg, William
May 11 1802 Arnsperger, Christopher to Fister, Catharine
Sep 14 1801 Arnsperger, John to Smith, Mary
Sep 26 1805 Arter, Elizabeth to Leather, George
May 28 1810 Arthur, Charles to Smith, Elizabeth
Nov 21 1806 Arthur, John to Weaver, Catharine
Jan 14 1809 Arthur, Margaret Ann to Shoemaker, Stephen
Apr 12 1779 Asbill, Mary to Cutelr Edw'd
Aug 16 1800 Asdell, Sally to Woodard, James
Jun  5 1784 Ashman, Henry to Moyer, Elizabeth
Aug 19 1780 Ashman, Margaret to Alfort, John
Oct  4 1779 Asque, John to Woolverton, Sarah
Feb 21 1785 Ater, Abraham to Reighe, Catharine
Mar 30 1799 Ater, Abraham to Ephlen, Charity
```

```
Jun 11 1791 Athein, Horatio to Showne, Mary
Jan 27 1798 Athey, Joseph to Wheeling, Mariah
Aug  4 1784 Atkins, Anna to Griffith, Wm.
Dec  4 1810 Atkins, Rachel to Bower, William F.
Sep  4 1797 Atwell, John to Lewis, Anne
Sep 29 1796 Atwood, Elizabeth to Green, William
Mar  9 1789 Aubert, Martin to Teterley, Catharine
Jan  3 1797 Auman, Catherine to Prill, Samuel
May 26 1803 Aury, Sarah to Erhart, Frederick
Oct 10 1799 Avalon, Philip to Conner, Elizabeth
Mar 14 1793 Avenpold, Jane to Ayton, Richard
Sep 29 1780 Aves, Ann to Hornblower, Wm.
Oct  3 1803 Awbry, Stilly to Bradon, Barteson
Feb 17 1806 Ayres, Daniel to Howard, Rebecca
Jul 28 1803 Ayton, Jane to Magruder, Edward
Mar 14 1793 Ayton, Richard to Avenpold, Jane

Jul  9 1803 Babylon, Peter to Barnhart, Catherine
Jun 21 1787 Badan, Mary to Harrison, Nathan
Apr  9 1808 Baer, Catherine to Getzendanner, Thomas
Jan 24 1789 Baer, John to Thomas, Mary
Nov 15 1808 Baer, John to Hoffman, Catherine
Jun  7 1783 Bagens, John to Whitenack, Catherine
Mar 14 1783 Bagerly, Sarah to Osborn, David
Jan  3 1791 Baggerly, Mary to Kile, Nicholas
Jun  4 1785 Baighle, Susannah to Ifert, Jeremiah
Sep 16 1805 Bail, Sarah to Lindsay, John
Feb 16 1809 Bail, Sophia to Mackley, Martin
Dec 17 1804 Bail, William to Kline, Elizabeth
Sep 16 1790 Bailey, Joseph to Hedges, Susana
Jan  3 1801 Bailey, Richard to Houseman, Catherine
Sep  2 1784 Bailey, William to Rachob, Mary
Jun 18 1796 Bailey, William to Ferrin, Phebe
Nov  6 1810 Bailey, William, Jr. to McDaniel, Sarah
Apr 12 1790 Bainbridge, Absalom to Beatty, Elizabeth
Sep 26 1781 Bainbridge, Catziah to Bainbridge, Edmond
Sep 26 1781 Bainbridge, Edmond to Bainbridge, Catziah
Nov  6 1779 Bair, Henry to Shellman, Eliz'th
Apr  1 1802 Baker, Adam to Hains, Mary
Sep 17 1794 Baker, Adam to Layman, Juliana
Aug  3 1807 Baker, Anne to Groshon, John
Feb  3 1803 Baker, Anne to Harvey, Seth
Nov 25 1790 Baker, Basil to Linch, Ann
Jun 13 1807 Baker, Brooke to Otto, Elizabeth
Mar 29 1789 Baker, Catharine to Baker, Frederick
Nov 15 1799 Baker, Catherine to Hoffert, Jacob
Jan 23 1805 Baker, Catherine to Lane, John
Aug 25 1783 Baker, Christian to Chreichbaum, Mary
Sep  9 1806 Baker, Christina to Motter, John
May 31 1803 Baker, Conrad to Frushour, Catharine
Feb 14 1810 Baker, Dorsey to Kinley, Elizabeth
Mar  7 1797 Baker, Elizabeth to Waters, Benjamin
Dec 12 1807 Baker, Elizbeth to Castle, Otho
Jan  9 1803 Baker, Eve to Crumpacker, Abraham
Jun 14 1797 Baker, Frederick to Buzzard, Susanna
```

```
Mar 29 1789 Baker, Frederick to Baker, Catharine
Apr 16 1800 Baker, Hannah to Getzendanner, Henry
Sep 15 1797 Baker, Henry to Coke, Precilla
Jun  4 1800 Baker, Henry to Phillips, Susanna
Apr 26 1810 Baker, Jacob to Coller, Catherine
Feb  1 1799 Baker, John to Harder, Polly
Dec  7 1799 Baker, Larkin to Mark, Margaret
Sep  8 1783 Baker, Mary to Geesee, Fred'k Henry
Dec 25 1793 Baker, Peggey to Duttero, Mr.
Jun 21 1789 Baker, Peter to Foy, Elizabeth
Feb 12 1799 Baker, Philip to Stoker, Margaret
Nov 10 1808 Baker, Philip to Repp, Elizabeth
Dec 23 1809 Baker, Philip to Stottlemier, Magdalene
Mar 23 1805 Baker, Rachel to Grabill, Moses
Dec 31 1779 Baker, Rosanna to Shover, Henry
Jan 18 1803 Baker, Silvanius to Clay, Anne
Apr 17 1802 Baker, Thomas to Possamun, Christina
Dec 14 1803 Baker, Thomas, Junr to Ramsour, Mary
Jan 29 1798 Baker, Walter to Richardson, Ursula
Nov 23 1802 Balding, John to Mcguffin, Jane
Nov 20 1802 Baldwin, Joseph to Francis, Elizabeth
Apr 18 1810 Baldwin, Nancy to Preston, Charles
Oct 15 1798 Baldwin, Pheby to Shoemaker, Abraham
May 16 1780 Baldwin, Ruth to Carrens, Thomas
Sep 26 1807 Baldwin, Susanna to Preston, Abraham
Jan  9 1808 Baldwin, Thomas to Pool, Basil
Mar 20 1809 Baldwin, Verlinda to Hopkins, Philip
Nov 27 1797 Bale, Elizabeth to Loeman, Mich'l
Oct  1 1796 Bale, John to Murry, Honor
Jun 26 1795 Bale, Lydia to Clancey, Roger
May 26 1784 Bale, Ruth to Taylor, Jesse
Dec 23 1801 Baley, Jane to Murphy, Samuel
Aug  7 1806 Ball, Catherine to Magnass, James
Mar 31 1779 Ball, Dan'l to Boyer, Catharine
Jan 15 1810 Ball, Horatio to Frazier, Rhoda
Feb 20 1779 Ball, James to Hinton, Rachel
Dec 14 1807 Ball, James to White, Mary
Nov 28 1804 Ball, Samuel to Crutchley, Rachel
Jan  9 1804 Ball, Teresa to Turner, Elie
Dec 19 1807 Ball, Vachel to Henry, Sarah
Feb  2 1796 Ballanger, Ann to Waters, Josiah
Sep  9 1786 Balsell, Christian to Yantz, Catharine
May  7 1782 Balser, John to Lydey, Elizabeth
Jul 30 1799 Balser, Susannah to Crist, John
Nov 21 1797 Baltin, Mary to Gordon, Joseph
May  9 1809 Baltzell, Catherine to Geesy, John
Jul 21 1797 Baltzell, Catherine to Hedges, Joseph
Nov 23 1799 Baltzell, Daniel to Kittinger, Susanna
Jul 10 1782 Baltzell, Elizabeth to Mahaney, Dan'l
Jun  7 1790 Baltzell, Elizabeth to Rice, Michael
May  6 1796 Baltzell, Jacob to Campbell, Anna
Aug 15 1801 Baltzell, Jacob to Meddert, Mary
Oct 15 1801 Baltzell, John to Pimmell, Elizabeth
Oct 27 1810 Baltzell, Margaret to McGowan, Terance
Sep 26 1804 Baltzell, Mary to Debrule, James C.
```

```
Aug 18 1809 Baltzell, Polly to Spoon, Elias
Mar 21 1805 Baltzell, Susanna to Main, John
Feb  2 1803 Baltzer, Elizabeth to Kingla, Joseph
May 24 1801 Baltzer, Louisa to Gray, Nathaniel
Jan 10 1787 Balzell, Jacob to Christ, Charity
Oct 13 1787 Bander, Cath. to Houser, Jacob
Apr 19 1809 Banister, Tena to Mealy, William
Jul 18 1789 Bankard, Abraham to Erb, Modelena
Jan 10 1792 Bankard, Esther to Hines, Patrick
Jun  9 1801 Bankard, Lawrence to Flegle, Mary
Sep 12 1810 Bankard, Mary to Herring, Frederick
Aug  9 1788 Bantz, Henry to Smith, Catherine
Jan 29 1798 Barber, Ann to Peak, John
Oct 30 1804 Barber, Permelia to Davis, John
Jan 28 1797 Barber, Samuel to Mockabee, Ann
May  6 1794 Barber, Sarah to Ward, John
Sep 27 1806 Bard, Jacob to Crist, Susanna
May  5 1778 Bardle, Ann to Beale, Benjamin
Aug 14 1790 Bare, Eve Margaret to Staley, Melchor
Jan 28 1786 Bare, George to Adams, Mary
Jan 29 1791 Bare, George to Cublentz, Elizabeth
Apr 12 1788 Bare, George Junr to Hauer, Catharine
May 13 1797 Bare, John to Brown, Elizabeth
Mar 21 1788 Bare, Mary to Wampler, Jacob
Jul 15 1786 Bare, Mary Ann to Getzendanner, Christian
Jun 17 1793 Bare, Susanna to Hobbs, Joseph
Apr 11 1801 Barger, Susanna to Wadsworth, William
Apr  8 1797 Bargesar, Daniel to Gates, Sarah
Oct  5 1793 Bargesser, Catherine to Shots, Philip
Feb 19 1785 Barker, William to Griffith, Susanna
Apr  8 1810 Barker, Wm. to Dorff, Mary
May 28 1779 Barkman, Peter to Crandler, Ulianna
Feb 18 1779 Barkshire, Henry to Burton, Cresilla
Dec 17 1779 Barlow, Zachariah to Hickman, Eleanor
Oct  3 1809 Barnard, Benjamin to Dern, Elizabeth
Dec  9 1797 Barnard, Michael to Strong, Caty
May  8 1804 Barnder, Daniel to Martain, Eve
May 14 1795 Barnes, Ann to Beck, Anthony
Oct 12 1780 Barnes, Caleb to Walker, Margaret
Aug 27 1787 Barnes, David to Hall, Elizbeth
Sep 29 1794 Barnes, Dawson to Poole, Mary
Oct 17 1801 Barnes, Dorsey to Parrish, Ruth
Feb 23 1792 Barnes, Elizabeth to Evans, David
May 27 1783 Barnes, James to Jarvis, Sarah
Dec 24 1795 Barnes, James to Harrison, Nancy
Jul 15 1786 Barnes, John to Taylor, Debitha
Dec 21 1801 Barnes, John to Perill, Clarissa
Dec 12 1793 Barnes, Louisa to Bowens, Thomas
Oct  1 1788 Barnes, Michael to Kemp, Elizabeth
Jan 17 1809 Barnes, Nancy to Mount, George
Oct 19 1804 Barnes, Orphey to Gladman, Thomas
Dec 24 1808 Barnes, Owen to Cushen, Mary
Dec  1 1795 Barnes, Sarah to Evans, John
Jan  3 1795 Barnes, Thomas to King, Ann
May 15 1788 Barnes, Vachel to McDougal, Charity
```

```
Sep 12 1791 Barnes, William to Onion, Deborah
Jan 28 1794 Barnes, Zadock to Poulson, Elizabeth
Apr 25 1796 Barnet, Luke to Pinkley, Catharine
Mar 18 1796 Barnet, Robert to Kemp, Margaret
Nov  4 1778 Barnett, Ann to Hedges, Josiah
Jun 22 1782 Barnett, Archibald to Lucas, Elizabeth
Jun 14 1779 Barnett, Jane to Flannigan, Lackey
Nov 25 1780 Barnett, Mary to McDaid, James
May 29 1786 Barnett, Robert to Stallings, Nancey
Nov 23 1780 Barnett, William to Piggman, Sarah
Jul  9 1803 Barnhart, Catherine to Babylon, Peter
Feb 11 1787 Barnhart, Catherine to Miller, John
Feb  8 1806 Barnhart, Elizabeth to Ecker, Abraham
Feb  5 1801 Barnhart, John to Kinsey, Barbara
Sep  9 1795 Barnhart, Peter to Hains, Elizabeth
Feb 13 1808 Barnhart, Rachel to Decker, Jacob
Apr 25 1808 Barnhart, William to Anders, Anne
Dec  6 1810 Barnhold, Mary to Thompson, John P.
Apr  5 1801 Barnhold, Nancy to Ritchie, John
Aug 19 1794 Barns, Eleanor to Barns, Ephraim
Aug 19 1794 Barns, Ephraim to Barns, Eleanor
Oct  5 1794 Barnthisell, Christopher to Grove, Catharine
Nov 26 1782 Barr, Hugh to James, Priscilla
Sep 19 1797 Barrack, Frederick to Simon, Mary
Sep  5 1806 Barrick, Barbara to Cramer, Henry
May 27 1778 Barrick, Catherine to Devilbiss, Adam
Mar 21 1806 Barrick, Catherine to Cramer, Frederick
Jun 21 1780 Barrick, Charity to Snyder, John
Feb 15 1793 Barrick, Christian to Hoover, Catharine
May  1 1783 Barrick, George to Waters, Nancy
Nov  1 1805 Barrick, George to Cramer, Margaret
Sep  9 1780 Barrick, Henry to Keller, Margaret
Jul  1 1809 Barrick, Henry to Sadler, Catherine
Oct  2 1802 Barrick, Margaret to Hoffman, John
Apr 17 1801 Barrick, Mary to Barrick, Peter
Mar 20 1804 Barrick, Michael to Bingett, Mary
Apr 17 1801 Barrick, Peter to Barrick, Mary
Feb 18 1804 Barrick, Sarah to Binger, John
May 22 1778 Barrick, William to Heartsock, Catherine
Sep 29 1792 Barrick, William to Scholes, Mary
Sep  8 1810 Barrick, William to Romack, Sarah
Apr 26 1810 Barrickman, Henry to Champer, Rebeca
Apr  1 1797 Barrington, Joseph to Fisher, Martha
Apr 23 1810 Bartgis, Mathias E. to Dertzabaugh, Margaret
May 17 1802 Bartholemew, Catharine to Buddenburgh, Jacob
Jun 16 1803 Bartholow, Aaron to Reem, Elsey Catharine
Aug 29 1798 Bartholow, Thomas to Nelson, Ann
Nov 11 1806 Bartlett, James to Taylor, Mary
Mar 21 1783 Bartlett, Sarah to Fooks, George
Jan 20 1800 Bartley, Joseph to Delozier, Susannah
Oct 21 1800 Barton, Axions to Smith, Joseph
Dec  2 1803 Barton, Nicholas to Maxfield, Anne
Dec 19 1803 Baruger, Henry to Titlo, Mary
Oct 13 1800 Basford, Rachel to Kinley, William
Nov 21 1780 Bash, Andrew to Hanes, Barbara
```

```
Dec  7 1808 Bassford, Mary to Clarke, John
Sep  2 1807 Bassford, Nancy to Crum, Isaac
Aug 10 1779 Bastian, Anthony to Fogle, Catharine
Mar 22 1780 Bastian, Sarah to Lock, John
Dec 12 1795 Batson, George to Calbfleish, Susanna
Aug 21 1806 Baty, Mary to Elliot, Mr.
Aug 22 1809 Bauder, Daniel to Parason, Sarah
Oct 18 1782 Baugh, Elizabeth to Fessler, John
May 13 1801 Baugh, Valentine to Collenberger, Catherine
Apr 15 1809 Baughman, Adam to McVicker, Sarah
May 17 1806 Bauman, Jacob to Linton, Charlotte
Nov 16 1807 Baumgardner, Daniel to Eppert, Catharine
Aug 22 1810 Baumgardner, Jacob to Koons, Magdalene
Jan 17 1807 Bausman, Benjamin to Bireley, Elizabeth
Oct  8 1809 Bawden, James to Greer, Polly
Jul 31 1806 Bawen, Francis to Tierly, Sarah
Sep 25 1802 Baxter, John to Dell, Lydia
Apr  3 1797 Baxter, Rachel to Poulson, Cornelius
Apr 15 1784 Bayard, John Hodge to Edelen, Rebecca
Oct  8 1788 Bayard, John Morris to Carrick, Margaret
Jan  6 1807 Bayer, Elizabeth to Heisler, Henry
Jan  4 1785 Bayer, Mich'l to Delaplank, Catherine
Jul 26 1808 Bayfield, Jane to Porter, Isaiah
Nov 11 1779 Bayley, Sam'l to Campbell, Mary
Aug 26 1783 Bayman, Mary to Frey, George
Nov 15 1779 Bayman, Thos. to Smith, Mary
Aug 27 1781 Bayne, Elizabeth to Dawson, Nicholas
Aug 31 1779 Beaghell, Christena to Furrow, Mathias
Mar 10 1792 Beaghly, Catherine to Gettert, Valentine
May  5 1778 Beale, Benjamin to Bardle, Ann
Nov 11 1791 Beale, Davault to Hildebrand, Mary
Feb 27 1798 Beale, Eleanor to Sewal (Sewell), Andrew
Sep 13 1796 Beale, Rebeckah to Wilson, Thomas P.
Nov  4 1806 Beall, Asa to Clancy, Elizabeth
Jun 27 1795 Beall, Bethan to Carter, Arthur
Apr  3 1786 Beall, Colmore to Shekells, Mary
Nov  2 1791 Beall, Colmore to Offutt, Jean
Apr 17 1790 Beall, Dan'l to Bingan, Catharine
Oct 17 1783 Beall, Elisha to Perry, Jane
Jan 18 1791 Beall, Elizabeth to Bernard, Noland
Apr  5 1797 Beall, Elizabeth to Busey, Thomas
Jan 18 1791 Beall, Elizabeth to Noland, Bernard
Oct 19 1790 Beall, George to Hamilton, Margaret
Mar 10 1806 Beall, Harriet to Alldridge, John
Jul  2 1805 Beall, Jacob to Labe, Mary
Dec 27 1805 Beall, James to Benson, Margaret Smith
Feb  1 1809 Beall, John to Tool, Elizabeth
Nov 26 1796 Beall, John B. to Beatty, Eleanor
Dec 11 1802 Beall, John Lee to Norwood, Anna
Mar  3 1803 Beall, John, Junr. to Tinderman, Elizabeth
Jan 13 1785 Beall, Joseph to Biggs, Henrietta
Dec 18 1790 Beall, Mary to Carter, Richard
Dec  5 1789 Beall, Mary Ann to Simms, J. Clebborn
Feb  5 1788 Beall, Nathaniel to Head, Ann
Mar  7 1780 Beall, Ninian to Stricker, Ann Maria
```

```
Oct  9 1779 Beall, Peter to Weddle, Margaret
Sep  3 1790 Beall, Priscilla to Williams, Edward
Aug 11 1787 Beall, Robert to Aldrige, Ann
Jun 15 1809 Beall, Sarah to Hayes, James
Aug 12 1805 Beall, Susanna to Weddle, John
Jun  9 1793 Beall, Susannah to Edwards, Headen
Jun  5 1790 Beall, Theodore to Greenfield, Susanna Eve
Apr  2 1803 Beall, Theodore to Smith, Catherine Sim
Apr 12 1799 Beall, Thomas Brooke to West, Harriet
Jun 21 1800 Beall, Tobitha to Swearingen, Joseph
Dec 29 1796 Beall, Upton to Price, Matilda
Dec 19 1798 Beall, William to Walker, Elizabeth
Apr 18 1803 Bealmer, William to Gill, Sally
Sep 20 1786 Beam, Jacob to Myers, Mary
Feb 12 1785 Beamer, Adam to Albaugh, Mary
Mar 21 1780 Beamer, Ann to Ringer, Jacob
Jul 29 1789 Beamer, Lucy to Leeply, John
Aug  1 1808 Beamer, Margaret to Nokes, Gilbert
Sep  4 1786 Beamer, Matthias to Boyer, Christena
Apr 12 1804 Beamer, Peter to Earhart, Elizabeth
Oct  8 1785 Beames, Barbara to Myers, Jacob (of Yost)
Apr  8 1801 Bean, Benjamin to Tenley, Eleanor
Sep 23 1797 Beane, William to Garaner, Elizabeth
Aug 14 1789 Beanes, Francis to Haff, Martha
Aug  8 1809 Beans, William to France, Elizabeth
Feb  5 1802 Bear, Michael to Walker, Catharine
Sep 12 1807 Beard, Catherine to Shott, Adam
May  9 1793 Beard, Margaret to Smith, John
Dec 23 1791 Beard, William to Roberts, Patty
Jun  1 1782 Beare, William to Rudecill, Elizabeth
Feb  8 1783 Bearinger, Barbara to Weaver, George
Jun 20 1786 Bearinger, Eve to Boyer, Abraham
Feb 17 1787 Beatty, Cathe. to Ritchie, John
Nov 26 1796 Beatty, Eleanor to Beall, John B.
Jul  7 1785 Beatty, Elijah to Hagan, Susanna
Sep  4 1802 Beatty, Elijah to Wigle, Sarah
Sep 25 1790 Beatty, Elizabeth to Charlton, John W.
Apr 12 1790 Beatty, Elizabeth to Bainbridge, Absalom
Jul  3 1799 Beatty, Henrietta to Parkinson, William
Dec  6 1810 Beatty, John Michael to Hughes, Charlotte
Oct 31 1810 Beatty, Lewis Augustis to Gist, Sarah
Oct  7 1795 Beatty, Lydia to Magruder, D. Ninian
Nov 24 1805 Beatty, Mahlon to Anderson, Sally
Nov 28 1783 Beatty, Mary to Ogle, Alexander
Dec 19 1789 Beatty, Mary to Stull, Daniel
Apr 19 1788 Beatty, Sophia to Rochester, Nathaniel
May 19 1787 Beatty, Susanna to Gomber, Jacob
May 26 1779 Beatty, Thos. to Waters, Jane
May 27 1791 Beaumont, Grace to Perrill, Alexander
Feb 23 1797 Beavers, Susanna to Licklider, George
Dec  8 1795 Beayer, Rebecca to Frazier, Peter
Mar 15 1794 Bechtell, George to Eller, Esther
Mar 12 1808 Bechtol, Lewis to Wieland, Catherine
May 14 1795 Beck, Anthony to Barnes, Ann
Dec 23 1797 Beck, Jeremiah to Night, Mary
```

```
Mar  7 1800 Beckebaugh, Susanna to Hay, Jacob
May  6 1797 Beckenbaugh, Christena to Marker, Daniel
Oct  6 1803 Beckenbaugh, Elizabeth to Critezer, Jacob
Aug 21 1797 Beckenbaugh, Eve to Bowles, John
Oct 21 1791 Beckenbaugh, George to Simmerman, Elizabeth
Dec 15 1784 Beckenbaugh, George Peter to Keffauver, Susanna
Feb 19 1801 Beckenbaugh, Jacob to Zimmerman, Catherine
Sep 19 1798 Beckenbaugh, Philipena to Woghter, George
May  9 1801 Beckener, Maria to Webler, George Peter
Sep  5 1786 Becker, Henry, Jr. to Miller, Catherine
Jul 25 1801 Beckerbach, Elizabeth to Hase, Fred'k Christopher
Dec 22 1792 Beckibaugh, George to Powlas, Mary
Feb 18 1792 Beckibaugh, Margr. to Bowlas, Jacob
Mar 10 1795 Beckibaugh, Susanna to Gaver, Dan'l
Sep  5 1794 Beckinbaugh, Barbara to Campbell, Jacob
Sep 23 1786 Beckwith, David to Justice, Catharine
Dec 24 1806 Beckwith, Mary to Tice, Henry
Jul 11 1809 Beckwith, Susanna to Pyott, James
Mar 28 1788 Beckwith, William to Elder, Martha
Feb  1 1806 Becraft, Catherine to Moldsworth, George
Apr 26 1804 Becraft, Elizabeth to Blackburn, William
Jan  1 1806 Becraft, Peter to Penn, Sarah
Jan 16 1810 Becraft, Rechel to Wilson, William
May 25 1802 Becraft, Sophia to Preston, John
Mar 26 1794 Beeler, George to Mullidore, Elizabeth
Jun  4 1778 Beever, William to Temple, Susannah
Feb 22 1805 Beigler, Madelena to Ahalt, Henry
Feb 10 1810 Bell, Benjamin to Hays, Amelia
Sep 22 1807 Bell, Jacob to Tinterman, Elizbeth
Mar 19 1807 Bell, John to Shelton, Lethe Ann
Jan 28 1799 Bell, Mary Ann to Spitzenburgh, Henry
Mar 16 1793 Belt, Eleanor to West, Erasmus
Nov  9 1796 Belt, Jeremiah to West, Ann
Apr  5 1791 Belt, John to Hyfield, Sarah
Dec 16 1790 Belt, Lloyd to Thomas, Eliz'th Causlet Metcalfe
Nov  3 1807 Belt, Priscilla to Jamison, Samuel
Jan 17 1807 Belwood, Elizabeth to Jarboe, George
Feb 27 1790 Bence, Jacob to Kemp, Barbara
Nov  3 1796 Bennet, Elizabeth to McClain, Joshua
Jan 20 1808 Bennet, Robert to Lawrence, Elizabeth
Jan  6 1800 Bennet, William to White, Letha
Dec 20 1779 Bennett Jesse to Knight, Prescilla
Nov 24 1780 Bennett, Benjamin to James, Rebecca
Apr 11 1788 Bennett, Daniel to Johnson, Sarah
Dec 29 1795 Bennett, John to Benton, Cassandra
Apr 29 1786 Bennett, John to Plummer, Mary
Dec 18 1792 Bennit, Jeffries to Benton, Eleanor
Mar 14 1795 Bennit, Nathan to Holland, Deborah
Nov 15 1809 Benson, Elizabeth to Miles, Greenberry
Dec 27 1805 Benson, Margaret Smith to Beall, James
Jan 28 1807 Benson, Ruth to Wilcoxen, William
May  4 1784 Bentley, Ruth to Head, Richard
Apr  6 1782 Bentley, Abner to Wood, Ruth
Apr  4 1795 Bentley, Absalom to Bentley, Ruth
Apr  4 1795 Bentley, Ruth to Bentley, Absalom
```

```
Dec 25 1786 Bentley, Sarah to Thornberry, John
Mar 15 1781 Bentley, Solomon to Wood, Rebecka
Apr 11 1797 Benton, Ann to Wallace, Charles
Dec 29 1795 Benton, Cassandra to Bennett, John
Dec 18 1792 Benton, Eleanor to Bennit, Jeffries
Jan 24 1804 Benton, Thomas to Nicholls, Pheby
Feb 14 1786 Bents, Margaret to Line, Henry
Apr  5 1788 Bentz (or Pence), George to Gumbare, Elizabeth
Mar 30 1778 Bentz, Catherine to Shellmon, Jacob
Jan  4 1799 Bentz, Jacob to Steckle, Catherine
Mar 28 1800 Bentzhoff, Elizabeth to Pittinger, William
Apr 24 1794 Berger, Catherine to Harding, George
Oct 26 1808 Berger, Magdalena to Young, Andrew
Apr  7 1779 Berger, Philipeana to Tabler, Melchor
Aug 10 1784 Berghman, Christopher to Pantz, Maria
Dec  1 1781 Berkman, Catherine to Fethercoil, Jno.
Jun  3 1779 Berkman, Peter to Litchard, Catharine
Jan 18 1791 Bernard, Noland to Beall, Elizabeth
Feb 11 1791 Berrier, Phebe to Swaney, John
Dec  8 1792 Berrier, Susanna to Dern, Isaac
Sep  8 1778 Berry, Christe to Gillaspie, David
Oct 21 1800 Berry, Richard to Howard, Margaret Young
Jun  8 1797 Berryer, Abraham to Hughes, Margaret
Dec 26 1810 Berryer, Margaret to Gillmeyer, John L.
Nov 30 1803 Bess, Michael to Armstrong, Nelly
Nov 20 1787 Bevard, John to Smith, Esther
Mar  7 1810 Bevington, Betsy to McMullen, William
Oct 19 1785 Bevington, Mary to Garnett, And'w
Nov  5 1785 Beyer, David to Crum, Sarah
May 12 1789 Biddle, Eve to Shriner, Peter
Apr 11 1800 Bie, George to Kline, Margaret
Oct 28 1784 Bier, John to Snider, Uliana
Nov 10 1798 Bier, Philip, Jun. to Miller, May
Dec 10 1810 Bierly, Jacob to Sowers, Leanna
Nov 25 1778 Biggon, Heugh to Hewey, Sarah
May  6 1803 Biggs, Catherine to Knouff, John
Oct 17 1795 Biggs, Fred'k to Wilson, Mary
Jan 13 1785 Biggs, Henrietta to Beall, Jospeh
Jun 25 1785 Biggs, Jacob to Moon, Eve
Dec 23 1794 Biggs, Jacob to Borghman, Christena
Nov 20 1782 Biggs, John to Willson, Prescilla
Dec 29 1808 Biggs, Joseph to Caff, Mary
Dec 11 1809 Biggs, Mary Wilson to Pitsel, Henry
Sep 26 1801 Biggs, William to McDaniel, Susanna
May  4 1807 Biggs, William to Furney, Catherine
Apr 23 1807 Bigham, David to Adair, Sarah
Jul  2 1810 Bigham, John to McIntire, Sarah
Mar 20 1799 Bigham, Thomas to McNair, Margaret
Apr 17 1790 Bingan, Catharine to Beall, Dan'l
Dec  8 1792 Binger, Barbara to Stone, John
Feb 18 1804 Binger, John to Barrick, Sarah
Mar 20 1804 Bingett, Mary to Barrick, Michael
Jul 10 1807 Binkley, Nancy to Crissinger, John
Sep 11 1800 Binns, Alexander to Wileman, Ann
Jan  4 1790 Binns, Simon to Wildman, Sarah
```

```
Aug  5 1782 Bird, Ann to Wiles, William
Dec 10 1780 Bird, Elizabeth to Cunningham, Peter
Jan  6 1795 Bird, Mary to Hoskinson, Thomas
Mar 30 1795 Bird, Sam'l to Dyson, Sarah
Jan 17 1807 Bireley, Elizabeth to Bausman, Benjamin
Sep  9 1797 Bireley, Elizabeth to Bontz, John
Dec  3 1807 Bireley, William to Myers, Charlotte
Sep  8 1810 Birely, Elizabeth to Hawk, Jacob
Mar 15 1809 Birely, Lewis to Zimmerman, Catherine
Oct  1 1787 Birely, Magdaline to Sease, Paul
Jun 17 1808 Birely, Margaret to Hartsock, Nicholas
Dec 24 1799 Biser, Catherine to Wilyard, Abraham
Mar  5 1808 Biser, Daniel to Routzan, Catharine
Dec 27 1808 Biser, Daniel to Harley, Sohpia
Nov 20 1805 Biser, Elizabeth to Keller, Henry
Jun 11 1810 Biser, Esther to Fluke, Jacob
Apr 10 1800 Biser, Jacob to Cost, Peggy
Mar 19 1804 Biser, John to Gaver, Lydia
Apr 14 1810 Biser, John to Slusser, Polly
Feb  6 1805 Biser, Mary to Gaver, David
Aug 18 1800 Bishop, Elizabeth to Kocugh, Mathias
Mar  5 1790 Bissett, Eliza. to Ducker, John
Dec  1 1780 Bissett, Elizabeth to Gartrell, Jehosophat
Jul 21 1797 Bittle, John to Mullinieux, Elizabeth
Apr 12 1799 Bixler, Elizabeth to Grabill, Moses
Nov 28 1803 Black, Elizabeth to Whitmore, John
Jan  2 1808 Black, Eve to Sinn, Jacob
Nov 29 1799 Black, Henry to Whitmore, Susanna
Feb  7 1806 Black, John to Singer, Catherine
Nov 18 1783 Black, Margaret to Gaver, John
May 14 1785 Black, Mary to Hickson, Thomas
Oct 28 1796 Blackburn, Ann to Pool, George
Dec 18 1805 Blackburn, Catherine to Preston, Frederick
Sep  7 1803 Blackburn, Elizabeth to Shelton, Thomas
Feb  4 1791 Blackburn, Mary to Aldridge, Thomas
Dec 15 1802 Blackburn, Sarah to Poole, Beale
Oct 29 1796 Blackburn, Thomas to Squire, Jane
Apr 26 1804 Blackburn, William to Becraft, Elizabeth
Feb 11 1779 Blackburn, Wm. to Carr, Ann
May  8 1779 Blackmore, Elizabeth to Winson, William
Feb  6 1782 Blair, Mary to Rodgers, John
Aug 20 1807 Blessing, Eve to Blessing, Philip
Aug 20 1807 Blessing, Philip to Blessing, Eve
Mar 25 1802 Blewer, Elizabeth to Proby, John
Jan  7 1793 Blickenstaffer, David to Shurtz, Uliana
Aug 31 1799 Blickenstaffer, Yost to Fuller, Margaret
Jan  2 1803 Blinderwood, William to Marshall, Ruth
Oct  3 1798 Bloom, John to Engel, Elizabeth
Mar 17 1804 Boak, Eliza to Stouffer, Jacob
Mar 26 1800 Boblon, Andrew to Waggoner, Susanna
May 12 1805 Bodall, George to Nusz, Mary
Dec  3 1795 Boden, Mary to Katultigh, Henry
Oct  7 1800 Boden, Samuel to Main, Susanna
Apr 13 1798 Bodensick, Justine Charlotte to Bush, John George
Dec 14 1780 Bodington, Pheby to Smith, William
```

```
Dec  7 1784 Bogen, Anthony Frederick to Koontz, Mary
Mar 15 1798 Boggess, Elizabeth to Stump, Joseph
Aug 27 1794 Boggs, James to Stickle, Margaret
Jun  5 1810 Boham, Polly to Roger, John
Oct 12 1804 Bohr, Michael to Burrier, Modlena
Apr 11 1803 Bohrer, Elizabeth to Brunner, Valentine
Nov 20 1804 Bolan, George to Wathan, Sarah
Jun 20 1795 Bolan, Margaret to Hall, John
Jul  8 1809 Bolen, Nancy to Caruthers, James
Mar  5 1783 Boley, Juliana to Reaves, Leon'd
Apr 28 1787 Bolie, Catharine to Keplinger, John
Jul  8 1809 Bolon, Abegail to Lickey, William
Dec 29 1801 Bolsky, Henry to Snoudagle, Margaret
Jan 29 1803 Boly, Elizabeth to Kolb, Jacob
Dec 25 1809 Boly, Jacob to Keplinger, Polly
Apr  1 1809 Bond, Hebe G. to Lowry, Thomas
Jan 21 1804 Bone, Susanna to Shoe, Philip, Jr.
Apr 13 1782 Bonham, Deborah to Flemming, Arthur
Apr 24 1779 Bonham, Jemimah to Nellson, George
Sep 24 1789 Bonham, Malachi to Williamson, Mary
Aug 25 1792 Bonham, Marey to Whitcraft, Edward
Dec 20 1785 Bonham, Rachel to Dorsey, John Lawrence
Sep  9 1797 Bontz, John to Bireley, Elizabeth
Aug 21 1790 Booger, Jacob to Crist, Elizabeth
Oct  1 1786 Boogher, Charlotte to Mantz, Isaac
Dec 30 1809 Boogher, Charlotte to Trout, Jacob
Aug  5 1780 Boogher, Elleanor to Measell, Jacob
Oct 16 1791 Boogher, Frederick to Hultz, Christena Margareta
Apr 22 1780 Bookey, Mathias to Grush, Christena
Feb 24 1808 Boon, Catherine to Iler, Jacob
Dec 25 1809 Boone, John to Collins, Rebecca
Mar 14 1808 Boone, Nicholas to Razeler, Christena
Jun 30 1795 Bobse, Barbara to Duphorn, Simon
Oct  2 1805 Booth, Edward to Mitchell, Dinah
Dec 23 1794 Borghman, Christena to Biggs, Jacob
Nov 19 1805 Boring, Hannah to Reynolds, Joseph
Jan 23 1797 Boring, Joshua to Camack, Jane
Mar 24 1794 Boroff, Valentine to Coze, Margaret
Sep 26 1809 Bortle, Elizabeth to Snowdigle, George
Apr  6 1778 Boseman, Richard to Holtz, Susanna
Sep 24 1787 Bosley, Mary Ann to Roberts, Archibald
Jun  2 1808 Bost, Henry to Winpigler, Susanna
Nov 10 1804 Bost, Jacob to Kerlin, Elizabeth
Mar 23 1809 Bost, John to Friddel, Mary
Oct 24 1807 Bost, Rahamah to Hoffman, George
Jan 21 1808 Bost, Samuel to Ramsberg, Catherine
Jul 24 1807 Bostian, John to Russell, Mary
Feb 20 1810 Bostian, Mary to Devilbiss, Caspar
Jun 11 1807 Bostian, Philip to Bostion, Sarah
Jun 11 1807 Bostion, Sarah to Bostian, Philip
Jan  9 1792 Boteler, Alexander to Philpott, Elizabeth
Sep 27 1806 Boteler, Ann to Cunningham, Charles
Sep 12 1797 Boteler, Arthur to Swearingen, Elizabeth
Feb  9 1799 Boteler, Catherine to Conn, William
Jan 25 1806 Boteler, Elias to Evitt, Susanna
```

```
Mar  1 1796 Boteler, Elizabeth to Slegle, Frederick
Aug 24 1793 Boteler, Henry to Eastburn, Mary
Nov 14 1809 Boteler, Joseph L. (Lingan) to Hackney, Sarah E.
May 17 1790 Boteler, Sarah to Eastburn, Robinson
Sep  2 1801 Boteler, Thomas to Garrott, Hannah
Sep 18 1798 Bottenfield, Jacob to Emeric, Elizabeth
Apr 13 1793 Bough, Barbra to Fessler, John
Sep 18 1779 Bourmaster, John W. to Dowlan, Mary Eve
Nov  4 1788 Bourne, Alice to Moore, Zachariah
Apr  9 1803 Bourrier, Jacob to Nusbaum, Catherine
Nov 27 1778 Bousom, John to Weddin, Elizabeth
Dec  9 1780 Bowden, Thomas to Mahany, Eleanor
Jun  6 1778 Bowden, William to Ryley, Elizabeth
Dec 12 1793 Bowens, Thomas to Barnes, Louisa
Jun 17 1780 Bower, Martin to Handshew, Barbara
Nov 17 1780 Bower, Philip to Perry, Sarah
Dec  4 1810 Bower, William F. to Atkins, Rachel
Mar 22 1809 Bowers, Margaret to Cook, Thomas
May 11 1807 Bowers, Susannah to Freeze, George
Feb 21 1781 Bowersmith, Cath. to Deerdarf, Abm.
May 20 1807 Bowersock, Magdalene to Kiefer, George
Sep 20 1798 Bowie, Peter to Clements, Mary
Dec 19 1788 Bowie, William to Card, Ann
Jan 25 1779 Bowlaney, Janey to Flower, Samuel
Feb 18 1792 Bowlas, Jacob to Beckibaugh, Margr.
Mar 15 1800 Bowlas, Margaret to Crist, Valentine
Dec 25 1809 Bowlas, Mary to Ramsberg, Casper
Nov 24 1785 Bowlass, Susannah to Collins, Matthew
Aug 21 1797 Bowles, John to Beckenbaugh, Eve
Oct 13 1801 Bowles, Mary to Coblentz, John
Feb 20 1787 Bowling, Samuel to Plummer, Mary Ann
Apr 26 1798 Bowlis, Henry to Routzawn, Elizabeth
Sep 10 1808 Bowman, Elizabeth to Simon, Joseph
Feb  6 1806 Bowman, Jacob to Linton, Charlotte
Feb 13 1809 Bowman, Samuel to Dill, Elizabeth
Oct  5 1784 Bowsinger, Henry to Shrader, Barbara
Jun 26 1783 Boyd, Andrew to McCay, Mary
Aug 10 1800 Boyd, Edward to Hoffman, Mary
Jan 13 1802 Boyd, Mary to Anderson, Hugh
Apr  9 1800 Boyd, Mary to Falconer, George Washington
Jul  5 1808 Boyd, Mary Anne to Hunt, Job
Jan 28 1809 Boyd, Ruth to Jennings, John
Dec 14 1798 Boyds, Mary to Mathews, Jacob
Jun 20 1786 Boyer, Abraham to Bearinger, Eve
Jul  4 1779 Boyer, Adam to Mantz, Charlotte
Mar 31 1779 Boyer, Catharine to Ball, Dan'l
Sep  4 1786 Boyer, Christena to Beamer, Matthias
Sep 24 1787 Boyer, Elizabeth to Hedges, Peter
Jul 25 1779 Boyer, Jacob to Link, Catharine
Dec 21 1796 Boyer, John to Burckhart, Mary
Apr 24 1790 Boyer, Mary to Hoff, Peter
Feb 24 1781 Boyer, Mary to Markell, Wm.
Feb 10 1779 Boyer, Nancey to Bricher, John
Aug 17 1809 Boyer, Sally to Wilson, Greenbury
Feb 18 1792 Boyer, Sarah to Ourey, Samuel
```

```
May 10 1808 Boyer, Thomas to Metcalf, Hannah
Feb 19 1789 Boylan, Thomas to Good, Mary
Aug 21 1779 Boyle, Ann to Bryley, Simon
Oct 30 1781 Boyle, Catharine to Trucks, John
Apr 23 1796 Boyle, Daniel to Carrico, Susanna
Nov 12 1801 Boyle, Daniel to Brooke, Mary Henrietta
Jan 22 1797 Boyle, John to Talbott, Ann
Nov 24 1809 Boyle, Peter to Livers, Elizabeth
Nov  1 1779 Boyr, Joseph to Stoll, Mary
Aug  9 1779 Boyrley, Eliz'th to Juit, Jacob
May 31 1782 Boyrley, Frederick to Motter, Eliz'th
Mar 18 1779 Boyrley, George to Juch (or Inch), Eliz'th
Nov 25 1807 Brabham, William to Wicuff, Susanna
Feb 23 1809 Braddock, John to Hilton, Mary
Oct 17 1795 Bradey, Jane to McAtee, Thomas
Sep 20 1804 Bradfield, Charlotte to James, David
Nov  4 1802 Bradfield, Hannah to Fitch, James
Dec 22 1795 Bradie, Lydia to Malone, Bartholomew Murphy
Jul 29 1782 Bradley, Dan'l to Lester, Ann
Sep 15 1808 Bradley, Nancy to Warner, George
Jul  8 1794 Bradley, Patrick to James, Rachel
Jan 30 1807 Bradley, Patrick to Burch, Nancy
Jan 16 1799 Bradley, Sarah to Turner, Lewis
Nov 18 1779 Bradley, Wm. to Fulliston, Jane
Oct  3 1803 Bradon, Barteson to Awbry, Stilly
Mar 13 1805 Brady, Susanna to Jones, Samuel
Sep  7 1805 Brain, John to Clem, Catherine
Nov 18 1803 Brain, Rebecka to Darst, John
Dec 12 1807 Brain, Sarah to Sulser, Peter
May 18 1786 Braithwaite, William to Brookover, Kitty
Dec  3 1804 Brandenberg, Catherine to Dehavin, John
May  8 1780 Brandenberger, Sam'l to Hargerhyma, Madilaine
Feb 22 1782 Brandenbergh, Fred'k to Sibert, Eliz'th
May 31 1782 Brandenbergh, Fred'k to Sibert, Eliz'th
Jul 10 1793 Brandenbergh, Henry to Gorner, Elizabeth
Sep 15 1808 Brandenburg, Hannah to Wile, George
May  9 1808 Brandenburg, Jacob to Wile, Catharine
Apr 12 1794 Brandenburg, John to Gorner, Phebe
Jun 15 1795 Brandenburg, William to Martin, Christena
Sep 13 1806 Brandenburg, William to Long, Christiana
Apr  3 1804 Brandenburgh, Henry to Gepheart, Elizabeth
Apr 23 1801 Brandenburgh, Mary to Michael, Jacob
Oct 18 1809 Brandenburgh, Susanna to Craver, John
Feb  6 1786 Brandt, Christian to Walter, Rosanna
Nov  3 1787 Branson, Tamar to Hoggins, John
May 14 1799 Brashear, Ely to Magrueder, Julia
Jan  8 1798 Brashear, Martha to Zerick, Daniel
Jun 11 1803 Brashear, Theodore to Jones, Priscilla
Sep 26 1778 Brashears, Cavey to Anderson, William
Apr 28 1792 Brashears, Dr. Belt to Cook, Ann
Nov 21 1790 Brashears, Henry to Mahony, John
Mar 12 1796 Brashears, Mary to Anderson, Robert
Jan  4 1791 Brashears, Tabitha to Pearre, Alexander
Sep 25 1800 Brashears, Theodore to Schue, Solme
Aug 18 1792 Brathelow, Michael to Nelson, Ann
```

```
Jun 11 1795 Braughan, Elizabeth to Scoby, Robert
Sep 13 1799 Bravo, Jacob to Nixon, Rebecca
Mar 30 1807 Brawn, Vachel to Hagan, Sarah
Feb  7 1783 Brawner, Elizabeth to Ridge, Cornelius
Sep 21 1807 Brawner, Elizabeth to Richardson, Elijah
Feb 11 1804 Brawner, Jeremiah to Keepers, Mary Anne
Jul 19 1786 Brawner, Lucy to Jenings, Richard
Nov 12 1807 Brawner, Lucy to Werts, Jacob
Feb 16 1798 Brawner, Thomas, Junr. to Need, Elizabeth
Apr 15 1789 Brayfield, John Baptist to Whitmire, Uliana
Apr 13 1796 Brayfield, Samuel to Pancoast, Jane
Oct 17 1778 Brayn, Joseph to Mathews, Martha
Jun 25 1808 Bredy, Elizabeth to Bumbaugh, John Henry
Oct 30 1783 Brendlinger, Sarah to Kenott, Conrad
May 22 1802 Brengle, Catharine to Reel, Michael
Dec  2 1797 Brengle, Catherine to Shule, John
Oct 18 1788 Brengle, Christian to Devilbiss, Elizbeth
Jan  5 1793 Brengle, Elizabeth to Brother, Henry
Nov 21 1791 Brengle, Elizabeth to Shope, Jacob
Oct 21 1800 Brengle, Jacob to Cookerly, Amelia
Mar 27 1803 Brengle, John to Zealer, Elizabeth
Jun 20 1788 Brengle, Lawrence to Sheffey, Catherine
May  9 1791 Brengle, Mary to Geyer, Daniel
Aug 16 1800 Brengle, Nicholas to Mantz, Mary
Apr 30 1803 Brengle, Peter to Mantz, Catharine
Jul 28 1800 Breson, Rosanna Cecili to Lashea, George
Oct  5 1802 Brewer, John to Mobley, Sinah
Apr  1 1786 Brewer, Sarah to Jones, Richard
Feb 10 1779 Bricher, John to Boyer, Nancey
Dec  6 1804 Brien, John to McPherson, Harriot
Dec 31 1784 Brightwell, John to Dodson, Mary
Mar 25 1781 Brightwell, Nussey to Hinckle, Jno.
Aug 20 1785 Brightwell, William to Waddle, Mary
Feb 13 1804 Brikett, James to Harris, Judith
Sep  4 1806 Brim, Catherine to Colglaser, Emanuel
Sep  1 1798 Brim, Elizabeth to Derr, John
Sep 13 1800 Brim, Polly to Lape, Jacob
Nov 28 1800 Briscoe, James to Brunner, Mary
May  7 1801 Briscoe, James to Brunner, Mary
Feb 14 1784 Briscoe, John to Magruder, Eleanor
Jul  1 1795 Briscoe, John to Delashmutt, Jane
Apr 28 1800 Briscoe, John to Scoggins, Elizabeth
Jun 29 1786 Briscoe, Mary Harbert to Tarlton, Jeremiah
Feb  5 1795 Briscoe, Nancy to Hopkins, Benj.
Mar  3 1792 Briscoe, Ralph to Delashmutt, Sarah
Jan 13 1797 Briscoe, Rebeckah to McKay, Benj'n
Mar 11 1797 Brish, Henry to Murry, Hariette
May 14 1807 Brish, Sophia to Nicholls, Henry
Sep 13 1788 Brishe, David to Pentz, Barbara
Apr 30 1790 Brishe, Mary to McClain, William
Sep 10 1806 Brodebeck, Elizabeth to Creager, Daniel
Apr  1 1779 Brooke, Ann Elizabeth to Thompson, Joseph
Nov 12 1801 Brooke, Mary Henrietta to Boyle, Daniel
Mar  2 1807 Brookover, Eleanor to Cartnall, Jacob
May 18 1786 Brookover, Kitty to Braithwaite, William
```

```
Mar  7 1786 Brookover, Thomas to Thomas, Mary
Mar 29 1809 Brookover, William to Marker, Elizabeth
May 13 1780 Brooner, Elias to Zimmerman, Mary Ann
Oct  9 1779 Brooner, John to Delauter, Susanna
Jan  5 1793 Brother, Henry to Brengle, Elizabeth
Apr  3 1809 Brother, Jacob, Junr to Shriver, Elizabeth
Jan  8 1795 Brother, Valentine to Shell, Margaret
Oct  1 1802 Brower, Jacob to England, Hannah
Sep 17 1810 Brown, Bidanna to Carr, Isaac
May  6 1806 Brown, Catherine to Cobenhafer, Jacob
Sep 11 1810 Brown, Clement to Johnson, Mary Eizabeth
May 11 1785 Brown, Darcus to Harvey, James
Jan 11 1798 Brown, Eleanor to Turner, Abraham
May 13 1797 Brown, Elizabeth to Bare, John
Oct 20 1794 Brown, Elizabeth to Hurst, John
Jun  4 1798 Brown, Elizabeth to Riley, Henry
Dec 27 1803 Brown, Ephraim to Sellman, Margaret
Nov  5 1801 Brown, Fielder to Heague, Hannah
Jul 23 1796 Brown, Frederick to Engle, Catharine
Jun  4 1793 Brown, Henry to Stevenson, Ann
Jun 22 1797 Brown, Henry to Wise, Catharine
Mar 20 1800 Brown, Isom to Gore, Mary
Dec  1 1800 Brown, James to Staups, Mary
Apr 18 1801 Brown, James to Stevenson, Mary
Jul 23 1804 Brown, John to Edwards, Sarah
Jun  7 1809 Brown, John to Simon, Polly
Aug 28 1787 Brown, Joseph to Stouder, Sarah
Nov 18 1805 Brown, Josiah to Stansbury, Sarah
Apr 12 1803 Brown, Lydia to Sullivan, John
Mar 28 1805 Brown, Mary to Cassell, George
Nov 28 1810 Brown, Mary to Jackson, John
Sep  2 1782 Brown, Mary to Smith, William
Mar 25 1786 Brown, Michael to Yantz, Rosanna
Apr  6 1782 Brown, Nancy to Kittle, William
Jun  5 1809 Brown, Nicholas to Stansbury, Ruth
Apr 15 1799 Brown, Rebecca to Colby, William
Jul 18 1793 Brown, Rebecca to Shilling, Murray
Sep 18 1802 Brown, Rosini to Miller, Solomon
Aug 21 1791 Brown, Samuel to Inman, Deborah
Oct 15 1800 Brown, Sarah to Waters, James
May 11 1778 Brown, Thomas to Chambers, Lydia Ann
Aug 14 1810 Brown, Thomas to Sowers, Susanna
Dec 27 1808 Brown, Sarah to Howard, Greenbury
Nov  3 1795 Browning, Cassandra to Clarke, Seth
Feb 24 1789 Browning, Delilah to Butler, William
Apr 22 1791 Browning, Edward to Soper, Priscilla
Mar 12 1788 Browning, Elias to Cullom, Susannah
May 24 1787 Browning, Elizabeth to Koon, Henry
Nov 19 1785 Browning, Elizabeth to Purdum, James
May 30 1796 Browning, Joseph to Haff, Mary
Dec 28 1793 Browning, Lewis to Philips, Margaret
Dec 14 1793 Browning, Mary to Browning, Zadock
May 10 1784 Browning, Nancy to Fulton, Nathaniel
Sep 23 1801 Browning, Rachel to Foster, Richard
Feb 10 1792 Browning, Sam'l to Hobbs, Nancy
```

```
Dec 14 1793 Browning, Zadock to Browning, Mary
May 18 1809 Brubaker, Samuel to Gorner, Barbara
Oct 27 1798 Brubecher, Elizabeth to Reed, Abraham
Oct 30 1805 Bruce, Elizabeth Key to Scott, John
Sep  9 1805 Brugh, Esther to Slutman, Peter
Apr 20 1780 Bruher, Marbara to Hutchinson, Archibald
Jan 17 1800 Bruner, Catherine to Taylor, George
Jun 23 1780 Bruner, Catherine to Woolfe, Peter
May 14 1804 Bruner, Charlotte to Smith, John
Oct  9 1784 Bruner, Margaret to Jordan, David
Oct  4 1782 Bruner, Peter to Gunn, Margaret
Apr 14 1803 Brunner, Catherine to Hollar, Charles
Jun  5 1804 Brunner, Elias to Wolfe, Catharine
Jul  9 1796 Brunner, Elizabeth to Ramsberg, Stephen
May 27 1797 Brunner, Elizabeth to Shull, Christian
Aug 29 1784 Brunner, Jacob to Kline, Margaret
Aug 12 1786 Brunner, Jacob to Snyder, Magdalene
Oct  3 1807 Brunner, Jacob to Doll, Margaret
Apr 15 1805 Brunner, Margaret to Kemp, Frederick
Nov 28 1800 Brunner, Mary to Briscoe, James
May  7 1801 Brunner, Mary to Briscoe, James
Jul 25 1809 Brunner, Mary to Hyme, Andrew, Jr.
Apr 25 1789 Brunner, Peter of Peter to Sinn, Catherine
Apr 11 1803 Brunner, Valentine to Bohrer, Elizabeth
Aug 29 1793 Bryan, James to Hall, Amey
Jan 16 1780 Bryan, John to Carrill, Eliz'th
Aug  6 1806 Bryan, Mary to Clary, Samuel
Jul 18 1806 Bryan, Mary to Hill, Thomas
Sep 29 1808 Bryan, Mary to Weddle, George
Jul 24 1793 Bryan, Thomas to Plummer, Massy
Aug 21 1779 Bryley, Simon to Boyle, Ann
Jan 26 1801 Bucey, Elizabeth to Rine, Michael
Sep 26 1778 Bucey, Henry to Trueman, Ann
Aug 11 1792 Bucey, Henry to Maccatee, Anne
Jan  6 1800 Bucey, John Bean to McAtee, Helan
Jan 12 1795 Bucey, Mary to Purdy, William
Oct 11 1792 Bucey, Mary to Stoner, Jacob
Nov 29 1800 Buchanan, John to Hockensmith, Martha
Apr 28 1792 Buchanan, Mary to Hughes, Joseph
May 11 1779 Buckey, Ann M. to Prauff, Jacob
Apr 21 1787 Buckey, George to Haas, Christena
May  8 1810 Buckey, John to Hauser, Susan
Jul 12 1792 Buckey, Margaret to Sawyer, Peter
Jan  7 1793 Buckey, Mary to Smith, Matthias
Mar 22 1806 Buckey, Michael to Pyfer, Catherine
Apr 13 1794 Buckey, Peter to Martena, Christena
May 16 1796 Buckey, Peter to Salmon, Mary
Jan 29 1793 Buckey, Valentine to Ramsbergh, Charlotte
Mar  5 1798 Buckias, Elizabeth to Dern, Frederick
Apr  9 1796 Buckias, John, Jr. to Wey, Elizabeth
Jun 18 1796 Buckias, Mary to Cross, Lewis
Jan 16 1802 Buckie, George to Dadisman, Peggy
Aug  8 1778 Buckingham, Hannah to Leatherwood, Samuel
Oct 12 1809 Buckingham, Nancy to Durbin, Ephraim
Jan 26 1784 Buckman, Sarah to Smith, Henry of George
```

```
Sep  5 1801 Bucky, Catherine to England, Andrew
May 17 1802 Buddenburgh, Jacob to Bartholemew, Catharine
May 18 1786 Buglar, Henry to Flukein, Barbara
May 16 1809 Bumbaugh, John to Carr, Hannah
Jun 25 1808 Bumbaugh, John Henry to Bredy, Elizabeth
Apr 23 1778 Bunn, Rebecca to Humbert, Peter
Oct 20 1803 Burall, Catherine to Murry, Stephen
Jan 30 1807 Burch, Nancy to Bradley, Patrick
Nov  5 1805 Burch, Thomas to Tydy, Elizabeth
Mar 17 1779 Burchell, Catherine to Matthews, Wm.
Sep 12 1795 Burckhart, George to Hedge, Hannah
Jan  4 1806 Burckhart, George to Castle, Elizabeth
Oct  5 1793 Burckhart, Joseph to Stephanus, Margaret
Dec 21 1796 Burckhart, Mary to Boyer, John
May 28 1794 Burckhartt, Barbara to Stipe, John
Feb  2 1790 Burckhartt, Catherine to Deal, John
Jul 21 1798 Burckhartt, Elizabeth to Stophel, Jacob
Jun 20 1798 Burckhartt, John to Markle, Catherine
Apr 15 1786 Burckhartt, Nathaniel to Simmons, Margaret
Sep  5 1784 Burckhartt, Pheby to Shees, Sebastian
Jun  9 1785 Burckitt, George Junr to Hobbs, Ann
Aug  9 1794 Burgee, Elizabeth to Marlow, Horatio
Sep 28 1801 Burgee, Martha to Garrott, Nicholas D.
Jun 26 1797 Burgee, Mary to Hall, Barruck
Dec  7 1790 Burgee, Nancy to Fowler, John
Dec 18 1792 Burgee, Rebecca to Purdy, Edmund
May 14 1805 Burgee, Singleton to Ijams, Jane
May 14 1805 Burgee, Thomas to Waters, Anne
Apr  3 1806 Burges, James to Harvey, Eunice
Sep  9 1795 Burges, Mary to Shekel, John
Dec  1 1809 Burges, Samuel to Warfield, Elizabeth
Nov  5 1790 Burges, William to Caran, Nicholls
Aug 17 1802 Burgess, Caleb to Warfield, Anne
Feb  3 1806 Burgess, Matilda to Simpson, Joshua
Jan 22 1794 Burgess, Onner to Hobbs, John, Junr.
Feb 19 1787 Burgess, Sarah to Hook, Dan'l
Apr  5 1803 Burgess, West to Warfield, Rachel
May 17 1793 Burgher, Adam to Smith, Susanna
aug 27 1781 Burgher, Catherine to Leonard, Christian
May 25 1807 Burk, Margaret to Raw, John
Jun  1 1805 Burk, Michael to Crabbs, Matty
Nov 12 1810 Burk, Michael to Fuss, Elizabeth
Mar 17 1792 Burkett, Margaret to Hall, Joseph
Aug 14 1809 Burkhart, Catherine to Heffner, Jacob
Jul 31 1809 Burkhart, Magdalen to Matthews, David
Mar 31 1798 Burkhart, Margaret to Curts, Nicholas
Sep 10 1783 Burkhart, Margaret to Gross, William
Oct 10 1800 Burkhart, Susanna to Hoover, Philip
Oct 21 1780 Burkitt, Christopher to Hobbs, Eliz'th
May 17 1792 Burkitt, Joshua to Nellson, Elizabeth
Feb 11 1806 Burn, Eleanor to Trundel, James
Jun 12 1779 Burn, Eliz'th to Elder, James
Jul 24 1779 Burn, Heugh to Temple, Sarah
Aug 19 1785 Burnee, Thomas to Nicewarner, Barbara
Sep 27 1787 Burnes, Elizabeth to Walker, Thomas
```

Aug 10 1800 Burnes, Mary to Ferral, William
Aug  4 1787 Burniston, Joseph to Grove, Juliana
Jul  4 1782 Burniston, Rebecca to Myers, Jacob
Oct 15 1796 Burns, Catherine to Vanhorn, Dennis
Dec 22 1806 Burns, Ed'd. H. to Castle, Mary
Feb 20 1799 Burns, Martha to Williams, John
Jan 17 1804 Burns, Susanna to Higgins, John
Jul 22 1780 Burrell, George to Lince, Elizabeth
Feb 13 1782 Burrell, Milley to Hague, Amos
Jul 28 1803 Burrier, Barbara to Lyons, John
Sep  6 1796 Burrier, Elizabeth to Walls, John
Jan 11 1804 Burrier, Esther to Nusbaum, John
Mar 30 1802 Burrier, Margaret to Nusbaum, Abraham
Sep  4 1800 Burrier, Mary to Waltz, Jacob
Oct 12 1804 Burrier, Modlena to Bohr, Michael
Sep 11 1807 Burrier, Philip to Nusbaum, Mary
Jun 28 1794 Burris, Thomas to Lanham, Ann
Mar 30 1782 Burrow, Lucy to Sehon, John
Feb 18 1779 Burton, Cresilla to Barkshire, Henry
Jul 13 1779 Burton, Hannah to Gilbert, Thos.
May  1 1779 Burton, Henry to Hill, Catherine
Jun  5 1790 Burton, Jacob to Swearingen, Mary
Mar 21 1810 Burton, William to Tudders, Rebecca
Dec 18 1804 Busey, Rebecca to McDavid, Daniel
Apr  5 1797 Busey, Thomas to Beall, Elizabeth
Mar 29 1803 Bush, Catherine to Creager, Jacob
Apr 13 1798 Bush, John George to Bodensick, Justine Charlotte
Sep 14 1779 Buskerk, Margaret to Francks, Henry Taylor
Jan 18 1806 Bussard, Catherine to Speelman, John
Jun  6 1809 Bussard, Catherine to Weaver, John
Mar 26 1808 Bussard, Eleanor to Smith, Jacob
Sep 14 1778 Bussard, Jacob to Sheffer, Mary
Mar  9 1809 Bussard, Jacob to Holtzman, Magdalena
Jan 30 1808 Bussard, Judith to Davy, Henry
Sep  7 1803 Bussard, Mary to Humbert, Michael
Jan  5 1809 Bussard, Rachel to Flewhart, John
Dec 19 1807 Bussard, Samuel, Jr. to Sueman, Eleanor, Jr.
Mar  4 1806 Bussard, Sarah to Road, George
Jul  7 1794 Bussard, Susanna to Runkle, Joseph
Aug 15 1806 Bussard, William to Harner, Magdalena
Jan 13 1792 Butler, Tobias to Smith, Elizabeth
Aug  1 1778 Butler, Joseph to Ogle, Mary
Jan 26 1807 Butler, Margaret to Staley, Solomon
Apr 13 1786 Butler, Peter to Silver, Anne
May 20 1786 Butler, Richard to Fischer, Amelia
Dec 23 1800 Butler, Susanna to Gedon, Daniel
Mar 21 1799 Butler, Susanna M. to Magruder, John R.
Dec 19 1795 Butler, Thomas to Gittings, Jane
Jul 14 1794 Butler, Tobias, Junr to Crist, Catherine
Oct 10 1788 Butler, William to Giddings, Delilah
Feb 24 1789 Butler, William to Browning, Delilah
Apr 22 1806 Butler, William to Deal, Julia W.
Jan  8 1799(1779?) Butler, Elizabeth to Head, Cecilius
Jun  3 1801 Butler, Sarah to Hedges, Stephen
Aug 17 1801 Button, Samuel to Haller, Elizabeth

```
Nov 13 1798 Buxton, John to Soper, Mercey
May 29 1794 Buzzard, Barbara to Stimmell, Peter
Jun 12 1795 Buzzard, Jno. to Hufford, Nancy
Jun 14 1797 Buzzard, Susanna to Baker, Frederick
Feb 16 1779 Byfield, Robert to Falconer, Mary
Jan  2 1787 Byrne, William to Hildebrand, Mary

Dec 19 1789 Cabler, Caroline Elizabeth to Stanley, Thomas
Dec 29 1808 Caff, Mary to Biggs, Joseph
Mar 14 1804 Cail, Christena to Geesy, Jacob
Oct  3 1808 Cain, Benjamin to Davis, Sarah
Feb 28 1779 Cain, Catherine to Greengrass, John
Jan  4 1797 Cain, John to Gaver, Molly
Feb 24 1800 Cain, Mary to Frazier, Levi
Dec 12 1795 Calbfleish, Susanna to Batson, George
Dec 30 1790 Calder, Nathaniel to Chew, Cassandra
Mar 22 1803 Calf, Martin to Ward, Margaret
Dec 29 1778 Calhoon, James to McAtee, Catherine
Mar  5 1791 Calliman, Zilpha to Perrill, Thomas
Jan 23 1783 Calmes, George to Price, Mary
Nov  6 1779 Calon, Catherine to Stottlemire, George
Oct  6 1781 Calpfleish, John to Foutz, Catherine
Jan 23 1797 Camack, Jane to Boring, Joshua
Dec 17 1793 Camden, Charles to Camden, Elizabeth
Dec 17 1793 Camden, Elizabeth to Camden, Charles
Jan  7 1793 Camden, Henry to Sprigg, Mary
Apr 25 1806 Campbell, Ann to Phillips, Noah
May  6 1796 Campbell, Anna to Baltzell, Jacob
Jan 23 1792 Campbell, Archibald to McDonald, Sarah
Mar 22 1808 Campbell, Benjamin to Lawyer, Catherine
Dec 23 1799 Campbell, Bennet to Devilbiss, Catharine
Dec  7 1808 Campbell, Elizabeth to Wireman, John
Dec 24 1793 Campbell, Eneas to Cheney, Henrietta
Sep  5 1794 Campbell, Jacob to Beckinbaugh, Barbara
Nov  2 1779 Campbell, James to Sehorn, Clare
Sep  9 1785 Campbell, James to Hyatt, Linney
Mar 26 1794 Campbell, James to Sewell, Sarah
Mar 16 1784 Campbell, John to Carter, Mary
Dec 23 1796 Campbell, John to Hobbs, Elizabeth
Dec 23 1802 Campbell, John to Liday, Barbara
Apr  9 1796 Campbell, John, Junr. to Cumming, Ann
Nov 11 1779 Campbell, Mary to Bayley, Sam'l
Apr 26 1792 Campbell, Mary to Howard, Cornelius
Jul 21 1797 Campbell, Mary to Sefton, Charles
May  9 1778 Campbell, Mathias to Voagh, Teney
Dec 19 1795 Campbell, Matthew to Stull, Susanna
Feb 20 1779 Campbell, Matty to Creable, Jacob
Oct  5 1808 Campbell, Richard C. to Zimmerman, Barbara
Dec 28 1802 Campbell, Rosanna to Crutsley, Elias
Mar  3 1785 Campbell, Sarah to McMinn, George
Mar 17 1807 Campbell, Susanna to Potts, William, Jr.
Dec  1 1788 Campbell, Susanna to Wickham, Robert
Nov 20 1787 Campden, Esther to Sargent, John
Mar  6 1780 Candle, James to Richards, Ann
Oct 23 1790 Cannon, John to Linganfelter, Elizabeth
```

```
Sep 19 1810 Cannon, Margaret to Rowzer, Daniel
Nov  3 1806 Cannon, Moses to Davis, Mary
Nov  5 1790 Caran, Nicholls to Burges, William
Apr 12 1800 Carbery, John Baptist to Schnertzel, Susanna
Dec  8 1792 Carbury, Henry to Schnertzell, Cevilla (Sybilla)
Dec 19 1788 Card, Ann to Bowie, William
Jul 20 1779 Carey, James to Hodge, Mary
Jul 17 1795 Carey, James to Carlisle, Charlotte
Feb  9 1792 Carl, David to Grove, Barbara
Jul 17 1795 Carlisle, Charlotte to Carey, James
Oct  3 1797 Carmack, Elizabeth to Duvall, Claudius
Dec 30 1799 Carmack, Elizabeth to Dern, William
Jan  8 1807 Carmack, John to Delaplane, Mary
Feb  2 1808 Carmack, Sarah to Herdman, George
Aug 16 1791 Carmack, William to Richards, Sarah
Aug 27 1810 Carmichael, Daniel to Hardy, Nancy
Nov 24 1797 Carmick, Sarah to Fulton, Alexander
Dec 22 1810 Carmickel, Margaret to Green, George
May 11 1805 Carn, Barbara to Fry, John
Oct  7 1808 Carn, Elizabeth to Holtzapple, Daniel
Mar 12 1805 Carn, Frederick to Crist, Susanna
Oct 12 1799 Carn, Madelena to Shoe, Solomon
Nov 10 1809 Carnan, Polly to Michael, Henry
May 31 1790 Carne, Margaret to Weisman, Conrad
May  9 1809 Carnes, Elizabeth to Conrad, Jossreph
Dec 25 1786 Carney, Ann to Goslin, Henry
Nov 13 1793 Carney, John to Crist, Elizabeth
Jan 30 1781 Carney, Mich'l to English, Margaret
Dec 24 1810 Carns, Henry to Combs, Susanna
Dec  7 1802 Carns, Mary to Heigle, Charles
Oct  1 1808 Carny, Patrick to Ritt, Martha
Oct  1 1797 Carper, Philip to Drill, Catherine
Feb 11 1779 Carr, Ann to Blackburn, Wm.
May 16 1809 Carr, Hannah to Bumbaugh, John
Sep 17 1810 Carr, Isaac to Brown, Bidanna
May 16 1780 Carrens, Thomas to Baldwin, Ruth
Oct  8 1788 Carrick, Margaret to Bayard, John Morris
Apr 23 1796 Carrico, Susanna to Boyle, Daniel
Jan 16 1780 Carrill, Eliz'th to Bryan, John
Jan 29 1779 Carrill, Wm. to Fee, Eliz'th
Dec 31 1803 Carrins, Elinder to McCoy, Zephaniah
Oct 27 1806 Carrolton, Thomas to Pittle, Mary
Oct 11 1807 Carruthers, Phebe to Kerrick, Thomas
Jun 27 1795 Carter, Arthur to Beall, Bethan
Sep  6 1783 Carter, John to Hambleton, Mary
Mar  3 1790 Carter, John to Thomas, Ann
May 16 1805 Carter, Joseph to Fisher, Catherine
Jun 28 1796 Carter, Joshua to Springer, Catherine
Mar 16 1784 Carter, Mary to Campbell, John
Mar 11 1788 Carter, Mary to Coale, James
Apr 20 1798 Carter, Rachel to Graham, Reubin
Dec 18 1790 Carter, Richard to Beall, Mary
Mar  6 1780 Carter, Thomas to Roach, Mary
Mar 14 1780 Cartey, Mary to Hatton, Wm.
Mar  4 1780 Cartey, Peggy to Pain, Michael
```

```
Mar  1 1780 Cartey, Thomas to Nicholls, Margaret
Oct  9 1783 Cartnail, Eliz'th to Graves, Thomas
Mar  2 1807 Cartnall, Jacob to Brookover, Eleanor
Sep 18 1805 Carty, Catherine to Thomas, John
Dec 11 1801 Carty, George to Tippis, Barbara
Jun  7 1804 Carty, George to Thomas, Susannah
May 21 1800 Carty, Thomas to Markle, Juliet
Jul  8 1809 Caruthers, James to Bolen, Nancy
May 16 1809 Cary, Maria B. to Ritchie, Robert
Jun  2 1793 Cary, William to Fritchie, Mariah Barbara
Aug 22 1802 Case, Alexander to Crowdy, Elizabeth
Nov  7 1803 Casemon, Elizabeth to Everhart, Martin
Sep 13 1810 Casey, Daniel to Frances, Nancy
Sep 26 1804 Casey, James to Tavenay, Rebecca
Dec 10 1783 Cash, Dorcas to Plummer, James
Feb 24 1794 Cash, Henrietta to Jones, Joseph
Oct 30 1801 Cash, Isaiah to Seal, Mary
Apr  4 1796 Cash, Jonathan to Fitzgerald, Sarah
May 12 1789 Cash, Mary to Plummer, Joseph
Apr  8 1780 Cash, Nancey to Roads, Jacob
Mar 18 1779 Cash, Ruth to Hinton, Richard
Mar 26 1779 Cash, Wm. to Nicholls, Casse
Oct 26 1809 Cassel, Rachel to Nicodemus, Andrew
Apr 23 1782 Cassell, Abraham to Linganfelter, Catherine
Dec  7 1810 Cassell, Catherine to Nicodemus, Henry
Aug 23 1779 Cassell, Eliz'th to Hufford, Dan'l
Mar 28 1805 Cassell, George to Brown, Mary
Jun 21 1806 Cassell, Nancy to Griffin, Thomas
Mar 17 1791 Cassell, Rachael to Waggoner, John, Pipe Creek
Jun 10 1780 Castle, Ann to Staley, Jacob
Jan  4 1806 Castle, Elizabeth to Burckhart, George
Oct 17 1778 Castle, Elizabeth to Sechrist, Charles
Mar 19 1808 Castle, Elizbeth to Castle, Samuel
Nov 22 1806 Castle, George V. to Horine, Catharine
Jan 21 1807 Castle, James Sampson to Tabler, Elizabeth
Apr 15 1808 Castle, Jemima to Stottlemier, David
Oct 18 1802 Castle, John to Taylor, Elizbeth
Sep 22 1807 Castle, John to Darner, Mary
Dec 22 1806 Castle, Mary to Burns, Ed'd. H.
Aug 27 1804 Castle, Mary to Keefaver, George
Dec 12 1807 Castle, Otho to Baker, Elizbeth
Mar 19 1808 Castle, Samuel to Castle, Elizbeth
Apr 30 1808 Castle, Thomas to Long, Barbara
Dec 26 1795 Caufman, Catherine to Smith, Balser
Jun  9 1802 Caufman, George to Iler, Mary
Apr  7 1798 Caufman, Henry to Hardman, Elizabeth
Dec 14 1791 Caufman, Mary to Leasher, Jacob
May  8 1778 Cavener, Mary to Forster, Moses
Dec 23 1790 Cawood, Rebecca to Heighten, Josias
Nov 28 1799 Ceas, Esther to Tritt, Peter
Oct 22 1805 Cecil, Aden to Tool, Sarah
Jan 29 1798 Cecil, Benjamin to Fisher, Ann
Feb 24 1798 Cecil, John to Linton, Mary
Jun 27 1804 Cecil, Levi to Toole, Martha
Jun  8 1782 Cecill, Elizabeth to Tool, James
```

```
Dec  6 1797 Cecill, George to Linton, Elizabeth
Feb  3 1807 Cecill, Samuel to Roads, Honora
Aug 11 1779 Censor, Christena to Fleagle, Valentine
Jun 15 1778 Cepharton, Mary to Pebble, Peter
Mar 23 1805 Cerby, Eleanor to Larkins, William
Apr  4 1808 Cettick, Barbara to Cramer, Solomon
Nov 17 1779 Chadbourne, Joseph to Gates, Ann
Feb 10 1793 Chamberlane, Nanny to McEntire, Alexander
May 11 1778 Chambers, Lydia Ann to Brown, Thomas
Dec  5 1796 Chamblin, Jane to Warner, Samuel
Oct 28 1797 Chamblin, Nancy to Chamblin, William
Oct 28 1797 Chamblin, William to Chamblin, Nancy
Oct 10 1806 Champer, Mary to Furry, Abraham
Apr 26 1810 Champer, Rebeca to Barrickman, Henry
Dec  6 1799 Chandler, Elizabeth to Warthen, Wilfred
Apr  9 1782 Chandler, Nathan to Davis, Cicely
Feb  2 1808 Chaney, Ann to Garder, Samuel
Mar  4 1797 Charles, Caterow to Christ, Catharine
Sep 25 1790 Charlton, John W. to Beatty, Elizabeth
Dec 24 1793 Cheney, Henrietta to Campbell, Eneas
Dec 30 1790 Chew, Cassandra to Calder, Nathaniel
Apr  6 1801 Chew, Elizabeth to Jacobs, Presley
Jul  1 1786 Chillcoal, Benjamin to McClain, Comfort
Jun  3 1809 Chilton, Ann Mackall to Mullikin, William Beans
Jun  8 1796 Chinn, Elizabeth to Wilson, John
Sep 23 1780 Chisholm, Margaret to Culliston, Jeremiah
Dec 30 1789 Chisholm, Rebeckah to Copeland, James
Dec 17 1790 Chiswell, Rebeckah to White, Benjamin
Mar  8 1794 Chopper, Catherine to Rightstine, William
Aug 25 1783 Chreichbaum, Mary to Baker, Christian
Mar  4 1797 Christ, Catharine to Charles, Caterow
Jan 10 1787 Christ, Charity to Balzell, Jacob
Aug 11 1800 Christian, Elizabeth to Neale, Bernard
Nov 10 1792 Chun, Lancelot to Ridgely, Martha
Feb 25 1787 Churchman, John Frederick to Tucker, Mary
Sep 18 1780 Cile, Peter to King, Eliz'th
Oct  3 1810 Cimmings, Joseph to Custer, Polly
Dec 13 1804 Cissell, Archibald to Robinson, Sarah
Aug 17 1779 Clabaugh, Charles to Hill, Eliz'th
Nov  1 1805 Clabaugh, John to Harris, Martha
Apr  3 1779 Clabaugh, Judey to Hill, Abram
May 11 1810 Clabaugh, Mary to Lee, James
Feb 18 1809 Clabaugh, Thomas to Good, Polly
Nov 23 1798 Clagett, Henry to Hawkins, Julia
Jan 29 1796 Clance, Barbara to Smith, Lewis
Apr  7 1798 Clance, Mary to Grimes, William
Jul 19 1785 Clancey, John to Yustice, Elizabeth
Jun 26 1795 Clancey, Roger to Bale, Lydia
May 28 1803 Clancy, Eleanor to Fellows, William
Nov  4 1806 Clancy, Elizabeth to Beall, Asa
Jul 17 1779 Clann, Betty to Harrison, John
Aug 30 1783 Clapham, Josias Colo. to Johnson, Dorcas
Dec 22 1806 Clapham, Rebecca to Luckett, Sam'l
Sep 26 1797 Clapham, Sam'l to Johnson, Elizabeth
May 12 1808 Clapsaddle, Susanna to Kuser, Samuel
```

```
Mar  7 1780 Clarey, Eleanor to Spurrier, Levin
Nov  3 1781 Clarey, John to Walker, Sarah
Mar 20 1779 Clark, Elizabeth to Ancrum, Jacob
Jan 13 1797 Clark, Elizabeth to Peck, David
Nov 17 1807 Clark, James to Head, Elizabeth
May 27 1789 Clark, Rachel to Sappington, James
Sep 21 1784 Clark, Thomas to Mansfield, Susanna
Feb  9 1806 Clarke, Elizabeth to Crawford, Samuel
Apr 16 1799 Clarke, Elizabeth to Gittings, Asa
Feb  5 1807 Clarke, Frderick to Grise, Mary
Dec  7 1808 Clarke, John to Bassford, Mary
Nov  3 1795 Clarke, Seth to Browning, Cassandra
Dec 17 1789 Clary, Ashford Dowden to Smith, Elizabeth
Jul 18 1795 Clary, Ashford Dowden to Neighbours, Sarah
Jan  6 1804 Clary, Benjamin to Hiner, Susannah
Apr 16 1810 Clary, Charlotte to Todd, Benjamin
Jan  3 1789 Clary, Daniel to Penn, Rachel
Dec  6 1800 Clary, Daniel to Spurrier, Ann
Feb 28 1801 Clary, Eleanor to Spurrier, Ralph
Jul  4 1808 Clary, Henrietta to Pierpoint, John
Jun 12 1802 Clary, Henry to Mullenax, Eleanor
Aug 12 1806 Clary, Jesse to Longsworth, Elizabeth
Nov 14 1800 Clary, John to Thomas, Ann
Jan 14 1806 Clary, Mary to Warner, Jacob
May  8 1788 Clary, Rachel to Israel, John
Aug  6 1806 Clary, Samuel to Bryan, Mary
Mar 11 1807 Clary, Samuel to Harrison, Cordelia
Oct 31 1809 Clary, Susanna to Norris, Upton
Oct 12 1803 Clary, William to Spurrier, Avis
May 20 1793 Clary, Zachariah to Penn, Delilah
Jun 30 1805 Claspy, Elizabeth to Gooldsberry, Tady
Jan 10 1793 Clay, Adam to Hardiger, Elizabeth
Jan 18 1803 Clay, Anne to Baker, Silvanius
Dec 28 1810 Clay, George to White, Nancy
Aug 21 1790 Clay, John to Jones, Nancy
Sep 19 1780 Clay, Mary to Koontz, Jacob
Jan 23 1795 Clay, Mary to Rine, Valentine
Jun  6 1803 Clay, Rebecca to Fawner, John
Mar 19 1795 Clay, Samuel to Grimes, Rachel
Mar 18 1781 Clefford, Michael to Eatan, Pheby
Sep  7 1805 Clem, Catherine to Brain, John
Jan  7 1799 Clem, Catherine to Shook, Jacob
Sep 13 1800 Clem, George to Durst, Catherine
Mar 15 1809 Clem, John to Stimmell, Susanna
Nov 10 1804 Clem, Mary to Umbaugh, George
Dec  5 1794 Clements, Basil to Green, Cloe
Sep 20 1798 Clements, Mary to Bowie, Peter
Feb  8 1793 Clements, Mary Ann Violetta to Green, Samuel
Jul 24 1797 Clements, William to Hardey, Winifred
Jul 18 1789 Clements, Wm. H. to Jenkins, Eleanor
Nov 22 1809 Clemson, James to Howard, Mary
Aug 17 1795 Clemson, Mary to Whitehill, John
Nov  1 1803 Clemson, Peggy to James, Daniel
Apr 18 1778 Cline, Catherine to Scutchall, George
Mar 23 1778 Cline, Elizabeth to Smedley, Jacob
```

```
Jul 19 1778 Cline, Henry to Jumper, Cary
Jan  9 1810 Clinehoof, Jane to Longwell, Mathew
Sep 21 1785 Clinerd, Francis to Weltzhamer, Sarah
Oct 27 1806 Clingan, Archibald to Fergerson, Ann
Apr 16 1806 Clingan, Margaret to Thompson, Samuel
Mar 21 1801 Clingan, Mary A. G. to McKaleb, John
Mar 16 1809 Clingan, Nancy to Alexander, William
Jun  6 1794 Clinton, Thomas to Michael, Catharine
Dec  4 1802 Clise, Elizabeth to Stoner, John
Feb 19 1802 Clise, John to Wheatcroft, Ann
Sep 27 1809 Clise, Margaret to Graver, Peter
Nov 28 1797 Cloninger, Philip to Hennickhouser, Modelina
Mar 22 1802 Close, Henry to Neat, Magdalene
Aug 25 1778 Coale, Casiah to Cumming, James
Dec  2 1788 Coale, Dennis to Dawson, Ann
Mar 30 1790 Coale, Henrietta to Emmit, William, Esq.
Nov 21 1797 Coale, Isaac to Ridgely, Sarah
Mar 11 1788 Coale, James to Carter, Mary
May 22 1796 Coale, Keziah to Stevens, Edward
May 24 1801 Coale, Vincent to Stewart, Eleanor
May  6 1806 Cobenhafer, Jacob to Brown, Catherine
Dec 25 1801 Cobeth, John to McElroy, Priscilla
Aug  6 1807 Coblentz, George to Hemp, Catherine
Oct 13 1801 Coblentz, John to Bowles, Mary
May 19 1802 Coblentz, Philip to Culler, Elizabeth
Mar 23 1803 Coblentz, Philip to Zimmerman, Elizabeth
Nov 30 1799 Cochran, Eleanor to Dorsey, John
May 19 1783 Cochran, Jane to Richards, Daniel
Mar 26 1801 Cochran, John to Starling, Rachel
Oct 29 1779 Cochron, Heugh to Hobston, Eliz'th
Mar 28 1778 Cock, Catharine to Archebald, Samuel
Dec 15 1783 Cock, Sam'l to Ogle, Mary
Oct 25 1806 Cocke, Martha to Grahame, Augustus
May 25 1809 Cockey, William to Graff, Catherine
Apr 21 1778 Coe, Edith to Wells, Richard
Sep 30 1780 Coe, Jemimah to Wills, Henry
Nov  8 1784 Coe, Jesse to Norris, Abrillea
Sep  1 1778 Coe, Mary to Whitmore, John
Dec 21 1785 Coffee, John Dowden to Roberts, Darcus
Mar 28 1780 Coffin, Lemuel to Creable, Catherine
May  5 1778 Coffin, Sarah to Hazelwood, Thomas
Mar  6 1805 Cogh, Elizabeth to Harbaugh, John, Junr.
Jul  7 1792 Coic, George to King, Elizabeth
Sep 15 1797 Coke, Precilla to Baker, Henry
Jan 10 1809 Colbert, John to Richards, Mary
Dec 12 1778 Colbert, Simon to Reed, Eleanor
Apr 15 1799 Colby, William to Brown, Rebecca
Oct  1 1808 Colclasier, Elizabeth to Judy, Jacob
Sep  7 1786 Cole, Richard to McSherry, Catherine
Aug 27 1799 Cole, William H. to Magors, Elizabeth
Dec  9 1779 Colebank, Mary to Traufle, Samuel
Mar 23 1810 Colegate, George to McCannon, Mary
Mar 21 1782 Coleman, Charity to Renner, Wm.
Aug  5 1809 Coleman, John to Ecleman, Susanna
Feb 27 1792 Coleman, Joseph to Justice, Rebeckah
```

```
Oct 10 1786 Coleshine, Earnest to Showe, Eliz'th
Sep  4 1806 Colglaser, Emanuel to Brim, Catherine
May 13 1801 Collenberger, Catherine to Baugh, Valentine
Apr 26 1810 Coller, Catherine to Baker, Jacob
Apr  4 1805 Collerflower, Elizabeth to Garrott, Joseph
Nov 16 1791 Colliberger, John to Dutrow, Susanna
Sep 16 1802 Collins, Eleanor to Newman, Joshua
Jan  7 1792 Collins, Elizabeth to McKeough, Patrick
Mar 30 1809 Collins, Henry to Eppert, Elizabeth
Aug 12 1791 Collins, Hodijah to Gromatt, Mary
Sep 16 1809 Collins, Levy to Comfer, Margaret
Nov 23 1809 Collins, Mary to Moren, John
Nov 24 1785 Collins, Matthew to Bowlass, Susannah
Feb  5 1780 Collins, Patrick to Pepper, Eliz'th
Nov 18 1788 Collins, Prudence to Thornbury, Thomas
Dec 25 1809 Collins, Rebecca to Boone, John
Jan 23 1800 Collins, Senah to Albaugh, Daniel
Apr 29 1793 Colman, Mary Magdalena to Routsong, Henry
Jan 26 1809 Colour, Philip to Fiester, Mary
May 26 1807 Columber, Mary to Merchant, Charles
Jul 11 1786 Combs, Rebeckah to Triplett, Reuben
Dec 24 1810 Combs, Susanna to Carns, Henry
Oct 24 1794 Comfer, Catherine to Shafer, Tobias
Sep 16 1809 Comfer, Margaret to Collins, Levy
Oct 14 1807 Comper, Susanna to Hines, Hugh
Jun 29 1778 Compston, John to Knotts, Sarah
Sep 30 1806 Compton, Elizabeth to Hill, Benjamin
Aug 20 1795 Compton, John to Jacobs, Elizabeth
Jun 28 1806 Compton, John to Delashmut, Elisabeth
Oct 27 1798 Compton, Joseph to Paine, Ann
Oct 13 1787 Conden, Wm. to Penn, Sarah
Oct 16 1797 Condon, David to Gotsailech, Catharena
Apr  5 1796 Condon, Eleanor to Parrish, Aquilla
Mar 26 1796 Condon, Elizabeth to McDonald, William
Mar  4 1808 Condon, Frances to Pickett, Charles
Apr 20 1805 Condon, James to Ackers, Sarah
Oct  7 1790 Condon, Mary to Keener, John
Jan  6 1787 Condon, Rich'd to Franklin, Arey
Nov 22 1809 Condon, William to Gray, Rebecca
Oct 20 1786 Condon, Wm. to Welsch, Ruth
Dec  8 1789 Condon, Zachariah to Elliott, Rachel
Dec 17 1799 Condon, Zachariah to Todd, Eleanor
May 17 1802 Conn, Mary to Cost, Jacob
Feb  9 1799 Conn, William to Boteler, Catherine
Jul 28 1809 Connard, Polly to Mouls, Philip
Aug 22 1807 Connelly, Ann to Zimmerman, John
Dec 31 1791 Connelly, Ann Statia to Newhouse, John
Aug 14 1793 Conner, Barbara to Rhine, Rudy
Dec 20 1803 Conner, David to Williams, Martha
May  4 1799 Conner, Eleanor to Garrot, Aeneas
Oct 10 1799 Conner, Elizabeth to Avalon, Philip
Sep 25 1778 Conner, James to Sipes, Eliz'th
Aug  7 1790 Conner, Lawrence to Appleby, Elizabeth
Nov 30 1793 Conner, Mary to Mason, Archibald
Jun 11 1808 Conner, Thomas to Martin, Elizabeth
```

```
Dec  6 1802 Conner, William to Haines, Catherine
Feb 16 1790 Conrad, Elizabeth to Oatner, John
Apr 16 1787 Conrad, Henry to Late, Mary
May  9 1809 Conrad, Josseph to Carnes, Elizabeth
May  4 1805 Conradt, George I. to Steiner, Elizabeth
Nov  8 1810 Conradt, Magdalane to Miller, Christian G.
Aug 22 1797 Conrod, Susanna to Rowe, Jacob
Feb  4 1809 Conroy, Andrew to Aldridge, Rebecca
May 19 1795 Conroy, Edward to Angus, Jemima
Aug 10 1787 Coogle, Adam to Nave, Catherine
Apr 28 1792 Cook, Ann to Brashears, Dr. Belt
Oct 22 1798 Cook, Anne to Fischer, Jonas
Jan 30 1809 Cook, Christian to Oram, Anne
Jun 25 1792 Cook, Elizabeth to Whips, Samuel
Jun  1 1779 Cook, Henry to Lambert, Mary
Apr 10 1779 Cook, John to Willson, Susannah
Jul 11 1795 Cook, John to Nixendorff, Catherine
May  5 1810 Cook, John to Root, Sarah
Aug 11 1800 Cook, Reasin to Low, Polly
Mar 22 1809 Cook, Thomas to Bowers, Margaret
Jul  4 1809 Cooke, Sophia to Duvall, John
Oct 21 1800 Cookerly, Amelia to Brengle, Jacob
Mar 24 1804 Cookerly, John to Smith, Margaret
Sep  9 1796 Cookerly, John, Jr. to Fleming, Alice
Dec 18 1802 Cookerly, William to Hughes, Darkey
May 10 1784 Cookus, Michael to Kile, Elizabeth
Apr  3 1804 Cooley, Edward to Talbott, Elizabeth
Jun 17 1799 Cooley, Eleanor to Young, Benjamin
Jun  7 1806 Cooley, Mary to Adlum, John, Jr.
Jun  3 1799 Coomes, Baalis to Richardson, Sarah
Dec  4 1802 Coomes, Joseph to McMickim, Martha
Dec 13 1809 Coomes, Raphael to Craton, Mary
Apr 13 1783 Coonce, Catherine to Tabler, Michael
Aug  5 1780 Coonce, John to Roar, Catherine
Oct 10 1786 Cooper, Adam to Hamilton, Rebeckah
Nov  8 1779 Cooper, Archb'd to Ramsey, Mary
Feb  6 1797 Cooper, Elizabeth to Gale, Thomas
Dec  7 1786 Cooper, James to Ramsey, Naomy
Aug 18 1807 Cooper, James to McHenry, Anne
Apr  1 1800 Cooper, Mary to Filson, Samuel
May 17 1794 Cooper, Mary to Lowrey, Ceazer
Nov  5 1801 Cooper, Robert to Witherow, Jane
Aug 22 1791 Cooper, Robert to Harlin, Catherine
Dec 17 1779 Cooper, Wm. to Harrison, Mary
Mar  8 1780 Cooperider, Elias to Iseminger, Susanna
Apr 29 1797 Coore, Christena to Townsend, Benjamin
Dec 30 1789 Copeland, James to Chisholm, Rebeckah
May 29 1809 Copeland, John to Shoemaker, Elizabeth
Jun 19 1790 Copenhaver, John to Miller, Barbara
Dec  2 1797 Coplan, Rebecca to Osborn, Daniel
Aug 16 1804 Coplentz, Mary Ann to Kuller, John
Oct 14 1783 Coppersmith, Catherine to Younge, Peter
Feb 18 1808 Coppersmith, Henry to Eichelberger, Magdalena
Jul 13 1805 Coppersmith, Modelena to Groff, Joseph
May  3 1801 Cordell, Lucy to Adams, Robert
```

```
Feb 20 1799 Corell, Elizabeth to Martin, John
Mar 11 1786 Cornall, John to O'Neall, Jennet
May  8 1785 Cossell, Dan'l to Ollix, Mary
Nov 26 1787 Cossell, Mary to Shriock, Daniel
Aug 11 1794 Cossen, Nicholas to Wilson, Rebeckah
Dec  9 1799 Cost, Catherine to Johnson, William
Apr 29 1790 Cost, Catherine to Mullendore, David
Mar 31 1809 Cost, Christian to Simmons, Marianne
Dec 22 1797 Cost, Elizabeth to Golman, Jacob
Dec 29 1798 Cost, George to Harshman, Mary
Dec  2 1799 Cost, Jacob to Croas, Mary Magdalene
May 17 1802 Cost, Jacob to Conn, Mary
May 25 1783 Cost, Margaret to Picking, Robert
Apr 10 1800 Cost, Peggy to Biser, Jacob
Nov 13 1810 Cost, Polly to Whipp, George
Aug 30 1794 Cost, Uhly to Mullindore, John
Jan 29 1779 Cotton, Elizabeth to Street, George
Aug  5 1807 Cough, Jacob to Senseny, Mary
Nov  1 1799 Coulter, Alexander to Jenings, Rebecca
Mar  6 1799 Covell, Mary Ann to Hatherly, Benjamin
Feb 20 1808 Coventry, John to Philips, Amelia
Mar 18 1791 Coventry, Rachel to Jones, Francis
Sep 10 1804 Cover, Daniel to Stouffer, Hannah
May 31 1785 Cover, Jacob to Rudecill, Elizabeth
Oct 31 1809 Cover, Mary to Hiner, John
Dec 21 1809 Cover, Mary to Smith, Frederick
Apr 18 1786 Covill, Susanna to Haddery, Benjamin
Sep 19 1807 Covill, Vashti to Forrest, Jeremiah
May 14 1782 Cowell, Elizabeth to Root, Daniel
Jan 15 1800 Cowley, John to Young, Sarah
Aug 25 1783 Cox, Agnes to Moxley, Sam'l
Apr  5 1799 Cox, Anne to Swaidner, Adam
Aug 14 1787 Cox, Elisha to Frasier, Milley
Jul 13 1806 Cox, Elizabeth to Shaugh, Jacob
Oct  9 1806 Cox, Samuel to Wilson, Ann
Sep 20 1783 Cox, William to Lintz, Catherine
Mar 24 1794 Coze, Margaret to Boroff, Valentine
Sep  5 1805 Crabb, Mary to Elliott, Solomon
May  3 1787 Crabb, Ralph to Thomas, Mary
Jan  4 1795 Crabb, Thomas to Adlum, Mary
Oct 27 1797 Crabbs, Elizabeth to Strong, George
Aug  2 1805 Crabbs, Elizabeth to Troxel, George
Feb 21 1803 Crabbs, Frederick to Oler, Catherine
Jun  1 1805 Crabbs, Matty to Burk, Michael
Jul  4 1795 Craber, Bostian to Hutchison, Allear
Apr 21 1810 Crable, Elizabeth to Stevens, Thomas H.
Oct  4 1798 Crabs, Jeremiah to Crabs, Mary
Mar 23 1809 Crabs, Joseph to Zallinger, Elizabeth
Jan 18 1798 Crabs, Margaret to Harris, Thomas
Oct  4 1798 Crabs, Mary to Crabs, Jeremiah
Jan 19 1809 Crabs, Peter to Grimes, Ruth
Nov 19 1783 Crabster, John to Little, Susanna
Dec 21 1801 Craft, Elizabeth to Murray, Stephen
May 31 1779 Craigg, Roger to Ford, Mary
Jun 13 1785 Crail, Wm. to Lewis, Mary
```

Nov 16 1778 Crale, Mary to Howard, John
Nov  9 1807 Cramer, Barbara to Marckel, William
Apr 30 1792 Cramer, Christena to Hedges, Andrew
Apr 23 1807 Cramer, Elizabeth to Hartsock, George
Aug  7 1798 Cramer, Elizabeth to Specht, Lewis
Mar 21 1806 Cramer, Frederick to Barrick, Catherine
Sep  5 1806 Cramer, Henry to Barrick, Barbara
Aug 21 1793 Cramer, John to Crise, Mary
Mar 27 1797 Cramer, John to Stimmell, Catherine
Apr 15 1797 Cramer, John to Hoover, Margaret
Mar 27 1807 Cramer, John to Goslin, Rachel
Nov  1 1805 Cramer, Margaret to Barrick, George
Nov  9 1795 Cramer, Margaret to Rights, Ludwick
Sep 13 1779 Cramer, Mich'l to Winpigler, Mary
Apr  4 1808 Cramer, Solomon to Cettick, Barbara
Nov  9 1808 Cramer, Susanna to Flenner, Abraham
Apr 26 1805 Cramer, Thomas to Putman, Mary
Oct  2 1802 Cramer, William to Hoover, Margaret
Jan 23 1794 Cramier, George to Reppert, Elizabeth
Dec 24 1800 Cramlett, Elizabeth to Munlix, Charles
Jul  4 1794 Cramphin, Josiah to Philpott, Ann
Jul 26 1794 Crampton, Eleanor to Jenkins, John
Apr  8 1797 Crampton, Philipena to Amerson, Charles
May 28 1779 Crandler, Ulianna to Barkman, Peter
Mar 14 1794 Craps, John to Innes, Sarah
Jun 23 1809 Crapster, Basil to Dorsey, Harriet
Nov 27 1810 Crapster, Mary to Hickson, Henry
Nov 12 1808 Crapster, Peter to Hobbs, Elizabeth C.
Dec 13 1809 Craton, Mary to Coomes, Raphael
Apr  1 1805 Craven, Eleanor to Owing, Robert
Mar  8 1810 Craven, Mahlon to Iden, Hannah
Oct  9 1798 Craver, Catherine to Lefever, Elias
Jul 12 1805 Craver, John to Fry, Mary
Oct 18 1809 Craver, John to Brandenburgh, Susanna
Jan 28 1805 Crawford, Aaron to Ingman, Sarah
Oct  5 1797 Crawford, Elizabeth to Ensey, Dennis
Apr 26 1797 Crawford, Elizabeth to Fisher, Ludwick
Mar  5 1793 Crawford, John to Guynn, Ann
Feb  9 1806 Crawford, Samuel to Clarke, Elizabeth
Mar 30 1795 Crawl, Isaac to Mathews, Mary
Oct 22 1781 Crawmer, Ludwick to Ryley, Elizabeth
Mar 28 1780 Creable, Catherine to Coffin, Lemuel
Feb 20 1779 Creable, Jacob to Campbell, Matty
Oct 21 1780 Creagar, Catharine to Ridge, Edward
Apr 19 1788 Creagar, Elizbeth to Link, Jacob
Mar  9 1803 Creager, Amelia to Crum, Nathan
Mar 28 1809 Creager, Casper to Smith, Barbara
Feb 14 1801 Creager, Catherine to Link, Daniel
May 30 1800 Creager, Christian to Woolf, Mary
Nov 25 1809 Creager, Cornelius to Getherd, Mary
Sep 10 1806 Creager, Daniel to Brodebeck, Elizabeth
Oct 13 1810 Creager, Daniel to Eyler, Mary
May 11 1802 Creager, David to Weck, Margaret
Aug 10 1787 Creager, Elizabeth to Springer, Edward
Mar 24 1802 Creager, Elizabeth to Tallhelm, Peter

```
Oct  1 1792 Creager, Elizabeth to Wilhide, Conrad
Apr 17 1806 Creager, Frederick to Shreup, Mary
Apr  7 1807 Creager, George, Esq. to Appler, Peggy
Nov  2 1805 Creager, George, Jr. to Salmon, Margaret
Jan 11 1796 Creager, Hannah to Crum, Ephraim
Mar 11 1809 Creager, Henry to Protzman, Sophia
Mar 29 1803 Creager, Jacob to Bush, Catherine
Jun  4 1802 Creager, John to Iler, Eve
May 10 1808 Creager, Lewis, Dr. to Hauer, Susanna
Mar 21 1798 Creager, Margaret to Delauder, John
Dec 27 1806 Creager, Michael to Renner, Catherine
Oct 29 1791 Creager, Phoebe to Fout, Henry
Nov 21 1803 Creager, Rachael to Harbaugh, Samuel
Apr 17 1801 Creager, Solomon to Smith, Mary
Aug 21 1778 Creale, Richard to Livingston, Eve
Mar  7 1789 Cregar, Adam to Springer, Susanna
Aug 27 1787 Cregar, John to Hedge, Phebe
Dec  6 1799 Creger, Jacob to Smith, Catherine
Nov  9 1799 Creger, Peter to Albaugh, Eve
May 28 1790 Crepell, Rachel to Hardin, Richard
May 20 1802 Cress, Jacob to Adams, Mary
Feb  7 1797 Cretin, James to Genings, Lucy
Jan 11 1806 Cretin, Lucy to Hughes, James
Jan  3 1807 Crideler, Elizabeth to Crothers, James
Aug 22 1789 Crigloe, William to Myers, Catherine
May 22 1778 Cringland, Elizabeth to Ryley, Patrick
Dec 27 1778 Crips, Mary to McCollom, David
May 14 1796 Crise, Eve to Vickery, Nathan
Dec 13 1788 Crise, Henry to Folk, Barbara
Aug 21 1793 Crise, Mary to Cramer, John
Sep 30 1801 Crise, Peter to Ludey, Susanna
Jul 10 1807 Crissinger, John to Binkley, Nancy
Jul 14 1794 Crist, Catherine to Butler, Tobias, Junr
Aug 21 1790 Crist, Elizabeth to Booger, Jacob
Nov 13 1793 Crist, Elizabeth to Carney, John
Apr 28 1796 Crist, Elizabeth to Price, Edward
Mar 10 1795 Crist, Henry to Head, Lucy
Mar  6 1796 Crist, Jacob to Reid, Sarah
Jul 30 1799 Crist, John to Balser, Susannah
Jun  8 1805 Crist, John to Umford, Catherine
Dec  8 1801 Crist, Margaret to Miller, John Samuel
Oct 27 1796 Crist, Mary to Lear, Michael
Feb 27 1798 Crist, Mary Cathereny to Devilbiss, John H.
Apr 15 1797 Crist, Peter to Mong, Margaret
Nov 20 1806 Crist, Rosanna to Delaplane, Joseph
Sep 27 1806 Crist, Susanna to Bard, Jacob
Mar 12 1805 Crist, Susanna to Carn, Frederick
Mar 15 1800 Crist, Valentine to Bowlas, Margaret
Oct  6 1803 Critezer, Jacob to Beckenbaugh, Elizabeth
Dec  2 1799 Croas, Mary Magdalene to Cost, Jacob
Aug 23 1794 Croft, Frederick to Weddle, Catherine
Aug 13 1792 Crom, Mary to Kerr, George
Oct  2 1794 Cromes, Aden to Williams, Pamelia
Feb 14 1803 Cromwell, John to Kephart, Margaret
Nov 11 1806 Cromwell, John to Kephart, Catherine
```

```
Apr 14 1807 Cromwell, Joseph M. to Anderson, Elizabeth
Nov 20 1806 Cromwell, Oliver to Gebhart, Harriet
May 13 1802 Cromwell, Richard to Grubb, Elizabeth
Apr 28 1785 Cromwell, Susanna to Dent, George
Jan 21 1799 Cromwell, William to Groff, Sarah
May 21 1779 Crone, Robert to Hagan, Nancy
Apr 29 1797 Cronice, Susanna to Lmbright, Henry
Apr 14 1781 Cronie, Henry to Overlast, Barbara
Aug  8 1801 Cronise, Catherine to Stoufer, Joseph
May 14 1788 Cronise, Eve to Zimmerman, Michael
Oct  8 1805 Cronise, Henry to Knouff, Elizabeth
Apr 14 1806 Cronise, Jacob to Fundenburgh, Catherine
Dec 30 1806 Cronise, John to Saum, Rachel
May 13 1797 Cronise, John, Junr. to Kemp, Eve
Feb  5 1781 Cronise, Susanna to Sunpower, Adam
Sep 12 1787 Cross, Barbara to Thompson, John
Apr 15 1798 Cross, George to Gradey, Anne
Feb  2 1782 Cross, Henry to Shoup, Catherine
Jun 18 1796 Cross, Lewis to Buckias, Mary
May  4 1803 Cross, Martha to Annin, Samuel
May  6 1793 Crossmug, John to Riley, Elizabeth
May  7 1810 Crossnickle, Eliz. to Harb, Jacob
Jan  3 1807 Crothers, James to Crideler, Elizabeth
Jun  8 1793 Crouse, Catharine to Sharrats, John
Jan 15 1810 Crouse, Frederick to Gwinn, Mary
May 28 1804 Crouse, Hannah to Louderman, George
May 20 1780 Crouse, John to Umstatt, Catherine
May 14 1803 Crow, Mary to Hedges, Joseph
Nov  4 1794 Crow, Sarah to Davage, Henry
Aug 22 1802 Crowdy, Elizabeth to Case, Alexander
Sep 15 1792 Crowell, John to Dagar, Susan
Apr 17 1779 Crowl, Barbara to Young, Leonard
Dec  7 1805 Crowl, Elizabeth to Hains, Jacob
Apr  7 1780 Crowl, Mich'l to Hosplehawn, Mary
Aug  2 1796 Crown, Conrad to Shroyer, Catherine
Mar  6 1797 Crum, Abraham to Ringer, Susanna
Jan 11 1796 Crum, Ephraim to Creager, Hannah
Apr 10 1802 Crum, Henry to Hoffman, Barbara
Nov 28 1791 Crum, Isaac to Plummer, Susanna
Sep  2 1807 Crum, Isaac to Bassford, Nancy
Mar  5 1785 Crum, John to Crum, Mary
Feb  2 1793 Crum, John to Crum, Rebeckah
Sep 19 1805 Crum, John to Miller, Eleanor
Feb  8 1806 Crum, John to Miller, Mary
Mar  5 1785 Crum, Mary to Crum, John
Mar  9 1803 Crum, Nathan to Creager, Amelia
Feb  2 1793 Crum, Rebeckah to Crum, John
Nov  5 1785 Crum, Sarah to Beyer, David
Jan 27 1801 Crum, William, Junior to Davis, Rebecca
Dec  7 1792 Crum, Wm. to Wise, Amelia
Dec 28 1793 Crum, Wm. to Levy, Elizabeth
Jul 11 1805 Crumbacker, Mary to Hammond, Thomas John
Jul 30 1803 Crumbaugh, David to Renner, Catharine
Jun  9 1806 Crumbine, John to Weaver, Sophia
Jan  9 1803 Crumpacker, Abraham to Baker, Eve
```

```
Jun  4 1809 Crumpvine, Jacob to Allex, Catherine
Jun 25 1781 Crusey, Rob't to Wells, Jane
Jan 18 1806 Crusoe, John to Kennedy, Lucy
Jul 17 1809 Crutchler, Vincent to Smith, Barbara
Nov 28 1804 Crutchley, Rachel to Ball, Samuel
Jan  5 1797 Cruthers, Ann to Keith, Price
Dec 28 1802 Crutsley, Elias to Campbell, Rosanna
Apr 25 1806 Crutzley, Dinah to Ourant, Jacob
Jan 29 1791 Cublentz, Elizabeth to Bare, George
Aug 19 1782 Culbertson, Samuel to McKean, Eleanor
Jan  6 1809 Culler, Barbara to Albaugh, Peter
Nov 24 1797 Culler, Caty to Ramsberg, George
May 19 1802 Culler, Elizabeth to Coblentz, Philip
Apr  6 1809 Culler, Henry to Fister, Anne
Dec 23 1795 Culler, Jacob to Storm, Mary
Jun  2 1802 Culler, Jacob to Long, Barbara
May 25 1805 Culler, Mary to Woodward, Nathaniel
Sep 23 1780 Culliston, Jeremiah to Chisholm, Margaret
Sep  4 1783 Cullom, Abigail to Owen, John
Mar 12 1788 Cullom, Susannah to Browning, Elias
Oct 12 1790 Cullom, William to Northcraft, Elizabeth
Nov  6 1790 Culp, Henry to Adlum, Catherine
Apr 13 1790 Culp, Michael to Grosh, Maria Sophia
Apr  9 1796 Cumming, Ann to Campbell, John, Junr.
May 22 1780 Cumming, Catherine to Simpson, Richard, Jr.
Aug 25 1778 Cumming, James to Coale, Casiah
Mar 17 1780 Cumming, Jane to McElfresh, John
Apr 14 1803 Cumming, John to Spurrier, Ann Louisa
Oct 21 1803 Cummings, Alice Ann to Shipley, Ezahiel
Mar 28 1793 Cummings, Elizabeth to Mathers, Tho
Nov 19 1798 Cumston, Joshua to Grable, Eve
Dec 21 1805 Cunningham, Aaron to Lemar, Eleanor
Sep 27 1806 Cunningham, Charles to Boteler, Ann
Dec 10 1780 Cunningham, Peter to Bird, Elizabeth
Dec 19 1801 Curffman, Henry to Tipple, Catherine
Aug 29 1807 Curfman, Christian to Tannehill, Harriot
May 14 1804 Curfman, Michael to Tipple, Sarah
Apr 25 1807 Curfman, Peter to McMullen, Susanna
Oct 13 1810 Curlin, Elizabeth to White, Elisha
Jan 19 1791 Curran, Biddy to Adams, Joseph
Jul 21 1783 Currance, Mary to Shaver, Tobias
Jan  4 1802 Currens, Anne to McKean, William
Feb 28 1809 Currens, William to Smith, Elizabeth
Jan 18 1793 Curry, Charles to Flood, Provey
Nov  8 1800 Curry, William to Dean, Sarah
Aug 31 1778 Curtis, Henry to Fulston, Hannah
Sep  3 1808 Curtis, Henry to Albaugh, Sarah
Apr  3 1802 Curtis, Mary to Furney, Abraham
Aug  7 1783 Curtis, Susanna to Moffett, John
Mar 31 1798 Curts, Nicholas to Burkhart, Margaret
Dec 17 1780 Curtz, Barbara to Sewalt, Jacob
Dec 24 1808 Cushen, Mary to Barnes, Owen
Apr 13 1790 Cushman, Eleanor to Greenwell, Philbert
Dec 14 1802 Cushour, Peter to Risler, Elizabeth
Sep  9 1803 Custard, Jonas to Hoffman, Catherine
```

```
Oct  3 1810 Custer, Polly to Cimmings, Joseph
Apr 12 1779 Cutler, Edw'd to Asbill, Mary
Dec  4 1798 Cutsail, Elizabeth to Thompson, Samuel
Nov 30 1807 Cutshall, Eve to Mayhue, Zedock
Apr  3 1784 Cutshall, George to Hammond, Hannah

Dec 27 1808 Dade, Townsend T. to Simmons, Ruth
Dec 22 1804 Dadisman, Elizabeth to Hanes, Jeremiah
Jan 16 1802 Dadisman, Peggy to Buckie, George
Sep 15 1792 Dagar, Susan to Crowell, John
Feb 29 1804 Dagen, John to Myers, Elizabeth
Apr 11 1807 Dahoff, Hannah to Lemmon, Samuel
Dec 17 1793 Dale, John Petere to Lemon, Catherine
Dec  8 1804 Daley, Nancy to McGarey, William
May 12 1778 Dalton, Hannah to Farroll, Thomas
Mar  4 1799 Dament, Daniel to Dickensheets, Hannah
Jun 28 1808 Damon, John to Fridinger, Esther
May  4 1800 Daniel, Jane to Talbott, Joseph
Feb  8 1795 Dannell, Isabel to Stewart, James
Jan 29 1780 Dannelly, Peggy to Thomas, Daniel
Feb 22 1802 Danner, Catherine to Schnerr, Charles
Oct  7 1799 Danner, Zachariah to Sawyer, Margaret
Apr 17 1779 Danniwolf, Elizabeth to Hart, Benj'n
May 24 1792 Darbey, Caleb to Gartrill, Sarah
Feb  3 1780 Darbey, Sarah to Phillips, Caleb
Aug 14 1779 Darlon, Remela to Addison, Robert
Sep  3 1785 Darnall, Henry to Leek, Mary
Nov  3 1788 Darnall, Philip to Perrill, Lucy
Jun 28 1808 Darnall, Ralph to Kolenburg, Hannah
May 19 1809 Darner, Barbara to Snerr, Henry
Sep 22 1807 Darner, Mary to Castle, John
Jul 27 1795 Darr, Catherine to Guy, Samuel
Apr 22 1780 Darr, Eliz'th to Getzendanner, Geo.
Apr 22 1780 Darr, Eliz'th to Kitzadanner, Geo.
Nov 28 1795 Darr, John to Stoner, Catherine
Mar  9 1805 Darr, John to Smith, Esther
Sep 18 1806 Darsh, Henry to Richter, Catherine
Nov 18 1803 Darst, John to Brain, Rebecka
May  3 1804 Daub, John to Routzan, Catherine
Nov  5 1795 Daugherty, George to Gerhart, Catherine
Nov  4 1794 Davage, Henry to Crow, Sarah
Jun 28 1796 Davey, John to Dorsey, Ruth
Nov 17 1796 Davidson, David to Harris, Dorcus
May 19 1800 Davis, Ambrose to White, Bewly
Jul 12 1796 Davis, Ann to Myers, Henry
Sep  7 1809 Davis, Anna to Geyton, Vincent
Jun 23 1786 Davis, Barnabas to Hobbs, Elizabeth
Oct 30 1792 Davis, Benjamin to Weaver, Catherine
Sep  5 1787 Davis, Cassandra to Hearn, Elijah
Sep 16 1779 Davis, Catherine to Sellman, Gassaway
Jan 23 1786 Davis, Christena to Hickman, Christopher
Apr  9 1782 Davis, Cicely to Chandler, Nathan
Oct 23 1804 Davis, David to Thompson, Sarah
Sep  2 1786 Davis, Drucilla to Hill, Nathan
Oct 28 1798 Davis, Eleanor to Ferrel, George
```

```
Apr  9 1789 Davis, Eleanor to Spurrier, Joseph
Aug  3 1779 Davis, Elizabeth to Harrison, Josias
Sep  1 1789 Davis, Elizabeth to Heckenmiller, John Conrad
Mar  4 1797 Davis, Elizabeth to Hammond, Lot
Apr 15 1798 Davis, Elizabeth to Martin, George
Jul 16 1806 Davis, Elizabeth to Sulliman, Jacob
Apr 11 1791 Davis, Elizabeth to Welsch, Philip
Apr 10 1795 Davis, Frances Brown to Molton, Wilfred
May  1 1790 Davis, Francis to Elliot, Sarah
Aug  4 1810 Davis, Isaac to Norris, Elizabeth
Apr  4 1795 Davis, Jarret to McDonald, Elizabeth
May  4 1782 Davis, John to Potter, Mary
Dec 19 1787 Davis, John to Widmeyer, Elizabeth
Nov 23 1802 Davis, John to Padget, Elizabeth
Oct 30 1804 Davis, John to Barber, Permelia
Nov  2 1809 Davis, John to Walker, Peggy
Dec  7 1799 Davis, Jonathan to Smith, Mary
Mar 24 1806 Davis, Josep to Ward, Maryan
Aug  6 1779 Davis, Joseph to How, Ann
Jul 30 1792 Davis, Levi to Whitmyer, Eleanor
Jul 10 1787 Davis, Lucretia to Philips, William
Sep 20 1804 Davis, Lucy to Soper, James
Sep 15 1783 Davis, Ludwick to Yates, Susanna
Oct  9 1807 Davis, Luke to Duvall, May
Nov  3 1806 Davis, Mary to Cannon, Moses
Nov  4 1778 Davis, Mary to Harrison, Wm.
Apr 21 1810 Davis, Mary to Penn, Samuel
Aug  3 1793 Davis, Mary to Veatch, Solomon
Jan 25 1786 Davis, Mary to Welsh, Henry
Jan 25 1804 Davis, Mary to Willson, John
Dec 19 1788 Davis, Mathias to Maynard, Rachel
Feb  9 1779 Davis, Nancey to Richardson, Wm.
Oct  4 1795 Davis, Nancy to Elliot, John
Mar  6 1794 Davis, Nancy to Goldie, Jacob
Jun 16 1792 Davis, Nancy Weaver to Veatch, John
Mar 10 1784 Davis, Rachel to Fleming, John
Jan 27 1801 Davis, Rebecca to Crum, William, Junior
Nov 10 1796 Davis, Reuben to Taylor, Eleanor
Mar 15 1782 Davis, Rezin to Phillips, Nancey
Jul 26 1809 Davis, Richard to Lewis, Sophia
Sep  2 1800 Davis, Samuel to Walls, Rachel
Oct  6 1809 Davis, Samuel to Musgrove, Eleanor
Oct  3 1808 Davis, Sarah to Cain, Benjamin
Feb  8 1785 Davis, Sarah to Flemming, Arthur
Apr 30 1794 Davis, Sarah to Falconer, Elisha
Dec 29 1799 Davis, Sarah to Newman, Stacey
Dec  6 1803 Davis, Sarah to Sleighmaker, Alexander
May 16 1807 Davis, Sarah to Salmon, William
Mar 20 1788 Davis, Sarah to Hain, Caleb
Apr 16 1803 Davis, Solomon to O'Neale, Elizabeth
Feb 29 1804 Davis, William to Rine, Elizabeth
Feb 15 1785 Davis, William Luckett to Hungerford, Elizabeth
Nov 11 1794 Davis, Zachariah to Hyatt, Elizabeth
Jan 30 1808 Davy, Henry to Bussard, Judith
Dec  2 1788 Dawson, Ann to Coale, Dennis
```

```
Feb 18 1784 Dawson, Ann to Dawson, Richard
Mar 21 1782 Dawson, Benjamin to Simmons, Mary
Jan 29 1780 Dawson, Elizabeth to Roland, Gaidon
Apr 12 1788 Dawson, John to Hagan, Mary
Sep 22 1806 Dawson, John to Hays, Anne
Aug 27 1781 Dawson, Nicholas to Bayne, Elizabeth
Sep  7 1797 Dawson, Peggy to Haff, William M.
Oct 13 1795 Dawson, Priscilla to Hauer, Nicholas
Feb 18 1784 Dawson, Richard to Dawson, Ann
Jul 29 1809 Dawson, Thomas to Allnutt, Susanna H.
Apr 22 1789 Dawson, William to Gilbert, Ann
Oct  1 1796 Days, Henry to Tall, Ruth
Apr  8 1785 De Coine, Sarah to McKardile, Isaac
Apr 22 1783 De Reitzenstein, Frederick to Shonkmeyer,
             Catherine Eliz'th
Feb  7 1792 Deaghe, Mary to Stoner, Daniel
Feb  2 1790 Deal, John to Burckhartt, Catherine
Jan 18 1806 Deal, John to Trout, Philpena
Apr 22 1806 Deal, Julia W. to Butler, William
Dec 18 1790 Deal, Peter to Elliot, Mary
Nov 18 1794 Deale, Henry to Eckard, Mary
Nov  7 1778 Deame, Robert to Reynolds, Eliz'th
Dec 15 1798 Dean, Barnabas to Frushour, Elizabeth
Jan  6 1800 Dean, Bernard to Frushour, Elizabeth
Mar 14 1807 Dean, Elizabeth to Gaver, Daniel
Mar 20 1809 Dean, Jacob to Malone, Sidney
Nov  8 1800 Dean, Sarah to Curry, William
Feb 17 1810 Dean, Stewart to Patterson, Mary
Jan 17 1805 Dean, William to Reynolds, Allice
Jun 25 1778 Deaver, Abraham to Lakin, Ann
Apr  2 1810 Deaver, Abraham to Matthews, Margaret
Sep 22 1806 Deaver, Basil to Everhart, Mary Ann
Dec 31 1804 Deaver, Levi to Griffith, Sophia
Oct 19 1808 Deaver, Levi to House, Nancy
Jan  5 1810 Deaver, Margaret to Frazier, Horatio
Dec 26 1799 Deaver, Misel to Frazier, Sarah
Jul 22 1803 Deavers, Joshua to Matthews, Hannah
Dec 14 1797 Deberry, George to Upcraft, Caty
Jul 31 1787 Deberry, Sarah to Rieston, Samuel
Mar 24 1809 Debery, John to Shreup, Catherine
Aug 23 1800 Debery, Rachel to Fox, Peter
Sep 26 1804 Debrule, James C. to Baltzell, Mary
Jun 29 1793 Decker, Anna to Meloy, John
Feb 13 1808 Decker, Jacob to Barnhart, Rachel
Jun  5 1780 Declve, Magdaline to Able, John
Feb 21 1781 Deerdarf, Abm. to Bowersmith, Cath.
Sep 25 1809 Deever, Reuben to Roads, Mary
Nov 10 1792 Dehaven, Andrew to Kemp, Esther
Dec  3 1804 Dehavin, John to Brandenberg, Catherine
Jan 30 1792 Dehoff, Hannah to Myers, John
Sep 11 1789 Dehoof, Philip to Ebbert, Elizabeth
Jan  4 1810 Delaplane, Jacob to Vallentine, Sarah
Nov 20 1806 Delaplane, Joseph to Crist, Rosanna
Nov  2 1792 Delaplane, Joshua to Dern, Mary
Jan  8 1807 Delaplane, Mary to Carmack, John
Jan  4 1785 Delaplank, Catherine to Bayer, Mich'l
```

```
Jul  7 1780 Delashmitt, Anne to Warfield, Richard
Jun 28 1806 Delashmut, Elisabeth to Compton, John
Jun 12 1809 Delashmutt, Artemese to Higdon, Thomas
Jun 14 1782 Delashmutt, Basil to Jacobs, Mary
Dec 26 1796 Delashmutt, Elizabeth to Walling, William
Jul  1 1795 Delashmutt, Jane to Briscoe, John
Feb 22 1779 Delashmutt, Lindsey to Trammell, Sarah
Mar  3 1792 Delashmutt, Sarah to Briscoe, Ralph
Dec 29 1797 Delashmutt, Sarah to Shimer, Isaac
Aug 19 1809 Delashumutt, Trammell to Moriarty, Mary W.
Feb  2 1790 Delauder, Catherine to Wirtz, Michael
Apr 18 1807 Delauder, Jacob to Michael, Elizabeth
Mar 21 1798 Delauder, John to Creager, Margaret
Jun 14 1806 Delaughter, Catherine to Slusser, Henry
Dec  1 1806 Delauter, David to Smith, Elizabeth
Jan  3 1786 Delauter, Elizabeth to Faling, Henry
Oct  9 1779 Delauter, Susanna to Brooner, John
Sep 20 1799 Deleplane, Daniel to Dern, Sophia
Mar  1 1806 Deleplane, Daniel to Norris, Catherine
Dec  3 1794 Dell, John to Peagae, Polly
Feb 21 1801 Dell, John Adam to Durbin, Rebecca
Sep 25 1802 Dell, Lydia to Baxter, John
Jan 20 1800 Delozier, Susannah to Bartley, Joseph
Oct 28 1805 Demcey, Thomas to Thomas, Mary
May 13 1807 Dempsey, Joseph to Lookenpeel, Mary
Feb  9 1810 Denison, Mary to Latshaw, John
Oct 14 1803 Dent, Aquila to Thomas, Catherine
Apr 28 1785 Dent, George to Cromwell, Susanna
Oct  8 1778 Dentlinger, Margaret to Miller, Jacob
May 13 1780 Depos, Jacob to Nicholls, Charlotte
Apr 21 1790 Dern, Catharine to Rice, James
Oct  3 1809 Dern, Elizabeth to Barnard, Benjamin
Sep 30 1786 Dern, Elizabeth to Knouff, Jacob
May 27 1796 Dern, Frances to Haff, Abraham, Jr.
Mar  5 1798 Dern, Frederick to Buckias, Elizabeth
May 19 1806 Dern, Frederick to Ott, Elizabeth
Dec  8 1792 Dern, Isaac to Berrier, Susanna
Nov  2 1792 Dern, Mary to Delaplane, Joshua
Sep  8 1788 Dern, Mary to Hedge, Caleb
Oct  3 1783 Dern, Nancy to Rice, James
Sep 20 1799 Dern, Sophia to Deleplane, Daniel
Sep  7 1797 Dern, Susanna to Stallins, William
Dec 30 1799 Dern, William to Carmack, Elizabeth
Jul  5 1803 Dern, William, Junr. to Lambrecht, Margaret
Aug  2 1783 Derr, Christena to Shryock, Valentine
Mar 17 1795 Derr, Eve to Holtzman, Conrad
Feb  2 1787 Derr, Jacob to Wintz, Margaret
Mar 29 1806 Derr, Jacob to Reel, Barbara
May  2 1810 Derr, Jacob to Long, Margaret
Sep  1 1798 Derr, John to Brim, Elizabeth
Feb 22 1782 Derr, Margaret to Grose, Henry
Feb 22 1800 Derr, Susanna to Miller, Henry
May 22 1786 Derr, Susannah to Devilbiss, Casper
Apr  8 1803 Derr, Thomas to Stoner, Barbara
Apr 23 1810 Dertzabaugh, Margaret to Bartgis, Mathias E.
```

```
Aug 13 1808 Dertzbaugh, Elizabeth to Killion, Philip
Oct 19 1799 Dertzebaugh, John to Knouff, Christena
Apr 26 1784 Deshong, William to Harris, Jane
May 24 1801 Devaney, James to Turner, Anna
Oct  3 1801 Devilbis, Margaret to Heckaturn, George
May 27 1778 Devilbiss, Adam to Barrick, Catherine
Sep 15 1792 Devilbiss, Appelona to Gramer, Adam
Feb 20 1810 Devilbiss, Caspar to Bostian, Mary
May 22 1786 Devilbiss, Casper to Derr, Susannah
Dec 23 1799 Devilbiss, Catharine to Campbell, Bennet
Aug 23 1794 Devilbiss, Catherine to Sadler, John
Oct 18 1788 Devilbiss, Elizbeth to Brengle, Christian
Mar 13 1798 Devilbiss, George to Karr, Martha
Jul 16 1805 Devilbiss, George to Devilbiss, Rebecca
Nov 14 1807 Devilbiss, John to Devilbiss, Martha
Feb 27 1798 Devilbiss, John H. to Crist, Mary Cathereny
Aug 23 1809 Devilbiss, Margaret to Angleberger, George
Nov 14 1807 Devilbiss, Martha to Devilbiss, John
Nov  5 1795 Devilbiss, Philippena to Grumbauch, Simon
Jul 16 1805 Devilbiss, Rebecca to Devilbiss, George
Nov  6 1802 Devilbiss, Rosanna to Steel, Jacob
Apr 15 1809 Devilbiss, Samuel to Kerr, Elizabeth
Apr  9 1782 Devit, Valentine to Williams, Mary
Oct  7 1810 Devoy, Mary Ann to Stedman, William
May 12 1794 Dewees, Sarah to Hodgkiss, Michael
Jan  7 1797 Dewire, Leonard to Linaweaver, Margaret
May 27 1809 Dick, John to Feagler, Catherine
Feb 26 1808 Dick, Levi to Shroyer, Elizabeth
Sep 22 1809 Dick, Philip to Morningstar, Elizabeth
Aug 17 1801 Dick, Susanna to Snyder, William
Apr  8 1799 Dick, Susannah to Frushour, Jacob
Jan  8 1782 Dickensheets, Cathe. to Markley, Gabriel
Apr 11 1791 Dickensheets, Elizabeth to Dudderer, Samuel
Mar  4 1799 Dickensheets, Hannah to Dament, Daniel
Sep 18 1779 Dickensheets, Mary to Markel, Adam
Apr 23 1779 Dickoutt, Elizabeth to Youtzell, Christian
May 26 1806 Dicks, John to Steward, Mary
Jan 23 1797 Dickson, Ann to Poole, William, Jr.
Aug  3 1782 Dickson, Mary to Hedges, Shardrick
May 24 1802 Difebaugh, Catherine to Euty, Philip
Feb 13 1809 Dill, Elizabeth to Bowman, Samuel
Jul  9 1778 Dillan, Rosanna to Gander, George
Apr  7 1806 Dillaplane, Margaret to Miller, Peter
Sep  6 1806 Dillehay, Thomas L. to Stonebraker, Anna
Jun  3 1809 Dilly, Benjamin to Evans, Anne
Oct 24 1795 Dilworth, John to Williams, Priscilla
Oct 25 1809 Dinsmore, Thomas to Taylor, Margaret
Sep 19 1797 Ditto, Catherine to Eli, David
Aug 21 1801 Divers, John to Holland, Mary
Jan 23 1799 Dix, Sarah to Knight, Elijah
May  2 1803 Dixen, John Calhoun to Razor, Elizabeth
Oct 30 1808 Dixon, William to Keppeling, Elizabeth
May  9 1798 Dixson, John Hattin to Tobery, Mary
Sep 22 1778 Dobson, William to Ray, Mary
Apr 16 1798 Dodds, Philip to Smith, Susanna
```

```
Apr 26 1797 Dodds, Samuel to Manahan, Margaret
Sep 17 1791 Dodds, Sarah to Smith, Adam
May 12 1789 Dodson, Esther to Farquhar, Rob't
Dec 31 1784 Dodson, Mary to Brightwell, John
Oct  7 1797 Doefler, Caty to Nuss, Frederick
Nov 26 1807 Dofler, Sybilla to Smith, Joseph
May  3 1803 Doll, Catharine to Gebhart, George
Nov 17 1798 Doll, Charlotte to Steckle, Solomon
Dec  5 1795 Doll, Charlotte to Hart, Peter
Jul  5 1791 Doll, Elizabeth to Hoffman, Valentine
Jan 28 1800 Doll, John to Kurtz, Susannah
Oct  3 1807 Doll, Margaret to Brunner, Jacob
Nov 12 1807 Doll, Susanna to Lear, George
Aug  6 1781 Donaldson, Ann to Rawlings, Solomon
Jan  8 1781 Donavan, Catherine to Goodacre, Wm.
Mar 21 1778 Donn, Mary to Stipe, James
Mar  9 1803 Donnavan, William to Tinderman, Susanna
May  4 1800 Donovan, John to Hannah, Margaret
Oct 15 1806 Donovan, Susanna to Shields, Barnet
Apr 29 1789 Donoven, William to Trenter, Esther
Jun 16 1810 Donston, Thomas to Gaivin, Barbara
Feb 17 1781 Dorchester, Wm. to Trencer, Mary
Feb 19 1787 Dorff, Catharine to Hollar, Mich'l
Nov 19 1808 Dorff, George to Weaver, Mary
Apr  8 1810 Dorff, Mary to Barker, Wm.
May 17 1802 Dorsey, Allen to Smith, Elizabeth
Mar 15 1810 Dorsey, Ann W. to Sprigg, Otho
Mar 25 1807 Dorsey, Ariminta to Hammond, George
Mar 25 1782 Dorsey, Basil to Richardson, Tabitha
Aug  1 1792 Dorsey, Basil to Harris, Harriet
Mar 27 1802 Dorsey, Edward to Klein, Mary
Nov 26 1802 Dorsey, Edward to Warfield, Ruth
Dec 17 1810 Dorsey, Eli, Junr. to Johnson, Sarah
Dec 15 1803 Dorsey, Elizabeth to Waters, Ignatius
Dec 23 1788 Dorsey, Evan to Lawrence, Susanna
Feb 24 1784 Dorsey, Greenbury to Hobbs, Sarah
Jun 23 1809 Dorsey, Harriet to Crapster, Basil
Dec 13 1786 Dorsey, Henrietta to Hobbs, Wm. of Sam'l
Nov 30 1799 Dorsey, John to Cochran, Eleanor
Dec 20 1785 Dorsey, John Lawrence to Bonham, Rachel
Oct  8 1807 Dorsey, John W. to Howard, Deborah
Mar  5 1788 Dorsey, Johnsa to Hammond, Sarah
Sep 15 1795 Dorsey, Joshua, Esq. to Kennedy, Janet
Dec 31 1798 Dorsey, Josias to Dorsey, Sophia
May 13 1793 Dorsey, Lucy to Sprigg, Thomas
Apr 14 1807 Dorsey, Luke to Worman, Barbara
Mar 28 1810 Dorsey, Maria to Randall, Vachel, W.
Dec 24 1806 Dorsey, Mary to Sollers, Sabrit
Sep  6 1796 Dorsey, Mich'l of Jno. to Poole, Elizabeth
Feb  7 1791 Dorsey, Oner to Puffinberger, Adam
Mar 17 1804 Dorsey, Rachel to Grimes, Orlando
May  4 1778 Dorsey, Rachel to McElfresh, John, Jr.
Jun 28 1796 Dorsey, Ruth to Davey, John
Dec 31 1798 Dorsey, Sophia to Dorsey, Josias
Jan 27 1789 Dorsey, Sophia to Dorsey, Wm. Jr.
```

```
Dec  6 1797 Dorsey, Sophia to Petticoat, George
Aug  1 1799 Dorsey, Sophia to Sheredine, Upton
Nov 22 1803 Dorsey, Susan to Howard, Samuel
Nov 23 1780 Dorsey, Trusilla to Mobley, Lewis
Feb 28 1792 Dorsey, Vachael to Poole, Ann
May 21 1793 Dorsey, William to Hobbs, Rachel
Apr  2 1781 Dorsey, Wm. to Worthington, Eliz'th
Jan 27 1789 Dorsey, Wm. Jr. to Dorsey, Sophia
Apr 23 1791 Doss, Margaret to Geyer, Adam
Jan 17 1787 Dotson, Elizabeth to Justice, Nicholas
Apr 12 1804 Doub, Valentine to Kemp, Esther
Nov 17 1807 Dougherty, Edward to Fardin, Rachel
May 29 1807 Dougherty, Nancy to Ponder, Abraham
Jan  9 1796 Douglass, Charles to Hall, Rebeckah
Oct  9 1807 Doup, Rosannah to Keller, Jacob
Jul  4 1809 Douty, James to Harn, Corrella
Nov 16 1807 Dow, John to Stires, Rhoda
Feb  6 1792 Dowden, Michael to Dunn, Mary
Aug 23 1798 Dowdle, Elizabeth to Noland, Gregary
May 22 1795 Dowdle, Margaret to Ransdale, Stephen Chilton
Dec  5 1806 Dowdle, Mary to Muret, James
Sep 18 1779 Dowlan, Mary Eve to Bourmaster, John W.
Nov 22 1798 Dowlen, Martha to Potts, Jonas
Jan  2 1794 Dowling, Edward to Gordon, Mary
Feb 16 1795 Downey, Alexander to Tucker, Mary
Feb 11 1797 Downey, Mary to Westenhaver, Christian
Aug  6 1810 Downey, Rebecca to Lyons, George
Sep 22 1784 Downing, James to Waters, Acena
Feb  2 1786 Downing, Sarah to Tucker, Littleton
Sep 13 1786 Doyle, John to Adamson, Sophia
Sep 16 1806 Doyle, William to Stauffer, Mariah
Oct 17 1780 Drake, Wm. to Hinckle, Eliz'th
Dec  6 1804 Draper (or Traper), Thomas to Zimmerman, Mary
May  3 1781 Drew, Mich'l to Woolf, Eliz'th
Aug  5 1806 Dribets, Powell to Hargraw, Judith
Oct  1 1797 Drill, Catherine to Carper, Philip
May  2 1809 Drill, Christian to Leakins, Elizabeth
Jun  4 1807 Drill, Elizabeth to Warthen, Francis
Jun  5 1802 Drill, Jacob to Niswanger, Mary
Oct 14 1797 Drill, Mary to Schley, Matthias
Dec 19 1808 Driscoll, Deborah to Ways, Brice
Oct 23 1803 Drish, Jean to Hammerly, John
Sep 16 1786 Drone, Wm. to Sheckells, Susanna
Mar 25 1793 Drowry, Ignatius to Goldsborough, Mary
Oct  6 1807 Drue, Elizabeth to Roderick, Jacob
Nov 19 1798 Drumon, James to Starling, Sarah
Aug  1 1780 Dryden, Wm. to Kisinger, Philipeana
Mar  5 1790 Ducker, John to Bissett, Eliza.
Jan 27 1780 Duckett, Eliz'th to Hammond, Ormond
Apr 29 1809 Dudderer, Margaret to Thornburgh, Ephraim
Apr 11 1791 Dudderer, Samuel to Dickensheets, Elizabeth
Mar  8 1803 Dudderer, Sarah to Funson, John
Sep  3 1808 Dudderer, Sarah to Manahan, Jonas
Apr 11 1809 Dudderer, William to Shriner, Margaret
Mar 10 1806 Duddero, Catherine to Wren, George
```

```
Dec  3 1800 Duddero, Michael to Ringer, Mary
Mar  1 1800 Duffey, Allen to Gasslin, Sarah
Feb 22 1790 Duffield, Leah to Hedges, William
Jun  3 1779 Duffle, Mary to Knox, Thos.
Nov 12 1804 Duffy, Henrietta to House, John
Apr 20 1805 Dugan, Jinnet to Freeman, John
Nov 25 1805 Dugas, Louis Jean Jacques to Morris, Ann Louisa
Sep 22 1808 Dunen, Rebeccah to Kelly, John
Aug  3 1802 Dunham, James C. to Hoover, Ann
Nov 15 1805 Duning, William to Harrey, Nancy
Jan 19 1792 Dunkin, Mary to McIntire, John
Feb  6 1792 Dunn, Mary to Dowden, Michael
Apr 24 1798 Dunn, Thomas to Warthan, Mary
May 30 1794 Dunn, William to Hawne, Christina
Mar  4 1786 Dunning, John to Mansfield, Ruth
Jun 30 1795 Duphorn, Simon to Boose, Barbara
Jan 29 1789 Durbin, Cornelius to Harrison, Mary
Mar  3 1802 Durbin, Elinder to Mattingly, Samuel
Oct 12 1809 Durbin, Ephraim to Buckingham, Nancy
Jul  1 1791 Durbin, John to Poulson, Margaret
Nov 30 1805 Durbin, Margaret to Lindsey, David
Jun 14 1805 Durbin, Rachael to Hide, Jonethan
Feb 15 1779 Durbin, Rachel to Polson, James
Feb 21 1801 Durbin, Rebecca to Dell, John Adam
Jul 12 1790 Durff, Elizabeth to Sifert, Mathias
Nov 21 1780 Durff, Jacob to Grindler, Juliana
Aug  3 1803 Durham, Peggy to Sicafucer, John
Sep 13 1800 Durst, Catherine to Clem, George
Dec 31 1805 Durst, Mary to Ramsberg, John
Jan 15 1785 Dust, John to Pritchett, Elizabeth
Nov 16 1791 Dutrow, Susanna to Colliberger, John
Aug 21 1779 Dutterar, John to Summer, Catherine
Jan 21 1799 Dutterer, Conrad to Soolser, Susannah
Aug  5 1794 Duttero, Conrad to Kerr, Frances
Aug 27 1792 Duttero, John to Worman, Susanna
Nov 20 1795 Duttero, John to Nusbaum, Mary
Mar  2 1810 Duttero, John to Hoffman, Polly
May  6 1790 Duttero, Margaret to Stull, John
Dec 25 1793 Duttero, Mr. to Baker, Peggey
Aug 20 1794 Duttero, Patty to Rice, Perry
Aug 20 1805 Duttero, Rosina to Sowers, Peter
Apr 23 1784 Duvall, Ann to Duvall, Levi
Feb  9 1799 Duvall, Benjamin to Thompson, Sarah
Jan 12 1805 Duvall, Benjamin to Ijams, Rebecca
Feb 22 1809 Duvall, Charity to Harn, Caleb
Oct  3 1797 Duvall, Claudius to Carmack, Elizabeth
Dec 11 1803 Duvall, Elisha to Gross, Phebe
May 21 1787 Duvall, Elizabeth to Owen, Hezekiah
Jan  1 1785 Duvall, Elizabeth to Simpson, Benjamin
May  7 1804 Duvall, Grafton to Hawkins, Elizabeth W.
Dec  3 1803 Duvall, James to Purdy, Catherine
Jul  4 1809 Duvall, John to Cooke, Sophia
Apr 23 1784 Duvall, Levi to Duvall, Ann
Jul 17 1801 Duvall, Mareen, H. to Price, Hannah
Jul  8 1789 Duvall, Marsen to Howard, Rachel
```

```
Oct 29 1792 Duvall, Marsh Mareen to Wilson, Rebeckah
Dec  2 1795 Duvall, Marsh Mareen to Fowler, Ann
Oct  9 1807 Duvall, May to Davis, Luke
Aug 14 1807 Duvall, Samuel to Allison, Mary
Feb 10 1794 Duvall, Sarah to Ijams, Thomas Plummer
Sep 11 1807 Duvall, Thomas to Richards, Susanna
Jan 16 1799 Dwyre, Jane to Wallace, Robert
May  8 1793 Dyer, Elizabeth to Wells, Richard, Dr.
May 31 1796 Dyer, Mary to Hughes, Francis
Aug 28 1790 Dyson, John Baptist to O'Nele, Mary
Jan  9 1786 Dyson, Mary to O'Neale, Barton
Mar 30 1795 Dyson, Sarah to Bird, Sam'l

Dec 29 1810 Eader, Abraham of Jno. to Hill, Elizabeth
Oct 18 1788 Eader, Adam to Kitterman, Elizabeth
Aug 28 1807 Eader, Nancy to Keller, Henry
Apr 12 1804 Earhart, Elizabeth to Beamer, Peter
Oct 17 1796 Earle, Jane to Watson, Walter
Jun  8 1809 Early, John to Gibberthorp, Sarah
Nov 27 1810 Earnst, Hester to Earnst, William
Jun 21 1785 Earnst, Jacob to Smith, Mary
Nov 27 1810 Earnst, William to Earnst, Hester
Aug 24 1793 Eastburn, Mary to Boteler, Henry
May 17 1790 Eastburn, Robinson to Boteler, Sarah
Nov  7 1791 Eastburn, Uness to Martheny, Wm.
Aug 31 1801 Easterday, Abraham to Fout, Modelena
Jun  5 1795 Easterday, Christian to Geddis, Cath.
Sep 15 1807 Easterday, Christian to Landers, Nancy
Jan  5 1805 Easterday, Conrad to Ahalt, Catherine
Dec 27 1806 Easterday, Elizabeth to Stockman, Philip
Sep  9 1796 Easterday, Jacob to Landers, Rachel
Jan 14 1805 Easterday, Julianna to Slifer, David
Dec  9 1806 Easton, Mary to Goodman, Jacob
Nov 16 1783 Easton, Mary to Leashorn, Conrad
Jul 19 1778 Easton, Ruth to Parnell, Bedwell
Jun 27 1803 Eastup, Sarah Cartwright to Squires, Asa
Mar 18 1781 Eatan, Pheby to Clefford, Michael
Feb 25 1804 Eater, Abraham to Koenig, Susanna
Nov 26 1810 Eater, Ann to Anderson, Jonathan M.
Jan 31 1781 Eater, Mary Magdalene to Plumb, George
Apr 25 1785 Eater, Wendelena to Whitmar, Lazarus
Sep 13 1806 Eaton, Isaac to Metzger, Rebeccah
Feb 20 1804 Eaton, Leonard to Palmer, Mary
Sep 11 1789 Ebbert, Elizabeth to Dehoof, Philip
Nov 10 1802 Ebbert, Henry to Tice, Mary
Feb 11 1800 Ebbert, John to Fritchie, Rebecca
Jan  7 1804 Ebbert, Susanna to Hardman, Henry
Aug 27 1804 Ebbert, Valentine to Spoon, Catherine
Jan  7 1809 Ebert, Frederick to Hague, Mary Ann
Nov  2 1793 Ebert, George Adam to Fout, Catherine
Sep  5 1801 Ebert, George Adam to Fout, Nancy
Oct 30 1783 Ebert, John to Ming, Margaret
Jul 27 1809 Ebert, Michael to Kelly, Elizabeth
Apr 19 1779 Ebert, Philip to Swadner, Mary
Nov 11 1809 Eberts, Jacob to Stimmell, Susanna
```

```
Nov  4 1803 Ebright, Mary Ann to Holter, John
Aug  6 1799 Eby, Jacob to Renner, Mary
Jan  7 1809 Eby, Mary to Shank, John
Dec 17 1783 Eck, Catherine to Shaw, Basil
Mar  5 1802 Eck, Elizabeth to Stansberry, Elijah
Nov 18 1794 Eckard, Mary to Deale, Henry
Oct  9 1805 Eckart, Henry to Gloss, Magdalena
Feb  8 1806 Ecker, Abraham to Barnhart, Elizabeth
Sep 13 1806 Eckhart, Anthony to Sheetinghelm, Catherine
Mar 22 1779 Eckman,  Christena to Snowdagle, Peter
Jan 27 1806 Eckman, Barbara to Pittinger, William
Jan  1 1808 Eckman, George to Shreup, Modelena
Jul 29 1797 Eckman, Jacob to Pitenger, Catherine
Dec 28 1799 Eckman, Michael to Jacob, Mary
Aug  5 1809 Ecleman, Susanna to Coleman, John
May 11 1778 Edeldire(?), James to Hammond, Mary
Jan 12 1801 Edelen, Ann to Knott, Philip
May 10 1782 Edelen, Clarissa to Thomas, Nathan
Apr 15 1784 Edelen, Rebecca to Bayard, John Hodge
Feb 26 1784 Edelin, Eleanor to Lynn, John
Jun  9 1793 Edwards, Headen to Beall, Susannah
Feb 24 1794 Edwards, John to Winfield, Ann
Jan 11 1779 Edwards, Mary to Powell, William
Aug 30 1797 Edwards, Robert to Heggins, Rebecca
Jul 23 1804 Edwards, Sarah to Brown, John
Mar 24 1801 Egnew, Henry to Fetterling, Elizabeth
Jun 18 1805 Eibert, Catherine to Michael, George
Sep  9 1778 Eichelberger, Christianna to Hawn, Michael
Nov 22 1810 Eichelberger, Elizabeth to Smith, Lewis
Apr 17 1806 Eichelberger, Jacob to Fout, Margaret
Jul 30 1803 Eichelberger, John to Zimmerman, Catherine
Feb 18 1808 Eichelberger, Magdalena to Coppersmith, Henry
Feb 28 1795 Eichelberger, Mary to Welty, Barnabas
Aug  7 1792 Eichenbrode, Daniel to Yost, Elizabeth
Dec  5 1807 Eickhofe, Elizabeth to Ramsberg, Stephen
Sep 26 1803 Eigenbrode, Christian to Iler, Margaret
Apr 11 1800 Eigenbrode, John to Singer, Susannah
Apr 29 1807 Eighenbrode, Margaret to Herring, Isaac
Oct 13 1808 Eiler, Samuel to Lavich, Mary
Dec 11 1806 Eiler, Susannah to Mayers, James
Jan 30 1804 Elder, Annie to Murphy, William, Jr.
Apr  1 1780 Elder, Eleanor to Guthrie, Wm.
Jun 12 1779 Elder, James to Burn, Eliz'th
May  7 1792 Elder, James to Hughes, Kitty
Apr 27 1808 Elder, Joseph to Head, Lucy
Mar 28 1788 Elder, Martha to Beckwith, William
Mar  3 1783 Elder, Mary to Harris, John
Apr 25 1806 Elder, Mary to Keepers, James
Jan  3 1808 Elger, Ann to Thrift, Charles
Aug 22 1793 Elginger, Modelena to Groteyon, Christian
Sep 19 1797 Eli, David to Ditto, Catherine
Apr 15 1797 Elias, George to Linaweaver, Catharine
Jun 16 1807 Eliott, Thomas to Fowler, Sarah
Feb 11 1790 Ellenbarch, John to Flock, Marg't
Mar 15 1794 Eller, Esther to Bechtell, George
```

```
Jun 28 1800 Eller, Magdalena to Staup, Peter
Aug 31 1803 Eller, Mary to Shoup, Christian
Jul 11 1805 Eller, Susanna to Sigler, Michael
May 26 1804 Ellette, Margarette to Starr, John
Dec 12 1782 Elligan, Mary to Riggs, John
Jan 10 1795 Elliot, Anna to Plummer, Mesheck
Oct  4 1795 Elliot, John to Davis, Nancy
Dec 18 1790 Elliot, Mary to Deal, Peter
Aug 21 1806 Elliot, Mr. to Baty, Mary
May  1 1790 Elliot, Sarah to Davis, Francis
Feb  3 1796 Elliot, Thomas to Hinton, Mary
Dec 12 1807 Elliott, Joel to Gibson, Hannah
Jun 21 1810 Elliott, Lydia to Leaming, Jacob
Jul 17 1790 Elliott, Margaret to Wayman, John
Dec  8 1789 Elliott, Rachel to Condon, Zachariah
Sep  1 1803 Elliott, Rebecca to Griffith, Isaac
May 14 1803 Elliott, Ruth to Gibson, Samuel
Sep  5 1805 Elliott, Solomon to Crabb, Mary
Oct  7 1791 Ellis, Eliazar to Onion, Rebecca
Dec 29 1809 Ellis, John to Stimmell, Elizabeth
Nov 24 1806 Ellis, Joseph to Roany, Mary
Mar 18 1794 Ellis, Mary to Lewis, Thomas
Sep  5 1789 Ellis, Rachel to Sheats, Henry
Sep 11 1797 Ellis, Ruthey to Thomas, Aquilla
Sep  8 1810 Ellis, Samuel to Patterson, Jane
May 27 1784 Ellis, Thomas to Meredith, Hannah
Nov 19 1808 Ellison, Sarah to Linton, Edward
Jan 29 1806 Ellison, Thomas to House, Eleanor
Jul 14 1781 Ely, David to Myers, Susanna
Sep 18 1798 Emeric , Elizabeth to Bottenfield, Jacob
Mar  1 1800 Emerson, Samuel to Sprecher, Rachel
Mar 30 1790 Emmit, William, Esq. to Coale, Henrietta
Dec  6 1808 Emmit, William, Esq. to Shellman, Susanna
May 24 1810 Emmitt, Abm. J. to Moore, Jane
Dec 16 1779 Emmory, Adam to Hipps, Sarah
Oct  3 1798 Engel, Elizabeth to Bloom, John
Jan 20 1806 England, Amos to Glissan, Rebecca
Sep  5 1801 England, Andrew to Bucky, Catherine
Mar 29 1806 England, Asa to Walker, Elizabeth
Oct  1 1802 England, Hannah to Brower, Jacob
Oct 29 1802 England, Joseph to Tipple, Mary
Sep 23 1802 England, Margaret to Williams, Jacob
Nov  5 1799 England, Mary to Ewin (Erwin), William
Dec 10 1800 England, Samuel to Townsend, Charlotte
Jul 23 1796 Engle, Catharine to Brown, Frederick
Dec  3 1789 Engle, George to Young, Catharine
Sep  7 1799 Engle, George to Young, Susannah
May  1 1797 Engle, Magdalen to Houck, Matthias
Nov 28 1801 Engle, Margaret to McDanel, John
Aug 17 1799 Engle, Peter to Renner, Mary
Mar 20 1800 Engle, Peter to Kramer, Elizabeth
Oct  1 1785 Englebrecht, John to Houx, Margaret
Feb 22 1787 Englebricht, Cathe. to Miller, George
Jun 27 1795 Englebright, Michael to Stull, Elizabeth
Feb  5 1790 Engler, Peter to Hoffman, Susanna
```

```
Feb  4 1809 Engles, Eleanor to Powell, Nathan
Apr  4 1810 Engles, Elein to Powell, Nathaniel
Aug 24 1782 Engles, Mary Ann to Kersner, Michael
Dec 14 1809 Engles, Silas to Hauer, Ann Maria
Jan 30 1781 English, Margaret to Carney, Mich'l
Nov 12 1801 Ennis, George to Williard, Mary
Oct  5 1797 Ensey, Dennis to Crawford, Elizabeth
Sep 27 1802 Ensey, Eleanor to Arnold, Ephraim
Feb  4 1808 Ensey, Grace to West, Clinton
Apr 27 1808 Ensey, Grace to West, Clinton
Mar 30 1799 Ephlen, Charity to Ater, Abraham
Nov 16 1807 Eppert, Catharine to Baumgardner, Daniel
Apr  6 1798 Eppert, Catherine to Zimmerman, Benjamin
Mar 30 1809 Eppert, Elizabeth to Collins, Henry
May  7 1787 Eppert, Henry to Swaidner, Elizabeth
Jul 18 1789 Erb, Modelena to Bankard, Abraham
Mar 27 1798 Erb, Peter to Grove, Barbara
Jan  5 1809 Erbert, Barbara to Hague, Andrew
May 26 1803 Erhart, Frederick to Aury, Sarah
Aug 22 1794 Essex, Elizabeth to Shaven, William
Nov 17 1792 Estep, Sarah to Tilliard, Edward C.
May  2 1809 Esther, Elizabeth to Nusz, Mich'l
Jun 30 1789 Etsler, Daniel to Albaugh, Mary
Apr  2 1803 Eutey, Mary to Orr, Thomas
May 24 1802 Euty, Philip to Difebaugh, Catherine
Sep 11 1797 Evans, Alty to Smith, James
Jun  3 1809 Evans, Anne to Dilly, Benjamin
Mar  5 1787 Evans, Caleb to Waddle, Eve
Dec 19 1805 Evans, Catherine to Rose, Christopher
Dec 18 1789 Evans, Charles to Lamb, Ann
Feb 23 1792 Evans, David to Barnes, Elizabeth
Sep  6 1781 Evans, Drusey to Hillery, Wm.
Nov 14 1796 Evans, Eleazer to Nicholls, Mary
Jan 21 1782 Evans, Elijah to Morris, Mary
Feb  2 1786 Evans, James to Meek, Sarah
Dec  1 1795 Evans, John to Barnes, Sarah
Apr  1 1800 Evans, John to Owings, Meranda
Sep 25 1789 Evans, Mary to Stephenson, Nathan
Oct 27 1782 Evans, Rebecka to Waldeck, Henry
Jul 17 1794 Evans, Robert to Smith, Eve
Apr 14 1783 Evans, Tacey to Fowler, Zedekiah
Aug 23 1809 Everding, Christian to Martzen, Christena
Aug  4 1803 Everhart, Elizabeth to Jackson, Jacob
Feb  8 1800 Everhart, Jacob to Shoemaker, Anne
Jan  4 1779 Everhart, Martin to Fulsin, Christena
Apr  7 1781 Everhart, Martin to Mock (Moek?), Mary Eve
Nov  7 1803 Everhart, Martin to Casemon, Elizabeth
Feb 27 1781 Everhart, Mary to Lambaugh, Henry
Feb  8 1808 Everhart, Mary to Whetton, John
Aug 16 1786 Everhart, Mary to Yost, Ludwick
Sep 22 1806 Everhart, Mary Ann to Deaver, Basil
Feb 20 1809 Everhart, Nancy to Larken, Thomas
Dec  5 1810 Everhart, William to Wedden, Lucy
Mar 20 1779 Everley, Elizabeth to Shibeler, George
Jun 13 1797 Everley, Peter to Wistman, Ulianna
```

```
Dec  2 1793 Everly, Barbara to Grove, Peter
May 27 1783 Everly, John to Isaminger, Elizabeth
Jan 21 1809 Evers, David to McDaniel, Rachel
Apr  6 1784 Evilleng, Mary Ann to Reybergh, William
Jun  4 1810 Evins, Catherine to Murry, John
Aug 26 1799 Evis, Solema to Hall, John
Dec 31 1803 Evit, Mary to Nichols, Peter
Jan 25 1806 Evitt, Susanna to Boteler, Elias
Jan 17 1784 Evitt, Woodward to Hiseler, Catherine
Aug 27 1797 Ewers, Jonathan to Gregg, Ann
Nov  5 1799 Ewin (Erwin), William to England, Mary
Oct 13 1810 Eyler, Mary to Creager, Daniel

Dec 12 1809 Fairman, Daniel to Keplinger, Catharine
Apr  9 1798 Falconear, John Barkley to Shane, Ann Maria
Apr 30 1794 Falconer, Elisha to Davis, Sarah
Apr  9 1800 Falconer, George Washington to Boyd, Mary
Dec 13 1783 Falconer, Margery to Maddon, John
Feb 16 1779 Falconer, Mary to Byfield, Robert
Jan  3 1786 Faling, Henry to Delauter, Elizabeth
Jan  6 1810 Falkner, Elisha to Norwood, Eleanor
Jul 29 1784 Faller, Catharine to Thompson, Thomas
Nov 17 1807 Fardin, Rachel to Dougherty, Edward
May 22 1794 Faris, Christian to Mantz, Elizabeth
Mar 26 1779 Faris, John to Mcdonnah, Sarah
Nov 23 1789 Farmer, William to Penn, Mary
Jun  4 1801 Farnsworth, Catherine to Massey, Samuel
Mar 14 1796 Farquhar, Amos to Moore, Jane
Mar 23 1784 Farquhar, James to Moore, Sarah
May 12 1789 Farquhar, Rob't to Dodson, Esther
Nov 25 1791 Farquhar, Susan to Willson, Henry
Aug 10 1805 Farquhar, William P. to Messler, Mary
May 12 1778 Farroll, Thomas to Dalton, Hannah
Jul  7 1798 Farthing, Eleanor to Foist, John
Sep 25 1809 Farthing, Elizabeth to Joy, Benedict
Jan  5 1801 Farthing, James to Oat, Margaret
May  6 1786 Farthing, Rebeckah to Lashorn, John
Jun 21 1779 Farver, Adam to Keplar, Eliz'th
May  8 1783 Farver, John to Arnold, Rachel
Feb 22 1808 Fauble, Catherine to Hovey, George Jacob
Apr 18 1795 Fauble, Jacob to Hubbard, Susanna
Dec 15 1807 Favorite, Abraham to Schryock, Elizabeth
Mar 28 1809 Favorite, Frederick to Young, Elizabeth
Oct 14 1803 Favorite, George to Matthews, Magdalena
Mar 27 1790 Faw, Abraham to Steiner, Mary
May  9 1804 Fawley, Henry to Spring, Christina
Jun  6 1803 Fawner, John to Clay, Rebecca
May 27 1809 Feagler, Catherine to Dick, John
Oct 21 1805 Febus, James to Rolins, Sally
Jan 29 1779 Fee, Eliz'th to Carrill, Wm.
Dec 23 1808 Feet, Henry to Alexander, Elizabeth
Jan 15 1785 Feichter, George to Snyder, Catherine
Nov 25 1806 Feister, Jacob to Long, Elizabeth
Apr 18 1801 Felius, Barbara to Zudy, Casper
May  6 1800 Felius, Conrad to Schley, Catherine
```

```
Apr 18 1801 Felius, Jacob to Gremit, Elizabeth
May 28 1803 Fellows, William to Clancy, Eleanor
Nov 23 1798 Felton, John to McHenry, Eleanor
Dec 16 1787 Fenell, Stephen to Perry, Margaret
Nov 26 1778 Fenton, Eleanor to Messer, Wm.
Mar  6 1807 Fenwick, Catherine to Jamison, Ignatius
Oct 27 1806 Fergerson, Ann to Clingan, Archibald
Sep  9 1809 Ferich (?), John to Smith, Ann
Nov  2 1793 Fero, Henry to Wigal, Mary
Aug 10 1800 Ferral, William to Burnes, Mary
Feb 12 1808 Ferras, Elizabeth to Wilson, Thomas
Oct 28 1798 Ferrel, George to Davis, Eleanor
Jul 21 1810 Ferret, Margaret to Mayer, Caesar
Jun 18 1796 Ferrin, Phebe to Bailey, William
Oct 18 1782 Fessler, John to Baugh, Elizabeth
Apr 13 1793 Fessler, John to Bough, Barbara
Dec  1 1781 Fethercoil, Jno. to Berkman, Catherine
Mar 24 1801 Fetterling, Elizabeth to Egnew, Henry
Jan 23 1802 Fiege, John to Harris, Elizabeth
Oct 15 1782 Fiege, Philip to Hummel, Chrisstena
Jan 26 1809 Fiester, Mary to Colour, Philip
Aug 16 1810 Fighter,George to Lamback, Neomy
Jul 31 1792 Filius, John to Yates, Elizabeth
Apr  1 1800 Filson, Samuel to Cooper, Mary
Apr 10 1798 Filuse (Filius?), Joseph to Sleicherlan, Elizabeth
Mar 16 1808 Findlace, Margaret to Sharm, James
Oct 28 1806 Fine, Elizabeth to Rhodes, Henry
Feb 18 1779 Fine, Mary to Meyers, Frederick
Mar  8 1805 Fine, Sarah to Parish, James
May 10 1806 Fingbaum, Elizabeth to Hartsock, William
Oct 22 1810 Fink, Henry to Layman, Betsey
Nov 25 1809 Fink, John to McFarlin, Nancy
Aug 11 1807 Finkbone, Mary to Sargent, Jacob
Oct  1 1806 Finley, Maria to McKesson, James
Mar 13 1805 Fir, Miner to Murry, Nancy
Nov 29 1806 Firecoat, Elizabeth to Whittington, James
Sep 12 1800 Firehauk, Christena to Hilton, Clemm
Dec 16 1793 Firestone, Catherine to Long, Charles
Dec 23 1801 Firestone, Jacob to Hummel, Mary
Apr 24 1805 Firmwald, Catharine to Sepp, Leonard
Nov 18 1806 Firor, Mary to Harbaugh, Christian
Apr 10 1797 Fischer, Adam to Rowe, Elizabeth
May 20 1786 Fischer, Amelia to Butler, Richard
Jan 25 1789 Fischer, Catherine to Wintz, Jacob
May 11 1805 Fischer, Elizabeth to Shafer, Nicholas
Oct 22 1798 Fischer, Jonas to Cook, Anne
Oct 24 1803 Fish, John Benton to Kephart, Susanna
Dec 24 1807 Fish, Richard to Harrison, Aschah
Jul  1 1809 Fishbeck, John to O'Bannion, Lydia
Apr 23 1802 Fishburn, David to Saltkill, Mary
Apr  1 1809 Fishburn, Susanna to Hall, Richard
Jan 29 1798 Fisher, Ann to Cecil, Benjamin
Aug 22 1810 Fisher, Asau to Gassaway, Sarah
May 16 1805 Fisher, Catherine to Carter, Joseph
Oct 26 1778 Fisher, Catherine to Fleagle, Charles
Jul 25 1804 Fisher, Elisha to Fowler, Mary
```

```
Nov 17 1782 Fisher, Elizbeth to Howard, George
Aug 16 1810 Fisher, Esau to Gassaway, Sarah
Apr 26 1797 Fisher, Ludwick to Crawford, Elizabeth
Apr  1 1797 Fisher, Martha to Barrington, Joseph
Dec 11 1797 Fisher, Priscilla to Turner, Joshua
Jun  7 1808 Fisher, Valentine to Holtzman, Charlotte
Apr 14 1800 Fiste, Barbara to Padgit, William
Apr 27 1795 Fiste, Philip to Simmerman, Margaret
Apr  6 1809 Fister, Anne to Culler, Henry
May 11 1802 Fister, Catharine to Arnsperger, Christopher
Jan 11 1799 Fister, Henry to Johnson, Drusilla
Nov 17 1808 Fister, John to Smith, Mary
Nov  4 1802 Fitch, James to Bradfield, Hannah
Dec 22 1801 Fitzgerald, Edward to Jefferson, Rebecca
Mar  2 1807 Fitzgerald, Elizabeth to Jefferson, Henry
Apr  4 1796 Fitzgerald, Sarah to Cash, Jonathan
Jun 24 1791 Fitzgerald, Wm. to Purdum, Molley
Jul 13 1791 Fitzpatrick, Dennis to Trott, Susanna
Nov 17 1796 Flack, Mary to Thomas, Isaac
Jul 23 1804 Flanigan, John to Waters, Amelia
Oct 14 1802 Flanigan, Malachi to Timmons, Lettitia
Feb  9 1809 Flanigan, Malachi to Gittings, Anna
Jun 14 1779 Flannigan, Lackey to Barnett, Jane
Jul 30 1810 Flannigan, Samuel to Kernell, Catharine
Oct 26 1778 Fleagle, Charles to Fisher, Catherine
Oct 20 1787 Fleagle, Mary to Stoner, David
Aug 11 1779 Fleagle, Valentine to Censor, Christena
Jun 15 1808 Fleck, Adam to Hiner, Elizabeth
Nov 15 1798 Fleck, Catherine to Shroyer, David
Feb  8 1800 Fleck, John to Snyder, Barbara
Jun  9 1801 Flegle, Mary to Bankard, Lawrence
Sep  9 1796 Fleming, Alice to Cookerly, John, Jr.
May 14 1810 Fleming, Ally to Otto, John
Apr 15 1809 Fleming, Caleb to Plummer, Eleanor
Mar 10 1784 Fleming, John to Davis, Rachel
Feb 28 1809 Fleming, Rachel to Welsh, Nicholas
Mar 13 1809 Fleming, Robert, Junr. to Love, Mary
Oct 13 1780 Flemming, Alley to Reynolds, Heugh
Apr 13 1782 Flemming, Arthur to Bonham, Deborah
Feb  8 1785 Flemming, Arthur to Davis, Sarah
Nov 28 1780 Flemming, Barbara to Ridge, Wm.
Apr  5 1782 Flemming, Barbara to Hardey, Arnold
Nov  9 1808 Flenner, Abraham to Cramer, Susanna
Nov 21 1803 Flenner, George to Yantes, Elizabeth
Jul  5 1794 Fletcher, Philip to Sullivan, Mary
Jan  5 1809 Flewhart, John to Bussard, Rachel
Feb 11 1790 Flock, Marg't to Ellenbarch, John
Jan 18 1793 Flood, Provey to Curry, Charles
Apr 22 1782 Flood, Sarah to Musgrove, Anthony
Nov  6 1792 Flout, Christopher to Hughes, Hannah
Jan 25 1779 Flower, Samuel to Bowlaney, Janey
Apr  5 1779 Flower, Thomas to Murphey, Mary
Aug  8 1809 Fluck, Molly to Toup, Frederick
Apr 17 1779 Flucke, John to Young, Eve
Jan 11 1787 Flucke, Mathias to Young, Cathe.
```

```
Jul  7 1797 Flucke, Peter to Haines, Mary
May  7 1785 Fluhart, Massey to Ridgley, Mary
May 27 1790 Fluke, Barbara to Staley, Mechor
Dec  5 1808 Fluke, Barbara to Willy, John
Mar 18 1807 Fluke, Catherine to Miller, Jacob
Jun 11 1810 Fluke, Jacob to Biser, Esther
Apr  2 1801 Fluke, John to Shroyer, Elizabeth
May 18 1786 Flukein, Barbara to Buglar, Henry
Mar 18 1797 Flyde, John to Powlass, Elizabeth
Aug  6 1808 Foacht, Rachel to Appler, David
Jan 26 1785 Fogle, Adam to Scaggs, Eliz'th
Aug  7 1787 Fogle, Adam to Hammett, Sarah
Aug 10 1779 Fogle, Catharine to Bastian, Anthony
Jul  4 1778 Fogle, Catherine to Heartsock, William
Jul 12 1793 Fogle, Christian to Norwood, Mary
Jun 11 1779 Fogle, Eliz'th to Groseman, Simon
Jul 30 1782 Fogle, Susannah to Willson, Thomas
Nov 27 1809 Fogler, Catherine to Hardy, Jonathan
Apr  9 1803 Fogler, Henry to Werner, Modalena
Jul  7 1798 Foist, John to Farthing, Eleanor
Dec 13 1788 Folk, Barbara to Crise, Henry
Mar 21 1783 Fooks, George to Bartlett, Sarah
Jan  9 1786 Ford, Cassandra to Harding, Elias
May 31 1779 Ford, Mary to Craigg, Roger
Mar 30 1793 Formwalt, Jacob to Garnhart, Cathe.
Jan 29 1810 Forney, Mary to Shriner, Abraham
Sep 19 1807 Forrest, Jeremiah to Covill, Vashti
May  8 1778 Forster, Moses to Cavener, Mary
May  5 1800 Fortney, David to Lewis, Elizabeth
Jan  2 1779 Forward, William to Harland, Hannah
Sep 23 1801 Foster, Richard to Browning, Rachel
Aug 14 1784 Fouble, Jacob to Gibbs, Margaret
Oct 25 1785 Fouch, Jemima to Hawling, John Wilespen
Nov 11 1786 Fouck, George to Kemp, Elizabeth
Mar 22 1790 Fout, Ann Maria to Link, Thomas
Dec 30 1802 Fout, Baltzer to Stilly, Mary
Aug  6 1796 Fout, Barbara to Fout, Daniel
Nov  2 1793 Fout, Catherine to Ebert, George Adam
Aug 23 1800 Fout, Charlotte to Linton, William
Aug  6 1796 Fout, Daniel to Fout, Barbara
Oct  6 1792 Fout, Elizabeth to Myers, Mich'l
Oct 29 1791 Fout, Henry to Creager, Phoebe
May  8 1804 Fout, Henry to Weaver, Christina
Jun 12 1805 Fout, Henry to Goslin, Nancy
Feb  6 1797 Fout, Jacob to Smith, Margaret
Apr 17 1806 Fout, Margaret to Eichelberger, Jacob
Mar 27 1795 Fout, Mary to Smith, John
Nov 23 1789 Fout, Michael to Hufferd, Catherine
Aug 31 1801 Fout, Modelena to Easterday, Abraham
Sep  5 1801 Fout, Nancy to Ebert, George Adam
Sep 20 1800 Fout, Peter to Piper, Mary
Sep  5 1785 Fout, Rebeckah to Getzendanner, John
Sep  5 1785 Fout, Rebeckah to Ketzindanner, John
Aug 23 1806 Fout, William to Adams, Magdalena
May  7 1787 Foutch, Heughey to Johnson, Elizabeth
```

```
Mar 18 1797 Foutch, Mary to Minnick, George
Oct  6 1781 Foutz, Catherine to Calpfleish, John
Nov  3 1795 Foutz, Magdalen to Miller, John of Dan.
Aug 16 1800 Foutz, Margaret to Foutz, Wm.
Jan  6 1787 Foutz, Margaret to Ollip, Adam
Jul 18 1780 Foutz, Rachel to Miller, Andrew
Aug 16 1800 Foutz, Wm. to Foutz, Margaret
Dec  2 1795 Fowler, Ann to Duvall, Marsh Mareen
Jun 22 1796 Fowler, Anna to Williams, William
May  6 1808 Fowler, Anne to Gassaway, Thomas
Apr  1 1809 Fowler, Benjamin to Fry, Eleanor
Dec 26 1808 Fowler, Eleanor to Kingsbury, Horatio
Sep 25 1778 Fowler, Eliz'th to Myler, Matthew
Dec  9 1782 Fowler, Elizabeth to Williams, Rezin
Dec  7 1790 Fowler, John to Burgee, Nancy
Apr 20 1798 Fowler, John to Huff, Mary
Dec 15 1810 Fowler, John to Leatherwood, Elizabeth
Jul 25 1804 Fowler, Mary to Fisher, Elisha
Jun 16 1807 Fowler, Sarah to Eliott, Thomas
Apr 14 1783 Fowler, Zedekiah to Evans, Tacey
Nov  2 1798 Fox, Adam to Garver, Ann
Nov  7 1807 Fox, Catherine to Smith, Alexander
Dec  7 1805 Fox, Elizabeth to Lighter, John
May 19 1794 Fox, Henry to Frey, Catherine
Jan 18 1799 Fox, Henry to Zimmerman, Leah
Jun 28 1799 Fox, Henry to Garver, Mary
Sep 15 1798 Fox, John to Simon, Catherine
Jul 12 1806 Fox, Margaret to Tallhammer, Matthias
Nov  1 1799 Fox, Peter to Oyler, Mary
Aug 23 1800 Fox, Peter to Debery, Rachel
Sep 12 1800 Fox, Peter to Hall, Bridget Ingen
Apr 18 1794 Fox, Uriah to Sedwith, Grace
Apr  2 1781 Foy, Catherine to Gattert, Valentine
Jun 21 1789 Foy, Elizabeth to Baker, Peter
Apr 25 1797 Foy, Joseph to Angling, Permelia
Feb  6 1787 Foye, Henry to Piecken, Mary
Sep 28 1804 Fralick, Elizabeth to Smith, John
Aug  8 1809 France, Elizabeth to Beans, William
Dec 23 1808 Frances, Catherine to Holland, William
Sep 13 1810 Frances, Nancy to Casey, Daniel
Nov 20 1802 Francis, Elizabeth to Baldwin, Joseph
Sep 14 1779 Francks, Henry Taylor to Buskerk, Margaret
Jan  6 1787 Franklin, Arey to Condon, Rich'd
Sep 19 1808 Franklin, Elizabeth to Pim, Thomas
Jan 30 1810 Franklin, Pamelia to Pickett, Sevin
Nov 22 1798 Franklin, Rezon to Goshedg, Elizabeth
Sep  8 1810 Franklin, Thomas to Mackey, Margaret
Jun 12 1781 Fraser, Wm. to Giddings, Verlinda
Nov 23 1804 Frasier, Henry to Martin, Mary
Feb  7 1783 Frasier, Margaret to Seargeant, Elijah
Nov  8 1789 Frasier, Mary to Morris, Jonathan
Aug 14 1787 Frasier, Milley to Cox, Elisha
Jul 27 1798 Frazier, Elizabeth to Jarbes, Bennet
Dec 14 1789 Frazier, Elizabeth to Marlow, Thomas
Feb  6 1802 Frazier, George to Frazier, Jane
```

```
Feb  9 1805 Frazier, Harriet to Frazier, Maryland
Jan  5 1810 Frazier, Horatio to Deaver, Margaret
Feb  6 1802 Frazier, Jane to Frazier, George
Sep  6 1798 Frazier, John to Good, Barbara
Dec 15 1810 Frazier, John to Himsworth, Mary
Feb 24 1800 Frazier, Levi to Cain, Mary
Feb  9 1805 Frazier, Maryland to Frazier, Harriet
Dec  8 1795 Frazier, Peter to Beayer, Rebecca
Jan 15 1810 Frazier, Rhoda to Ball, Horatio
Dec 26 1799 Frazier, Sarah to Deaver, Misel
Feb  8 1800 Frazier, Tobitha to Smith, Walter
Jan 23 1810 Fread, Mary to Varner, John
Jun  2 1779 Free, Mary to Valentine, Jacob
Nov  1 1797 Freed, Peter to Hennickhouser, Charity
May 31 1779 Freeman, Eleanor to Shultz, Alex'dr
Apr 20 1805 Freeman, John to Dugan, Jinnet
Mar 27 1806 Frees, Jacob to Waters, Ann
Nov 20 1797 Freet, Ann to Stoub, Adam
May 11 1807 Freeze, George to Bowers, Susannah
Jun 18 1799 Freeze, Michael to Grabill, Catherine
Feb 17 1802 French, Otho to Anderson, Elizabeth
Jul 14 1805 French, Peter to Holtzman, Christianna
May 19 1794 Frey, Catherine to Fox, Henry
May 25 1805 Frey, Elizabeth to Kaufman, David
Sep 21 1779 Frey, Elizabeth to Valentine, Henry
Aug 26 1783 Frey, George to Bayman, Mary
Jan 29 1796 Frey, Isaac to Stone, Mary
Mar  9 1792 Frey, Mary to Mangins, Matthias
Aug 15 1809 Frey, Samuel to Shriver, Susan
Jan  5 1808 Friar, Elizabeth to Jenkins, Felix
Apr 11 1795 Friberger, George to Shoup, Sophia
Mar 23 1809 Friddel, Mary to Bost, John
Apr 27 1805 Friddle, David to Hargate, Mary
Jun 28 1808 Fridinger, Esther to Damon, John
Dec 14 1804 Frieberger, George to Mortar, Catherine
Nov 11 1805 Fringer, Stephen to Shipley, Anne
Apr  3 1781 Frinton, Thos. to Hutchcraft, Margaret
May 17 1806 Fritchie, John to Hauer, Barbara
Jun  2 1793 Fritchie, Mariah Barbara to Cary, William
Feb 11 1800 Fritchie, Rebecca to Ebbert, John
Feb 28 1780 Frizzle, Jacob to McKinley, Margaret
Aug  1 1801 Fronck, Mary to Grim, John
Jan 16 1780 Froud, James to Sage, Mary
Sep 24 1799 Frushour, Adam, Junr. to Wandle, Margaret
Oct 24 1808 Frushour, Barbara to Mulhorn, Edward R.
May 31 1803 Frushour, Catharine to Baker, Conrad
Dec 15 1798 Frushour, Elizabeth to Dean, Barnabas
Jan  6 1800 Frushour, Elizabeth to Dean, Bernard
Oct  6 1809 Frushour, George to Ungleberger, Elizabeth
Apr  8 1799 Frushour, Jacob to Dick, Susannah
May  5 1809 Frushour, Jacob to Knouff, Catherine
Jul 21 1810 Frushour, John to Angleberger, Mary
Mar 26 1796 Frushour, Mary to Rose, Frederick
Jun 14 1794 Frushour, Mary to Zealer, George
Apr 21 1804 Frushour, Susanna to Shroyer, Jacob
```

```
Dec 15 1808 Frutch, Catherine to Scaggs, Richard
Apr  1 1809 Fry, Eleanor to Fowler, Benjamin
Jun 21 1804 Fry, Elizabeth to Shroyer, Thomas
Jun 16 1794 Fry, Enoch to Holtzapple, Soloma
May 11 1805 Fry, John to Carn, Barbara
Dec 30 1806 Fry, John to Stine, Elizabeth
Jul 12 1805 Fry, Mary to Craver, John
Jun 11 1794 Fry, Rosanna to Measel, Frederick, Junior
Aug  6 1796 Frydinger, Nicholas to Kemp, Esther
Aug 31 1799 Fuller, Margaret to Blickenstaffer, Yost
Mar 20 1792 Fuller, Nancy to Mumford, James, Jr.
Nov 18 1779 Fulliston, Jane to Bradley, Wm.
May 11 1779 Fullum, Mich'l to Ropp, Mary
Apr  5 1800 Fulmer, Lewis to Goodman, Mary
Jan  4 1779 Fulsin, Christena to Everhart, Martin
Aug 31 1778 Fulston, Hannah to Curtis, Henry
Nov 24 1797 Fulton, Alexander to Carmick, Sarah
Sep 23 1802 Fulton, Elizabeth to Jacobs, Dorsey
Jun  3 1794 Fulton, George to Hedges, Margaret
May 10 1784 Fulton, Nathaniel to Browning, Nancy
Jan 22 1791 Fultz, Susanna Margaret to Raymer, Michael
Jan 26 1796 Fundeberg, Barbara to Strawsberger, John
Apr 14 1806 Fundenburgh, Catherine to Cronise, Jacob
Jul 24 1810 Funderberg, Elizabeth to Swigart, Peter
Dec 17 1803 Funk, George to Grim, Catherine
Mar  8 1803 Funson, John to Dudderer, Sarah
Apr  3 1802 Furney, Abraham to Curtis, Mary
May  4 1807 Furney, Catherine to Biggs, William
Apr 12 1784 Furney, Henry to Horine, Judey
Sep 11 1793 Furney, Mary to Timmons, Charles
May  3 1797 Furnival, Louise Sophia to Amelong, Frederick M.
May 20 1803 Furrier, Jacob to Morningstar, Juliana
Aug 31 1779 Furrow, Mathias to Beaghell, Christena
Oct 10 1806 Furry, Abraham to Champer, Mary
Nov 12 1810 Fuss, Elizabeth to Burk, Michael
Mar 12 1790 Fye, Joseph to McClain, Ann

Aug 19 1803 Gabeler, Teresa to Madeira, John
Jul 30 1804 Gabler, Gotlip to Moderd, Susanna
Dec 11 1798 Gabler, Lotty to Speelman, Henry
Apr 18 1795 Gadultig, George to Hole, Catharine
Jan 25 1794 Gaither, Henrietta to Poole, Dennis
Jan 26 1797 Gaither, Rachael to Hammond, Thomas John
Jun 16 1810 Gaivin, Barbara to Donston, Thomas
Feb  6 1797 Gale, Thomas to Cooper, Elizabeth
Mar 13 1805 Galt, John to Klinehoff, Sarah
Dec 28 1809 Games, John to Hays, Sarah
Jul  9 1778 Gander, George to Dillan, Rosanna
Aug  4 1779 Gannon, Ann to Pickett, John
Nov  7 1782 Ganntt, Thomas to Potts, Sarah
Oct  5 1797 Gantt, Daniel to Anderson, Lucy
Jan 29 1798 Gantt, Eleanor to Higdon, John
Sep 23 1797 Garaner, Elizabeth to Beane, William
Feb  2 1808 Garder, Samuel to Chaney, Ann
Jul 22 1784 Gardner, Angel to Yesterday, Michael
```

```
Mar 26 1798 Gardner, Henry to Reel, Elizabeth
Jan  5 1801 Gardner, Malon to Nixon, Ann
Dec 24 1800 Garhart, Jacob to Kiler, Esther
May 21 1798 Garner, Luke to Powell, Hannah
Oct 19 1785 Garnett, And'w to Bevington, Mary
Feb 18 1780 Garnett, Geo. to Mosserley, Eliz'th
Mar 30 1793 Garnhart, Cathe. to Formwalt, Jacob
Sep 16 1801 Garnhart, Margaret to Ott, Philip
Aug 27 1800 Garott, Ann to Gittings, Erasmus
Jan 18 1779 Garrett, Allen to Philpott, Mary Barton
Oct 27 1784 Garrett, Mary to Hackney, Jacob
Nov 15 1808 Garrison, Elizabeth to Lilly, Richard
May  4 1799 Garrot, Aeneas to Conner, Eleanor
Dec  3 1781 Garrott, Cassandra to Philpott, Zachariah
Apr 15 1801 Garrott, Elizabeth to Garrott, John Philpot
Feb 28 1805 Garrott, Erasmus to Garrott, Sarah
Sep  2 1801 Garrott, Hannah to Boteler, Thomas
Apr 15 1801 Garrott, John Philpot to Garrott, Elizabeth
Apr  4 1805 Garrott, Joseph to Collerflower, Elizabeth
Sep 28 1801 Garrott, Nicholas D. to Burgee, Martha
Feb 28 1805 Garrott, Sarah to Garrott, Erasmus
Dec  1 1780 Gartrell, Jehosophat to Bissett, Elizabeth
May 24 1792 Gartrill, Sarah to Darbey, Caleb
Nov  2 1798 Garver, Ann to Fox, Adam
Apr  2 1803 Garver, Christian to Morningstar, Mary
Jun 28 1799 Garver, Mary to Fox, Henry
Nov  7 1789 Gassaway, Nancy to Gassaway, Samuel
Jul 13 1807 Gassaway, Providence to Ijams, John
Oct 12 1778 Gassaway, Ricahrd to Arnold, Ann
Nov  7 1789 Gassaway, Samuel to Gassaway, Nancy
Aug 22 1810 Gassaway, Sarah to Fisher, Asau
Aug 16 1810 Gassaway, Sarah to Fisher, Esau
May  6 1808 Gassaway, Thomas to Fowler, Anne
May 11 1778 Gassiway, Rebecca to Stull, Lawrence
Mar  1 1800 Gasslin, Sarah to Duffey, Allen
Feb 23 1801 Gater, Rachel to Kemp, Peter Jun.
Nov 17 1779 Gates, Ann to Chadbourne, Joseph
May 21 1800 Gates, George to Riggs, Mary
Apr  8 1797 Gates, Sarah to Bargesar, Daniel
Feb 22 1805 Gatrill, John to Hall, Ariana
Apr  2 1781 Gattert, Valentine to Foy, Catherine
Oct 15 1789 Gatton, Ann to Reed, James
Sep 29 1782 Gatton, Azariah to Veneble, Hesse
Jul 22 1783 Gatton, Rebeckah to Rankins, William
Jul  1 1785 Gatton, Richard to Veatch, Jemima
Sep 29 1786 Gatton, Sylvester, G. to Robey, Anna
Nov 16 1779 Gatton, Verlinda to Lewis, Jno.
Apr  6 1798 Gaugh, Elizabeth to Shryock, Matthias
Nov 13 1808 Gaugh, Eve to Leatherman, John
Mar 22 1806 Gaugh, John to Snook, Elizabeth
Jul 17 1797 Gaunt, Peggy to King, Nicholas
Mar 10 1795 Gaver, Dan'l to Beckibaugh, Susanna
Mar 14 1807 Gaver, Daniel to Dean, Elizabeth
Feb  6 1805 Gaver, David to Biser, Mary
Apr  9 1805 Gaver, Elizabeth to Shoup, Christian
```

```
Oct 29 1803 Gaver, Gideon to Tritt, Mary
Nov 18 1783 Gaver, John to Black, Margaret
Mar 19 1804 Gaver, Lydia to Biser, John
Jan  4 1797 Gaver, Molly to Cain, John
May 18 1779 Gaver, Valentine to Smitten, Eliz'th
Nov  4 1778 Gavin, Sarah to White, Thomas
Dec  4 1779 Gay, Henry to Silverin, Judy
May  3 1803 Gebhart, George to Doll, Catharine
Nov 20 1806 Gebhart, Harriet to Cromwell, Oliver
Dec 23 1801 Gebhart, John to Heastond, Sarah
Aug 16 1796 Gebhart, Peter to Haas, Elizabeth
Nov 11 1793 Gebhart, Solomon to Werner, Catherine
Apr  3 1804 Gepheart, Elizabeth to Brandenburgh, Henry
Jun  5 1795 Geddis, Cath. to Easterday, Christian
Dec 23 1800 Gedon, Daniel to Butler, Susanna
May 25 1778 Gedultig, Conrad to Snider, Catharine
Sep  8 1783 Geesee, Fred'k Henry to Baker, Mary
Jan 12 1799 Geesey, Henry to Ramack, Rosina
Mar 14 1804 Geesy, Jacob to Cail, Christena
May  9 1809 Geesy, John to Baltzell, Catherine
Nov 12 1807 Gelwicks, George C. to Nixdorff, Mary
Feb  7 1797 Genings, Lucy to Cretin, James
Dec 26 1801 Gentles, Elizabeth to McDaniel, William
Apr 10 1806 George, John to Woods, Elizabeth
Nov  5 1795 Gerhart, Catherine to Daugherty, George
Feb 28 1810 German, Alletha to Watkins, Rezin
Nov 25 1809 Getherd, Mary to Creager, Cornelius
Mar 10 1792 Gettert, Valentine to Beaghly, Catherine
Oct 13 1787 Getzadanner, Thos. to Koontz, Mary Ann
Jun 11 1794 Getzendanner, Balser to Stull, Phillipena
Sep 10 1801 Getzendanner, Catherine to Houck, George
Apr  1 1786 Getzendanner, Christ'n to Ramsbergh, Cathe.
Jul 15 1786 Getzendanner, Christian to Bare, Mary Ann
Jan  7 1797 Getzendanner, Elizabeth to Getzendanner, Jacob of Adam
Mar  5 1808 Getzendanner, Elizabeth to Keefer, Henry
Apr 22 1780 Getzendanner, Geo. to Darr, Eliz'th
Apr 16 1800 Getzendanner, Henry to Baker, Hannah
Dec  4 1800 Getzendanner, Jacob to Stophel, Catherine
Jan  7 1797 Getzendanner, Jacob of Adam to Getzendanner, Elizabeth
Sep  5 1785 Getzendanner, John to Fout, Rebeckah
May 30 1789 Getzendanner, John to Tabler, Catherine
Nov 26 1786 Getzendanner, Magdalena to Welfley, David
Nov 11 1793 Getzendanner, Marg't to Kemp, Jacob
Feb  1 1806 Getzendanner, Margaret to Houck, Jacob
Dec 10 1796 Getzendanner, Margaret to Neff, Jacob
Apr 20 1805 Getzendanner, Margaret to Smith, George
Apr  9 1808 Getzendanner, Thomas to Baer, Catherine
Apr 23 1791 Geyer, Adam to Doss, Margaret
Mar  4 1810 Geyer, Barbara to Rote, Joseph
Aug 15 1806 Geyer, Conrad to Rocker, Barbara
May  9 1791 Geyer, Daniel to Brengle, Mary
Aug 29 1809 Geyer, Eliza Catherine to Hagar, Samuel
Nov  1 1804 Geyer, Frederick to Smith, Mary
Feb  7 1795 Geyer, Henry to Ireland, Elizbeth
Jul 25 1794 Geyer, Jacob to Lemaster, Elizabeth
```

```
Sep  7 1809 Geyton, Vincent to Davis, Anna
Mar 19 1785 Giar, John to Sheffey, Elizabeth
Jun  8 1809 Gibberthorp, Sarah to Early, John
Dec 26 1805 Gibbony, John to Jones, Esther
Aug 20 1796 Gibbs, John to McDonald, Susanna
Aug 14 1784 Gibbs, Margaret to Fouble, Jacob
Dec 12 1807 Gibson, Hannah to Elliott, Joel
May 14 1803 Gibson, Samuel to Elliott, Ruth
Nov  4 1792 Gibson, Thomas to Heughs, Nancy
Aug  9 1809 Gibson, Thomas to Myers, Catherine
Feb 17 1800 Giddings, Alley to Grove, George
Oct 10 1788 Giddings, Delilah to Butler, William
Apr 30 1793 Giddings, Thomas to Perry, Lyda
Jun 12 1781 Giddings, Verlinda to Fraser, Wm.
May  1 1784 Gier, George to Thomas, Mary
Aug 26 1795 Giesbert, Daniel to Michael, Elizabeth
Mar  7 1798 Giestbert, Sarah to Michael, Jacob
Oct 21 1807 Gigar, Catherine to Prower, David
Apr 30 1803 Gigar, John to Nuss, Mary
Apr 22 1789 Gilbert, Ann to Dawson, William
Mar 27 1787 Gilbert, Catharine to Shilling, William
Sep  7 1805 Gilbert, Catherine to Main, Frederick
Nov  3 1787 Gilbert, Elizabeth to Jacobs, Benja.
Sep 19 1808 Gilbert, Hannah to Ludy, Henry
Feb 17 1810 Gilbert, Henry to Loraw, Eve
Aug 13 1803 Gilbert, Peter to Larkin, Elizabeth
Mar 26 1805 Gilbert, Polly to Moor, William
Oct 31 1780 Gilbert, Susanna to Wright, Alexander
Jul 13 1779 Gilbert, Thos. to Burton, Hannah
Apr 18 1803 Gill, Sally to Bealmer, William
Sep  8 1778 Gillaspie, David to Berry, Christe
Aug 16 1800 Gillaspie, Mary to Sansell, Peter
Jul 25 1803 Gillaspie, Nancy to Spangler, John
Apr 23 1798 Gilleland, John to Hays, Mary
Mar  3 1787 Gillion, Philip to Rowe, Catherine
Mar 17 1802 Gilliss, Porcius to Leekings, Becky
Dec 26 1810 Gillmeyer, John L. to Berryer, Margaret
Sep  1 1808 Gilpin, William to Reed, Margaret
Dec 14 1779 Gire, Catherine to Swayne, Charles
Jun 20 1793 Gire, Susannah to Templin, William
Sep  4 1798 Gisberd, Abraham to Jenkins, Sarah
Nov 22 1798 Gisburts, Deboro to Pepper, Frederick
Jun 21 1800 Giseberd, Guy to Thomas, Rebecca
Nov  3 1803 Gisebert, Jonathan to Michael, Catherine
Jun  2 1792 Gisebert, Susanna to Michael, Adam
Nov 10 1795 Gisenir, John, Esq. to Good, Mary
Aug 21 1809 Gist, George to Jones, Rachel
May 16 1806 Gist, Independent to Gist, Rachel
May 16 1806 Gist, Rachel to Gist, Independent
Oct 31 1810 Gist, Sarah to Beatty, Lewis Augustis
May 29 1803 Giting, Abraham to Sheffey, Mary
Feb 10 1793 Gittinger, Cabey to Mitchell, Theodore
May 15 1802 Gittinger, Elizabeth to Woolf, Jacob
Feb  9 1809 Gittings, Anna to Flanigan, Malachi
Apr 16 1799 Gittings, Asa to Clarke, Elizabeth
```

Mar 21 1795 Gittings, Cassandra to Morrison, James
Nov 21 1792 Gittings, Elizab Garrott to Rawlings, Benja.
Aug 27 1800 Gittings, Erasmus to Garott, Ann
Feb 17 1807 Gittings, James to Mitchell, Cassandra
Dec 19 1795 Gittings, Jane to Butler, Thomas
Feb  2 1807 Gittings, Juliet to Talbutt, Hendley
Nov 10 1807 Gittings, Teresa to Talbott, John
Dec 29 1795 Gitts, Barbara to Smith, Peter
Jun 14 1788 Gitzadanner, Elizabeth to Hoffman, Philip
Jun  9 1784 Gitzadanner, Jacob to Moyer, Elizabeth
Oct 31 1800 Gizebert, Jane to Michael, Andrew
Apr 19 1809 Gladhill, Jane to Griffith, John
Oct 19 1804 Gladman, Thomas to Barnes, Orphey
Sep 12 1796 Glasscock, Susanna to Peck, William
Jun  9 1792 Glaze, Eleanor to Poole, Joseph
Oct 27 1801 Glisan, James to White, Esther
Jan 20 1806 Glissan, Rebecca to England, Amos
Oct 14 1807 Glissan, Sarah to Wolfe, Abraham
Feb  4 1797 Glissan, Solomon to Stallings, Elizabeth
Oct  9 1805 Gloss, Magdalena to Eckart, Henry
May 29 1793 Goar, Thomas to Smith, Marcy
Feb  5 1785 Godman, Patsy to Tucker, Jonathan
Jul 30 1801 Goings, Joseph to Windsor, Nancy
Apr  4 1805 Goings, Roswell to Lett, Monica
Mar  6 1794 Goldie, Jacob to Davis, Nancy
Oct 16 1780 Goldie, Mary to Wandle, Jacob
Jun 30 1805 Goldsberry, Tady to Claspy, Elizabeth
Nov 22 1803 Goldsbery, Nancey to Rogers, Joshua
Mar 25 1793 Goldsborough, Mary to Drowry, Ignatius
Dec 22 1797 Golman, Jacob to Cost, Elizabeth
Apr  5 1788 Gombare, Elizabeth to Pence, George
May 19 1787 Gomber, Jacob to Beatty, Susanna
Sep  6 1798 Good, Barbara to Frazier, John
Nov  1 1796 Good, Elizabeth to McGuigan, Arthur
Nov 30 1793 Good, John to Thomas, Elizabeth
Feb 19 1789 Good, Mary to Boylan, Thomas
Nov 10 1795 Good, Mary to Gisenir, John, Esq.
Feb 18 1809 Good, Polly to Clabaugh, Thomas
Jan  8 1781 Goodacre, Wm. to Donavan, Catherine
Jan 15 1803 Goodill, George to Ryan, Elenor
Nov 18 1803 Goodley, Polly to Allder, John
Feb 11 1807 Goodlin, Elizabeth to Porter, Nicholas
Oct 13 1808 Goodly, Joseph to Hurdle, Susanna
Nov  7 1795 Goodman, Ann to Isentrey, George
May  8 1784 Goodman, Anne to Myer, Henry
Mar 17 1779 Goodman, Barbara to Naylor, Isaac Jones
Nov 12 1800 Goodman, Catherine to Staley, Joseph
Jul 30 1796 Goodman, Jacob to Jones, Catherine
Dec  9 1806 Goodman, Jacob to Easton, Mary
Apr  5 1800 Goodman, Mary to Fulmer, Lewis
Nov 10 1806 Goodman, Rachel to Kessler, Jacob
Oct 20 1780 Goodman, Rebecca to Shoup, Peter
Jun 11 1809 Goodman, William to Rhoads, Elizabeth
Oct 27 1788 Goodman, William,Senr. to Morris, Mary
Nov 21 1797 Gordon, Joseph to Baltin, Mary

```
Jan  2 1794 Gordon, Mary to Dowling, Edward
Mar 26 1806 Gore, Elizabeth to Jenkins, Wm.
Mar 20 1800 Gore, Mary to Brown, Isom
Aug  3 1801 Gore, Sally to Gregg, Mahlon
May 18 1809 Gorner, Barbara to Brubaker, Samuel
Jul 10 1793 Gorner, Elizabeth to Brandenbergh, Henry
Oct 19 1799 Gorner, Mary to Weaver, John
Apr 12 1794 Gorner, Phebe to Brandenburg, John
Oct 10 1810 Gorney, Joseph to Haller, Catherine
Nov 22 1798 Goshedg, Elizabeth to Franklin, Rezon
Aug 14 1803 Goslin, Ambrose to Shafer, Anne
Dec 25 1786 Goslin, Henry to Carney, Ann
Jun 12 1805 Goslin, Nancy to Fout, Henry
Mar 27 1807 Goslin, Rachel to Cramer, John
Feb 24 1807 Goslin, Sarah to Koon, John
Nov  1 1798 Gosnel, Peter to Hill, Emma
Sep  3 1802 Gosnell, John to Lavely, Elizabeth
Oct 16 1797 Gotsailech, Catharena to Condon, David
Nov 26 1792 Gott, Susanna to Harris, Samuel
Mar 26 1806 Gover, Elizabeth to Hoff, Garrott
Aug 18 1804 Grabell, Susan to Smith, David
Jun 18 1799 Grabill, Catherine to Freeze, Michael
Apr 12 1799 Grabill, Moses to Bixler, Elizabeth
Mar 23 1805 Grabill, Moses to Baker, Rachel
Nov 23 1795 Grable, Barbara to Pixler, Jacob
Nov 19 1798 Grable, Eve to Cumston, Joshua
Jun 24 1806 Grace, William to Hawn, Elizabeth
Apr 15 1798 Gradey, Anne to Cross, George
May 25 1809 Graff, Catherine to Cockey, William
Feb 28 1807 Graham, Jonas to Thomson, Mary
Apr 20 1798 Graham, Reubin to Carter, Rachel
Oct 25 1806 Grahame, Augustus to Cocke, Martha
Jan 12 1788 Grahame, John Colin to Johnson, Ann Jennings
Sep 15 1792 Gramer, Adam to Devilbiss, Appelona
May 14 1799 Grant, Susanna to Lamb, Owen
Sep 27 1809 Graver, Peter to Clise, Margaret
Jan 12 1786 Graves, Priscilla to Ansell, Samuel
Oct  9 1783 Graves, Thomas to Cartnail, Eliz'th
Sep 12 1807 Gray, John to Mayhue, Mary
Jan 27 1807 Gray, Joseph to Scoggins, Rachel
May 24 1801 Gray, Nathaniel to Baltzer, Louisa
Apr 21 1798 Gray, Polly to Greenwell, John Basil
Nov 22 1809 Gray, Rebecca to Condon, William
May 24 1804 Graybell, Anne to Wood, Joseph
Feb  3 1780 Grear, Sarah to Larymore, Thomas
Oct  1 1798 Greeher, Robert to Warren, Mary
Mar 25 1778 Green, Ann to Padgett, Benjamin
Sep 29 1782 Green, Charles to Taysor, Margaret
Dec 20 1806 Green, Charlotte to Salmon, Richard
Dec  5 1794 Green, Cloe to Clements, Basil
Dec 22 1810 Green, George to Carmickel, Margaret
Apr 19 1806 Green, John to Miller, Nancy
Jun 23 1806 Green, Jonathan to Long, Elizabeth
Oct 10 1796 Green, Luke to Wilson, Peggy
Mar 25 1796 Green, Sam'l to Wrench, Susanna
```

Feb  8 1793 Green, Samuel to Clements, Mary Ann Violetta
Sep 29 1796 Green, William to Atwood, Elizabeth
Jan 28 1804 Greenamyer, Barbara to Hinkle, John
Apr 28 1810 Greenawalt, Christian to Smith, Mary
Sep  2 1803 Greene, William to Owings, Betsy
Jun  5 1790 Greenfield, Susanna Eve to Beall, Theodore
Feb 28 1779 Greengrass, John to Cain, Catherine
Apr  6 1806 Greenlease, James to Kendel, Catherine
Nov 18 1803 Greenwald, Margaret to Keefer, George
Jan 13 1796 Greenwell, Elizabeth to Mugg, John
Dec 30 1803 Greenwell, Helen to Tucker, Jonathan Ross
Apr 21 1798 Greenwell, John Basil to Gray, Polly
Nov  9 1801 Greenwell, Mary to Kirk, Thomas, Junr.
Nov 26 1793 Greenwell, Mary to Yorick, Michael
Apr 13 1790 Greenwell, Philbert to Cushman, Eleanor
Dec 23 1807 Greenwell, Sarah to Moran, Robert
Nov 26 1810 Greenwood, Eleanor to Powell, Thomas
Sep 16 1797 Greenwood, Mary to Josse, Anthony
Nov 24 1806 Greer, Anne to McGaughey, James
Oct  8 1809 Greer, Polly to Bawden, James
Aug 27 1797 Gregg, Ann to Ewers, Jonathan
Aug  3 1801 Gregg, Mahlon to Gore, Sally
Sep 13 1808 Gregg, Ruth to Hickson, Samuel
Jun  5 1795 Gregg, Thomas to Smith, Anne
Jul 10 1803 Greggs, Rebecca to Steere, Isaac
Nov 20 1810 Gregory, Henry to Miller, Elizabeth
Dec 22 1806 Gregrory, Mary to Miller, Thomas
Apr 18 1801 Gremit, Elizabeth to Felius, Jacob
Jun 15 1779 Griffey, Agnes to McGowan, Sam'l
Apr 12 1783 Griffin, Ann to Silver, George
Feb 22 1782 Griffin, Elizabeth to Jacobs, Joseph
Jun 21 1806 Griffin, Thomas to Cassell, Nancy
Feb 17 1785 Griffin, Zadock to Hunter, Susanna
Sep  5 1796 Griffith, Abraham to Thompson, Elizabeth
May  3 1790 Griffith, Ann to Taylor, Henry
Nov  2 1787 Griffith, Caleb to Richardson, Mary
Aug 22 1778 Griffith, Chisholm to Scott, Mary Ann
Feb  3 1803 Griffith, Drucilla to Pile, Robert
Aug 27 1781 Griffith, Elisha to Woolf, Catherine
May  5 1807 Griffith, Elizabeth to Hoot, Samuel
Sep 16 1797 Griffith, Henry to Stewart, Hessey
Sep  1 1803 Griffith, Isaac to Elliott, Rebecca
Apr  4 1809 Griffith, John to Powell, Delilah
Apr 19 1809 Griffith, John to Gladhill, Jane
Nov  1 1783 Griffith, Joshua to Ridgley, Elizabeth
Feb 22 1781 Griffith, Lidia to McElfish, Philip
Mar 10 1809 Griffith, Lyde to Wayman, Amelia
Dec 29 1804 Griffith, Peggy to Proctor, Abraham
Jul  7 1783 Griffith, Philamond to Jacob, Eleanor
Nov 20 1788 Griffith, Rachel to Mobley, Edward
Oct 19 1789 Griffith, Richard to Tice, Margaret
Jun  2 1796 Griffith, Richard to Thomas, Ann
Oct 30 1800 Griffith, Samuel to Streems, Eve
Dec 31 1804 Griffith, Sophia to Deaver, Levi
Feb 19 1785 Griffith, Susanna to Barker, William

```
Aug  4 1784 Griffith, Wm. to Atkins, Anna
Jan  5 1806 Grigg, Elizabeth to Hogue, Jesse
Oct 24 1808 Grigg, Phebe to Michael, Christopher
Dec 17 1803 Grim, Catherine to Funk, George
May 16 1805 Grim, Christena to Shronk, John
Aug  4 1803 Grim, Daniel to Staup, Sarah
Aug  1 1801 Grim, John to Fronck, Mary
Dec 15 1792 Grimbolt, Genevieve Emilie to De K. Legaud, Peter
            Marie Guilie
Jan 27 1801 Grimes, Amelia to Pickett, Ezekiel
Oct 29 1793 Grimes, Basil to Picket, Betsy
Mar 20 1779 Grimes, Catherine to Moore, Wm.
Mar 16 1808 Grimes, Eleanor to Ridgely, Frederick
Dec 17 1805 Grimes, Elias to Ott, Mary
Jul 20 1795 Grimes, Elizabeth to Grimes, William
Mar 19 1798 Grimes, Frederick to Randall, Margaret
Jun  8 1778 Grimes, Jane to Allen, Philip
Dec 16 1778 Grimes, Jane to Harris, Robert
May  3 1808 Grimes, Joshua to Harman, Harriet
May 17 1806 Grimes, Lot to Otto, Catherine
Feb 26 1810 Grimes, Margaret to Hagan, John
Mar 17 1804 Grimes, Orlando to Dorsey, Rachel
Mar 24 1803 Grimes, Orphey to Wilson, Michael
Jan 17 1793 Grimes, Priscilla to Kelly, Dennis
Mar 19 1795 Grimes, Rachel to Clay, Samuel
Jan 19 1809 Grimes, Ruth to Crabs, Peter
Jul  3 1805 Grimes, Samuel to Staub, Catherine
Jun 13 1797 Grimes, Sarah to Hearn, Greenbury
Aug 29 1782 Grimes, Sarah to Todd, Basil
Apr 15 1790 Grimes, Susanna to Parker, Gilbert
Jul 20 1795 Grimes, William to Grimes, Elizabeth
Apr  7 1798 Grimes, William to Clance, Mary
Nov 21 1780 Grindler, Juliana to Durff, Jacob
Feb  5 1807 Grise, Mary to Clarke, Frderick
May 19 1795 Groce, Cathe. Eliza. to Niehoof, Balser
Jul 13 1805 Groff, Joseph to Coppersmith, Modelena
Jan 21 1799 Groff, Sarah to Cromwell, William
Jun 24 1808 Groft, Catherine to Suman, Isaac
Aug 12 1791 Gromatt, Mary to Collins, Hodijah
Nov 30 1780 Groom, James to Ricketts, Rebecca
Feb 22 1782 Grose, Henry to Derr, Margaret
Jun 11 1779 Groseman, Simon to Fogle, Eliz'th
Apr 16 1796 Grosh, Charlotte to Ramsberg, Jacob, Junr.
Apr 13 1790 Grosh, Maria Sophia to Culp, Michael
Apr 14 1795 Groshe, Eleanor to Hart, Thomas
Mar 31 1781 Groshner, Wm. to Welsh, Eliz'th
Feb 16 1801 Groshon, Elias to Lida, Margaret
Aug  3 1807 Groshon, John to Baker, Anne
Jun  6 1794 Groshong, Abraham to Waggoner, Elizabeth
Apr 24 1797 Gross, Margaret to Slunger, John
Dec 11 1803 Gross, Phebe to Duvall, Elisha
Sep 10 1783 Gross, William to Burkhart, Margaret
Aug 22 1793 Groteyon, Christian to Elginger, Modelena
Feb  9 1792 Grove, Barbara to Carl, David
Mar 27 1798 Grove, Barbara to Erb, Peter
Oct  5 1794 Grove, Catharine to Barnthisell, Christopher
```

```
Mar 19 1802 Grove, Catharine to Miller, Christopher
Aug 14 1789 Grove, Catherine to Righter, Peter
Dec  9 1802 Grove, Charlotte to Kiefer, Jacob
Jan 23 1793 Grove, Dolley to Shoup, Samuel
Oct 10 1793 Grove, Elizabeth to Thomas, Griffith
May 14 1791 Grove, Eve to Wilyard, Jacob
Feb 17 1800 Grove, George to Giddings, Alley
Jul 31 1798 Grove, Henry to Kephart, Judith
Aug  4 1787 Grove, Juliana to Burniston, Joseph
Oct 28 1797 Grove, Martin to Stemple, Catherine
Oct 17 1803 Grove, Mary to House, Stephen
May 21 1798 Grove, Mary to Smith, Henry
Nov 20 1783 Grove, Mary to Willett, Griffith
Dec  2 1793 Grove, Peter to Everly, Barbara
Aug 11 1798 Grove, Peter to Unglebower, Katy
Jul 18 1799 Grove, Rachel to Hinckle, John
May  8 1784 Grove, Sophia to Lutzell, Mich'l
Jun 29 1803 Grover, George to Hardy, Elizabeth
Nov  7 1780 Grover, Jonathan Mason to Musgrove, Sarah
Nov 23 1795 Grover, Priscilla to Mick, John
May 13 1802 Grubb, Elizabeth to Cromwell, Richard
Nov 22 1798 Gruber, David to Moore, Susy
Apr 12 1806 Gruber, Elizabeth to Mierhaffer, John
Nov  5 1795 Grumbauch, Simon to Devilbiss, Philippena
Apr 22 1780 Grush, Christena to Bookey, Mathias
Dec  9 1784 Guiseberts, And'w to Ridgley, Urith
Apr 29 1799 Gulick, Martha to Johnson, Casper
Apr  5 1788 Gumbare, Elizabeth to Bentz (or Pence), George
Dec 12 1779 Gumbare, John, Junr. to Mantz, Esther
Dec 27 1779 Gummert, Christian to Road, Margaret
Dec  1 1797 Gump, John to McGaghey, Mary
Feb 14 1791 Gun, Alexander to McKay, Margery
Apr 27 1789 Gunn, Christena to Miller, John
Oct  4 1782 Gunn, Margaret to Bruner, Peter
Apr  1 1780 Guthrie, Wm. to Elder, Eleanor
Jul 27 1795 Guy, Samuel to Darr, Catherine
Mar  5 1793 Guynn, Ann to Crawford, John
Jan 23 1804 Gwinn, Amelia to Philpott, Barton
Jan 14 1799 Gwinn, Elizabeth to Philpot, Charles
Aug  6 1803 Gwinn, Frances to Stansbury, William
Jan 15 1810 Gwinn, Mary to Crouse, Frederick

Apr 21 1787 Haas, Christena to Buckey, George
Aug 16 1796 Haas, Elizabeth to Gebhart, Peter
Aug 18 1788 Haas, Michael to Prishe, Sophia
Feb  9 1789 Haas, Susanna to Havener, Andrew
May  3 1785 Haas, Susanna to Ridenhour, Jacob
May 14 1785 Hackney, Benj'n Rhodes to Philpott, Elizabeth Warrent
Oct 27 1784 Hackney, Jacob to Garrett, Mary
Nov 14 1809 Hackney, Sarah E. to Boteler, Joseph L. (Lingan)
Apr 18 1786 Haddery, Benjamin to Covill, Susanna
Dec 21 1809 Haden, Mary to Woodman, William
May 27 1796 Haff, Abraham, Jr. to Dern, Frances
Aug 14 1789 Haff, Martha to Beanes, Francis
Apr 10 1786 Haff, Martha to James, John
```

| | | | |
|---|---|---|---|
| May | 30 | 1796 | Haff, Mary to Browning, Joseph |
| Jun | 3 | 1778 | Haff, Sarah to Hindes, Rudolph |
| Sep | 7 | 1797 | Haff, William M. to Dawson, Peggy |
| Apr | 9 | 1808 | Haffner, Elizabeth to Haffner, George |
| Apr | 9 | 1808 | Haffner, George to Haffner, Elizabeth |
| Apr | 9 | 1803 | Hagan, Ammishaddy to Hilton, Sarah |
| Feb | 12 | 1804 | Hagan, Dorothy to Shafer, Conrad |
| Feb | 19 | 1793 | Hagan, Elizabeth to McWilliams, John |
| Feb | 19 | 1793 | Hagan, Elizabeth to Williams, John |
| Jan | 29 | 1788 | Hagan, Francis to Ramsower, Margaret |
| Jun | 17 | 1780 | Hagan, Henry to Hyatt, Susanna |
| Aug | 1 | 1797 | Hagan, Hugh to Waggoner, Dorothy |
| Feb | 26 | 1810 | Hagan, John to Grimes, Margaret |
| Apr | 12 | 1788 | Hagan, Mary to Dawson, John |
| May | 21 | 1779 | Hagan, Nancy to Crone, Robert |
| May | 14 | 1809 | Hagan, Peter to Stilly, Nancy |
| Mar | 30 | 1807 | Hagan, Sarah to Brawn, Vachel |
| Jul | 7 | 1785 | Hagan, Susanna to Beatty, Elijah |
| Dec | 8 | 1781 | Hagar, George to Keefhaver, Magdalena |
| Nov | 17 | 1783 | Hagar, Jonathan to Orendorff, Mary |
| Aug | 29 | 1809 | Hagar, Samuel to Geyer, Eliza Catherine |
| Dec | 19 | 1778 | Hagerty, George to Kennedy, Elizabeth |
| Feb | 13 | 1782 | Hague, Amos to Burrell, Milley |
| Jan | 5 | 1809 | Hague, Andrew to Erbert, Barbara |
| Jan | 7 | 1809 | Hague, Mary Ann to Ebert, Frederick |
| Mar | 20 | 1788 | Hain, Caleb to Davis, Sarah |
| Apr | 24 | 1798 | Haine, Charles to Impson, Dorothy |
| Aug | 8 | 1806 | Haines, Catharine to Lescaleet, John |
| Dec | 6 | 1802 | Haines, Catherine to Conner, William |
| Apr | 7 | 1798 | Haines, John to Lipps, Mary |
| Aug | 2 | 1796 | Haines, Joseph to Shroyer, Mary |
| Jul | 7 | 1797 | Haines, Mary to Flucke, Peter |
| Sep | 9 | 1795 | Hains, Elizabeth to Barnhart, Peter |
| Dec | 7 | 1805 | Hains, Jacob to Crowl, Elizabeth |
| Apr | 1 | 1802 | Hains, Mary to Baker, Adam |
| Dec | 29 | 1788 | Hains, Nathan to Murray, Ann |
| Oct | 20 | 1810 | Hale, George to Wagner, Barbara |
| Apr | 15 | 1794 | Hale, Mary to Harvey, Basil |
| Aug | 29 | 1793 | Hall, Amey to Bryan, James |
| Aug | 25 | 1793 | Hall, Amey to Harbaugh, George, Jr. |
| Jun | 10 | 1790 | Hall, Ann to Justice, Ezekiel |
| Feb | 22 | 1805 | Hall, Ariana to Gatrill, John |
| Jun | 26 | 1797 | Hall, Barruck to Burgee, Mary |
| Apr | 20 | 1799 | Hall, Benjamin to Leakins, Elizabeth |
| Jul | 2 | 1801 | Hall, Benjamin to Ingman, Rachel |
| Sep | 12 | 1800 | Hall, Bridget Ingen to Fox, Peter |
| Feb | 14 | 1805 | Hall, Eleanor to McElfresh, John of John |
| May | 30 | 1804 | Hall, Elizabeth to Pitts, John, Rev. |
| Jan | 19 | 1808 | Hall, Elizabeth to Journey, Sabrit |
| Aug | 27 | 1787 | Hall, Elizbeth to Barnes, David |
| Mar | 13 | 1800 | Hall, Henry to Turner, Mary |
| Jun | 20 | 1795 | Hall, John to Bolan, Margaret |
| Aug | 26 | 1799 | Hall, John to Evis, Solema |
| Jul | 16 | 1801 | Hall, John to Hyatt, Elizabeth |
| Mar | 11 | 1784 | Hall, Joseph to Horner, Nancy |

```
Mar 17 1792 Hall, Joseph to Burkett, Margaret
Dec 12 1782 Hall, Lilee to Pool, William
Dec 13 1796 Hall, Margaret to Hall, Vachel
Mar  3 1810 Hall, Margaret to Smith, John
Jan 10 1806 Hall, Mary to Hilton, James
May 27 1805 Hall, Nicholas to Harris, Martha
Sep  9 1805 Hall, Nicholas to McElfresh, Anne
Aug 22 1807 Hall, Rachel to Molesworth, Samuel
Jan  9 1796 Hall, Rebeckah to Douglass, Charles
Apr  1 1809 Hall, Richard to Fishburn, Susanna
May 28 1803 Hall, Susanna to Moore, John
May 28 1803 Hall, Susanna to Moore, John
Jun  3 1802 Hall, Susanna to Teaner, Adam
Dec 13 1796 Hall, Vachel to Hall, Margaret
Oct 10 1810 Haller, Catherine to Gorney, Joseph
Aug 20 1808 Haller, Catherine to Walker, James
Aug 17 1801 Haller, Elizabeth to Button, Samuel
Aug 19 1793 Haller, Elizabeth to Woolfe, Henry
Apr  4 1805 Haller, Joshua to Hane, Catherine
Oct  6 1804 Halverstadt, Catherine to Keefer, Jacob
Sep  6 1783 Hambleton, Mary to Carter, John
Jul 20 1789 Hamilton, Eleanor to McDonald, Francis
Oct  4 1782 Hamilton, Elizabeth to Hobbbs, Elie
Jul 22 1800 Hamilton, Francis to Philpoott, Catherine
Jun 22 1795 Hamilton, John Alexander to Philpot, Eleanor
Nov 22 1794 Hamilton, John G. to Smallwood, Eliz.
Oct 19 1790 Hamilton, Margaret to Beall, George
Oct 10 1808 Hamilton, Phebe M. to Nabb, William
Oct 10 1786 Hamilton, Rebeckah to Cooper, Adam
Sep 26 1795 Hamilton, Robert to Andrew, Elizabeth
Oct 23 1803 Hammerly, John to Drish, Jean
Apr 27 1799 Hammersleigh, Charles to Shreup, Barbara
Jan 24 1795 Hammet, Rebeckah to Wilson, Jacob
Aug  7 1787 Hammett, Sarah to Fogle, Adam
Jun 21 1790 Hammond, Ann to Warfield, Henry
Apr 20 1799 Hammond, Arianna to Hammond, Upton
Oct  6 1803 Hammond, Charles to Hammond, Elizabeth
Oct  2 1795 Hammond, Elizabeth to Hammond, Philip
Oct  6 1803 Hammond, Elizabeth to Hammond, Charles
Mar 25 1807 Hammond, George to Dorsey, Ariminta
Apr  3 1784 Hammond, Hannah to Cutshall, George
Jun 16 1801 Hammond, John to Roberts, Rachel
Mar  4 1797 Hammond, Lot to Davis, Elizabeth
May 11 1778 Hammond, Mary to Edeldire(?), James
Dec 29 1798 Hammond, Mary to Johnson, Benjamin
Jun  8 1793 Hammond, Nathan to Worthington, Priscilla
Jan 27 1780 Hammond, Ormond to Duckett, Eliz'th
Oct  2 1795 Hammond, Philip to Hammond, Elizabeth
Mar  5 1788 Hammond, Sarah to Dorsey, Johnsa
Jan 26 1797 Hammond, Thomas John to Gaither, Rachael
Jul 11 1805 Hammond, Thomas John to Crumbacker, Mary
Feb  8 1806 Hammond, Tomsey to Pool, William
Apr 20 1799 Hammond, Upton to Hammond, Arianna
Apr  6 1805 Hampton, John to Abbott, Margaret
Nov 16 1789 Hamston, Mary to Mullikin, John
```

```
Jan 12 1780 Hande, Thomas to Whitmer, Catherine
Dec  1 1806 Handley, Dennis to Rusher, Elizabeth
Mar  1 1779 Handshaw, John to Knowse, Eliz'th
Jun 17 1780 Handshew, Barbara to Bower, Martin
Apr  4 1805 Hane, Catherine to Haller, Joshua
Nov 21 1780 Hanes, Barbara to Bash, Andrew
Dec 22 1804 Hanes, Jeremiah to Dadisman, Elizabeth
Dec 10 1799 Hankins, Sarah to Stevenson, John
Jun 10 1809 Hann, Elizabeth to Keefer, Jacob
Jan 18 1805 Hann, Philip to Keefer, Elizabeth
Oct 29 1801 Hanna, Jane to Myers, William
May  4 1800 Hannah, Margaret to Donovan, John
Nov  5 1803 Hannah, Woman of Colony to Williams, Robert (colored)
Dec 28 1795 Hannahe, Mary to Lynch, Abraham
Dec  5 1808 Hannis, Joseph to Patrick, Catherine
Jun 14 1791 Hansey, Eleanor to Miller, Dewalt
Oct 23 1784 Hanshugh, Fred'k to Whitehair, Mary
Oct  3 1809 Happener, John G. to Rep, Margaret
May  7 1810 Harb, Jacob to Crossnickle, Eliz.
Nov 18 1806 Harbaugh, Christian to Firor, Mary
Aug 25 1793 Harbaugh, George, Jr. to Hall, Amey
Mar  6 1805 Harbaugh, John, Junr. to Cogh, Elizabeth
Nov 21 1803 Harbaugh, Samuel to Creager, Rachael
Feb  1 1799 Harder, Polly to Baker, John
May 24 1801 Hardesty, William to Knouff, Lovice
Apr  5 1782 Hardey, Arnold to Flemming, Barbara
Jul 24 1797 Hardey, Winifred to Clements, William
Jan 10 1793 Hardiger, Elizabeth to Clay, Adam
May 28 1790 Hardin, Richard to Crepell, Rachel
Dec 29 1806 Harding, Amelia to Hobbs, John
Apr 13 1807 Harding, Cassandra to Rose, Henry
Sep 17 1802 Harding, Christian to Musseter, Barbara
Feb 24 1799 Harding, Eleanor to Harding, Elias
Jan  9 1786 Harding, Elias to Ford, Cassandra
Feb 24 1799 Harding, Elias to Harding, Eleanor
Jul 19 1808 Harding, Elizabeth to Skeal, Nicholas
May  6 1798 Harding, Elizabeth B. to Williams, Benjamin
Jan 17 1809 Harding, Elizabeth S. to Willson, Richard
Apr 24 1794 Harding, George to Berger, Catherine
Nov  3 1810 Harding, Jacob to Ruperd, Elizabeth
May 31 1804 Harding, John L. to Marshall, Eleanor
Dec  5 1795 Harding, Lewis to Jarret, Ann
Feb 13 1807 Harding, Lewis to Ridgely, Sarah
May  7 1796 Harding, Mary to Luckett, Philip
Jun 21 1783 Harding, Mary to Sprigg, Samuel
Oct 24 1804 Harding, Mary Ann to Simmons, Jacob
Mar 14 1798 Harding, Vachel to Parker, Mary
Apr 12 1786 Harding, Zephaniah to Howell, Sarah
Sep 11 1779 Hardman, Anna Maria to Oberfeld, Mathias
Apr  7 1798 Hardman, Elizabeth to Caufman, Henry
Mar 31 1804 Hardman, George to Strickstroke, Barbara
Jan  7 1804 Hardman, Henry to Ebbert, Susanna
Jun 27 1807 Hardman, Martin to Niswanger, Elizabeth
May 16 1795 Hardy, Ann to Smith, Benjamin
Sep 10 1792 Hardy, Darcus to Hempston, Christian
```

```
Jun 29 1803 Hardy, Elizabeth to Grover, George
Nov 27 1809 Hardy, Jonathan to Fogler, Catherine
Jun  9 1807 Hardy, Joseph to Ramsberg, Catherine
Mar  2 1799 Hardy, Mary to McAtee, George
Feb 19 1784 Hardy, Mary to Phillips, Jesse
Feb  5 1785 Hardy, Mary to Riggs, John
Aug 27 1810 Hardy, Nancy to Carmichael, Daniel
Dec 12 1784 Hardy, Rebeccah to Wheeler, Henry
Dec 25 1806 Hardy, Samuel to Hawk, Catherine
Jan  2 1809 Hardy, Susannah to Ramsberg, Jacob
Sep 24 1796 Hargant, John to McLaughlin, Sarah
Jun  1 1779 Hargate, Abraham to Pentrin, Mary
Aug 30 1806 Hargate, Abraham to Wilt, Susanna
Sep  9 1799 Hargate, Catherine to Wietrick, George
Apr 18 1810 Hargate, John to Thomas, Barbara
Apr 27 1805 Hargate, Mary to Friddle, David
May  8 1780 Hargerhyma, Madilaine to Brandenberger, Sam'l
Jan 17 1807 Harget, Catherine to Specht, Conrad
Nov 27 1806 Harget, Elizabeth to Winbeagler, Richard
Aug 26 1780 Hargishymeir, Catherine to Showes, Samuel
Aug  5 1806 Hargraw, Judith to Dribets, Powell
Jan 29 1780 Haring, Henry to Peckenpaugh, Catherine
Jan  2 1779 Harland, Hannah to Forward, William
Jun 18 1789 Harley, Joshua to Whitenacht, Elizabeth
Dec 27 1808 Harley, Sohpia to Biser, Daniel
Aug 22 1791 Harlin, Catherine to Cooper, Robert
Apr 18 1791 Harlin, James to Wood, Mary
Jan  5 1792 Harlin, Joshua to Wood, Sarah
Mar  9 1798 Harman, Christiana to Stemple, Henry
May  3 1808 Harman, Harriet to Grimes, Joshua
Dec 29 1800 Harman, Nicholas to Kennedy, Margaret
Mar 30 1799 Harmon, Jacob to Zealer, Margaret
May 17 1794 Harmon, John to Shryock, Elizabeth
Dec 26 1793 Harmon, Modelena to House, William
Feb 22 1809 Harn, Caleb to Duvall, Charity
Jul  4 1809 Harn, Corrella to Douty, James
Aug 15 1806 Harner, Magdalena to Bussard, William
Dec 24 1792 Harp, Susanna to Wigle, Leonard
Feb  7 1810 Harper, Nancy to Larkin, David
Dec 30 1800 Harper, Richard to Stevenson, Margaret
Dec 28 1806 Harper, Sarah to Shook, John
Mar 27 1790 Harple, Hannah to Sheats, Jacob
Nov 15 1805 Harrey, Nancy to Duning, William
Feb 15 1798 Harriade, Elizabeth to Neff, John
Feb  1 1806 Harriott, Peter to Waltz, Mary
Feb 22 1796 Harris, Catherine to Phillips, Elie
Nov 17 1796 Harris, Dorcus to Davidson, David
Jan 23 1802 Harris, Elizabeth to Fiege, John
Feb 21 1809 Harris, Elizabeth to Jones, John
Aug  1 1792 Harris, Harriet to Dorsey, Basil
Apr 26 1784 Harris, Jane to Deshong, William
Jun 20 1801 Harris, Jesse to Noyes, Darkey
Sep 22 1807 Harris, Jesse to Veach, Susanna
Mar  3 1783 Harris, John to Elder, Mary
Feb 13 1804 Harris, Judith to Brikett, James
```

```
Nov  1 1805 Harris, Martha to Clabaugh, John
May 27 1805 Harris, Martha to Hall, Nicholas
Jan 31 1804 Harris, Mary to Hatfield, John
Feb  6 1795 Harris, Mary to Matthews, Peter
Jun 12 1804 Harris, Mary to Spencer, William
Jan 26 1808 Harris, Nancy to Norris, John
Dec 21 1789 Harris, Priscilla to Hilton, James
Dec 16 1778 Harris, Robert to Grimes, Jane
May  6 1798 Harris, Ruth to Silman, Thomas
May 24 1786 Harris, Samuel to Koonce, Catherine
Nov 26 1792 Harris, Samuel to Gott, Susanna
Jun  8 1803 Harris, Sarah to Jamison, John
Jan 18 1798 Harris, Thomas to Crabs, Margaret
Apr 23 1808 Harrison, Alexander C. to Owings, Catherine
Aug 21 1810 Harrison, Anne to Anchors, Samuel
Dec 24 1807 Harrison, Aschah to Fish, Richard
Apr 18 1787 Harrison, Catherine, Miss to Tyler, John, Dr.
Mar 11 1807 Harrison, Cordelia to Clary, Samuel
Sep 11 1810 Harrison, Eleanor to Sherman, Benjamin
Jul 12 1792 Harrison, Eleanor to Turner, Thomas
Feb  2 1797 Harrison, Elizabeth, Miss to Nelson, Roger, Capt.
Jun 14 1804 Harrison, James to Williams, Eleanor
Sep 16 1805 Harrison, Jane to Mossberg, Christian
May 27 1783 Harrison, Jane Contee to Murdock, William
Jul 17 1779 Harrison, John to Clann, Betty
Jan 17 1807 Harrison, John to Hoffman, Elizabeth
Aug  3 1779 Harrison, Josias to Davis, Elizabeth
Mar  9 1780 Harrison, Kens to Saffle, Sarah
Dec 17 1779 Harrison, Mary to Cooper, Wm.
Jan 29 1789 Harrison, Mary to Durbin, Cornelius
Feb  2 1798 Harrison, Mary to Karr, Walter
Dec 24 1795 Harrison, Nancy to Barnes, James
Jun 21 1787 Harrison, Nathan to Badan, Mary
Dec  2 1784 Harrison, Phoebe to Wright, Eli
Jul 11 1801 Harrison, Ruth to Saffell, John
Feb 20 1788 Harrison, Samuel to Showne, Elizabeth
May 30 1805 Harrison, William to Musgrove, Mary
Nov  4 1778 Harrison, Wm. to Davis, Mary
Dec 16 1795 Harrris, Cordelia to Owings, Beall
Aug  9 1798 Harschell, Margaret to Stoneburner, Jacob
Dec 29 1798 Harshman, Mary to Cost, George
Sep  6 1794 Hart, Adam to Myers, Elizabeth
Apr 17 1779 Hart, Benj'n to Danniwolf, Elizabeth
Feb 22 1783 Hart, Catherine to Myrehaver, Peter
Oct 19 1778 Hart, Christ'n to Richards, Eliz'th
Oct 10 1796 Hart, Elizabeth to Richards, Brice
Feb 21 1789 Hart, Elizabeth to Smith, Peter
Aug  1 1789 Hart, Ellis to Howard, Ann
Feb 11 1786 Hart, Michael to Row, Mary
Dec  5 1795 Hart, Peter to Doll, Charlotte
Apr 14 1795 Hart, Thomas to Groshe, Eleanor
Mar 16 1782 Harter, Mary to Albaugh, David
Jun 24 1803 Hartman, Barbara to Huber, Jacob
Jun  5 1786 Hartman, John to Sheets, Catherine
Aug 20 1810 Harton, George to Wetsel, Betsy
```

```
Apr 23 1807 Hartsock, George to Cramer, Elizabeth
Jun 17 1808 Hartsock, Nicholas to Birely, Margaret
Apr 19 1805 Hartsock, Sarah to Morrow, James
May 10 1806 Hartsock, William to Fingbaum, Elizabeth
Oct 18 1796 Hartsoke, Catherine to Mumford, William
Jan 17 1795 Harvey, Ann to Spangler, Christian
Apr 15 1794 Harvey, Basil to Hale, Mary
May  5 1800 Harvey, Elizabeth to McCormack, John
Apr  3 1806 Harvey, Eunice to Burges, James
May 11 1785 Harvey, James to Brown, Darcus
Feb  3 1803 Harvey, Seth to Baker, Anne
Oct 28 1805 Harvy, Prissilla to Spurrier, Benjamin
Aug  5 1805 Harwood, Thomas N. to Noland, Polly
Jul 25 1801 Hase, Fred'k Christopher to Beckerbach, Elizabeth
Oct 13 1803 Hatcher, Margaret to Nichols, Jacob
Jan 31 1804 Hatfield, John to Harris, Mary
Mar  6 1799 Hatherly, Benjamin to Covell, Mary Ann
Mar 14 1780 Hatton, Wm. to Cartey, Mary
Dec 14 1809 Hauer, Ann Maria to Engles, Silas
May 17 1806 Hauer, Barbara to Fritchie, John
Apr 12 1788 Hauer, Catharine to Bare, George Junr
Mar 26 1807 Hauer, Elizabeth to Rohr, Jacob
Sep 21 1786 Hauer, Elizabeth to Steiner, John, Jr.
Oct  8 1803 Hauer, Georgeerine to Shellman, Catherine
Dec 15 1792 Hauer, Margaret to Stover, John
Nov 18 1792 Hauer, Mary to Springer, William
Oct 13 1795 Hauer, Nicholas to Dawson, Priscilla
May 10 1808 Hauer, Susanna to Creager, Lewis, Dr.
Jun 10 1791 Hauser, Adam to Yantz, Sibylla
May  8 1810 Hauser, Susan to Buckey, John
Aug 27 1808 Hauver, Catherine to Wilyard, Michael
Feb  9 1789 Havener, Andrew to Haas, Susanna
Dec 25 1806 Hawk, Catherine to Hardy, Samuel
Sep  8 1810 Hawk, Jacob to Birely, Elizabeth
Apr 16 1802 Hawk, Susanna to Shriner, Philip
May  7 1804 Hawkins, Elizabeth W. to Duvall, Grafton
Nov 23 1798 Hawkins, Julia to Clagett, Henry
Oct 25 1785 Hawling, John Wilespen to Fouch, Jemima
Jul 31 1802 Hawman, Barbara to Kiefer, Michael
Aug 18 1781 Hawman, Peter to Hildebrand, Elizabeth
Jun 24 1806 Hawn, Elizabeth to Grace, William
Nov 11 1799 Hawn, Lewis to Pearce, Elizabeth
Sep  9 1778 Hawn, Michael to Eichelberger, Christianna
Dec 12 1808 Hawn, William to Stuck, Catherine
May 30 1794 Hawne, Christina to Dunn, William
Apr  7 1797 Hay, Edmond to Whitacre, Sarah
Mar  7 1800 Hay, Jacob to Beckebaugh, Susanna
Jun 15 1809 Hayes, James to Beall, Sarah
Sep 24 1783 Hayes, Mary to Norris, William
Jun 15 1779 Hayes, Mary to Yeast, Philip
May  5 1802 Hayes, Zachariah to Norris, Mary Anne
Apr 11 1804 Haynes, Daniel to Moore, Elizabeth
Jun 14 1809 Hays, Abigail to Trail, William
Feb 10 1810 Hays, Amelia to Bell, Benjamin
Sep 22 1806 Hays, Anne to Dawson, John
```

```
Jan 19 1802 Hays, Anne to Waltham, Benedict
Jan 12 1802 Hays, Charles to Hilton, Sarah
Aug 25 1795 Hays, Eleanor to Kibby, Joseph
Mar  9 1797 Hays, George to Ridgley, Elizabeth
Jan 29 1796 Hays, John to Howard, Susanna
Feb  7 1791 Hays, Joseph to Wimmer, Deborah
Apr 23 1798 Hays, Mary to Gilleland, John
Dec  2 1788 Hays, Notley to Rawlings, Sarah
Sep 10 1796 Hays, Priscilla to Owings, Archibald
Feb 11 1789 Hays, Richard to Norris, Charlotte
Dec 28 1809 Hays, Sarah to Games, John
Dec  1 1786 Hays, Thomas to Wilkey, Ann
Jul 12 1797 Haywood, Isaac to Talbott, Ann
Aug 24 1782 Haze, Leonard to Simmonds, Eleanor
May  5 1778 Hazelwood, Thomas to Coffin, Sarah
Feb  5 1788 Head, Ann to Beall, Nathaniel
Feb 13 1779 Head, Biggar to Livers, ---
Jan  8 1799(1779?) Head, Cecilius to Butler, Elizabeth
Nov 17 1807 Head, Elizabeth to Clark, James
Oct  9 1778 Head, Elizabeth to Wood, Richard
Jan  2 1790 Head, Ignatius to Perry, Nancy
Jan 30 1806 Head, Jane to Howell, Henry
Mar 10 1795 Head, Lucy to Crist, Henry
Apr 27 1808 Head, Lucy to Elder, Joseph
Nov 17 1807 Head, Mary to Minghini, Joseph
May  4 1784 Head, Richard to Bentley, Ruth
Aug 27 1778 Head, Wm. Edward to Walker, Mary
Nov  5 1801 Heague, Hannah to Brown, Fielder
May 10 1779 Heanmyer, Jacob to Steiner, Catherine
Aug 18 1801 Hearn, Denton to Pickett, Rachel
Sep  5 1787 Hearn, Elijah to Davis, Cassandra
Jun 13 1797 Hearn, Greenbury to Grimes, Sarah
Jul  6 1798 Hearn, Mathias to Shipley, Amelia
May 22 1778 Heartsock, Catherine to Barrick, William
Jul  4 1778 Heartsock, William to Fogle, Catherine
Dec 23 1801 Heastond, Sarah to Gebhart, John
Aug 26 1779 Heater, Frederick to Shroiner, Mary Ann
Feb  2 1788 Hebb, Richard to Thomas, Ann
Jul  1 1783 Heck, Daniel to Mcclain, Elizabeth
Jun  4 1796 Heck, Eve Margaret to Hoffman, David
Jun  2 1778 Heckathorn, Philapoena to Mottis, Peter
Oct  3 1801 Heckaturn, George to Devilbis, Margaret
Sep  1 1789 Heckenmiller, John Conrad to Davis, Elizabeth
Sep  8 1788 Hedge, Caleb to Dern, Mary
Sep 12 1795 Hedge, Hannah to Burckhart, George
Jul 15 1797 Hedge, Mary to Zimmerman, Jacob
Nov 14 1799 Hedge, Moses to Waters, Catherine
Dec 28 1794 Hedge, Nicholas to Ritchie, Zeruiah
Aug 27 1787 Hedge, Phebe to Cregar, John
Apr 30 1792 Hedges, Andrew to Cramer, Christena
Jan 29 1805 Hedges, Andrew to Leatherman, Juliana
Dec  7 1799 Hedges, Anna to Julien, Rene
Jan 25 1802 Hedges, Isaac to Staley, Barbara
Aug 17 1784 Hedges, Jonas to Hedges, Mary Ann
Jul 21 1797 Hedges, Joseph to Baltzell, Catherine
```

May 14 1803 Hedges, Joseph to Crow, Mary
Nov  4 1778 Hedges, Josiah to Barnett, Ann
Jun  3 1794 Hedges, Margaret to Fulton, George
Dec 17 1790 Hedges, Mary to Rice, William
Aug 17 1784 Hedges, Mary Ann to Hedges, Jonas
Sep 24 1787 Hedges, Peter to Boyer, Elizabeth
Mar 17 1786 Hedges, Sarah to Keller, George
Aug  3 1782 Hedges, Shardrick to Dickson, Mary
Jun  3 1801 Hedges, Stephen to Butler, Sarah
Sep 16 1790 Hedges, Susana to Bailey, Joseph
Feb 22 1790 Hedges, William to Duffield, Leah
Feb 13 1804 Hedges, William to Yantes, Catharine
Apr 23 1778 Heffner, Catherine to Miller, David
Jul 28 1781 Heffner, Catherine to Pupp, Peter
Jul 25 1778 Heffner, Elizabeth to Abey, Peter
Jan  5 1807 Heffner, Elizabeth to Shoun, John
Apr  1 1786 Heffner, George, Jr. to Yantz, Eve Margaret
Dec  6 1790 Heffner, Gotlip to Shafer, Catharine
May 14 1801 Heffner, Jacob to Angleberger, Margaret
Aug 14 1809 Heffner, Jacob to Burkhart, Catherine
Oct  4 1806 Heffner, Margaret to Julien, Richard B.
May  1 1781 Heffner, Mary to Sheely, And'w
Oct  8 1779 Heffner, Mich'l to Reed, Margaret
Sep  6 1794 Heffner, Mich'l to Shafer, Elizabeth
Oct 25 1803 Heffner, Susanna to Yandes, George
Jan  2 1783 Hefner, Christena to Summers, Peter
Aug 30 1797 Heggins, Rebecca to Edwards, Robert
Dec 23 1790 Heighten, Josias to Cawood, Rebecca
Dec  7 1802 Heigle, Charles to Carns, Mary
Jan  6 1807 Heisler, Henry to Bayer, Elizabeth
Jun 21 1806 Heisley, Sophia to Rigney, John
Feb 19 1801 Heizer, John to Kemp, Catherine
Dec  4 1783 Hellen, Barbara to Kruse, John
Feb 24 1802 Heller, Christena to Shuff, Jonathan
Oct 14 1802 Hemmingsworth, Jeremiah to Hughes, Marzella
Aug  6 1807 Hemp, Catherine to Coblentz, George
May  8 1790 Hemp, Juliana to Shellhouse, Peter
Jan 15 1791 Hempston, Charity to Plummer, Zephaniah
Sep 10 1792 Hempston, Christian to Hardy, Darcus
Dec 20 1806 Hempy, Peter to Michael, Maryan
Jan  7 1797 Henderson, Griffith to Richardson, Hannah
Aug 14 1805 Henderson, James to Reed, Thomason
Nov  5 1809 Henderson, John to Stimble, Barbara
Apr 29 1784 Hendrickson, Susanna to White, Henry
Nov  1 1797 Hennickhouser, Charity to Freed, Peter
Nov 28 1797 Hennickhouser, Modelina to Cloninger, Philip
Oct  1 1803 Henry, Catherine to Weaver, Christian
Oct  8 1808 Henry, Charles to Shriner, Mary
Jul 15 1800 Henry, Daniel to Vanmetre, Rebecca
Jan  1 1804 Henry, Jane to Kline, David
Dec 19 1807 Henry, Sarah to Ball, Vachel
Jun  1 1800 Henry, Stephen to Vandevander, Jane
Feb 21 1807 Hensey, Patsy to Miller, Ludwick Lewis
Aug 28 1779 Henson, Biddy to Warner, John
Nov 15 1786 Herbert, Jeremiah to Hill, Mary

```
Feb  2 1808 Herdman, George to Carmack, Sarah
May  7 1793 Herpster, Frederick to Shollison, Mary
Nov  6 1810 Herrin, Jacob to Wertz, Elizabeth
Sep 12 1810 Herring, Frederick to Bankard, Mary
Apr  1 1799 Herring, Henry to Sailer, Mary
Apr 29 1807 Herring, Isaac to Eighenbrode, Margaret
Feb 13 1806 Herring, John to Shroyer, Mary
Aug 15 1807 Hersh, Catherine to Hummer, John
Jan 11 1799 Hershaberger, Eve to Runner, Michael, Jr.
Mar 21 1782 Hershberger, Dorathy to Kemp, Fred'k
May  7 1787 Hershberger, Henry to Ramsbergh, Catherine
Nov 21 1785 Hertzterfer, John to Reichart, Mary
May 15 1801 Hessong, John to Johnson, Margaret
Feb 20 1792 Heugh, John to Munro, Anne
Nov  4 1792 Heughs, Nancy to Gibson, Thomas
Jan  7 1804 Hewett, Rachel to Ourant, John
Nov 25 1778 Hewey, Sarah to Biggon, Heugh
Jul 30 1804 Hewitt, Ruth to Sargent, Jacob
Apr  4 1807 Hewlet, Mary to O'Flaherty, Michael
Sep 14 1789 Hickey, James to Linch, Mary Ann
Jan 23 1786 Hickman, Christopher to Davis, Christena
Dec 17 1779 Hickman, Eleanor to Barlow, Zachariah
Jul 18 1795 Hickman, Elizabeth to McIntosh, Michael
Apr 22 1800 Hickman, Jane to Luckett, John
Apr 27 1804 Hicks, Joseph to Storng, Mary
Nov 27 1810 Hickson, Henry to Crapster, Mary
Sep 13 1808 Hickson, Samuel to Gregg, Ruth
May 14 1785 Hickson, Thomas to Black, Mary
Jun 14 1805 Hide, Jonethan to Durbin, Rachael
May 28 1794 Hie, Mary to Lambert, John
Jan 29 1798 Higdon, John to Gantt, Eleanor
Sep 14 1793 Higdon, Margaret to Speak, James
Dec 20 1792 Higdon, Peter to Pierce, Anna
Jun 12 1809 Higdon, Thomas to Delashmutt, Artemese
Feb 23 1801 Higgins, James L. to Sheredine, Sophia
Jan 17 1804 Higgins, John to Burns, Susanna
Feb 18 1786 Higgins, Rachel to Tucker, Richard
Feb  4 1789 Highfield, Ann to Smith, John
Aug 31 1796 Highfield, John to Metz, Catherine
Jan 23 1793 Highfield, Mary to Miller, Robert
May 24 1788 Highler, Susanna to Morgan, John
Feb 11 1803 Hildebrand, Barbara to Linton, Benjamin
Aug 18 1781 Hildebrand, Elizabeth to Hawman, Peter
May 30 1807 Hildebrand, Elizabeth to Lantz, Curtius
Apr  1 1802 Hildebrand, Henry, Junr. to Lantz, Margaret
Mar  2 1801 Hildebrand, Jacob to Smith, Maria
Apr  3 1798 Hildebrand, John to Myers, Margaret
Nov 11 1791 Hildebrand, Mary to Beale, Davault
Jan  2 1787 Hildebrand, Mary to Byrne, William
Oct 27 1780 Hildebrand, Philipeana to Welfley, Christian
Apr 26 1785 Hilderbrick, George to Koontz, Mary Ann
Sep  4 1788 Hilke, Christian to Thomas, Barbary
Oct 17 1801 Hilkner, Barbara to McDanold, John
May 24 1800 Hill, Abraham to McCoune, Sarah
Apr  3 1779 Hill, Abram to Clabaugh, Judey
```

```
Sep  5 1778 Hill, Benj'n to Scaggs, Sarah
Sep 30 1806 Hill, Benjamin to Compton, Elizabeth
May  1 1779 Hill, Catherine to Burton, Henry
Apr  5 1802 Hill, Christian to Jefferson, Elizabeth
Aug 17 1779 Hill, Eliz'th to Clabaugh, Charles
Dec 29 1810 Hill, Elizabeth to Eader, Abraham of Jno.
Nov  1 1798 Hill, Emma to Gosnel, Peter
Sep 25 1788 Hill, Henry Roby to Tolbert, Ann
Sep 16 1778 Hill, Joseph, Jr. to Row, Margaret
Jun  8 1808 Hill, Lewis to Spencer, Jinett
Nov 15 1786 Hill, Mary to Herbert, Jeremiah
Sep  2 1786 Hill, Nathan to Davis, Drucilla
Dec 21 1786 Hill, Robert to Hyfield, Eleanor
Jan  7 1799 Hill, Ruth to Jenkins, Daniel
Apr 16 1783 Hill, Thomas to Howard, Sarah
Sep  7 1783 Hill, Thomas to Sullivan, Hannah
Feb 19 1793 Hill, Thomas to Wharton, Elizabeth
Jul 18 1806 Hill, Thomas to Bryan, Mary
Apr  3 1779 Hill, William to Perkinson, Mary
Oct 19 1789 Hilleary, Eleanor to Jacobs, Richard
Apr 30 1783 Hilleary, Ogbon to Purdy, Elizabeth
Jan 18 1802 Hilleary, Rebecca to Thomas, Philip
Nov 30 1804 Hilleary, Sarah to Norwood, Thomas
Dec  6 1796 Hilleary, Sarah to Skinner, Henry Smith
Feb 14 1781 Hillery, Eliz'th to Madden, Joseph
Apr 18 1804 Hillery, Osbon to King, Elenor
Feb  9 1782 Hillery, Thomas to Murphey, Ann
Sep  6 1781 Hillery, Wm. to Evans, Drusey
Apr 19 1804 Hilliard, James to Laurance, Mary
Jan 14 1789 Hilton, Andrew to Spalding, Catherine
Sep 12 1800 Hilton, Clemm to Firehauk, Christena
Feb 10 1790 Hilton, Eleanor to Wheeler, Thomas
Dec 21 1789 Hilton, James to Harris, Priscilla
Jan 10 1806 Hilton, James to Hall, Mary
Jun 16 1792 Hilton, Luke to Wilson, Margaret
Mar 24 1778 Hilton, Margaret to Morrow, Archebald
Feb 23 1809 Hilton, Mary to Braddock, John
Feb 10 1792 Hilton, Mary to Hinkley, Fred'k
Dec  5 1789 Hilton, Mary to Talbott, James
Jan 28 1791 Hilton, Matthew to Wheeler, Susanna
Apr  9 1803 Hilton, Sarah to Hagan, Ammishaddy
Jan 12 1802 Hilton, Sarah to Hays, Charles
Oct 27 1780 Hilton, Trueman to Patrick, Christena
Jan 26 1782 Hilton, Wm. to Nicholls, Elizabeth
Sep  5 1807 Himes, Catharine to Will, George
Dec 15 1810 Himsworth, Mary to Frazier, John
Oct 11 1785 Hinamon, Geo. to Howard, Elizabeth
Oct 17 1780 Hinckle, Eliz'th to Drake, Wm.
Mar 25 1781 Hinckle, Jno. to Brightwell, Nussey
Jul 18 1799 Hinckle, John to Grove, Rachel
Apr  3 1784 Hinckle, Margaret to Rhine, Casper
Jun  3 1778 Hindes, Rudolph to Haff, Sarah
Jun 15 1808 Hiner, Elizabeth to Fleck, Adam
Oct 31 1809 Hiner, John to Cover, Mary
May  9 1805 Hiner, Mary to Stull, Christopher
```

```
Jan  6 1804 Hiner, Susannah to Clary, Benjamin
Apr 28 1807 Hines, Elizabeth to Strong, Benjamin
Oct 14 1807 Hines, Hugh to Comper, Susanna
Apr 24 1810 Hines, Jacob to Hines, Susanna
Mar  9 1795 Hines, John to Roderick, Mary
Nov  4 1796 Hines, Nathaniel to Penn, Elizabeth
Jan 10 1792 Hines, Patrick to Bankard, Esther
Apr 24 1810 Hines, Susanna to Hines, Jacob
Oct 13 1798 Hinkle, Elizabeth to Hinkle, George
Mar 18 1804 Hinkle, Elizabeth to Nusz, Henry
Oct 13 1798 Hinkle, George to Hinkle, Elizabeth
Jan  6 1803 Hinkle, John to Runner, Eve
Jan 28 1804 Hinkle, John to Greenamyer, Barbara
Feb 10 1792 Hinkley, Fred'k to Hilton, Mary
Sep 23 1786 Hinton, John to McClain, Susan
Feb  3 1796 Hinton, Mary to Elliot, Thomas
Feb 20 1779 Hinton, Rachel to Ball, James
Nov 23 1779 Hinton, Rachel to Laton, Uriah
Mar 18 1779 Hinton, Richard to Cash, Ruth
Dec 16 1779 Hipps, Sarah to Emmory, Adam
Apr 17 1786 Hipsley, Charles to Poole, Sarah
Jan 17 1784 Hiseler, Catherine to Evitt, Woodward
Sep 29 1792 Hiseler, Elizabeth to Holler, Tobias
Sep 25 1784 Hiseler, Michael to Hoffman, Mary
May 28 1809 Hite, I. to Tilt, Margaret
May 28 1809 Hite, J. to Tilt, Margaret
Jun  9 1785 Hobbs, Ann to Burckitt, George Junr
Apr 29 1808 Hobbs, Anne to Hobbs, Brice
Oct 25 1800 Hobbs, Asenath to Ringland, John
Apr 29 1808 Hobbs, Brice to Hobbs, Anne
Jan 13 1783 Hobbs, Charles to Ogle, Elizabeth
Oct  4 1782 Hobbs, Elie to Hamilton, Elizabeth
Oct 21 1780 Hobbs, Eliz'th to Burkitt, Christopher
May 18 1804 Hobbs, Eliza to Maynard, Nathan
Dec 23 1796 Hobbs, Elizabeth to Campbell, John
Jun 23 1786 Hobbs, Elizabeth to Davis, Barnabas
Nov 16 1807 Hobbs, Elizabeth to Maynard, Brice
Nov 12 1808 Hobbs, Elizabeth C. to Crapster, Peter
Dec 29 1806 Hobbs, John to Harding, Amelia
Jan 22 1794 Hobbs, John, Junr. to Burgess, Onner
Jun 17 1793 Hobbs, Joseph to Bare, Susanna
Apr 17 1788 Hobbs, Joshua to Hobbs, Rachel
Apr 11 1803 Hobbs, Mary to Hobbs, Samuel
Feb 10 1792 Hobbs, Nancy to Browning, Sam'l
May 21 1793 Hobbs, Rachel to Dorsey, William
Apr 17 1788 Hobbs, Rachel to Hobbs, Joshua
Jan 19 1795 Hobbs, Rachel to Plummer, William
Apr 11 1803 Hobbs, Samuel to Hobbs, Mary
Feb 24 1784 Hobbs, Sarah to Dorsey, Greenbury
Jun 22 1790 Hobbs, Sarah to Lawrence, Samuel
Feb 13 1798 Hobbs, Thomas to Owings, Urith
May 30 1796 Hobbs, William C. to Schnertzell, Christina
Dec 13 1786 Hobbs, Wm. of Sam'l to Dorsey, Henrietta
Oct 30 1797 Hobbs, Zachariah to James, Susanna
Oct 29 1779 Hobston, Eliz'th to Cochron, Heugh
```

Jun 30 1805 Hockensmith, Catherine (License issued To same persons Jul 22 1805)
Jun  8 1799 Hockensmith, John to Sluss, Barbara
Nov 29 1800 Hockensmith, Martha to Buchanan, John
Jul 21 1782 Hockersmith, Mary to Whitmore, Benjamin
Mar 26 1803 Hockley, Catharine to Penn, Benjamin
Jul 20 1779 Hodge, Mary to Carey, James
May 12 1794 Hodgkiss, Michael to Dewees, Sarah
Mar 28 1794 Hodgkiss, Rachel to Metcalfe, Thomas
Oct  6 1790 Hodgkiss, Sarah to Roberts, William
Mar 26 1806 Hoff, Garrott to Gover, Elizabeth
Apr 24 1790 Hoff, Peter to Boyer, Mary
Nov 15 1799 Hoffert, Jacob to Baker, Catherine
Apr 10 1802 Hoffman, Barbara to Crum, Henry
Nov 15 1808 Hoffman, Catherine to Baer, John
Sep  9 1803 Hoffman, Catherine to Custard, Jonas
May 27 1809 Hoffman, Christena to McKinley, William
Jun  4 1796 Hoffman, David to Heck, Eve Margaret
Jan 17 1807 Hoffman, Elizabeth to Harrison, John
Dec 31 1802 Hoffman, Elizabeth to Sullivan, Jacob
Oct 24 1807 Hoffman, George to Bost, Rahamah
Oct 29 1808 Hoffman, George to Shirley, Mary
Oct  8 1791 Hoffman, George to Phillips, Eleanor
Apr 15 1784 Hoffman, Jacob to McClain, Mary
Jun 22 1801 Hoffman, John to Steiner, Elizabeth
Oct  2 1802 Hoffman, John to Barrick, Margaret
Oct 15 1806 Hoffman, John to Yandess, Barbara
Feb 15 1804 Hoffman, Margaret to Runner, Henry
Aug 10 1800 Hoffman, Mary to Boyd, Edward
Sep 25 1784 Hoffman, Mary to Hiseler, Michael
Mar  7 1808 Hoffman, Mary to Spealman, Jacob
Jun 14 1788 Hoffman, Philip to Gitzadanner, Elizabeth
Mar  2 1810 Hoffman, Polly to Duttero, John
Feb  5 1790 Hoffman, Susanna to Engler, Peter
Jul  5 1791 Hoffman, Valentine to Doll, Elizabeth
Nov 23 1794 Hoffner, Mich'l to Waughter, Catherine
Apr 21 1789 Hoffwider, Ann to Wilson, Thomas
Jan  5 1784 Hogg, Catherine to Morris, John
Nov  3 1787 Hoggins, John to Branson, Tamar
Jan 11 1791 Hoggins, Linney Ann to Plummer, William
Aug 19 1784 Hoggins, Richard to Knott, Elizabeth
Jan  5 1806 Hogue, Jesse to Grigg, Elizabeth
Apr 12 1810 Hogue, Samuel to Holmes, Elizabeth
Apr 18 1795 Hole, Catharine to Gadultig, George
Apr  9 1803 Hole, Elizabeth to Keefer, Henry
Nov 22 1798 Hole, John to Knott, Dorcus
Dec 28 1797 Hole, Mary to Lombright, Philip
Jan 29 1780 Hollan, Catharine to Hollan, William
Jan 14 1807 Hollan, Sarah to Nusz, Henry
Jan 29 1780 Hollan, William to Hollan, Catharine
Jul 24 1804 Holland, Ann to Hungerford, William B.
Oct 17 1801 Holland, Daniel to Powles, Catherine
Mar 14 1795 Holland, Deborah to Bennit, Nathan
Mar  3 1792 Holland, James to Welsh, Sarah
Nov 27 1802 Holland, John to Hughes, Elizabeth
Sep 12 1778 Holland, Jonathan to Ridgley, Drusilla

```
Mar 10 1789 Holland, Jonathan to Ridgley, Urith
Aug 21 1801 Holland, Mary to Divers, John
Feb 25 1782 Holland, Otho to Ridgley, Jane
Jul 27 1807 Holland, Rezin to Rhodes, Mary
Jan  7 1792 Holland, Samuel to Phillips, Nackey
Mar 12 1803 Holland, Sarah to Tibbets, Jerry
Dec 23 1808 Holland, William to Frances, Catherine
Feb 12 1781 Holland, Wm. to Weyman, Ann
Dec 25 1798 Holland, Zadock to Mockabee, Priscilla
Apr 22 1786 Hollar, Catharine to Peter, John
Apr 14 1803 Hollar, Charles to Brunner, Catherine
Feb 19 1787 Hollar, Mich'l to Dorff, Catharine
Aug 26 1798 Hollar, Michael of Godfrey to Rabourn, Catherine
Mar 21 1799 Hollenberger, Ann to Shriner, George
May  1 1797 Hollenberger, Catharine to Shingletaker, Jacob
May  6 1783 Holler, Christopher to Lutz, Barbara
Sep 29 1792 Holler, Tobias to Hiseler, Elizabeth
Jan 21 1793 Holman, Adam to Matthews, Elizabeth
Apr 12 1810 Holmes, Elizabeth to Hogue, Samuel
Dec 22 1802 Holmes, Elizabeth to Hughes, Samuel
Apr 29 1808 Holmes, Nancy to Logsdon, John
Sep 14 1810 Holprun, Catherine to Shunk, Christian
Aug  3 1798 Holt, Anne to Kist, Philip
Sep 15 1810 Holter, Daniel to Williams, Mary
Nov  4 1803 Holter, John to Ebright, Mary Ann
Jan 21 1800 Holtz, Margaret to Luten, Abraham
Nov 11 1809 Holtz, Michael to Straleman, Margaret
Jun 17 1785 Holtz, Nicholas to Simmerman, Susannah
Apr  6 1778 Holtz, Susanna to Boseman, Richard
Dec 27 1800 Holtzapple, Abraham to Knouff, Elizabeth
Oct  7 1808 Holtzapple, Daniel to Carn, Elizabeth
Jun 16 1794 Holtzapple, Soloma to Fry, Enoch
Jun  7 1808 Holtzman, Charlotte to Fisher, Valentine
Sep 24 1808 Holtzman, Christian to Weymer, Elizabeth
Jul 14 1805 Holtzman, Christianna to French, Peter
Mar 17 1795 Holtzman, Conrad to Derr, Eve
Mar 22 1781 Holtzman, Henry to Smith, Mary
May  6 1786 Holtzman, Jacob to Shell, Molly
Jul 10 1793 Holtzman, John to Alexander, Ann
Mar  9 1809 Holtzman, Magdalena to Bussard, Jacob
Nov  5 1805 Holtzman, Martin to Slates, Christena
Dec  8 1788 Holtzman, Mary to Towbridge, John
Dec 22 1795 Holtzman, Susanna to Scaggs, Richard
Nov 23 1804 Holverstot, David to Worman, Modalena
Nov 21 1806 Hommer, Lucia to Stull, John
Oct  1 1792 Honeling, Barbara to Williard, Peter
Jan 13 1802 Hood, Affa to Kelly, John
Jan 28 1809 Hood, John to Wolf, Tabitha
Jan 25 1808 Hood, Rachel to Wolfe, Henry H.
Apr 18 1801 Hoof, Henry to Smith, Mary
Feb 19 1787 Hook, Dan'l to Burgess, Sarah
Dec 11 1794 Hook, Isaac to White, Martha
Oct  1 1803 Hook, James (of Snowden) to Lynch, Kezia
Aug 12 1778 Hook, John Snowden to Ward, Elizabeth
Feb  4 1782 Hook, Purnell to Rice, Benjamin
```

```
Nov 14 1784 Hook, Stephen to Thrasher, Sarah
Apr 23 1803 Hooper, Eleanor to Lewis, William
Jan 15 1800 Hooper, John to Jenkins, Mary
Feb 17 1801 Hooper, Mary to Trago, Aquila
May  5 1807 Hoot, Samuel to Griffith, Elizabeth
May  3 1794 Hoover, Adam to Wever, Catherine
Aug  3 1802 Hoover, Ann to Dunham, James C.
Feb 15 1793 Hoover, Catharine to Barrick, Christian
Jun 29 1807 Hoover, Catherine to Weller, George
Apr 28 1800 Hoover, Elizabeth to Nunemaker, George
May 31 1810 Hoover, Jacob to Ridge, Betsey
Feb 17 1800 Hoover, John to Allison, Sarah
Sep 18 1802 Hoover, John to Riddle, Anne
Apr 15 1797 Hoover, Margaret to Cramer, John
Oct  2 1802 Hoover, Margaret to Cramer, William
Oct 10 1800 Hoover, Philip to Burkhart, Susanna
Sep 11 1804 Hope, Rachel to McGinniss, Robert
Feb  5 1795 Hopkins, Benj. to Briscoe, Nancy
Aug 15 1798 Hopkins, Elizabeth to McDaniel, Francis
Jun 15 1779 Hopkins, Elizabeth to Wallace, William
Mar 20 1809 Hopkins, Philip to Baldwin, Verlinda
Aug  9 1803 Hopper, Benjamin to Turner, Elizabeth
Aug 29 1791 Hoppermill, John to Warble, Margaret
Jul 19 1808 Hopwood, Elizabeth to Woodman, Thomas
Nov 22 1806 Horine, Catharine to Castle, George V.
Apr 12 1784 Horine, Judey to Furney, Henry
Oct 11 1802 Horine, Mary to Main, George
Oct 26 1785 Horine, Mary to Martz, Peter
Sep 18 1778 Horine, Susanna to Shrader, Henry
Nov 24 1809 Hornar, Alexander to Marshall, Sarah
Sep 29 1780 Hornblower, Wm. to Aves, Ann
Mar 11 1784 Horner, Nancy to Hall, Joseph
Apr  3 1798 Hort, Elizabeth to Morrison, John
Nov 27 1796 Hoskinson, Ann to Young, William
Jan  6 1795 Hoskinson, Thomas to Bird, Mary
Feb 15 1780 Hospelhaun, Margaret to Isenberger, Jacob
Apr  7 1780 Hosplehawn, Mary to Crowl, Mich'l
Aug 30 1780 Hosselton, Edward to Welton, Magdalene
Jan  8 1800 Hostler, John to Isenberg, Catherine
May 21 1796 Houck, Barbara to Zealer, George
Apr 23 1803 Houck, Catherine to Shriver, Henry
Sep 10 1801 Houck, George to Getzendanner, Catherine
Dec 23 1805 Houck, Jacob to Lowe, Catherine
Feb  1 1806 Houck, Jacob to Getzendanner, Margaret
Jun  1 1801 Houck, John, Junr. to Shoup, Mary
Apr 25 1795 Houck, Margaret to Kittinger, John
May  1 1797 Houck, Matthias to Engle, Magdalen
Mar 29 1782 Houcks, Jacob to Shultz, Catherine
Sep 20 1781 Houcks, Mathias to Morningstar, Susanna
Sep  4 1798 Hough, Rachel to James, Levi
Jan 16 1810 Houghf, John to Shepperd, Mary
Mar 11 1797 Houk, John to Sin, Elizabeth
Jun  6 1802 Houkman, Philip to Sinn, Sally
Aug 11 1783 House, Caleb to Pearpoint, Sarah
Feb  4 1782 House, Dan'l to Long, Elizabeth
```

```
Jul 25 1806 House, Daniel to Wedding, Tabitha
Jan 29 1806 House, Eleanor to Ellison, Thomas
Nov 23 1801 House, George to Segerfuse, Elizabeth
Nov 12 1804 House, John to Duffy, Henrietta
Oct 19 1808 House, Nancy to Deaver, Levi
Oct 17 1803 House, Stephen to Grove, Mary
Dec 26 1793 House, William to Harmon, Modelena
Oct  3 1805 House, William to Lemar, Susanna
Jan  3 1801 Houseman, Catherine to Bailey, Ricahrd
Apr 15 1806 Houser, Catherine to Thomas, William
Oct 13 1787 Houser, Jacob to Bander, Cath.
Oct 10 1791 Houser, Mary to Mayberry, Jesse
Oct  1 1785 Houx, Margaret to Englebrecht, John
Oct  1 1785 Houx, Margaret to Inglebrecht, John Conrad
Feb 22 1808 Hovey, George Jacob to Fauble, Catherine
Aug  6 1779 How, Ann to Davis, Joseph
Jul 16 1810 How, James to Ragan, Patty
Apr 26 1792 Howard, Cornelius to Campbell, Mary
Aug  1 1789 Howard, Ann to Hart, Ellis
Apr 23 1778 Howard, Catherine to Mantz, Peter, Majr.
Dec 13 1787 Howard, Darcus to Howard, Joseph
Oct  8 1807 Howard, Deborah to Dorsey, John W.
Dec 13 1788 Howard, Eleanor to Maynard, Henry
Feb  4 1796 Howard, Eleanor to Simmons, John H.
Mar 19 1794 Howard, Elisha to McAtee, Chloe
Oct 11 1785 Howard, Elizabeth to Hinamon, Geo.
Nov 17 1782 Howard, George to Fisher, Elizbeth
Dec 27 1808 Howard, Greenbury to Brown, Sarah
Jul 23 1785 Howard, Henry to Purdey, Ann
Oct 19 1779 Howard, Jac. to Veatch, Casiah
Nov 16 1778 Howard, John to Crale, Mary
Jan 25 1783 Howard, Joseph to Killkup, Sarah
Dec 13 1787 Howard, Joseph to Howard, Darcus
Aug 24 1792 Howard, Joshua to Warfield, Elizabeth
Oct 21 1800 Howard, Margaret Young to Berry, Richard
Oct 25 1796 Howard, Maria to Thomas, Samuel, Jr.
Nov 22 1809 Howard, Mary to Clemson, James
Dec 16 1780 Howard, Mary to Jefferson, Henry
Mar 21 1788 Howard, Priscilla to Judey, Jacob
Jul  8 1789 Howard, Rachel to Duvall, Marsen
Dec 27 1799 Howard, Rachel to Robertson, Samuel
Feb 17 1806 Howard, Rebecca to Ayres, Daniel
Jun 10 1797 Howard, Sam'l to Lyles, Elizabeth
Nov 22 1803 Howard, Samuel to Dorsey, Susan
Apr 16 1783 Howard, Sarah to Hill, Thomas
Jan 19 1792 Howard, Sarah to McElfresh, Joseph
Dec  2 1793 Howard, Sarah to Reed, Thomas
Feb 17 1792 Howard, Sarah to Winchester, Stephen, Esq.
Jan 29 1796 Howard, Susanna to Hays, John
Apr 23 1791 Howard, Thomas to Hughes, Ann
Apr  2 1782 Howe, John to Rop, Lowery
Jun 13 1778 Howe, William Rob't to Strider, Ann
Jan 30 1806 Howell, Henry to Head, Jane
Apr 12 1786 Howell, Sarah to Harding, Zephaniah
Nov 26 1798 Hows, Henny to Lloyd, Samuel
```

```
Mar 29 1806 Hoxie, Prudence to Shoe, John
Jun  1 1798 Hoy, Nicholas to Umstead, Rachel
Sep 29 1798 Hoy, Susannah to Wood, Bennet
Apr 18 1795 Hubbard, Susanna to Fauble, Jacob
Jun 24 1803 Huber, Jacob to Hartman, Barbara
Sep  1 1802 Huckel, Anna to Lavey, John
Oct 10 1804 Huckle, Sarah to Magraw, Henry
Apr 24 1778 Huff, Barbara to Kemp, John
Apr  1 1779 Huff, Elizabeth to Yesterday, Christian
Oct  5 1809 Huff, Liddy to Taylor, Joseph
Nov 17 1783 Huff, Martha to Roach, Edward
Apr 20 1798 Huff, Mary to Fowler, John
Aug 26 1786 Huff, Mary to Lyne, John
Oct 26 1809 Huffard, Catharine to McDanald, James
Dec 20 1806 Huffard, Susanna to Matthias, Griffith
Nov 23 1789 Hufferd, Catherine to Fout, Michael
Oct 28 1806 Huffert, Daniel to Zies, Barbara
Jul  1 1780 Huffman, Elizabeth to Piper, Philip
Aug 23 1779 Hufford, Dan'l to Cassell, Eliz'th
Jun 12 1795 Hufford, Nancy to Buzzard, Jno.
Mar  9 1797 Hughes, Agnes to Jordan, Alexander
Apr 23 1791 Hughes, Ann to Howard, Thomas
Dec  6 1810 Hughes, Charlotte to Beatty, John Michael
Dec 18 1802 Hughes, Darkey to Cookerly, William
Nov 27 1802 Hughes, Elizabeth to Holland, John
May 31 1796 Hughes, Francis to Dyer, Mary
Nov  6 1792 Hughes, Hannah to Flout, Christopher
Feb 22 1805 Hughes, Harriett to Taney, Joseph
Apr  2 1810 Hughes, Hugh to Winpigler, Elizabeth
Jan 11 1806 Hughes, James to Cretin, Lucy
Apr 28 1792 Hughes, Joseph to Buchanan, Mary
May  7 1792 Hughes, Kitty to Elder, James
Jun  8 1797 Hughes, Margaret to Berryer, Abraham
Oct 14 1802 Hughes, Marzella to Hemmingsworth, Jeremiah
Jan 13 1783 Hughes, Rachel to Peterson, William
Oct 14 1807 Hughes, Rhoda to O'Boyle, James
Dec 22 1802 Hughes, Samuel to Holmes, Elizabeth
May 15 1800 Hughes, Winnefred to Lilly, Ignatius
Apr 13 1805 Hull, James to Metz, Maria Elizabeth
Aug 29 1803 Hull, John to Woolf, Mary
Jan 20 1803 Huller, Susanna to Luday, John
Aug  4 1779 Hulse, Samuel to Knight, Margaret
Oct 16 1791 Hultz, Christena Margareta to Boogher, Frederick
Sep  7 1803 Humbert, Michael to Bussard, Mary
Apr 23 1778 Humbert, Peter to Bunn, Rebecca
Apr 19 1805 Humer, Eleanor to Koch, Henry
Mar 19 1796 Hummel, Catherine to Markey, David
Oct 15 1782 Hummel, Chrisstena to Fiege, Philip
Dec 23 1801 Hummel, Mary to Firestone, Jacob
Mar 12 1803 Hummer, Elizabeth to Kerr, Robert
Oct 16 1810 Hummer, Henry to Renner, Sally
Aug 15 1807 Hummer, John to Hersh, Catherine
Dec 14 1796 Humphrey, Mary to Osborne, Richard
Feb 15 1785 Hungerford, Elizabeth to Davis, William Luckett
Jul 24 1804 Hungerford, William B. to Holland, Ann
Jul  5 1808 Hunt, Job to Boyd, Mary Anne
```

```
Feb 17 1785 Hunter, Susanna to Griffin, Zadock
Dec  9 1796 Hunter, Thomas to Quynn, Ann
Mar 13 1799 Hurd, William to Waltz, Pheby
Oct 13 1808 Hurdle, Susanna to Goodly, Joseph
Oct 20 1794 Hurst, John to Brown, Elizabeth
Dec 25 1794 Hurst, William to Minor, Ann
May 20 1807 Huston, Elizabeth to Reid, James
Apr  3 1781 Hutchcraft, Margaret to Frinton, Thos.
Apr  3 1781 Hutchcraft, Margaret to Trinton, Thomas
Apr 20 1780 Hutchinson, Archibald to Bruher, Marbara
Oct 31 1782 Hutchinson, Sarah to Vanhorn, Dennis
Jul  4 1795 Hutchison, Allear to Craber, Bostian
Feb 28 1808 Hutton, Enos to Plummer, Rebeccah
Feb 24 1806 Hutzee, John to Shoemaker, Elizabeth
Jan  9 1808 Hutzell, Jacob to Kugle, Catherine
Dec 10 1791 Hutzell, Michael to Miller, Susanna
Feb 24 1810 Hutzell, Polly to Shoemaker, Daniel
Nov 11 1794 Hyatt, Elizabeth to Davis, Zachariah
Jul 16 1801 Hyatt, Elizabeth to Hall, John
Jan 14 1792 Hyatt, Jesse to Riggs, Nancy
Jan 18 1787 Hyatt, Leviney to Richards, William
Sep  9 1785 Hyatt, Linney to Campbell, James
Apr 13 1782 Hyatt, Sarah to Woolfe, John
Oct 29 1792 Hyatt, Sophia to Todd, Joshua
Jun 17 1780 Hyatt, Susanna to Hagan, Henry
Oct 24 1807 Hyatt, Susanna to Philips, John
Dec 21 1786 Hyfield, Eleanor to Hill, Robert
Apr  5 1791 Hyfield, Sarah to Belt, John
Jul 25 1809 Hyme, Andrew, Jr. to Brunner, Mary
Aug 25 1794 Hyme, Catherine to Mansparager, Daniel
Oct 21 1800 Hyme, David to Stockman, Ann
Dec 24 1799 Hyme, Elizabeth to Ridgely, Westall
Aug 28 1798 Hyme, Mary to Ridgely, Richard
Feb 28 1805 Hymes, George to Manspicker, Margaret
May 28 1810 Hymes, George to Winpigler, Sophia
Feb  7 1782 Hynes, Philip to Myers, Mary
Nov 19 1810 Hytchew, Mary to Metcalfe, Thomas

Jan 17 1783 Icoff, Adolph to Thomas, Mary
Apr 27 1805 Icoff, Charlotte to Routzang, Daniel
Mar  8 1810 Iden, Hannah to Craven, Mahlon
Nov 26 1808 Ifert, Jacob to Wissinger, Mary
Jun  4 1785 Ifert, Jeremiah to Baighle, Susannah
Mar 10 1804 Iiams, Plummer to Iiams, Rebecca
Mar 10 1804 Iiams, Rebecca to Iiams, Plummer
May 14 1805 Ijams, Jane to Burgee, Singleton
Mar 21 1782 Ijams, John to Waters, Mary
Jul 13 1807 Ijams, John to Gassaway, Providence
Jan 12 1805 Ijams, Rebecca to Duvall, Benjamin
Dec 17 1799 Ijams, Ruth to Mussetter, Christopher
Feb 10 1794 Ijams, Thomas Plummer to Duvall, Sarah
Nov 29 1808 Iler, Adam to Myers, Mary
Nov 29 1808 Iler, Anna to Wilyard, Elias
Jun  4 1802 Iler, Eve to Creager, John
Jun 23 1802 Iler, Jacob to Lukebaugh, Margaret
```

```
Feb 24 1808 Iler, Jacob to Boon, Catherine
Sep 26 1803 Iler, Margaret to Eigenbrode, Christian
Jun  9 1802 Iler, Mary to Caufman, George
Apr 24 1798 Impson, Dorothy to Haine, Charles
Mar 18 1779 Inch (or Juch), Eliz'th to Boyrley, George
Oct  1 1785 Inglebrecht, John Conrad to Houx, Margaret
Apr 14 1786 Ingles, Susanna to Mortar, Valentine
Aug 19 1805 Ingman, Ambrose to Pierce, Martha
Jan 13 1803 Ingman, Delila to Snider, Michael
Apr 21 1803 Ingman, Joshua to Ratliff, Amelia
Jul  2 1801 Ingman, Rachel to Hall, Benjamin
Jan 28 1805 Ingman, Sarah to Crawford, Aaron
Dec 25 1790 Ingram, Henrietta to Rodes, Jonathan
Aug 21 1791 Inman, Deborah to Brown, Samuel
Mar 14 1794 Innes, Sarah to Craps, John
Jan 11 1785 Ips, Sarah to Nicholls, James
Feb  7 1795 Ireland, Elizabeth to Geyer, Henry
Jun 23 1783 Ireland, Jonathan to Rice, Elizabeth
Apr 10 1810 Irons, Joseph to Lane, Mary
Oct  2 1797 Irons, Susanna to Norris, Thomas
Jan 16 1795 Isaac, Elizabth to Pepper, Henry
May 27 1783 Isaminger, Elizabeth to Everly, John
Dec  2 1779 Iseminger, Catherine to Yontsey, John
Sep 27 1783 Iseminger, Christena to Smith, Jacob
Jul 25 1783 Iseminger, Mary to Keefour, Jacob
Mar  8 1780 Iseminger, Susanna to Cooperider, Elias
Jan  8 1800 Isenberg, Catherine to Hostler, John
Mar 10 1804 Isenberg, Gabriel to Ogle, Lydia
Feb 12 1802 Isenberg, Polly to Lucas, Jesse
Sep 15 1783 Isenberger, Catherine to Trubey, Jacob
Nov 18 1788 Isenberger, Henry to Medtert, Catherine
Feb 15 1780 Isenberger, Jacob to Hospelhaun, Margaret
Sep 12 1796 Isenberger, Peter to Smouse, Marg't
Dec 12 1780 Isenbergh, Nicholas to Smouse, Mary
Oct  9 1778 Isenbergh, Susanna to Sollman, Adam
Oct 29 1808 Isentrager, Rachel to Monticu, Samuel
Nov  7 1795 Isentrey, George to Goodman, Ann
Oct 26 1779 Iser, Philip to Albaugh, Anna
Jun 26 1780 Israel, Basil to Mansfield, Eleanor
May  8 1788 Israel, John to Clary, Rachel
Sep 10 1800 Israel, Leer to Mackley, Richard
Sep 10 1800 Israel, Leer to Mackley, Richard

Mar 28 1810 Jackson, Bethsheba to Terry, Michael
Feb  9 1805 Jackson, Henry to Powell, Nancy
Aug  4 1803 Jackson, Jacob to Everhart, Elizabeth
Mar 11 1810 Jackson, James to Palmer, Rachel
Nov 28 1810 Jackson, John to Brown, Mary
Apr 14 1800 Jackson, Mary to Jones, Jacob
May  1 1804 Jackson, Mary to Laflaver, Jacob
Jul  7 1783 Jacob, Eleanor to Griffith, Philamond
Oct 22 1798 Jacob, Elizabeth to Kessler, George
Dec 28 1799 Jacob, Mary to Eckman, Michael
Mar  2 1779 Jacobie, John to Weane, Catherine
Feb  7 1801 Jacobs, Ann to Steward, Thomas
May  7 1802 Jacobs, Barbara to Leese, Henry
```

```
Nov  3 1787 Jacobs, Benja. to Gilbert, Elizabeth
May  5 1807 Jacobs, Catherine to Lynn, Jacob
Mar 27 1807 Jacobs, Catherine to Simmons, Peter
Sep 23 1802 Jacobs, Dorsey to Fulton, Elizabeth
Aug 20 1795 Jacobs, Elizabeth to Compton, John
Mar  9 1799 Jacobs, Eve to Linn, Isaac
Feb 23 1791 Jacobs, George to Perrill, Ann
Apr 21 1790 Jacobs, Henry to Williard, Catharine
Feb  6 1805 Jacobs, Joel to Keefer, Elizabeth
Feb 22 1782 Jacobs, Joseph to Griffin, Elizabeth
Jun 14 1782 Jacobs, Mary to Delashmutt, Basil
Oct 23 1809 Jacobs, Michael to Kelley, Anna Statia
Apr  6 1801 Jacobs, Presley to Chew, Elizabeth
Feb  8 1794 Jacobs, Rebeckah to Keadle, Gibson
Oct 19 1789 Jacobs, Richard to Hilleary, Eleanor
Nov 16 1778 Jacobs, Wm. to Stokes, Dorcas
Apr 28 1781 Jacobs, Wm. to Thomas, Sarah
Jun  2 1780 Jacques, Denton to Powell, Eliz'th
Dec 11 1795 James, Achsa to Poole, Brice
Feb 26 1787 James, Ann to Nicholls, James
Nov  1 1803 James, Daniel to Clemson, Peggy
Sep 20 1804 James, David to Bradfield, Charlotte
Oct 31 1807 James, Eli to Keptler, Elizabeth
Jan 18 1805 James, Esther to Thomas, William
Mar  7 1804 James, Fanny to Warfield, John
Apr 10 1786 James, John to Haff, Martha
Sep  4 1798 James, Levi to Hough, Rachel
Feb 27 1790 James, Margaret to Poole, Henry
Sep 12 1803 James, Polly to Maddox, John
Nov 26 1782 James, Priscilla to Barr, Hugh
Jul  8 1794 James, Rachel to Bradley, Patrick
Nov 24 1780 James, Rebecca to Bennett, Benjamin
Oct 30 1797 James, Susanna to Hobbs, Zachariah
May  2 1790 Jameson, Teresa to Smith, Joseph
Mar 28 1796 Jamison, Ignatius to Luckett, Lucy
Mar  6 1807 Jamison, Ignatius to Fenwick, Catherine
Jun  8 1803 Jamison, John to Harris, Sarah
Nov 18 1790 Jamison, Leonard to Smith, Mary
Nov  3 1807 Jamison, Samuel to Belt, Priscilla
Dec 27 1797 Janes, Elizabeth to Tinnely, Charles Brooke
Dec 20 1792 Janes, Thomas to Waters, Mary
Jul 27 1798 Jarbes, Bennet to Frazier, Elizabeth
Oct  6 1806 Jarboe, Ann to Phillpot, John
Nov  2 1807 Jarboe, Francis to McVicker, Sarah
Jan 17 1807 Jarboe, George to Belwood, Elizabeth
Jan 30 1808 Jarboe, Henrietta to Philpott, Samuel
Dec  5 1795 Jarret, Ann to Harding, Lewis
Apr  9 1800 Jarrett, John to Yores, Susannah
May 27 1783 Jarvis, Sarah to Barnes, James
Feb 18 1802 Jay, William to King, Anne
Aug 16 1796 Jeffers, Joseph to Robertson, Elizabeth
Jan  6 1783 Jefferson, Benjamin to Jefferson, Prescilla
Mar  2 1803 Jefferson, Deborah to Michael, John
Apr  5 1802 Jefferson, Elizabeth to Hill, Christian
Dec 16 1780 Jefferson, Henry to Howard, Mary
```

```
Mar  2 1807 Jefferson, Henry to Fitzgerald, Elizabeth
Dec  3 1806 Jefferson, Leonard to Nichols, Barbara
Jan  6 1783 Jefferson, Prescilla to Jefferson, Benjamin
Dec 22 1801 Jefferson, Rebecca to Fitzgerald, Edward
Dec 25 1790 Jemeson, Francis to Thompson, Ann
Mar  9 1780 Jemison, Charles to Molley, Mary
Feb 24 1779 Jemison, Mary Ann to Johnson, Charles
Nov  1 1799 Jenings, Rebecca to Coulter, Alexander
Jul 19 1786 Jenings, Richard to Brawner, Lucy
Jan  7 1799 Jenkins, Daniel to Hill, Ruth
Jul 18 1789 Jenkins, Eleanor to Clements, Wm. H.
Dec 29 1800 Jenkins, Eleanor to Locker, William
Jan  5 1808 Jenkins, Felix to Friar, Elizabeth
Nov 14 1809 Jenkins, Henry to Offett, Margaret
Aug 19 1778 Jenkins, Job to Tucker, Sarah Ann
Jan 19 1802 Jenkins, Job to Leakins, Mary
Jul 26 1794 Jenkins, John to Crampton, Eleanor
Jan 15 1800 Jenkins, Mary to Hooper, John
Dec 19 1785 Jenkins, Mary Ann to Ritchie, Abner
Mar 23 1799 Jenkins, Milley to Wattson, Zepheniah
Sep  4 1798 Jenkins, Sarah to Gisberd, Abraham
Aug 31 1801 Jenkins, William to Riggs, Elizabeth
Mar 26 1806 Jenkins, Wm. to Gore, Elizabeth
Jan 28 1809 Jennings, John to Boyd, Ruth
Dec  9 1805 Jenny, Mary to Purcell, John
May 27 1793 Jimeson, Samuel to Overtosh, Mary Elizabeth
Nov 17 1800 Johnson, Abigail to Johnson, Thomas
Dec 27 1791 Johnson, Ann to Nesmith, Isaac
Jan 26 1801 Johnson, Ann to Shryock, John
Jan 12 1788 Johnson, Ann Jennings to Grahame, John Colin
Sep  3 1778 Johnson, Basil to Tracey, Sarah
Oct 12 1779 Johnson, Benja. (Free Negro) to Todd, Lucy (Free
            Negro)
Dec 29 1798 Johnson, Benjamin to Hammond, Mary
Apr 29 1799 Johnson, Casper to Gulick, Martha
Mar  4 1806 Johnson, Catherine W. to Ross, William
Feb 24 1779 Johnson, Charles to Jemison, Mary Ann
Aug 30 1783 Johnson, Dorcas to Clapham, Josias Colo.
Jan 11 1799 Johnson, Drusilla to Fister, Henry
Feb  3 1802 Johnson, Eleanor to Johnson, Richard
Sep 26 1797 Johnson, Elizabeth to Clapham, Sam'l
Nov 28 1783 Johnson, Elizabeth to Wright, George
May  7 1787 Johnson, Elizabeth to Foutch, Heughey
Jul 19 1808 Johnson, Elizabeth to Miller, Jacob
Dec  4 1809 Johnson, Francis to Myers, Elizabeth
Oct 27 1786 Johnson, John to West, Susanna
May 28 1778 Johnson, Joseph to Miller, Catharine
Oct 23 1781 Johnson, Joseph to Yost, Barbara
May 11 1807 Johnson, Joseph to Yost, Eve
Mar 10 1810 Johnson, Joseph to Levy, Rebecca
May 27 1786 Johnson, Keziah to Williams, William
May 15 1801 Johnson, Margaret to Hessong, John
Dec  4 1788 Johnson, Mary to Taylor, Richard
Sep 11 1810 Johnson, Mary Eizabeth to Brown, Clement
Sep  6 1796 Johnson, Molly to Olliser, George
Mar 13 1794 Johnson, Noah to Spencer, Rachel
```

```
Feb 11 1802 Johnson, Rebecca to Johnson, Thomas
Mar 25 1799 Johnson, Rebecca to Lemaster, Richard
Jul 30 1782 Johnson, Rebecca to Robee, Patrick Moreland
Feb  3 1802 Johnson, Richard to Johnson, Eleanor
Oct 30 1790 Johnson, Robert to Sprigg, Ann
Feb  1 1781 Johnson, Roger to Thomas, Elizabeth
Apr 11 1788 Johnson, Sarah to Bennett, Daniel
Oct  8 1800 Johnson, Sarah to McKinzie, Henry
Dec 17 1810 Johnson, Sarah to Dorsey, Eli, Junr.
Jan  4 1794 Johnson, Susanna to Ogle, William
Nov 17 1800 Johnson, Thomas to Johnson, Abigail
Feb 11 1802 Johnson, Thomas to Johnson, Rebecca
Aug  1 1806 Johnson, Thomas to Nichols, Elizabeth
Dec 12 1806 Johnson, Thomas to Plummer, Cull
Apr 18 1805 Johnson, Washington to Poston, Elizabeth
Nov 30 1799 Johnson, William to Thomas, Casandra
Dec  9 1799 Johnson, William to Cost, Catherine
May 24 1800 Johnson, William to Miller, Magdalen
May 11 1805 Jones, Allen to Plummer, Rachael
Mar 18 1782 Jones, Catherine to Shontz, Michael
Jul 30 1796 Jones, Catherine to Goodman, Jacob
Apr  4 1787 Jones, Elizabeth to Lyles, Richard
Dec 22 1800 Jones, Elizabeth to Tabler, William
Dec 26 1805 Jones, Esther to Gibbony, John
Mar 18 1791 Jones, Francis to Coventry, Rachel
Apr 13 1787 Jones, Hanbury to Viers, Sarah
May 23 1794 Jones, Hanbury to Poole, Elizabeth
Apr 14 1800 Jones, Jacob to Jackson, Mary
Feb 21 1809 Jones, John to Harris, Elizabeth
Feb 24 1794 Jones, Joseph to Cash, Henrietta
Dec  7 1796 Jones, Joshua to Warfield, Ann
Nov 27 1779 Jones, Margaret to Plummer, William
Jul 19 1803 Jones, Mary to Tidy, James
Jan 28 1796 Jones, Mary Davidge to Kirk, Richard
Aug 21 1790 Jones, Nancy to Clay, John
Dec  9 1802 Jones, Patty to Kellison, Reynolds
Jun 11 1803 Jones, Priscilla to Brashear, Theodore
Aug 21 1809 Jones, Rachel to Gist, George
Apr  1 1786 Jones, Richard to Brewer, Sarah
Nov 10 1786 Jones, Richard to Allen, Elizabeth
Mar 13 1805 Jones, Samuel to Brady, Susanna
Jul 28 1803 Jones, Sarah White to Kendal, William
Dec 18 1809 Jones, Susanna to Anderson, Francis
Feb 15 1800 Jones, Susannah to Vernal, John
Feb 18 1807 Jones, Thomas to Martin, Charlotte
Mar 18 1802 Jones, Thomas B. to Lawrence, Nancy
Mar  9 1797 Jordan, Alexander to Hughes, Agnes
Oct  9 1784 Jordan, David to Bruner, Margaret
Aug  9 1805 Jordan, Linday to McElfresh, George
Jan 15 1791 Joss, George to Zimmerman, Catharine
Sep 16 1797 Josse, Anthony to Greenwood, Mary
Jan 19 1808 Journey, Sabrit to Hall, Elizabeth
Sep 25 1809 Joy, Benedict to Farthing, Elizabeth
Jun 10 1798 Joy, John to Smith, Elizabeth
Dec  7 1796 Joy, Stephen to Shively, Mary
```

Mar 18 1779 Juch (or Inch), Eliz'th to Boyrley, George
Mar 21 1788 Judey, Jacob to Howard, Priscilla
Oct  1 1808 Judy, Jacob to Colclasier, Elizabeth
Aug  9 1779 Juit, Jacob to Boyrley, Eliz'th
Dec  7 1799 Julien, Rene to Hedges, Anna
Oct  4 1806 Julien, Richard B. to Heffner, Margaret
Apr  2 1793 Juluck, Juliet to Sissell, Philip
Jul 19 1778 Jumper, Cary to Cline, Henry
Oct 10 1783 Jumper, Christian to Orem, Elizabeth
Sep 23 1786 Justice, Catharine to Beckwith, David
Jun 10 1790 Justice, Ezekiel to Hall, Ann
Jan 17 1787 Justice, Nicholas to Dotson, Elizabeth
Feb 27 1792 Justice, Rebeckah to Coleman, Joseph

Mar 14 1796 Kadle, Gibson to Lemaster, Martha
Jan 26 1809 Kahler, Jacob to Madeira, Rachel
May  9 1809 Kalb, Absalom to Larkin, Susanna
Feb  1 1805 Kale, George to Rusher, Susanna
Nov 29 1796 Kale, Mary to Minor, John
Jan  1 1810 Kar, Rachel to Renner, Adam
Feb 21 1799 Karn, Jacob to Thomas, Mary
Jun  7 1802 Karnant, Adam to Keefauver, Susanna
Mar 13 1798 Karr, Martha to Devilbiss, George
Feb  2 1798 Karr, Walter to Harrison, Mary
Dec  3 1795 Katultigh, Henry to Boden, Mary
May 25 1805 Kaufman, David to Frey, Elizabeth
Mar  8 1800 Kaufman, Mary to Wissinger, George
May 21 1791 Kavanagh, William to Toofoot, Mary
Jul 12 1797 Kaywood, Isac to Talbott, Ann
Feb  8 1794 Keadle, Gibson to Jacobs, Rebeckah
Aug 17 1805 Keans, Michael to Shroyer, Elizabeth
Apr 15 1784 Keefauver, Nicholas to Peckepaugh, Margaret
Jun  7 1802 Keefauver, Susanna to Karnant, Adam
Aug 27 1804 Keefaver, George to Castle, Mary
Dec 18 1786 Keefaver, Peter to Yost, Catherine
Aug 28 1804 Keefer, Catherine to Lambeth, John
Oct 30 1810 Keefer, Christian, Junr. to Rice, Eleanor
Jan 18 1805 Keefer, Elizabeth to Hann, Philip
Feb  6 1805 Keefer, Elizabeth to Jacobs, Joel
Nov 18 1803 Keefer, George to Greenwald, Margaret
Aug 20 1795 Keefer, Henry to Reed, Rachel
Apr  9 1803 Keefer, Henry to Hole, Elizabeth
Mar  5 1808 Keefer, Henry to Getzendanner, Elizabeth
Oct  6 1804 Keefer, Jacob to Halverstadt, Catherine
Jun 10 1809 Keefer, Jacob to Hann, Elizabeth
Dec 15 1795 Keefer, Mary to Smith, John of John
Dec 19 1804 Keefer, Samuel to Shaneholtz, Margaret
Nov 15 1809 Keefer, Susanna to Sheely, Frederick
Dec  8 1781 Keefhaver, Magdalena to Hagar, George
Jul 25 1783 Keefour, Jacob to Iseminger, Mary
Sep 20 1785 Keener, Andrew to Amelung, Fredericka
May 22 1795 Keener, Frederica to Sommerkemp, Philip
Oct  7 1790 Keener, John to Condon, Mary
Nov 20 1798 Keepers, Eleanor to Knouff, Andrew
Apr 25 1806 Keepers, James to Elder, Mary

```
Feb 11 1804 Keepers, Mary Anne to Brawner, Jeremiah
Nov  5 1803 Keerl, Henry to Kendel, Margaret
Jun 26 1809 Keesy, Henry to Scott, Abey
May 19 1801 Keever, Andrew to Smith, Peggy
Jan 23 1807 Keever, Andrew to Smith, Mary Magdalene
Apr 26 1800 Keever, Henry to Miller, Elizabeth
Dec 15 1784 Keffauver, Susanna to Beckenbaugh, George Peter
Nov 16 1807 Keiffer, Lewis to McDonald, Margaret
Jan  5 1797 Keith, Price to Cruthers, Ann
Nov  9 1807 Kellenberger, Joseph to Lamar, Rachel
Dec 21 1803 Keller, Catharine to Routshoin, George
Jul  2 1810 Keller, Catherine to Motter, Michael
Jan 30 1790 Keller, Conrad to Stallings, Elizabeth
Mar 15 1799 Keller, Elizabeth to Thomas, Valentine
Mar 17 1786 Keller, George to Hedges, Sarah
Apr 19 1803 Keller, George to Kephart, Mary
Nov 20 1805 Keller, Henry to Biser, Elizabeth
Aug 28 1807 Keller, Henry to Eader, Nancy
Nov 18 1781 Keller, Jacob to Thompson, Rebecca
Oct 11 1786 Keller, Jacob to Smith, Susannah
Jul 22 1797 Keller, Jacob to Slagle, Elizabeth
Oct  9 1807 Keller, Jacob to Doup, Rosannah
Apr 25 1778 Keller, John to Yost, Mary
Feb 23 1808 Keller, John to Tanner, Barbara
Aug 26 1785 Keller, Juliana to Smith, Middleton
Oct 12 1778 Keller, Madelene to Ale, Daniel
Sep  9 1780 Keller, Margaret to Barrick, Henry
Oct 16 1781 Keller, Mary to Mills, Richard
Sep 10 1803 Keller, Mary to Schultz, John
Oct 23 1809 Kelley, Anna Statia to Jacobs, Michael
Oct  4 1808 Kellison, Nancy to Row, James
Dec  9 1802 Kellison, Reynolds to Jones, Patty
Jan 17 1793 Kelly, Dennis to Grimes, Priscilla
May 25 1795 Kelly, Edward to Thompson, Mary
Jul 27 1809 Kelly, Elizabeth to Ebert, Michael
Jan 13 1802 Kelly, John to Hood, Affa
Sep 22 1808 Kelly, John to Dunen, Rebeccah
Mar  7 1798 Kelly, Monarchy to Titus, Tunis
Feb 24 1808 Kelly, Priscilla to McLaughlin, Michael
Apr 12 1800 Kelly, Rebecca to Lewis, Benedict
Mar 26 1796 Kelty, Cornelius to Livers, Ann
Mar 28 1804 Kemp, Andrew to Madare, Catherine
Feb 27 1790 Kemp, Barbara to Bence, Jacob
Feb 19 1801 Kemp, Catherine to Heizer, John
Nov 22 1804 Kemp, Catherine to Main, Adam
Oct  6 1810 Kemp, Catherine to Norwood, Joshua
Jan  7 1801 Kemp, Daniel to Norris, Catherine
Mar 14 1801 Kemp, David to Miller, Margaret
Nov 11 1786 Kemp, Elizabeth to Fouck, George
Oct  1 1788 Kemp, Elizabeth to Barnes, Michael
Jan  5 1803 Kemp, Elizabeth to Staley, Jacob
Nov 10 1792 Kemp, Esther to Dehaven, Andrew
Aug  6 1796 Kemp, Esther to Frydinger, Nicholas
Apr 12 1804 Kemp, Esther to Doub, Valentine
May 13 1797 Kemp, Eve to Cronise, John, Junr.
```

```
Mar 21 1782 Kemp, Fred'k to Hershberger, Dorathy
Aug 31 1780 Kemp, Frederick to Ritter, Susanna
Apr 15 1805 Kemp, Frederick to Brunner, Margaret
Mar 24 1804 Kemp, George to Snyder, Mary
Jul 19 1779 Kemp, Henry to Ritter, Modelane
Mar 10 1781 Kemp, Henry to Mathews, Margaret
May 19 1794 Kemp, Henry to Miller, Susanna
Nov 11 1793 Kemp, Jacob to Getzendanner, Marg't
Jun 24 1802 Kemp, Jacob to Runkles, Sarah
Apr 24 1778 Kemp, John to Huff, Barbara
Jun 12 1782 Kemp, John to Snow, Elizabeth
Oct  2 1809 Kemp, Joseph to Staley, Magdalene
Sep  6 1785 Kemp, Ludwick to Norris, Barbara
Mar 18 1796 Kemp, Margaret to Barnet, Robert
Jan  6 1801 Kemp, Margaret to Morley, Ezekiel
Sep 23 1778 Kemp, Peter to Seaman (or Leaman), Mary
Feb 23 1801 Kemp, Peter, Jun. to Gater, Rachel
Mar 24 1792 Kemp, Susanna to Miller, John
Jul 28 1803 Kendal, William to Jones, Sarah White
Nov  6 1798 Kendall, Aaron to Kirk, Sarah
Apr  6 1806 Kendel, Catherine to Greenlease, James
Nov  5 1803 Kendel, Margaret to Keerl, Henry
Mar  2 1799 Kennedy, Dennis to Richards, Eleanor
Dec 19 1778 Kennedy, Elizabeth to Hagerty, George
Sep  4 1803 Kennedy, Francis to Thomas, Margaret
Jun 30 1795 Kennedy, George to Scott, Eleanor
Sep 15 1795 Kennedy, Janet to Dorsey, Joshua, Esq.
Dec 15 1792 Kennedy, John to Sauffer, Mary Ann
Oct  3 1778 Kennedy, Joseph to King, Christianna
Jan 18 1806 Kennedy, Lucy to Crusoe, John
Dec 29 1800 Kennedy, Margaret to Harman, Nicholas
Oct 30 1783 Kenott, Conrad to Brendlinger, Sarah
May 11 1794 Kensell, Jacob to Smith, Catharine
Nov 12 1801 Kent, Isaac to Marks, Milly
Nov 11 1806 Kephart, Catherine to Cromwell, John
Nov 10 1793 Kephart, Catherine to Obleman, John
Mar 28 1799 Kephart, Elizabeth to Wisman, Jacob
Jun  6 1810 Kephart, John to Young, Eve
Jul 31 1798 Kephart, Judith to Grove, Henry
Feb 14 1803 Kephart, Margaret to Cromwell, John
Oct 24 1803 Kephart, Susanna to Fish, John Benton
Apr 19 1803 Kephart, Mary to Keller, George
Feb 12 1800 Kephart, Mary to Wistman, Valentine
Jul 25 1794 Kephart, Sarah to Trout, Wendle
Aug  7 1782 Kephart, Simon to Leipley, Susannah
Jun 21 1779 Keplar, Eliz'th to Farver, Adam
Mar 17 1788 Keplar, Fredericka to Wolheim, John William
Oct 11 1799 Kepler, Frances to Williard, John
Feb 22 1802 Kepler, John to Young, Molly
Feb 16 1803 Kepler, Mary to Whitmore, George
Jun  7 1783 Keplinger, Catherine to Tertzbaugh, John
Aug 24 1808 Keplinger, Catherine to O'Connor, Bernard
Dec 12 1809 Keplinger, Catharine to Fairman, Daniel
Jan  4 1783 Keplinger, Christena to Knouff, Adam
Apr 28 1787 Keplinger, John to Bolie, Catharine
```

```
Feb 16 1779 Keplinger, Mary to Louis, John
Dec 25 1809 Keplinger, Polly to Boly, Jacob
Oct 30 1808 Keppeling, Elizabeth to Dixon, William
Apr 14 1807 Keppler, Peter to Shafer, Elizabeth
Oct 31 1807 Keptler, Elizabeth to James, Eli
Nov 10 1804 Kerlin, Elizabeth to Bost, Jacob
Jul 30 1810 Kernell, Catharine to Flannigan, Samuel
Apr 15 1809 Kerr, Elizabeth to Devilbiss, Samuel
Aug  5 1794 Kerr, Frances to Duttero, Conrad
Aug 13 1792 Kerr, George to Crom, Mary
Jul 29 1793 Kerr, John to Rogers, Ann
Mar 12 1803 Kerr, Robert to Hummer, Elizabeth
Oct 11 1807 Kerrick, Thomas to Carruthers, Phebe
Aug 24 1782 Kersner, Michael to Engles, Mary Ann
Oct 22 1798 Kessler, George to Jacob, Elizabeth
Nov 10 1806 Kessler, Jacob to Goodman, Rachel
Mar  8 1794 Kessler, John to Waskey, Nancy
Apr 25 1795 Kessler, Mary to Showe, Henry
Mar 18 1786 Kessler, Peter to Power, Elizabeth
Aug  2 1805 Kessler, Peter to Smith, Anne
Sep  5 1785 Ketzindanner, John to Fout, Rebeckah
Jan  6 1806 Key, Ann Phebe Charlton to Taney, Roger Brooke
Sep 16 1805 Key, William to Willen, Martha
Aug 25 1795 Kibby, Joseph to Hays, Eleanor
May 20 1807 Kiefer, George to Bowersock, Magdalene
Dec  9 1802 Kiefer, Jacob to Grove, Charlotte
Jul 31 1802 Kiefer, Michael to Hawman, Barbara
Mar 23 1781 Kigar, Jno. to Shitzen, Esther
Mar 18 1791 Kile, Adam to Martin, Elizabeth
May 10 1784 Kile, Elizabeth to Cookus, Michael
Jan  3 1791 Kile, Nicholas to Baggerly, Mary
May 15 1799 Kiler, Daniel to Ward, Elizabeth
Dec 24 1800 Kiler, Esther to Garhart, Jacob
Apr 11 1808 Killen, Maria to Long, Reuben
Aug 13 1808 Killion, Philip to Dertzbaugh, Elizabeth
Jan 25 1783 Killkup, Sarah to Howard, Joseph
Mar  9 1782 Kimbell, Mary to Morris, Jonathan
Dec 19 1789 Kindle, Mary to Luter, Michael
Jan  3 1795 King, Ann to Barnes, Thomas
Feb 18 1802 King, Anne to Jay, William
Oct 23 1779 King, Catherine to Roar, Jacob
Mar 30 1779 King, Charles to Risener, Eliz'th
Apr  3 1779 King, Charles to Middagh, Mary
Oct  3 1778 King, Christianna to Kennedy, Joseph
Apr 18 1804 King, Elenor to Hillery, Osbon
Sep 18 1780 King, Eliz'th to Cile, Peter
Jul  7 1792 King, Elizabeth to Coic, George
Jul 20 1793 King, Elizabeth to Adkins, William
Dec  6 1788 King, George to Perry, Rachel
Jun 23 1798 King, John to Toup, Margaret
Sep 26 1783 King, Mary to Lodge, William
Mar 30 1810 King, Mary to Young, John
Jul 17 1797 King, Nicholas to Gaunt, Peggy
Feb 20 1792 King, Rachel to Rhode, Jacob
Apr 11 1805 King, Richard to Redburn, Elizabeth
```

```
Jul  2 1802 King, William to Newey, Sarah
Nov 27 1810 King, William R. to Thomas, Eleanor
Jun 29 1780 King, Wm. to Wright, Eliz'th
Feb  2 1803 Kingla, Joseph to Baltzer, Elizabeth
Dec 26 1808 Kingsbury, Horatio to Fowler, Eleanor
Feb 14 1810 Kinley, Elizabeth to Baker, Dorsey
Jan 17 1801 Kinley, Jacob to Norwood, Elizabeth
Oct 13 1800 Kinley, William to Basford, Rachel
Feb  5 1801 Kinsey, Barbara to Barnhart, John
Dec 31 1800 Kinzey, Annie to Shoemaker, Christian
Jan 20 1798 Kirfman, Adam to Randall, Doraty
Nov 13 1800 Kirk, George to Stewart, Peggy
Apr  9 1793 Kirk, Margaret to Soper, Samuel
Jan 28 1796 Kirk, Richard to Jones, Mary Davidge
Nov  6 1798 Kirk, Sarah to Kendall, Aaron
Nov  9 1801 Kirk, Thomas, Junr. to Greenwell, Mary
Aug 24 1782 Kirkt, Susannah to Myer, Jacob
Nov 15 1785 Kise, Catherine to Stanley, Thomas
Dec 23 1785 Kisinger, Mary to Shriner, Adam
Aug  1 1780 Kisinger, Philipeana to Dryden, Wm.
Apr  3 1790 Kissinger, Francis to Levy, Sarah
Aug  3 1798 Kist, Philip to Holt, Anne
Oct 18 1788 Kitterman, Elizabeth to Eader, Adam
Jan 20 1798 Kittinger, Jacob to Shafer, Barbara
Apr 25 1795 Kittinger, John to Houck, Margaret
Nov 23 1799 Kittinger, Susanna to Baltzell, Daniel
Jun 30 1805 Kittle, Silas to Hockensmith, Catherine (License
            issued to same person)
Apr  6 1782 Kittle, William to Brown, Nancy
Apr 22 1780 Kitzadanner, Geo. to Darr, Eliz'th
Oct 13 1787 Kitzadanner, Thos. to Koontz, Mary Ann
Mar 11 1809 Kitzmiller, Martin to McCraft, Mary
Oct  5 1784 Kizer, Catherine to Prist, George
Mar 27 1802 Klein, Mary to Dorsey, Edward
Feb 17 1780 Klien, Nicholas to Smith, Margaret
Jan  1 1804 Kline, David to Henry, Jane
Dec 17 1804 Kline, Elizabeth to Bail, William
Apr 17 1810 Kline, George to Marker, Elizabeth
Apr 11 1800 Kline, Margaret to Bie, George
Aug 29 1784 Kline, Margaret to Brunner, Jacob
Jun 26 1790 Kline, Stephen to Shultz, Margaret
Mar 13 1805 Klinehoff, Sarah to Galt, John
May 30 1780 Knave, Margaret to Robinson, And'w
Jan 23 1799 Knight, Elijah to Dix, Sarah
May  1 1790 Knight, James to Williamson, Ann
Dec  8 1804 Knight, James to McCleery, Mary
Jul 23 1790 Knight, Joshua to Phillips, Sophia
Jan  2 1802 Knight, Joshua to Marcus, Mary
Aug  4 1779 Knight, Margaret to Hulse, Samuel
Dec 20 1779 Knight, Prescilla to Bennett Jesse
Mar  6 1798 Knight, Rachel to Taylor, Aquilla
Dec 11 1807 Knight, Sarah to Wells, Thomas
Mar 16 1796 Knight, Thomas to Williamson, Elizabeth
Feb  2 1790 Knock, Basil to Pickett, Mary
Nov 22 1798 Knott, Dorcus to Hole, John
```

```
Aug 19 1784 Knott, Elizabeth to Hoggins, Richard
Nov  6 1809 Knott, Lena to Trunel, Silas
Jan 12 1801 Knott, Philip to Edelen, Ann
Jun 29 1778 Knotts, Sarah to Compston, John
Jan  4 1783 Knouff, Adam to Keplinger, Christena
Nov 20 1798 Knouff, Andrew to Keepers, Eleanor
Jun 25 1796 Knouff, Catherine to Williard, Philip
May  5 1809 Knouff, Catherine to Frushour, Jacob
Oct 19 1799 Knouff, Christena to Dertzebaugh, John
Oct  8 1805 Knouff, Elizabeth to Cronise, Henry
Dec 27 1800 Knouff, Elizabeth to Holtzapple, Abraham
Jan  1 1807 Knouff, Elizabeth to Valentine, George
Sep 30 1786 Knouff, Jacob to Dern, Elizabeth
May  6 1803 Knouff, John to Biggs, Catherine
May 24 1801 Knouff, Lovice to Hardesty, William
May 24 1806 Knouff, Mary M. to Newons, Thomas
Mar  1 1779 Knowse, Eliz'th to Handshaw, John
Nov 12 1803 Knox, Robert to Stephenson, Jane
Aug 18 1781 Knox, Susanna to Shipley, Basil
Jun  3 1779 Knox, Thos. to Duffle, Mary
Dec 14 1807 Koblentz, Daniel to Stockman, Catherine
Apr 19 1805 Koch, Henry to Humer, Eleanor
Aug 18 1800 Kocugh, Mathias to Bishop, Elizabeth
Feb 25 1804 Koenig, Susanna to Eater, Abraham
Feb  7 1804 Kogh, Charlotte to Study, Henry
May 24 1806 Kohlenberg, Caroline to Mitchell, Ignatius
Jan 27 1798 Kolb, Catherine to Stallings, Newman
Sep  3 1796 Kolb, George to Winnull, Ann
Jan 29 1803 Kolb, Jacob to Boly, Elizabeth
Jun 28 1808 Kolenburg, Hannah to Darnall, Ralph
Mar 11 1799 Koller, John to Troshon, Catherine
Aug 10 1787 Koogle, Adam to Nave, Catherine
May 24 1787 Koon, Henry to Browning, Elizabeth
Feb 24 1807 Koon, John to Goslin, Sarah
May 24 1786 Koonce, Catherine to Harris, Samuel
Aug 22 1810 Koons, Magdalene to Baumgardner, Jacob
Aug 24 1807 Koontz, Alice to Woolf, George
Nov 14 1807 Koontz, Anne to Tanzey, Arthur
Oct 28 1799 Koontz, Catherine to Martin, Jacob
Sep 30 1805 Koontz, Elizabeth to Shup, Solomon
Oct 25 1810 Koontz, George to Long, Catherine
Dec 24 1787 Koontz, Henry to Steiner, Marg't
Sep 19 1780 Koontz, Jacob to Clay, Mary
Jun 30 1808 Koontz, Jacob to Alexander, Elizabeth
Mar  1 1802 Koontz, Magdalena to Stover, Philip
Jun  6 1809 Koontz, Maria E. to Young, Samuel
Dec  7 1784 Koontz, Mary to Bogen, Anthony Frederick
Apr 26 1785 Koontz, Mary Ann to Hilderbrick, George
Oct 13 1787 Koontz, Mary Ann to Kitzadanner, Thos.
Oct 13 1787 Koontz, Mary Ann to Getzadanner, Thos.
Feb 16 1779 Koontz, Salomy to Smith, Jacob
Oct 21 1783 Koontza, Frederick to Shull, Elizabeth
Mar 20 1800 Kramer, Elizabeth to Engle, Peter
Nov 24 1783 Kreis, Christian to Turnwoolfe, Mary Eliz'th
Jun 25 1796 Krugg, Susanna to Mantz, John
```

```
Dec  4 1783 Kruse, John to Hellen, Barbara
Jan  9 1808 Kugle, Catherine to Hutzell, Jacob
Aug 16 1804 Kuller, John to Coplentz, Mary Ann
Jun  8 1805 Kuller, Susanna to Wilyard, George
Dec  7 1797 Kulp, William to Miller, Eve
Jan 28 1800 Kurtz, Susannah to Doll, John
May 12 1808 Kuser, Samuel to Clapsaddle, Susanna
May  6 1802 Kusic, Sarah to Spring, Frederick
Jan 21 1794 Kutz, Elizabeth to Smith, John Henry
Aug 27 1790 Kyser, Sarah to Toughman, Frederick

Oct 10 1807 Labe, Elizabeth to Wisinger, George
Jul  2 1805 Labe, Mary to Beall, Jacob
May  1 1804 Laflaver, Jacob to Jackson, Mary
Sep 24 1802 Lain, John to Pennybacker, Mary
Jun 25 1778 Lakin, Ann to Deaver, Abraham
Mar  3 1780 Lakin, Basil to Smith, Hannah
Nov 14 1783 Lakin, Mary to Aldridge, John
Oct 30 1780 Lakin, Rachel to Markin, Sam'l
Jul 18 1788 Lakins, Abraham to Ungles, Mary
Aug 23 1779 Laman, Jacob to Peterson, Hannah
Nov  9 1807 Lamar, Rachel to Kellenberger, Joseph
Oct 30 1788 Lamar, Sarah to Thrasher, Elias
Oct 18 1803 Lamar, William to Thrasher, Drusilla
Oct 26 1791 Lamarr, Henrietta to Thrasher, Elie
Dec 18 1789 Lamb, Ann to Evans, Charles
May 14 1799 Lamb, Owen to Grant, Susanna
Aug 16 1810 Lamback, Neomy to Fighter, George
Feb 27 1781 Lambaugh, Henry to Everhart, Mary
May 28 1794 Lambert, John to Hie, Mary
Jun  1 1779 Lambert, Mary to Cook, Henry
Aug 28 1804 Lambeth, John to Keefer, Catherine
Aug 25 1806 Lambrecht, Elizabeth to Sponcellar, John
Feb  7 1804 Lambrecht, George to Sponsaler, Rachel
Jul  5 1803 Lambrecht, Margaret to Dern, William, Junr.
Apr 17 1802 Lambright, John to Smith, Catherine
Aug 30 1809 Lambright, Mary to Yowler, George
Nov  5 1803 Lammerson, Richard to Penser, Barbara
Mar 25 1797 Lamon, Eve to Swaidner, Adam
Sep 15 1807 Landers, Nancy to Easterday, Christian
Sep  9 1796 Landers, Rachel to Easterday, Jacob
Dec 20 1806 Landes, Isaac to Stoner, Hannah
Feb 27 1807 Lane, George G. to Webb, Susanna
Jan 23 1805 Lane, John to Baker, Catherine
Feb  9 1807 Lane, John to Shook, Sarah
Apr 10 1810 Lane, Mary to Irons, Joseph
Jun 28 1794 Lanham, Ann to Burris, Thomas
Jan  6 1783 Lanham, Drusey to Roach, Richard
Nov 15 1803 Lanham, Elizabeth to Wedden, Ralph
Dec 22 1809 Lankton, Elizabeth to White, James
Apr 15 1800 Lantz, Catharine to Row, George
Mar 25 1806 Lantz, Catherine to Tritt, Paul
Dec 24 1801 Lantz, Christian to Tidy, Sophia
May 30 1807 Lantz, Curtius to Hildebrand, Elizabeth
Apr  1 1802 Lantz, Margaret to Hildebrand, Henry, Junr.
```

```
Dec 27 1806 Lantz, Mary to Linton, James
Dec  1 1810 Lantz, Susan to Mahaney, John
Sep 13 1800 Lape, Jacob to Brim, Polly
Nov  8 1785 Lapp, Henry to Sigler, Phoeby
Feb 20 1809 Larken, Thomas to Everhart, Nancy
Feb  7 1810 Larkin, David to Harper, Nancy
Aug 13 1803 Larkin, Elizabeth to Gilbert, Peter
May  9 1809 Larkin, Susanna to Kalb, Absalom
Mar 23 1805 Larkins, William to Cerby, Eleanor
Sep 26 1807 Larned, Augustus to Pool, Sarah
Feb  3 1780 Larymore, Thomas to Grear, Sarah
Jul 28 1800 Lashea, George to Breson, Rosanna Cecili
May  6 1786 Lashorn, John to Farthing, Rebeckah
Apr 16 1787 Late, Mary to Conrad, Henry
Sep 11 1809 Late, Michael to Umbaugh, Catherine
Nov 23 1779 Laton, Uriah to Hinton, Rachel
Feb  9 1810 Latshaw, John to Denison, Mary
Apr 19 1804 Laurance, Mary to Hilliard, James
Sep  3 1802 Lavely, Elizabeth to Gosnell, John
Apr 18 1797 Lavely, William to Livers, Tracy
Sep  1 1802 Lavey, John to Huckel, Anna
Oct 13 1808 Lavich, Mary to Eiler, Samuel
Nov  5 1784 Lawrence, Ann West to Mansell, Geo.
Jan 20 1808 Lawrence, Elizabeth to Bennet, Robert
Dec  7 1790 Lawrence, Elizabeth to Shreaves, William
Jan  1 1805 Lawrence, John S. to Shriner, Sarah Maria
Mar 18 1802 Lawrence, Nancy to Jones, Thomas B.
Nov  3 1804 Lawrence, Peggy to Talbott, Allen
Jan 30 1795 Lawrence, Rachel to Thompson, Andrew
Mar  6 1780 Lawrence, Richard to Warfield, Ann
Jun 22 1790 Lawrence, Samuel to Hobbs, Sarah
Dec 23 1788 Lawrence, Susanna to Dorsey, Evan
Mar 22 1808 Lawyer, Catherine to Campbell, Benjamin
Oct 22 1810 Layman, Betsey to Fink, Henry
Sep 17 1794 Layman, Juliana to Baker, Adam
Oct  2 1796 Leach, Walter to Lynch, Charlotte
Mar 26 1792 Leagere, Geo. to Pittinger, Elizabeth
Jan 30 1787 Leakin, Daniel to Skekel, Ann
May  2 1809 Leakins, Elizabeth to Drill, Christian
Apr 20 1799 Leakins, Elizabeth to Hall, Benjamin
Jan 19 1802 Leakins, Mary to Jenkins, Job
Mar 25 1790 Leakins, William to Mumford, Martha
Jun 21 1810 Leaming, Jacob to Elliott, Lydia
Jan 24 1781 Lear, Dan'l to Pancartson, Mary
Oct 17 1795 Lear, Fred'k to Miller, Catharine
Nov 12 1807 Lear, George to Doll, Susanna
Oct 27 1796 Lear, Michael to Crist, Mary
Apr 25 1795 Lease, George to Tice, Elizabeth
May 18 1789 Lease, Jacob to Thompson, Cassandra
Apr 27 1807 Lease, John to Stevens, Margaret
Dec 30 1797 Lease, Susannah to Vanfossen, Levi
Dec 14 1791 Leasher, Jacob to Caufman, Mary
Nov 16 1783 Leashorn, Conrad to Easton, Mary
Sep 17 1791 Leashorn, Elizabeth to Shots, John
Dec 24 1802 Leatch, Edward to Abright, Mary
```

```
Nov  4 1794 Leatch, Rebeckah to Rice, Joseph
Oct 29 1803 Leather, Catherine to Tom, George
Sep 26 1805 Leather, George to Arter, Elizabeth
Mar 26 1781 Leather, Margaret to Young, Conrad
Sep 29 1805 Leather, Mary to Tabler, Lewis
Apr 27 1810 Leatherman, Catherine to Young, Jacob
May 14 1807 Leatherman, Elizabeth to Sanderson, William R.
Aug 22 1782 Leatherman, Francis to Arnold, Anthony
Nov 20 1798 Leatherman, John to Miller, Catherine
Nov 13 1808 Leatherman, John to Gaugh, Eve
Jan 29 1805 Leatherman, Juliana to Hedges, Andrew
Oct 18 1803 Leatherman, Margaret to Shriver, Abraham
Apr 22 1802 Leatherman, Mary to Shriver, Isaac
Aug 25 1786 Leatherman, Peter to Swigart, Mary
Dec 15 1810 Leatherwood, Elizabeth to Fowler, John
Dec 22 1804 Leatherwood, Mary to Moore, Christian
Mar 23 1805 Leatherwood, Mary to Tener, Adam
Aug  8 1778 Leatherwood, Samuel to Buckingham, Hannah
May 11 1810 Lee, James to Clabaugh, Mary
Mar 10 1797 Lee, Rachael to Murrel, Robert
Sep  3 1785 Leek, Mary to Darnall, Henry
Mar 17 1802 Leekings, Becky to Gilliss, Porcius
Oct 20 1791 Leeply, George to Nicholls, Elizabeth
Jul 29 1789 Leeply, John to Beamer, Lucy
May 13 1796 Leese, Elizabeth to Thompson, Henry
May  7 1802 Leese, Henry to Jacobs, Barbara
Jun  4 1796 Lefaver, Daniel to Sulser, Margaret
Feb 20 1796 Lefaver, Elizabeth to Price, John
Sep  1 1798 Lefaver, Hester to Smith, Abraham
May 12 1800 Lefaver, John to Martz, Catherine
Oct  9 1798 Lefever, Elias to Craver, Catherine
Dec 15 1792 Legaud, Peter Marie Guilie De K. (?) to Grimbolt,
            Genevieve Emilie
Dec 15 1787 Leggit, Samuel to Parkes, Jane
Aug  7 1782 Leipley, Susannah to Kephart, Simon
Jun 27 1778 Leisle, Ann to Parkinson, John
Dec 21 1805 Lemar, Eleanor to Cunningham, Aaron
Oct  3 1805 Lemar, Susanna to House, William
Feb  6 1802 Lemar, Thomas to Wilyard, Mary
Jul 25 1794 Lemaster, Elizabeth to Geyer, Jacob
Jun  3 1807 Lemaster, Harriet to Philips, Wesley
Mar 14 1796 Lemaster, Martha to Kadle, Gibson
Mar 25 1799 Lemaster, Richard to Johnson, Rebecca
May 28 1801 Lemmon, Eve to Montgomery, Alexander
Jun 10 1797 Lemmon, Eve to Sweadner, Adam
Feb 23 1805 Lemmon, Hugh to Norris, Rachel
Apr 11 1807 Lemmon, Samuel to Dahoff, Hannah
Dec 17 1793 Lemon, Catherine to Dale, John Petere
Jan  7 1795 Lemon, Catherine to Rose, John
Feb 16 1810 Lemon, Jacob to Ridinger, Peggy
May  7 1800 Lenham, Robert C. to Penn, Rachel
Aug 17 1801 Leonard, Catherine to River, Jacob
Aug 27 1781 Leonard, Christian to Burgher, Catherine
Jun 25 1796 Leonard, Margaret to Mason, Martin
Aug  8 1806 Lescaleet, John to Haines, Catharine
```

```
Dec 20 1804 Lescolate, William to Mackey, Elizabeth
Jul 29 1782 Lester, Ann to Bradley, Dan'l
Apr  4 1805 Lett, Monica to Goings, Roswell
Dec 12 1805 Lett, Pamela to Mattox, George
Dec 22 1804 Levy, Abraham to Wigle, Ann Catharine
Sep 24 1791 Levy, David, Junr. to Sturrum, Mary
Dec 28 1793 Levy, Elizabeth to Crum, Wm.
Nov 21 1789 Levy, Jacob to Shroiner, Mary
Apr  6 1805 Levy, Jonathan to Stemple, Elizbeth
Mar 10 1810 Levy, Rebecca to Johnson, Joseph
May 21 1807 Levy, Rebecca to Zealler, Adam
Apr  3 1790 Levy, Sarah to Kissinger, Francis
Sep  4 1797 Lewis, Anne to Atwell, John
Apr 12 1800 Lewis, Benedict to Kelly, Rebecca
Dec 16 1809 Lewis, Delila to Reel, Leonard T.
Jan 18 1797 Lewis, Drusilla to Trundle, David
May  5 1800 Lewis, Elizabeth to Fortney, David
Mar  7 1804 Lewis, Elizabeth to Murphy, George
Nov 16 1779 Lewis, Jno. to Gatton, Verlinda
Jun 13 1785 Lewis, Mary to Crail, Wm.
Jul 26 1809 Lewis, Sophia to Davis, Richard
Mar  1 1810 Lewis, Susan to Porter, Isaiah
Mar 18 1794 Lewis, Thomas to Ellis, Mary
Jul  2 1798 Lewis, Thomas to Teshner, Sophia
Apr 23 1803 Lewis, William to Hooper, Eleanor
Oct 18 1803 Leyth, John to Thrasher, Martha
Jul  8 1809 Lickey, William to Bolon, Abegail
Feb 23 1797 Licklider, George to Beavers, Susanna
Feb 16 1801 Lida, Margaret to Groshon, Elias
Dec 23 1802 Liday, Barbara to Campbell, John
Oct 12 1782 Lieth, Samuel to Thrasher, Cassiah
Jan  1 1791 Liggat, Jane to Abricks, Hermanus
Apr  7 1810 Lighter, Jacob to Smith, Catherine
Dec  7 1805 Lighter, John to Fox, Elizabeth
Jul 21 1797 Lightner, John to Warner, Mary
May 17 1796 Lighty, John to Miller, Elizabeth
Jan  1 1779 Lilley, Henry to Whitehead, Sarah
May 15 1800 Lilly, Ignatius to Hughes, Winnefred
Nov 15 1808 Lilly, Richard to Garrison, Elizabeth
Apr 15 1797 Linaweaver, Catharine to Elias, George
Jan  7 1797 Linaweaver, Margaret to Dewire, Leonard
Jul 22 1780 Lince, Elizabeth to Burrell, George
Nov 25 1790 Linch, Ann to Baker, Basil
Sep 14 1789 Linch, Mary Ann to Hickey, James
Apr 14 1783 Linck, Adam to Ogle, Jane
Sep 16 1805 Lindsay, John to Bail, Sarah
Sep  3 1782 Lindsay, Thomas to Trentor, Margaret
Nov 27 1790 Lindsey, Alexander to Merstiller, Rebecka
Nov 30 1805 Lindsey, David to Durbin, Margaret
Sep 18 1789 Lindsey, George to McDonald, Elizabeth
Feb 14 1786 Line, Henry to Bents, Margaret
Aug 12 1797 Linganfelder, John to Mount, Ann
Mar 15 1793 Linganfelder, Mary to Waltz, Frederick
Apr 23 1782 Linganfelter, Catherine to Cassell, Abraham
Oct 23 1790 Linganfelter, Elizabeth to Cannon, John
```

```
Jul 25 1779 Link, Catharine to Boyer, Jacob
Feb 14 1801 Link, Daniel to Creager, Catherine
Apr 19 1788 Link, Jacob to Creagar, Elizbeth
Mar 22 1790 Link, Thomas to Fout, Ann Maria
Mar  9 1799 Linn, Isaac to Jacobs, Eve
Oct  3 1804 Linn, Modalena to Pepple, William
Apr 15 1810 Linthicum, Charles Griffith to Merriwether, Louisa
Oct  6 1809 Linthicum, Frederick to McElfresh, Elizabeth Smith
Dec 13 1802 Linthicum, Sarah to McElfresh, William
Feb 11 1803 Linton, Benjamin to Hildebrand, Barbara
Feb  6 1806 Linton, Charlotte to Bowman, Jacob
May 17 1806 Linton, Charlotte to Bauman, Jacob
Nov 19 1808 Linton, Edward to Ellison, Sarah
Dec  6 1797 Linton, Elizabeth to Cecill, George
Feb  4 1793 Linton, Isaac to Richards, Susanna
Dec 27 1806 Linton, James to Lantz, Mary
Apr 26 1808 Linton, Joshan to Upperwood, Joshua
Feb 24 1798 Linton, Mary to Cecil, John
Aug 23 1800 Linton, William to Fout, Charlotte
May 20 1778 Linton, Zachariah to Maynard, Mary
Sep 20 1783 Lintz, Catherine to Cox, William
Apr  7 1798 Lipps, Mary to Haines, John
Jun  3 1779 Litchard, Catharine to Berkman, Peter
Dec 17 1808 Litert, Henry to Miller, Anne
Oct  7 1806 Little, Mary to McGee, James
Jul 25 1778 Little, Michael to Quinner, Mary
Nov 19 1783 Little, Susanna to Crabster, John
Feb 13 1779 Livers, --- to Head, Biggar
Mar 26 1796 Livers, Ann to Kelty, Cornelius
Nov 24 1809 Livers, Elizabeth to Boyle, Peter
Apr 18 1797 Livers, Tracy to Lavely, William
Aug 21 1778 Livingston, Eve to Creale, Richard
Jun  1 1805 Lloyd, Elizabeth to Oden, Thomas
Nov 26 1798 Lloyd, Samuel to Hows, Henny
Mar 22 1780 Lock, John to Bastian, Sarah
Dec  7 1807 Lock, John to Stimmel, Elizbeth
Dec 29 1800 Locker, William to Jenkins, Eleanor
Sep 26 1783 Lodge, William to King, Mary
Oct  8 1798 Loehr, Elizabeth to Sinn, Philip
Nov 27 1797 Loeman, Mich'l to Bale, Elizabeth
Feb 23 1809 Logan, Margaret to Reid, Patrick
Mar 19 1778 Logan, William to Shelar, Margaret
Apr 29 1808 Logsdon, John to Holmes, Nancy
Apr 29 1797 Lombright, Henry to Cronice, Susanna
Dec 28 1797 Lombright, Philip to Hole, Mary
Jun 12 1779 Loney, Catharine to Anderson, John
Sep 28 1810 Long, Andrew to Mumford, Elizabeth
Jun  2 1802 Long, Barbara to Culler, Jacob
Apr 30 1808 Long, Barbara to Castle, Thomas
Jan 27 1806 Long, Barbara to Wildanger, George
Oct 25 1810 Long, Catherine to Koontz, George
Dec 16 1793 Long, Charles to Firestone, Catherine
Sep 13 1806 Long, Christiana to Brandenburg, William
Aug 10 1805 Long, Christianna to Staub, Christian
Nov 25 1806 Long, Elizabeth to Feister, Jacob
```

```
Jun 23 1806 Long, Elizabeth to Green, Jonathan
Feb  4 1782 Long, Elizabeth to House, Dan'l
May 26 1808 Long, John to Alexander, Catherine
May  2 1810 Long, Margaret to Derr, Jacob
Jun  7 1806 Long, Mary to Stimmel, Abraham
Apr 11 1808 Long, Reuben to Killen, Maria
Nov 13 1779 Long, Uliana to Miller, Jacob
Aug 12 1806 Longsworth, Elizabeth to Clary, Jesse
Jun  6 1785 Longsworth, Solomon to McElfresh, Lucretia
Jan  9 1810 Longwell, Mathew to Clinehoof, Jane
May 13 1807 Lookenpeel, Mary to Dempsey, Joseph
Jun 13 1804 Lookingbill, Peter to Worman, Elizabeth
Sep  4 1790 Lookingpeel, John to Worman, Sarah
Dec 31 1808 Lookinsland, David to Weller, Catherine
Feb 17 1810 Loraw, Eve to Gilbert, Henry
May 14 1785 Lott, Jacob to Michael, Cath.
May 28 1804 Louderman, George to Crouse, Hannah
Feb 16 1779 Louis, John to Keplinger, Mary
Nov  7 1784 Love, David to Ramsey, Nancey
Mar 13 1809 Love, Mary to Fleming, Robert, Junr.
Aug 27 1807 Low, John to Wickell, Barbara
Aug 11 1800 Low, Polly to Cook, Reasin
Jul 19 1778 Lowe, And'w to Peckenbaugh, Mary
Dec 23 1805 Lowe, Catherine to Houck, Jacob
Nov  1 1799 Lowe, Jacob to Rep, Susannah
May 26 1784 Lowman, Mary to Piles, Richard
Oct  8 1799 Lowman, Susannah to Matthews, Jacob
May 17 1794 Lowrey, Ceazer to Cooper, Mary
Jan  2 1802 Lowry, Susanna to Nicholls, Benjamin
Apr  1 1809 Lowry, Thomas to Bond, Hebe G.
Sep 18 1778 Loy, Charlotte to Shoup, George
Dec  2 1800 Loy, Elizabeth to Protsman, Henry
Oct 17 1807 Loy, Jacob to Ovelman, Elizbeth
Jul 27 1778 Loyd, Mary to Woods, George
Jun 22 1782 Lucas, Elizabeth to Barnett, Archibald
Feb 12 1802 Lucas, Jesse to Isenberg, Polly
Dec  1 1797 Lucas, John to Waters, Christena
Dec 28 1793 Lucas, Thomas to Simmons, Elizabeth
Jun 28 1788 Luckett, David to Luckett, Susanna
Jan 31 1781 Luckett, John to Munro, Kitty
Apr 22 1800 Luckett, John to Hickman, Jane
Mar 28 1796 Luckett, Lucy to Jamison, Ignatius
May  7 1796 Luckett, Philip to Harding, Mary
Dec 22 1806 Luckett, Sam'l to Clapham, Rebecca
Jun 28 1788 Luckett, Susanna to Luckett, David
Mar  7 1799 Lucorsh, Margaret to Reel, Frederick
Jan 20 1803 Luday, John to Huller, Susanna
Sep 30 1801 Ludey, Susanna to Crise, Peter
Sep 19 1808 Ludy, Henry to Gilbert, Hannah
Mar 28 1807 Ludy, Peter to Martin, Christena
Jun 23 1802 Lukebaugh, Margaret to Iler, Jacob
Nov  6 1799 Lung, Jacob to Rep, Susannah
Mar 13 1805 Luskelete, Polly to Walter, Jacob
Jul 20 1797 Lusty, Mary to Paxson, Joseph
Jan 21 1800 Luten, Abraham to Holtz, Margaret
```

```
Dec 19 1789 Luter, Michael to Kindle, Mary
Nov 16 1779 Luther, Christ'n to Sewell, Alley
Jan  8 1808 Lutler, Elizabeth to Willyard, Daniel
May  6 1783 Lutz, Barbara to Holler, Christopher
Mar 16 1802 Lutz, John to Miller, Polly
May  8 1784 Lutzell, Mich'l to Grove, Sophia
Sep 19 1808 Lyda, Jacob to Millhouse, Margaret
May 27 1780 Lyder, Henry to Staley, Catherine
May  7 1782 Lydey, Elizabeth to Balser, John
Jun 10 1797 Lyles, Elizabeth to Howard, Sam'l
Oct 30 1807 Lyles, Margaret to Perkins, Henry H.
Dec  1 1807 Lyles, Rebecca to Philips, Samuel
Apr  4 1787 Lyles, Richard to Jones, Elizabeth
Dec 28 1795 Lynch, Abraham to Hannahe, Mary
Oct  2 1796 Lynch, Charlotte to Leach, Walter
Feb 13 1779 Lynch, John to Ridgley, Mary
Oct  1 1803 Lynch, Kezia to Hook, James (of Snowden)
Aug 26 1786 Lyne, John to Huff, Mary
Aug  1 1794 Lynn, Catharine to Ambrose, John
Dec 21 1797 Lynn, Elizabeth to Thomas, Philip
May  5 1807 Lynn, Jacob to Jacobs, Catherine
Feb 26 1784 Lynn, John to Edelin, Eleanor
Jan 25 1806 Lyon, Isaac to Wagner, Catherine
Aug  6 1810 Lyons, George to Downey, Rebecca
Jul 28 1803 Lyons, John to Burrier, Barbara
Oct  7 1802 Lyster, David to Nichodemus, Rachel

Aug 11 1792 Maccatee, Anne to Bucey, Henry
Nov  4 1789 Mace, John to Nicholson, Ann
Aug 24 1802 Macfarlin, Robert to Main, Anne
Aug 24 1802 Macfarlin, Robert to Main, Anne
Nov 10 1785 Mackall, Susanna to Price, Thomas, Capt.
Dec 20 1791 Mackbee, Sarah Price to Parker, Hutchison
Jun 23 1788 Mackelfresh, Sarah to Wood, Henry
Dec 20 1804 Mackey, Elizabeth to Lescolate, William
Sep  8 1810 Mackey, Margaret to Franklin, Thomas
Nov 30 1810 Mackey, Mary to Reily, Daniel
Apr 30 1796 Mackey, Robert to Ragan, Sarah
Feb 16 1809 Mackley, Martin to Bail, Sophia
Sep 10 1800 Mackley, Richard to Israel, Leer
Sep 10 1800 Mackley, Richard to Israel, Leer
Mar 28 1804 Madare, Catherine to Kemp, Andrew
Feb 14 1781 Madden, Joseph to Hillery, Eliz'th
Aug  1 1810 Maddoc, Frederick to Riley, Mary
Apr  8 1780 Maddon, Jacob to Steward, Dolly
Dec 13 1783 Maddon, John to Falconer, Margery
Sep 12 1803 Maddox, John to James, Polly
Jan 15 1784 Maddox, Sarah to Smith, John
Aug 19 1803 Madeira, John to Gabeler, Teresa
Dec 30 1807 Madeira, Margaret to Moss(?), Charles
Oct  6 1801 Madeira, Mary to Tromberger, Jacob
Jan 26 1809 Madeira, Rachel to Kahler, Jacob
Apr 15 1786 Madera, Nicholas to Adamson, Susanna
Sep 28 1807 Magee, George W. to Senseney, Catherine
Apr 10 1797 Magers, Ann to Philips, Jason
```

```
Sep 20 1808 Magers, Elias to Weary, Mary
Oct  2 1801 Magers, Lawrence to White, Mary
Aug 10 1778 Maginnis, John to Moran, Hetty
Aug  7 1806 Magnass, James to Ball, Catherine
Aug 27 1799 Magors, Elizabeth to Cole, William H.
Oct 10 1804 Magraw, Henry to Huckle, Sarah
Nov 19 1805 Magruder, Alexander Contee to Thomas, Rebecca Bellicon
Oct  7 1795 Magruder, D. Ninian to Beatty, Lydia
May 12 1782 Magruder, Deborah to Ward, Peter
Jul 28 1803 Magruder, Edward to Ayton, Jane
Feb 14 1784 Magruder, Eleanor to Briscoe, John
Mar 21 1799 Magruder, John R. to Butler, Susanna M.
Jan 17 1798 Magruder, Mary to McAtee, Ignatius
May 14 1799 Magrueder, Julia to Brashear, Ely
Sep  6 1810 Mahagan, William to Selmon, Eve
Jul 10 1782 Mahaney, Dan'l to Baltzell, Elizabeth
Dec  1 1810 Mahaney, John to Lantz, Susan
Dec  9 1780 Mahany, Eleanor to Bowden, Thomas
May 15 1800 Mahoney, Barnaba to Waltz, Margaret
Apr 29 1796 Mahoney, Barnabas to Reel, Mary
Jan  6 1794 Mahony, James H. to Williams, Sarah
Nov 21 1790 Mahony, John to Brashears, Henry
Oct  6 1795 Mahony, Mary to Winhold, William
Nov 22 1804 Main, Adam to Kemp, Catherine
Aug 24 1802 Main, Anne to Macfarlin, Robert
Aug 24 1802 Main, Anne to Macfarlin, Robert
Mar  5 1802 Main, Charity to Miller, Leonard
Jun 14 1802 Main, Elizabeth to Spealman, John
Sep  7 1805 Main, Frederick to Gilbert, Catherine
Oct 11 1802 Main, George to Horine, Mary
Mar 21 1805 Main, John to Baltzell, Susanna
Mar 13 1802 Main, Polly to Smith, Matthias
Oct  7 1800 Main, Susanna to Boden, Samuel
Dec 22 1795 Malone, Bartholomew Murphy to Bradie, Lydia
Mar 20 1809 Malone, Sidney to Dean, Jacob
Nov 14 1807 Malory, Anne to Prather, Silas
Sep  3 1808 Manahan, Jonas to Dudderer, Sarah
Apr 26 1797 Manahan, Margaret to Dodds, Samuel
Aug 18 1801 Manahan, Thomas to Porters, Ruth
Oct 29 1795 Manakey, Catherine to Onions, William
Dec 22 1807 Mane, John to Mane, Susannah
Dec 22 1807 Mane, Susannah to Mane, John
Mar  9 1792 Mangins, Matthias to Frey, Mary
Oct 23 1800 Maniard, Ezra to Robertson, Hannah
Nov  5 1784 Mansell, Geo. to Lawrence, Ann West
Jun 26 1780 Mansfield, Eleanor to Israel, Basil
Mar  4 1786 Mansfield, Ruth to Dunning, John
Sep 21 1784 Mansfield, Susanna to Clark, Thomas
Jul 11 1780 Mansfield, Susanna to Welsh, John, Sr.
Aug 25 1794 Mansparager, Daniel to Hyme, Catherine
Feb 28 1805 Manspicker, Margaret to Hymes, George
Apr 30 1803 Mantz, Catharine to Brengle, Peter
Jul  4 1779 Mantz, Charlotte to Boyer, Adam
Oct 27 1782 Mantz, David to Miller, Elizabeth
May 22 1794 Mantz, Elizabeth to Faris, Christian
```

```
Dec 12 1779 Mantz, Esther to Gumbare, John, Junr.
Dec  6 1807 Mantz, Ezra to Ritchie, Maria P.A.D.
Oct  1 1786 Mantz, Isaac to Boogher, Charlotte
Mar 24 1803 Mantz, Isaac to Norris, Elizabeth
Jun 25 1796 Mantz, John to Krugg, Susanna
Aug 16 1800 Mantz, Mary to Brengle, Nicholas
Dec 12 1790 Mantz, Mary to Quynn, Allen, Jr.
Apr 23 1778 Mantz, Peter, Majr. to Howard, Catherine
Aug  1 1798 Marater, John to Nicholson, Elizabeth
Apr  2 1805 Marchel, Catherine to Marchel, Ezra
Apr  2 1805 Marchel, Ezra to Marchel, Catherine
Nov  9 1807 Marckel, William to Cramer, Barbara
Mar 28 1807 Marckell, Jonathan to Schriner, Rachel
Sep  5 1801 Marckley, Elizabeth to Pyles, John
Oct 18 1796 Marcus, Eleanor to Porter, Isaiah
Oct 27 1804 Marcus, Elizabeth to Norris, Otho
Jan  2 1802 Marcus, Mary to Knight, Joshua
Dec 22 1781 Margruder, Mary Ann to Murdock, Benjamin
Sep  7 1807 Mark, George to Purdy, Cynthia
Dec 17 1802 Mark, John to Purdy, Amelia
Dec  7 1799 Mark, Margaret to Baker, Larkin
Sep 18 1779 Markel, Adam to Dickensheets, Mary
Feb 24 1781 Markell, Wm. to Boyer, Mary
Dec 17 1806 Marker, Catharine to Patton, George
May  6 1797 Marker, Daniel to Beckenbaugh, Christena
Mar 29 1809 Marker, Elizabeth to Brookover, William
Apr 17 1810 Marker, Elizabeth to Kline, George
May 12 1801 Marker, George to Storm, Margaret
Feb 28 1780 Marker, Henry to Shotts, Clory
Mar 19 1796 Markey, David to Hummel, Catherine
Oct 30 1780 Markin, Sam'l to Lakin, Rachel
Jun 20 1798 Markle, Catherine to Burckhartt, John
Dec  7 1796 Markle, George to Smith, Catherine
May 21 1800 Markle, Juliet to Carty, Thomas
Jan  8 1782 Markley, Gabriel to Dickensheets, Cathe.
Nov 12 1801 Marks, Milly to Kent, Isaac
Dec  2 1802 Marks, Peggy to Murphy, John
Apr 30 1783 Marley, Mary to Ankrom, Aaron
Sep 27 1791 Marlow, Edward to Rice, Rebeckah
Aug  9 1794 Marlow, Horatio to Burgee, Elizabeth
Dec 14 1789 Marlow, Thomas to Frazier, Elizabeth
Jan 21 1807 Marquam, Philip to Poole, Charlotte
Nov 10 1806 Marquet, Elizabeth to Peltz, John
Dec 30 1779 Marshall, Alex'dr to Pearl, Susanna
May 31 1804 Marshall, Eleanor to Harding, John L.
Aug 11 1797 Marshall, Elizabeth to Rust, John
Apr  3 1790 Marshall, Grace to Murphy, John
Mar  4 1801 Marshall, Mary to Robertson, William
Oct  9 1800 Marshall, Priscilla to Riggs, Samuel
Jan  2 1803 Marshall, Ruth to Blinderwood, William
Jan  2 1803 Marshall, Ruth to Underwood, William B.
Jan 11 1798 Marshall, Samuel to McGeihan, Elizabeth
Nov 24 1809 Marshall, Sarah to Hornar, Alexander
May  8 1804 Martain, Eve to Barnder, Daniel
Apr 13 1794 Martena, Christena to Buckey, Peter
```

```
Nov  7 1791 Martheny, Wm. to Eastburn, Uness
Oct 24 1810 Martin, Barbara to Titlow, Thomas
Apr 18 1808 Martin, Catherine to Ott, Frederick
Feb 18 1807 Martin, Charlotte to Jones, Thomas
Jun 15 1795 Martin, Christena to Brandenburg, William
Mar 28 1807 Martin, Christena to Ludy, Peter
Sep 26 1807 Martin, Christian to Whilhite, Magdalene
Dec  1 1789 Martin, David to Reible, Catherine
Jun 11 1808 Martin, Elizabeth to Conner, Thomas
Mar 18 1791 Martin, Elizabeth to Kile, Adam
Aug 20 1807 Martin, Elizabeth to Touvell, Robert
Apr 15 1798 Martin, George to Davis, Elizabeth
Jan 18 1783 Martin, Jacob to Tabler, Elizabeth
Oct 28 1799 Martin, Jacob to Koontz, Catherine
Nov 28 1809 Martin, Jacob, Junr. to Rohr, Sophia
Sep 19 1795 Martin, John to Rinehart, Peggy
Feb 20 1799 Martin, John to Corell, Elizabeth
Aug 11 1806 Martin, John to Shaneholtz, Catherine
Nov 23 1804 Martin, Mary to Frasier, Henry
Mar 22 1806 Martin, Mary to Munde, Thaddeus
Dec 13 1808 Martin, Mary to Toms, John
Jun  2 1796 Martin, Peter to Ramey, Lydia
Jan 12 1801 Martin, Robert to Norris, Sarah
May 12 1800 Martz, Catherine to Lefaver, John
Aug 21 1809 Martz, George to Reese, Catherine
Nov  9 1783 Martz, Peter to Shroiner, Eliz'th
Oct 26 1785 Martz, Peter to Horine, Mary
Aug 23 1809 Martzen, Christena to Everding, Christian
Nov 30 1793 Mason, Archibald to Conner, Mary
Jun 25 1796 Mason, Martin to Leonard, Margaret
May 22 1800 Mason, Thomas to Shultz, Susanna
Oct 19 1808 Masoncup, George to Stanley, Elizbeth
Jun  4 1801 Massey, Samuel to Farnsworth, Catherine
Aug 13 1791 Mathern, Philip Nich's to Thomas, Barbara
Mar 28 1793 Mathers, Tho to Cummings, Elizabeth
Apr 20 1794 Mathews, Jacob to Struble, Sophia
Dec 14 1798 Mathews, Jacob to Boyds, Mary
Mar 10 1781 Mathews, Margaret to Kemp, Henry
Oct 17 1778 Mathews, Martha to Brayn, Joseph
Mar 30 1795 Mathews, Mary to Crawl, Isaac
Jul 22 1789 Matthers, Sarah to Mohler, Jacob
Jul 31 1809 Matthews, David to Burkhart, Magdalen
Dec 20 1803 Matthews, Edward to Stoner, Mary
Jan 21 1793 Matthews, Elizabeth to Holman, Adam
Jul 22 1803 Matthews, Hannah to Deavers, Joshua
Oct  8 1799 Matthews, Jacob to Lowman, Susannah
Oct 14 1803 Matthews, Magdalena to Favorite, George
Apr  2 1810 Matthews, Margaret to Deaver, Abraham
Feb  6 1795 Matthews, Peter to Harris, Mary
Mar 17 1779 Matthews, Wm. to Burchell, Catherine
Dec 20 1806 Matthias, Griffith to Huffard, Susanna
Apr  2 1808 Mattingly, Gabriel J. to Norris, Elizabeth
Mar  3 1802 Mattingly, Samuel to Durbin, Elinder
Dec 12 1805 Mattox, George to Lett, Pamela
Oct 15 1804 Mawgins, Barbara to Myers, John H.
```

```
Dec  2 1803 Maxfield, Anne to Barton, Nicholas
May 21 1810 Maxfield, Jernsey to McCutchen, Jesse
Aug 13 1808 Maxwell, Hetty to Philips, Solomon
Oct 24 1786 Maxwell, Thomas to Stickle, Mary
Oct 10 1791 Mayberry, Jesse to Houser, Mary
Jul 21 1810 Mayer, Caesar to Ferret, Margaret
Dec 11 1806 Mayers, James to Eiler, Susannah
Jul 20 1808 Maygers, Jerusha to Williams, Benjamin
Feb 15 1803 Mayhew, Matthew to Patten, Anne
Sep 12 1807 Mayhue, Mary to Gray, John
Nov 30 1807 Mayhue, Zedock to Cutshall, Eve
Sep 15 1801 Maynard, Ann to Pumphrey, Vachel
Nov 16 1807 Maynard, Brice to Hobbs, Elizabeth
Feb  6 1801 Maynard, Catherine to Maynard, Ephraim
Feb  6 1801 Maynard, Ephraim to Maynard, Catherine
Dec 13 1788 Maynard, Henry to Howard, Eleanor
May 20 1778 Maynard, Mary to Linton, Zachariah
Dec  9 1797 Maynard, Mary Ann to Welch, James
May 18 1804 Maynard, Nathan to Hobbs, Eliza
Dec 19 1788 Maynard, Rachel to Davis, Mathias
Oct 16 1787 Maynard, Sarah to Nelson, Basil
Apr 19 1809 McAlister, William to Slaymaker, Elizabeth
Dec 29 1778 McAtee, Catherine to Calhoon, James
Mar 19 1794 McAtee, Chloe to Howard, Elisha
Mar 17 1787 McAtee, Francis, X. to Reeder, Mary
Mar  2 1799 McAtee, George to Hardy, Mary
Jan  6 1800 McAtee, Helan to Bucey, John Bean
Jan 17 1798 McAtee, Ignatius to Magruder, Mary
Oct 17 1795 McAtee, Thomas to Bradey, Jane
Aug 30 1804 McBride, Edward to Thompson, Elizabeth
Sep 25 1780 McCain, Wm. to McDonnaugh, Mary
May 16 1809 McCann, Thos. to Norris, Elizabeth
Mar 23 1810 McCannon, Mary to Colegate, George
Jun 26 1783 McCay, Mary to Boyd, Andrew
Mar 12 1790 McClain, Ann to Fye, Joseph
Jul  1 1786 McClain, Comfort to Chillcoal, Benjamin
Mar  2 1791 McClain, Daniel to Mosteller, Anna
Jul  1 1783 Mcclain, Elizabeth to Heck, Daniel
Aug  4 1783 McClain, John to Yates, Eliz'th
Nov  3 1796 McClain, Joshua to Bennet, Elizabeth
Apr 15 1784 McClain, Mary to Hoffman, Jacob
Jan 24 1809 McClain, Sarah to Wilyard, John
Sep 23 1786 McClain, Susan to Hinton, John
Apr 30 1790 McClain, William to Brishe, Mary
Apr 25 1809 McClanihan, Michael to McCleery, Susanna
Apr 17 1806 McClay, John to Ward, Lydia
Feb 27 1810 McCleery, Elizabeth to Rodrock, John
Dec  8 1804 McCleery, Mary to Knight, James
Apr 25 1809 McCleery, Susanna to McClanihan, Michael
Dec 26 1803 McClelland, John to Miller, Mary
Jul 28 1790 McCloskey, James to Riggs, Henrietta
Dec 27 1778 McCollom, David to Crips, Mary
Apr 18 1785 Mccomsey, Robert to Warner, Catharine
May  5 1800 McCormack, John to Harvey, Elizabeth
Jun 14 1788 McCormick, James to Moore, Nancy
```

```
May 24 1800 McCoune, Sarah to Hill, Abraham
Dec 31 1803 McCoy, Zephaniah to Carrins, Elinder
Nov  4 1784 McCracken, John to Wood, Elizabeth
Mar 11 1809 McCraft, Mary to Kitzmiller, Martin
Feb  1 1792 McCrea, William to Thompson, Elizabeth
Feb  9 1807 McCue, John to McKean, Rosanna
Nov 24 1808 McCurdy, James to More, Martha
Dec 19 1782 McCusey, John to Simpson, Sarah
May 21 1810 McCutchen, Jesse to Maxfield, Jernsey
Mar 25 1796 McDade, Charles to Reed, Elizabeth
Nov 25 1780 McDaid, James to Barnett, Mary
Oct 26 1809 McDanald, James to Huffard, Catharine
Nov 28 1801 McDanel, John to Engle, Margaret
Aug 15 1798 McDaniel, Francis to Hopkins, Elizabeth
Jul 12 1803 McDaniel, Jonathan to Powhorn, Mary
Jan 21 1809 McDaniel, Rachel to Evers, David
Nov  6 1810 McDaniel, Sarah to Bailey, William, Jr.
Sep 26 1801 McDaniel, Susanna to Biggs, William
Dec 26 1801 McDaniel, William to Gentles, Elizabeth
Oct 17 1801 McDanold, John to Hilkner, Barbara
Dec 18 1804 McDavid, Daniel to Busey, Rebecca
Feb 18 1802 McDermot, Hugh to Smith, Margaret
Nov 12 1798 McDonald, Ann to Nelson, William
Apr  4 1795 McDonald, Elizabeth to Davis, Jarret
Aug  8 1789 McDonald, Elizabeth to Miller, Conrad
Jul 20 1789 McDonald, Francis to Hamilton, Eleanor
May  8 1780 McDonald, George to Sutherland, Catherine
Oct 10 1799 McDonald, James to Schriner, Elizabeth
Apr 17 1778 McDonald, Joseph to Neill, Anna
Nov 16 1807 McDonald, Margaret to Keiffer, Lewis
Sep  6 1794 McDonald, Mary to Steel, Solomon
Jan 23 1792 McDonald, Sarah to Campbell, Archibald
Aug 20 1796 McDonald, Susanna to Gibbs, John
Aug 24 1778 McDonald, Susanna to Porter, Thomas
Mar 26 1796 McDonald, William to Condon, Elizabeth
Mar 26 1779 Mcdonnah, Sarah to Faris, John
Sep 25 1780 McDonnaugh, Mary to McCain, Wm.
Sep 18 1789 McDonold, Elizabeth to Lindsey, George
May 15 1788 McDougal, Charity to Barnes, Vachel
Feb 22 1781 McElfish, Philip to Griffith, Lidia
Sep  9 1805 McElfresh, Anne to Hall, Nicholas
Mar  4 1808 McElfresh, Caleb to Shipley, Elizabeth Owings
Nov 25 1789 McElfresh, Charles to Smith, Ann
Feb 10 1809 McElfresh, Charles to Pitts, Elizabeth
Dec 13 1779 McElfresh, David to Nellson, Lucey
Oct  6 1809 McElfresh, Elizabeth Smith to Linthicum, Frederick
Aug  9 1805 McElfresh, George to Jordan, Linday
Mar 17 1780 McElfresh, John to Cumming, Jane
Feb 14 1805 McElfresh, John of John to Hall, Eleanor
May  4 1778 McElfresh, John, Jr. to Dorsey, Rachel
Jan 19 1792 McElfresh, Joseph to Howard, Sarah
Jun  6 1785 McElfresh, Lucretia to Longsworth, Solomon
Apr  4 1792 McElfresh, Rachel to Smith, John
Dec 13 1802 McElfresh, William to Linthicum, Sarah
Feb  9 1793 McElroy, Patrick to Thompson, Prisey
```

```
Dec 25 1801 McElroy, Priscilla to Cobeth, John
Feb 10 1793 McEntire, Alexander to Chamberlane, Nanny
Apr 21 1800 McFarland, Arthur to Pittenger, Magdalen
Nov 25 1809 McFarlin, Nancy to Fink, John
Dec  1 1797 McGaghey, Mary to Gump, John
Dec  3 1778 McGalvain, John to McKinley, Eliz'th
Apr 16 1796 McGarey, Barnabas to McGary, Mary
Dec  8 1804 McGarey, William to Daley, Nancy
Apr 16 1796 McGary, Mary to McGarey, Barnabas
Nov 24 1806 McGaughey, James to Greer, Anne
Oct  7 1806 McGee, James to Little, Mary
Jan 11 1798 McGeihan, Elizabeth to Marshall, Samuel
Jan 28 1786 McGill, Ann to Williams, Walter
Jun  9 1789 McGill, Eleanor to Thomas, John
Nov 28 1789 McGill, Patrick to West, Eleanor
Dec 30 1786 McGill, Sarah to West, Thomas
Sep 11 1804 McGinniss, Robert to Hope, Rachel
Apr  5 1798 McGlatherg, Elizabeth to Moller, Adolph
Jun 15 1779 McGowan, Sam'l to Griffey, Agnes
Oct 27 1810 McGowan, Terance to Baltzell, Margaret
Nov 23 1802 Mcguffin, Jane to Balding, John
Oct 13 1800 McGuffin, Jane to Riley, Edward
Nov  1 1796 McGuigan, Arthur to Good, Elizabeth
Sep  1 1797 McGuire, John to Rickard, Mary
Dec  2 1798 McGuyre, John to Shoff, Hanner
Aug 29 1791 Mchaffes, Jennet to Wells, James
Aug 18 1807 McHenry, Anne to Cooper, James
Nov 23 1798 McHenry, Eleanor to Felton, John
Sep 12 1794 McIntire, Daniel to Weaver, Margaret
Jan 19 1792 McIntire, John to Dunkin, Mary
Jul  2 1810 McIntire, Sarah to Bigham, John
Jul 18 1795 McIntosh, Michael to Hickman, Elizabeth
Mar 21 1801 McKaleb, John to Clingan, Mary A. G.
Apr  8 1785 McKardile, Isaac to De Coine, Sarah
Oct 23 1790 McKay, Ann to Shaw, Hugh
Jan 13 1797 McKay, Benj'n to Briscoe, Rebeckah
Feb 14 1791 McKay, Margery to Gun, Alexander
Aug 19 1782 McKean, Eleanor to Culbertson, Samuel
Feb  9 1807 McKean, Rosanna to McCue, John
Jan  4 1802 McKean, William to Currens, Anne
Nov 17 1806 McKenzie, Eleanor to Weaver, Daniel
Jan  7 1792 McKeough, Patrick to Collins, Elizabeth
Oct  1 1806 McKesson, James to Finley, Maria
Dec  3 1778 McKinley, Eliz'th to McGalvain, John
Feb 28 1780 McKinley, Margaret to Frizzle, Jacob
May 27 1809 McKinley, William to Hoffman, Christena
Nov  2 1808 McKinney, Charles to Saffron, Mary
May 25 1805 McKinnock, Letitia to White, Joseph
Oct  8 1800 McKinzie, Henry to Johnson, Sarah
Apr 22 1809 McKissock, Anne to Shields, William
Aug  3 1793 McKiver, Dan to Ramsey, Sarah
Nov 19 1810 McKomsey, Polly to Metcalfe, John P.
Feb 24 1808 McLaughlin, Michael to Kelly, Priscilla
Sep 24 1796 McLaughlin, Sarah to Hargant, John
Feb 28 1795 McLure, Margaretta to Rutter, Edward Hanson
```

```
Dec  4 1802 McMickim, Martha to Coomes, Joseph
Apr 16 1808 McMillan, Samuel to Wright, Mary Ann
Mar  3 1785 McMinn, George to Campbell, Sarah
Apr 25 1807 McMullen, Susanna to Curfman, Peter
Mar  7 1810 McMullen, William to Bevington, Betsy
Oct 23 1802 McNair, John to Musgrove, Sarah
Mar 20 1799 McNair, Margaret to Bigham, Thomas
Oct 19 1786 McNeale, Archibald to Whitmore, Sarah
Apr  7 1809 McPake, Mary to Wells, James
Dec  6 1804 McPherson, Harriot to Brien, John
Sep 11 1783 McPherson, John, Mr. to Smith, Sarah, Miss
Sep  7 1786 McSherry, Catherine to Cole, Richard
Apr 15 1809 McVicker, Sarah to Baughman, Adam
Nov  2 1807 McVicker, Sarah to Jarboe, Francis
Feb 19 1793 McWilliams, John to Hagan, Elizabeth
Nov 28 1807 McWilliams, Ruth to Moser, John
May 17 1806 Mealy, Michael to Merryman, Elizabeth
Apr 19 1809 Mealy, William to Banister, Tena
Apr 24 1800 Means, Anne to Vandivender, Isaac
Jun 11 1794 Measel, Frederick, Junior to Fry, Rosanna
May 13 1803 Measel, Mary Ann to Warnfelts, Jacob
Aug  5 1780 Measell, Jacob to Boogher, Elleanor
Nov 29 1798 Medcalfe, Elizabeth to Werner, William
Aug 15 1801 Meddert, Mary to Baltzell, Jacob
Nov 18 1788 Medtert, Catherine to Isenberger, Henry
Mar 20 1792 Meek, Christiopher to Summers, Betsey
Feb  2 1786 Meek, Sarah to Evans, James
Feb  7 1786 Meelhouse, John to Taylor, Polly
Jun 29 1793 Meloy, John to Decker, Anna
Jan 12 1788 Melvin, Elizabeth to Rice, Joseph
May 19 1808 Menchy, David to Norris, Mary
Jul 10 1801 Mendenall, Agnes to Nadenbousch, Philip
May  4 1807 Menser, Sarah to Sheffer, Philip
May 26 1807 Merchant, Charles to Columber, Mary
Dec 15 1808 Merchant, Mary to Vanhorn, Dennis
May 27 1784 Meredith, Hannah to Ellis, Thomas
Apr 15 1793 Meredith, Lyda to Adams, James
Oct 11 1785 Meredith, Mary to Webb, William
Aug 19 1790 Meredith, Norris to Norris, Mary
Sep 28 1798 Meredith, Thomas to Welch, Ruth
Feb  9 1797 Merick, John to Stears, Polly
Apr 15 1810 Merriwether, Louisa to Linthicum, Charles Griffith
May 17 1806 Merryman, Elizabeth to Mealy, Michael
May 15 1810 Merryman, Polly to Reesler, Jacob
Nov 27 1790 Merstiller, Rebecka to Lindsey, Alexander
Jul 19 1793 Messer, John to Werner, Mary
Nov 26 1778 Messer, Wm. to Fenton, Eleanor
Dec 17 1801 Messerly, George to Shafer, Mary
Dec 21 1789 Messing, Christian to Nagle, Sophia
May 31 1808 Messler, John to Wilson, Susanna
Aug 10 1805 Messler, Mary to Farquhar, William P.
Mar 14 1801 Messler, William to Sleek, Elizabeth
May 10 1808 Metcalf, Hannah to Boyer, Thomas
Nov 19 1810 Metcalfe, John P. to McKomsey, Polly
Mar 28 1794 Metcalfe, Thomas to Hodgkiss, Rachel
```

```
Nov 19 1810 Metcalfe, Thomas to Hytchew, Mary
Aug 27 1779 Methard, Catherine to Robinson, Edw'd
Apr 24 1804 Mettart, Margaret to Ruth, Henry
Aug 31 1796 Metz, Catherine to Highfield, John
Apr 13 1805 Metz, Maria Elizabeth to Hull, James
Dec 23 1797 Metz, Mary to Sintz, Adam
Sep 17 1810 Metzger, Louisa to Pancoast, Samuel
Sep 13 1806 Metzger, Rebeccah to Eaton, Isaac
Jul 21 1804 Metzger, Susanna to Tritt, Christian
Apr  8 1797 Meyer, Margaret to Weltzheimer, Lewis
Feb 18 1779 Meyers, Frederick to Fine, Mary
Jun  2 1792 Michael, Adam to Gisebert, Susanna
Oct 31 1800 Michael, Andrew to Gizebert, Jane
May 14 1785 Michael, Cath. to Lott, Jacob
Jun  6 1794 Michael, Catharine to Clinton, Thomas
Nov  3 1803 Michael, Catherine to Gisebert, Jonathan
Oct 24 1808 Michael, Christopher to Grigg, Phebe
Apr 18 1807 Michael, Elizabeth to Delauder, Jacob
Aug 26 1795 Michael, Elizabeth to Giesbert, Daniel
Jun 18 1805 Michael, George to Eibert, Catherine
Nov 10 1809 Michael, Henry to Carnan, Polly
Mar  7 1798 Michael, Jacob to Giestbert, Sarah
Apr 23 1801 Michael, Jacob to Brandenburgh, Mary
Aug 18 1810 Michael, Jacob to Ramsberg, Susanna
Mar  2 1803 Michael, John to Jefferson, Deborah
Dec 20 1806 Michael, Maryan to Hempy, Peter
Jul 27 1798 Michael, Sarah to Stottlemier, John
Apr 16 1783 Michael, William to Peckenbaugh, Barbara
Dec 18 1798 Michael, William to Razor, Margaret
Aug 21 1809 Michael, William to Shank, Elizabeth
Nov 23 1795 Mick, John to Grover, Priscilla
Apr  3 1779 Middagh, Mary to King, Charles
Apr 12 1806 Mierhaffer, John to Gruber, Elizabeth
Nov 15 1809 Miles, Greenberry to Benson, Elizabeth
Mar 15 1808 Miles, Seneath to Nelson, Elisha
Nov 22 1792 Millan, Ann to Reid, John
Jul 18 1780 Miller, Andrew to Foutz, Rachel
Oct 30 1799 Miller, Ann to Vennals, Richard
Jul 18 1795 Miller, Ann Mary to Shook, Walter
Dec 17 1808 Miller, Anne to Litert, Henry
Jun 19 1790 Miller, Barbara to Copenhaver, John
May 28 1778 Miller, Catharine to Johnson, Joseph
Oct 17 1795 Miller, Catharine to Lear, Fred'k
May  5 1778 Miller, Catharine to Norris, Samuel
Sep  5 1786 Miller, Catherine to Becker, Henry, Jr.
Nov 20 1798 Miller, Catherine to Leatherman, John
May 29 1802 Miller, Charlotte to Myers, John
Oct  3 1791 Miller, Christian to Wissinger, Elizabeth
Nov  8 1810 Miller, Christian G. to Conradt, Magdalane
Mar 19 1802 Miller, Christopher to Grove, Catharine
Aug  8 1789 Miller, Conrad to McDonald, Elizabeth
Apr 23 1778 Miller, David to Heffner, Catherine
Jun 14 1791 Miller, Dewalt to Hansey, Eleanor
Sep 19 1805 Miller, Eleanor to Crum, John
Nov 20 1810 Miller, Elizabeth to Gregory, Henry
```

```
Apr 26 1800 Miller, Elizabeth to Keever, Henry
May 17 1796 Miller, Elizabeth to Lighty, John
Oct 27 1782 Miller, Elizabeth to Mantz, David
Feb  7 1804 Miller, Elizabeth to Nicholson, Francis
Dec 22 1799 Miller, Elizabeth to Paxton, Thomas
Jun  9 1808 Miller, Elizabeth to Ridenour, Adam
Apr 23 1787 Miller, Elizabeth to Ramsbergh, John of Adam
Mar  2 1800 Miller, Elizabeth to Thompson, Robert
Feb  3 1794 Miller, Elizbeth to Reed, Alexander
Aug  9 1797 Miller, Esther to Robertson, Dan'l
Dec  7 1797 Miller, Eve to Kulp, William
Feb 22 1787 Miller, George to Englebricht, Cathe.
May 23 1808 Miller, George to Shafer, Mary
Dec  7 1802 Miller, Hannah to Young, Henry
Feb 22 1800 Miller, Henry to Derr, Susanna
Oct  8 1778 Miller, Jacob to Dentlinger, Margaret
Nov 13 1779 Miller, Jacob to Long, Uliana
Mar  9 1782 Miller, Jacob to Morningstar, Rosanna
Nov 20 1787 Miller, Jacob to Walter, Catherine
Jan 25 1800 Miller, Jacob to Rice, Ann
Aug 28 1802 Miller, Jacob to Storm, Margaret
Mar 18 1807 Miller, Jacob to Fluke, Catherine
Jul 19 1808 Miller, Jacob to Johnson, Elizabeth
Oct  3 1786 Miller, John to Street, Elizabeth
Feb 11 1787 Miller, John to Barnhart, Catherine
Apr 27 1789 Miller, John to Gunn, Christena
Jun 18 1791 Miller, John to Vanferson, Mary
Mar 24 1792 Miller, John to Kemp, Susanna
Nov  3 1795 Miller, John of Dan. to Foutz, Magdalen
Dec  8 1801 Miller, John Samuel to Crist, Margaret
Dec  7 1802 Miller, Jonathan to Neitich, Mary
Mar 23 1798 Miller, Joshua to Plummer, Deborah
Mar  5 1802 Miller, Leonard to Main, Charity
Feb 21 1807 Miller, Ludwick Lewis to Hensey, Patsy
May 24 1800 Miller, Magdalen to Johnson, William
Mar 14 1801 Miller, Margaret to Kemp David
Mar 27 1807 Miller, Margaret to Robinson, Alexander
Feb  8 1806 Miller, Mary to Crum, John
Dec 26 1803 Miller, Mary to McClelland, John
Apr 15 1807 Miller, Mary to Olden, William
Jul 18 1784 Miller, Mary to Wizart, John
Nov 10 1798 Miller, May to Bier, Philip, Jun.
Apr 19 1806 Miller, Nancy to Green, John
Oct 18 1781 Miller, Nicholas to Musgrove, Mary
Apr  7 1806 Miller, Peter to Dillaplane, Margaret
Mar 16 1802 Miller, Polly to Lutz, John
Aug 17 1805 Miller, Polly to Musselman, David
Jan 18 1779 Miller, Rachel to Smith, William
Jan 23 1793 Miller, Robert to Highfield, Mary
Sep 28 1809 Miller, Sarah to Robison, James
Sep 18 1802 Miller, Solomon to Brown, Rosini
Dec 10 1791 Miller, Susanna to Hutzell, Michael
May 19 1794 Miller, Susanna to Kemp, Henry
Dec 22 1806 Miller, Thomas to Gregrory, Mary
Sep 19 1808 Millhouse, Margaret to Lyda, Jacob
```

```
Jun 25 1795 Mills, Andrew to Stofell, Catherine
Mar  8 1786 Mills, Mary to Naylor, Alexander
Oct 16 1781 Mills, Richard to Keller, Mary
Oct 30 1783 Ming, Margaret to Ebert, John
Nov 17 1807 Minghini, Joseph to Head, Mary
Mar 18 1797 Minnick, George to Foutch, Mary
Dec 25 1794 Minor, Ann to Hurst, William
Nov 29 1796 Minor, John to Kale, Mary
Aug 28 1805 Mitchel, John to Shacklett, Elizabeth
Nov 26 1799 Mitchell, Alexander to Scott, Elizabeth
Jul 22 1799 Mitchell, Ann to Stouffer, Henry
Feb 17 1807 Mitchell, Cassandra to Gittings, James
Oct  2 1805 Mitchell, Dinah to Booth, Edward
Mar 26 1802 Mitchell, Elizabeth to Painter, William
May 24 1806 Mitchell, Ignatius to Kohlenberg, Caroline
Feb 10 1793 Mitchell, Theodore to Gittinger, Cabey
Apr  7 1800 Mobberley, Elizabeth to Richardson, Samuel P.
Nov 20 1788 Mobley, Edward to Griffith, Rachel
Oct 26 1802 Mobley, Harriett to Andrews, Charles
Nov 23 1780 Mobley, Lewis to Dorsey, Trusilla
Oct  5 1802 Mobley, Sinah to Brewer, John
Dec 12 1805 Moch, Catherine to Roads, George
Apr  7 1781 Mock (Moek?), Mary Eve to Everhart, Martin
Jun 15 1800 Mock, Jacob to Rawlings, Elizabeth
Jan 28 1797 Mockabee, Ann to Barber, Samuel
Dec 25 1798 Mockabee, Priscilla to Holland, Zadock
Feb 14 1780 Mockaboy, Elizabeth to Philpott, Charles Thomas
Jul 30 1804 Moderd, Susanna to Gabler, Gotlip
Aug  7 1783 Moffett, John to Curtis, Susanna
Jul 22 1789 Mohler, Jacob to Matthers, Sarah
Feb  1 1806 Moldsworth, George to Becraft, Catherine
Jan 26 1805 Molen, Barton to Penn, Rhody
Jan  8 1803 Moler, Margaret to Schnertzel, George
Jul 23 1800 Moler, Margaret to Sprigg, William
Aug 22 1807 Molesworth, Samuel to Hall, Rachel
Apr  5 1798 Moller, Adolph to McGlatherg, Elizabeth
Mar  9 1780 Molley, Mary to Jemison, Charles
Apr 10 1795 Molton, Wilfred to Davis, Frances Brown
Apr 15 1797 Mong, Margaret to Crist, Peter
May 28 1801 Montgomery, Alexander to Lemmon, Eve
Apr 10 1792 Montgomery, Jno. to Sedwick, Joshan
Oct 29 1808 Monticu, Samuel to Isentrager, Rachel
Nov 16 1801 Moody, James to Row, Catherine
Jun 25 1785 Moon, Eve to Biggs, Jacob
Dec  8 1803 Moor, Abner to Trout, Mary
Mar 26 1805 Moor, William to Gilbert, Polly
Dec 22 1804 Moore, Christian to Leatherwood, Mary
Apr 11 1804 Moore, Elizabeth to Haynes, Daniel
May 24 1810 Moore, Jane to Emmitt, Abm. J.
Mar 14 1796 Moore, Jane to Farquhar, Amos
May 28 1803 Moore, John to Hall, Susanna
May 28 1803 Moore, John to Hall, Susanna
Oct 31 1798 Moore, Mary to Yandes, George
Jun 14 1788 Moore, Nancy to McCormick, James
Mar 23 1784 Moore, Sarah to Farquhar, James
```

| | | | |
|---|---|---|---|
| Nov | 22 | 1798 | Moore, Susy to Gruber, David |
| Mar | 10 | 1789 | Moore, William to Young, Jane |
| Mar | 20 | 1779 | Moore, Wm. to Grimes, Catherine |
| Nov | 4 | 1788 | Moore, Zachariah to Bourne, Alice |
| Aug | 10 | 1778 | Moran, Hetty to Maginnis, John |
| Dec | 23 | 1807 | Moran, Robert to Greenwell, Sarah |
| Nov | 24 | 1808 | More, Martha to McCurdy, James |
| Nov | 23 | 1809 | Moren, John to Collins, Mary |
| May | 17 | 1802 | Morgan, Catharine to Arnold, John |
| Aug | 19 | 1794 | Morgan, Dorothy to Wright, William |
| May | 24 | 1788 | Morgan, John to Highler, Susanna |
| Aug | 19 | 1809 | Moriarty, Mary W. to Delashumutt, Trammell |
| Jan | 6 | 1801 | Morley, Ezekiel to Kemp, Margaret |
| Aug | 24 | 1808 | Morningstar, Catherine to Wilhite, Henry |
| Sep | 22 | 1809 | Morningstar, Elizabeth to Dick, Philip |
| Mar | 30 | 1805 | Morningstar, George to Switezer, Elizabeth |
| Aug | 18 | 1809 | Morningstar, John to Ream, Sarah |
| May | 20 | 1803 | Morningstar, Juliana to Furrier, Jacob |
| Apr | 2 | 1803 | Morningstar, Mary to Garver, Christian |
| Nov | 23 | 1781 | Morningstar, Philip to Morningstar, Solema |
| Mar | 9 | 1782 | Morningstar, Rosanna to Miller, Jacob |
| Nov | 23 | 1781 | Morningstar, Solema to Morningstar, Philip |
| Sep | 20 | 1781 | Morningstar, Susanna to Houcks, Mathias |
| Feb | 5 | 1803 | Morphy, Hannah to Ramsberg, John |
| Nov | 25 | 1805 | Morris, Ann Louisa to Dugas, Louis Jean Jacques |
| Jul | 23 | 1810 | Morris, Catharine Precilla to Anderson, Edward H. (Dr.) |
| Jan | 5 | 1784 | Morris, John to Hogg, Catherine |
| Mar | 26 | 1797 | Morris, John to Peck, Ann |
| Mar | 9 | 1782 | Morris, Jonathan to Kimbell, Mary |
| Nov | 8 | 1789 | Morris, Jonathan to Frasier, Mary |
| May | 20 | 1800 | Morris, Kezia to Stoner, Benedict |
| Aug | 27 | 1802 | Morris, Maria to Richard, John Hart |
| Jan | 21 | 1782 | Morris, Mary to Evans, Elijah |
| Oct | 27 | 1788 | Morris, Mary to Goodman, William,Senr. |
| Mar | 21 | 1795 | Morrison, James to Gittings, Cassandra |
| Apr | 3 | 1798 | Morrison, John to Hort, Elizabeth |
| Mar | 24 | 1778 | Morrow, Archebald to Hilton, Margaret |
| Apr | 19 | 1805 | Morrow, James to Hartsock, Sarah |
| Dec | 14 | 1804 | Mortar, Catherine to Frieberger, George |
| Apr | 14 | 1786 | Mortar, Valentine to Ingles, Susanna |
| Dec | 30 | 1806 | Mosburg, Henry to Winbigler, Mary |
| Feb | 6 | 1789 | Moser, Catherine to Ruedecill, Jacob |
| Nov | 28 | 1807 | Moser, John to McWilliams, Ruth |
| Dec | 30 | 1807 | Moss(?), Charles to Madeira, Margaret |
| Sep | 16 | 1805 | Mossberg, Christian to Harrison, Jane |
| Feb | 18 | 1780 | Mosserley, Eliz'th to Garnett, Geo. |
| Mar | 2 | 1791 | Mosteller, Anna to McClain, Daniel |
| May | 31 | 1782 | Motter, Eliz'th to Boyrley, Frederick |
| Sep | 9 | 1806 | Motter, John to Baker, Christina |
| Jul | 2 | 1810 | Motter, Michael to Keller, Catherine |
| Nov | 28 | 1808 | Motter, Sarah to Nusbaum, Henry |
| Jun | 2 | 1778 | Mottis, Peter to Heckathorn, Philapoena |
| Mar | 30 | 1780 | Mottis, Ulianna to Snuke, Peter |
| Sep | 11 | 1806 | Moul, Margaret to Pairpoint, Samuel |
| Dec | 18 | 1796 | Moule, Susanna to Ragan, Andrew |

```
Jul 28 1809 Mouls, Philip to Connard, Polly
Aug 12 1797 Mount, Ann to Linganfelder, John
Jan 17 1809 Mount, George to Barnes, Nancy
May 12 1794 Mount, John to Smith, Margaret
Sep 27 1790 Mowerer, Adam to Win, Magd'l
Nov 26 1794 Moxley, Nehemiah to Norwood, Elizabeth
Aug 25 1783 Moxley, Sam'l to Cox, Agnes
Jul 12 1785 Moyer, Barbara to Shoup, John
Jun  5 1784 Moyer, Elizabeth to Ashman, Henry
Jun  9 1784 Moyer, Elizabeth to Gitzadanner, Jacob
Oct 29 1798 Muckel, Eleanor to Nelson, Peter
Jan 13 1796 Mugg, John to Greenwell, Elizabeth
Nov 14 1778 Mugg, Marg't to Road, George
Oct 24 1808 Mulhorn, Edward R. to Frushour, Barbara
Apr 18 1791 Mullen, John W. to Unglesby, Ann
Jun 12 1802 Mullenax, Eleanor to Clary, Henry
Apr 29 1790 Mullendore, David to Cost, Catherine
Mar 26 1794 Mullidore, Elizabeth to Beeler, George
Nov 16 1789 Mullikin, John to Hamston, Mary
Jun  3 1809 Mullikin, William Beans to Chilton, Ann Mackall
Mar 28 1785 Mullindore, Jacob to Swisher, Susanna
Aug 30 1794 Mullindore, John to Cost, Uhly
Jul 21 1797 Mullinieux, Elizabeth to Bittle, John
Dec  6 1803 Mulvey, Mary to Stover, Philip
Sep 28 1810 Mumford, Elizabeth to Long, Andrew
Mar 20 1792 Mumford, James, Jr. to Fuller, Nancy
Mar  1 1800 Mumford, John to Sellers, Hannah
Mar 25 1790 Mumford, Martha to Leakins, William
Oct 24 1789 Mumford, Mary to Wright, Joseph
Oct 18 1796 Mumford, William to Hartsoke, Catherine
Mar 27 1785 Muncaster, Ann to Stone, Walter Hanson
Mar 22 1806 Munde, Thaddeus to Martin, Mary
Dec 16 1781 Mungin, Rosanna to Noland, Barney
Dec 24 1800 Munlix, Charles to Cramlett, Elizabeth
Feb 20 1792 Munro, Anne to Heugh, John
Jan 31 1781 Munro, Kitty to Luckett, John
Dec  5 1806 Munshoure, John to Smith, Sarah
Dec 19 1799 Murdoch, Eleanor to Potts, Richard, Esq.
Dec 22 1781 Murdock, Benjamin to Margruder, Mary Ann
Oct 19 1809 Murdock, Harriot to Tyler, William B.
May 27 1783 Murdock, William to Harrison, Jane Contee
Apr 21 1810 Murdock, William to Small, Ann
Dec  5 1806 Muret, James to Dowdle, Mary
Feb  9 1782 Murphey, Ann to Hillery, Thomas
Dec 30 1793 Murphey, Drusilla to Norwood, James
Sep  7 1790 Murphey, Duncan to Siars, Prethenia
Feb 13 1792 Murphey, James to Smith, Eleanor
Oct 26 1797 Murphey, Joshua to Peck, Ann
Apr  5 1779 Murphey, Mary to Flower, Thomas
Mar  7 1804 Murphy, George to Lewis, Elizabeth
Apr  3 1790 Murphy, John to Marshall, Grace
Dec  2 1802 Murphy, John to Marks, Peggy
Apr 25 1806 Murphy, Joseph Aquila to White, Elizbeth Smith
Feb 15 1800 Murphy, Lawrence to Staups, Catherine
Dec 23 1801 Murphy, Samuel to Baley, Jane
```

```
Oct 25 1810 Murphy, William to Sands, Elizabeth
Jan 30 1804 Murphy, William, Jr. to Elder, Annie
Dec 29 1788 Murray, Ann to Hains, Nathan
Sep  6 1800 Murray, Joseph to Redman, Ann
May 20 1806 Murray, Rachael to Steiner, Henry
Jan 21 1808 Murray, Solomon to Strong, Elizabeth
Dec 21 1801 Murray, Stephen to Craft, Elizabeth
Mar 10 1797 Murrel, Robert to Lee, Rachael
Mar 11 1797 Murry, Hariette to Brish, Henry
Oct  1 1796 Murry, Honor to Bale, John
Jun  4 1810 Murry, John to Evins, Catherine
Oct 22 1799 Murry, Mary to Shrigly, Enoch
Mar 13 1805 Murry, Nancy to Fir, Miner
Jan 15 1801 Murry, Sarah to Welch, Benjamin
Oct 20 1803 Murry, Stephen to Burall, Catherine
Apr 10 1810 Muse, Nancy to Tinkens, Simon
Jan 13 1801 Museter, John to Williams, Ann
Apr 22 1782 Musgrove, Anthony to Flood, Sarah
Oct  6 1809 Musgrove, Eleanor to Davis, Samuel
Oct 11 1797 Musgrove, Gilbert to Whittington, Dorcas
May 30 1805 Musgrove, Mary to Harrison, William
Oct 18 1781 Musgrove, Mary to Miller, Nicholas
Feb 26 1784 Musgrove, Nathan to Selby, Ann
Nov  7 1780 Musgrove, Sarah to Grover, Jonathan Mason
Oct 23 1802 Musgrove, Sarah to McNair, John
Aug 17 1805 Musselman, David to Miller, Polly
Sep 17 1802 Musseter, Barbara to Harding, Christian
Feb 27 1792 Mussetter, Christian to Sauffer, Regina
Dec 17 1799 Mussetter, Christopher to Ijams, Ruth
Mar 22 1806 Myer, Barbara to Righting, Andrew
Nov 23 1784 Myer, Barbara to Wigle, John
May  8 1784 Myer, Henry to Goodman, Anne
Aug 24 1782 Myer, Jacob to Kirkt, Susannah
Apr 13 1796 Myer, Sam to Need, Catherine
Mar 12 1807 Myers, Adam to Worman, Margaret
Nov 23 1809 Myers, Catharine to Adams, William
Aug 22 1789 Myers, Catherine to Crigloe, William
Aug  9 1809 Myers, Catherine to Gibson, Thomas
Nov  5 1791 Myers, Catherine to Rachel, Daniel
Dec  3 1807 Myers, Charlotte to Bireley, William
Feb 29 1804 Myers, Elizabeth to Dagen, John
Sep  6 1794 Myers, Elizabeth to Hart, Adam
Dec  4 1809 Myers, Elizabeth to Johnson, Francis
Sep 27 1783 Myers, Eve to Shultz, David
Jun 12 1784 Myers, George to Zimmerman, Margaret
Jul 29 1809 Myers, George to Simmons, Elizabeth
Apr  1 1802 Myers, George Frederick to Thomas, Catharine
Jul 12 1796 Myers, Henry to Davis, Ann
Jul  4 1782 Myers, Jacob to Burniston, Rebecca
Oct  8 1785 Myers, Jacob (of Yost) to Beames, Barbara
Sep  5 1782 Myers, John to Adams, Mary Ann
Jan 30 1792 Myers, John to Dehoff, Hannah
Mar 17 1796 Myers, John to Anderson, Ann
May 29 1802 Myers, John to Miller, Charlotte
Oct 15 1804 Myers, John H. to Mawgins, Barbara
```

```
Jan  1 1801 Myers, Jonathan to Pryor, Elizabeth
Apr  3 1798 Myers, Margaret to Hildebrand, John
Sep 20 1786 Myers, Mary to Beam, Jacob
Feb  7 1782 Myers, Mary to Hynes, Philip
Nov 29 1808 Myers, Mary to Iler, Adam
Oct  6 1792 Myers, Mich'l to Fout, Elizabeth
Aug  9 1800 Myers, Peggy to Young, Andrew
Apr  1 1795 Myers, Phebe to Plumley, Oliver
Aug  6 1806 Myers, Samuel to Snyder, Mary
May 25 1809 Myers, Sarah to Albaugh, David
Jul 14 1781 Myers, Susanna to Ely, David
Oct 29 1801 Myers, William to Hanna, Jane
Sep 25 1778 Myler, Matthew to Fowler, Eliz'th
Feb 22 1783 Myrehaver, Peter to Hart, Catherine

Oct 10 1808 Nabb, William to Hamilton, Phebe M.
Jul 10 1801 Nadenbousch, Philip to Mendenall, Agnes
Mar  4 1800 Nagle, Sebastian, Jr. to Shafer, Modelena
Dec 21 1789 Nagle, Sophia to Messing, Christian
May  7 1787 Naile, Henry to Rogers, Mary
Jun  5 1793 Nailor, Jane to Stevens, John
Aug 10 1787 Nave, Catherine to Coogle, Adam
Aug 10 1787 Nave, Catherine to Koogle, Adam
Mar  8 1786 Naylor, Alexander to Mills, Mary
Mar 17 1779 Naylor, Isaac Jones to Goodman, Barbara
Aug 11 1800 Neale, Bernard to Christian, Elizabeth
Mar 22 1802 Neat, Magdalene to Close, Henry
Apr 13 1796 Need, Catherine to Myer, Sam
May  3 1803 Need, Christopher to O'Bryan, Catharine
Feb 16 1798 Need, Elizabeth to Brawner, Thomas, Junr.
May  5 1785 Need, Mary to Rice, Andrew
Oct 30 1797 Neff, Adam to Utt, Elizabeth
Dec 24 1784 Neff, Ann to Nicodemus, John
Dec 10 1796 Neff, Jacob to Getzendanner, Margaret
Feb 15 1798 Neff, John to Harriade, Elizabeth
Dec 27 1793 Negro Betty to Peck, John
Mar 22 1799 Neighbours, Nathan to Price, Sarah
Jul 18 1795 Neighbours, Sarah to Clary, Ashford Dowden
Apr 17 1778 Neill, Anna to McDonald, Joseph
Dec  7 1802 Neitich, Mary to Miller, Jonathan
May 17 1792 Nellson, Elizabeth to Burkitt, Joshua
Apr 24 1779 Nellson, George to Bonham, Jemimah
Dec 24 1779 Nellson, Henry to Poole, Sophia
Dec 13 1779 Nellson, Lucey to McElfresh, David
Jan  6 1810 Nelson, Amos to Williams, Lucy
Aug 18 1792 Nelson, Ann to Brathelow, Michael
Aug 29 1798 Nelson, Ann to Bartholow, Thomas
Oct 16 1787 Nelson, Basil to Maynard, Sarah
Aug  1 1810 Nelson, Betsy to Wintrode, John
Mar 15 1808 Nelson, Elisha to Miles, Seneath
Oct 29 1798 Nelson, Peter to Muckel, Eleanor
Feb 26 1788 Nelson, Roger to Sim, Mary
Feb  2 1797 Nelson, Roger, Capt. to Harrison, Elizabeth, Miss
Nov 12 1798 Nelson, William to McDonald, Ann
Dec 27 1791 Nesmith, Isaac to Johnson, Ann
```

```
Aug  9 1780 Nevin, Eliz'th to Richards, Richard
Jul  2 1802 Newey, Sarah to King, William
Dec 31 1791 Newhouse, John to Connelly, Ann Statia
Oct 14 1809 Newman, George to Powell, Susanna
Sep 16 1802 Newman, Joshua to Collins, Eleanor
Dec 29 1799 Newman, Stacey to Davis, Sarah
May 24 1806 Newons, Thomas to Knouff, Mary M.
Mar 21 1804 Nicewanger, Christian to Tucker, Leah
Aug 19 1785 Nicewarner, Barbara to Burnee, Thomas
Dec 21 1780 Nicewonger, John to Noffsinger, Ann
Oct  7 1802 Nichodemus, Rachel to Lyster, David
Jan  2 1802 Nicholls, Benjamin to Lowry, Susanna
Mar 26 1779 Nicholls, Casse to Cash, Wm.
May 13 1780 Nicholls, Charlotte to Depos, Jacob
Jan 26 1782 Nicholls, Elizabeth to Hilton, Wm.
Jun 18 1788 Nicholls, Elizabeth to Whip, Peter
Oct 20 1791 Nicholls, Elizabeth to Leeply, George
May 14 1807 Nicholls, Henry to Brish, Sophia
Jan 11 1785 Nicholls, James to Ips, Sarah
Feb 26 1787 Nicholls, James to James, Ann
Nov 28 1785 Nicholls, John Haymond to Wilcoxon, Cassandra
Mar  1 1780 Nicholls, Margaret to Cartey, Thomas
Nov 14 1796 Nicholls, Mary to Evans, Eleazer
Jan 24 1804 Nicholls, Pheby to Benton, Thomas
Sep  8 1785 Nicholls, William to Offutt, Charity
Dec  3 1806 Nichols, Barbara to Jefferson, Leonard
Aug  1 1806 Nichols, Elizabeth to Johnson, Thomas
Oct 13 1803 Nichols, Jacob to Hatcher, Margaret
Oct 15 1801 Nichols, Nancy to Russell, John
Dec 31 1803 Nichols, Peter to Evit, Mary
Nov  4 1789 Nicholson, Ann to Mace, John
Aug  1 1798 Nicholson, Elizabeth to Marater, John
Feb  7 1804 Nicholson, Francis to Miller, Elizabeth
Dec  3 1803 Nicholson, Margaret to Tinson, William
May 26 1803 Nickam, Peter to Young, Elizabeth
Oct 31 1797 Nickey, Sarah to Switser, Lawrence
Oct 26 1809 Nicodemus, Andrew to Cassel, Rachel
Dec  7 1810 Nicodemus, Henry to Cassell, Catherine
Dec 24 1784 Nicodemus, John to Neff, Ann
Jun 25 1796 Niehoff, John Daniel to Ramsberg, Catherine
May 19 1795 Niehoof, Balser to Groce, Cathe. Eliza.
Jan  8 1793 Niehoof, Nicholas to Yowler, Eva
Mar 26 1810 Nigh, John to Yoncum, Barbara
Dec 23 1797 Night, Mary to Beck, Jeremiah
Jun 27 1807 Niswanger, Elizabeth to Hardman, Martin
Jun  5 1802 Niswanger, Mary to Drill, Jacob
Nov 12 1807 Nixdorff, Mary to Gelwicks, George C.
Jul 11 1795 Nixendorff, Catherine to Cook, John
Jan 17 1804 Nixendorff, Susanna to Waltz, George
Jan  5 1801 Nixon, Ann to Gardner, Malon
Dec 20 1809 Nixon, Jonathan to Savidge, Elizabeth
Sep 13 1799 Nixon, Rebecca to Bravo, Jacob
Oct 19 1778 Noble, Mary to Richardson, John
Dec 21 1780 Noffsinger, Ann to Nicewonger, John
Aug  1 1808 Nokes, Gilbert to Beamer, Margaret
```

```
Dec 16 1781 Noland, Barney to Mungin, Rosanna
Jan 18 1791 Noland, Bernard to Beall, Elizabeth
Aug 23 1798 Noland, Gregary to Dowdle, Elizabeth
Jul 21 1787 Noland, John to Watkins, Ann
Apr 18 1786 Noland, Michael to Sickman, Mary
Aug  5 1805 Noland, Polly to Harwood, Thomas N.
Nov 12 1785 Nollert, Margaret to Teal, Henry
Dec 11 1785 Norman, Charity to Scurlock, William
Nov  8 1784 Norris, Abrillea to Coe, Jesse
Sep  6 1785 Norris, Barbara to Kemp, Ludwick
Jun  1 1790 Norris, Barnabas to Oatner, Barbara
Mar  2 1804 Norris, Catharine to Umstadt, David
Mar  1 1806 Norris, Catherine to Deleplane, Daniel
Jan  7 1801 Norris, Catherine to Kemp, Daniel
Feb 11 1789 Norris, Charlotte to Hays, Richard
Oct 30 1797 Norris, Eleanor to Raitt, Hammond
Aug  4 1810 Norris, Elizabeth to Davis, Isaac
Apr  2 1808 Norris, Elizabeth to Mattingly, Gabriel J.
Mar 24 1803 Norris, Elizabeth to Mantz, Isaac
May 16 1809 Norris, Elizabeth to McCann, Thos.
Apr 14 1796 Norris, George to Talbot, Eleanor
Jan 13 1784 Norris, John to Norris, Rachel
Mar 18 1795 Norris, John to Rigdon, Elizabeth
Dec 15 1800 Norris, John to Raitt, Mary
Nov 24 1807 Norris, John to Thomas, Sarah
Jan 26 1808 Norris, John to Harris, Nancy
May 19 1808 Norris, Mary to Menchy, David
Aug 19 1790 Norris, Mary to Meredith, Norris
May  5 1802 Norris, Mary Anne to Hayes, Zachariah
Oct 27 1804 Norris, Otho to Marcus, Elizabeth
Feb 23 1805 Norris, Rachel to Lemmon, Hugh
Jan 13 1784 Norris, Rachel to Norris, John
Dec  8 1810 Norris, Rachel to Smelser, John
May  5 1778 Norris, Samuel to Miller, Catharine
Jan 12 1801 Norris, Sarah to Martin, Robert
May 13 1807 Norris, Tabitha to Starr, Jesse
Oct  2 1797 Norris, Thomas to Irons, Susanna
Oct 31 1809 Norris, Upton to Clary, Susanna
Sep 24 1783 Norris, William to Hayes, Mary
Feb 12 1791 Norris, William to Silver, Elizabeth Margaret
Jul 18 1807 Norris, William to Talbott, Rebecca
Mar 24 1798 Norriss, Elizabeth to Steel, James S.
Oct 12 1790 Northcraft, Elizabeth to Cullom, William
Dec 11 1802 Norwood, Anna to Beall, John Lee
Jan  6 1810 Norwood, Eleanor to Falkner, Elisha
Jan 17 1801 Norwood, Elizabeth to Kinley, Jacob
Nov 26 1794 Norwood, Elizabeth to Moxley, Nehemiah
Dec 30 1793 Norwood, James to Murphey, Drusilla
Apr  7 1787 Norwood, Jemima to Poole, Samuel
Oct  6 1810 Norwood, Joshua to Kemp, Catherine
Jul 12 1793 Norwood, Mary to Fogle, Christian
Dec 20 1783 Norwood, Mary to Poole, John
Nov 23 1798 Norwood, Mary to Smith, Jacob
Sep 15 1802 Norwood, Matilda to Watkins, Joseph
Nov 30 1804 Norwood, Thomas to Hilleary, Sarah
```

```
Jun 20 1801 Noyes, Darkey to Harris, Jesse
Jun 13 1801 Nugent, Henry to Redman, Catherine
Apr 10 1779 Null, Mary to Vanderlin, Nicholas
Apr 28 1800 Nunemaker, George to Hoover, Elizabeth
Mar 30 1802 Nusbaum, Abraham to Burrier, Margaret
Apr  9 1803 Nusbaum, Catherine to Bourrier, Jacob
Aug  4 1810 Nusbaum, Daniel to Sowers, Mary
Feb 21 1792 Nusbaum, David to Waltz, Eve
Aug  6 1806 Nusbaum, David to Steward, Catherine
Nov 28 1808 Nusbaum, Henry to Motter, Sarah
Nov 21 1808 Nusbaum, Jacob to Snyder, Susanna
Jan 11 1804 Nusbaum, John to Burrier, Esther
Sep 11 1807 Nusbaum, Mary to Burrier, Philip
Nov 20 1795 Nusbaum, Mary to Duttero, John
May 10 1810 Nusbaum, Sally to Snyder, Abraham
Oct  7 1797 Nuss, Frederick to Doefler, Caty
Apr 30 1803 Nuss, Mary to Gigar, John
Oct 18 1809 Nussbame, Solomon to Walse, Mary
Apr  3 1809 Nussear, Michael R. to Will, Kitty
Mar 18 1804 Nusz, Henry to Hinkle, Elizabeth
Jan 14 1807 Nusz, Henry to Hollan, Sarah
May 12 1805 Nusz, Mary to Bodall, George
May  2 1809 Nusz, Mich'l to Esther, Elizabeth

Jul  1 1809 O'Bannion, Lydia to Fishbeck, John
Oct 14 1807 O'Boyle, James to Hughes, Rhoda
May  3 1803 O'Bryan, Catharine to Need, Christopher
Oct  9 1790 O'Bryan, Dennis to Perry, Mary Ann
Apr 29 1809 O'Conner, Bernard to Salkeld, Phebe
Aug 26 1809 O'Conner, Bernard to Salkeld, Phebe
Aug 24 1808 O'Connor, Bernard to Keplinger, Catherine
Jan 14 1808 O'Ferral, Catherine to Shroyer, Jacob
Apr  4 1807 O'Flaherty, Michael to Hewlet, Mary
Jan  9 1786 O'Neale, Barton to Dyson, Mary
Apr 16 1803 O'Neale, Elizabeth to Davis, Solomon
Mar 11 1786 O'Neall, Jennet to Cornall, John
Aug 28 1790 O'Nele, Mary to Dyson, John Baptist
Jan  5 1801 Oat, Margaret to Farthing, James
May 11 1799 Oat, Susannah to Shafer, John
Jun  1 1790 Oatner, Barbara to Norris, Barnabas
Feb 16 1790 Oatner, John to Conrad, Elizabeth
Sep 11 1779 Oberfeld, Mathias to Hardman, Anna Maria
Nov 10 1793 Obleman, John to Kephart, Catherine
Jun  1 1805 Oden, Thomas to Lloyd, Elizabeth
Nov 14 1809 Offett, Margaret to Jenkins, Henry
Sep  8 1785 Offutt, Charity to Nicholls, William
Nov  2 1791 Offutt, Jean to Beall, Colmore
Aug 10 1802 Ogbern, Benjamin to Willis, Lydia
May 15 1786 Ogbern, Mary to Robertson, Zachariah
Mar 30 1808 Ogg, William to Arnold, Susanna
Nov 28 1783 Ogle, Alexander to Beatty, Mary
Jan 13 1783 Ogle, Elizabeth to Hobbs, Charles
Apr 14 1783 Ogle, Jane to Linck, Adam
Oct 30 1809 Ogle, Joseph to Valentine, Elizabeth
Mar 10 1804 Ogle, Lydia to Isenberg, Gabriel
```

```
Jan  8 1799 Ogle, Margaret to Ogle, William
Nov  6 1802 Ogle, Margaret to Thomas, Michael
Dec  4 1781 Ogle, Martha to Wood, John
Aug  1 1778 Ogle, Mary to Butler, Joseph
Dec 15 1783 Ogle, Mary to Cock, Sam'l
Nov 11 1803 Ogle, Peter to Stultz, Mary
Jan  4 1794 Ogle, William to Johnson, Susanna
Jan  8 1799 Ogle, William to Ogle, Margaret
Apr 30 1804 Ohler, Barbara to Shaffer, John
Feb  9 1810 Ohler, John to Rife, Catherine
Apr 15 1807 Olden, William to Miller, Mary
Aug  6 1803 Oldwine, Charles to Shrader, Elizabeth
Feb 21 1803 Oler, Catherine to Crabbs, Frederick
Feb 24 1789 Ollex, Elizabeth to Schell, Henry
Jan  6 1787 Ollip, Adam to Foutz, Margaret
Sep  6 1796 Olliser, George to Johnson, Molly
May  8 1785 Ollix, Mary to Cossell, Dan'l
Aug 19 1784 Onion, Ann to Poole, William
Sep 12 1791 Onion, Deborah to Barnes, William
Oct  7 1791 Onion, Rebecca to Ellis, Eliazar
Oct 29 1795 Onions, William to Manakey, Catherine
Jun  2 1800 Oppold, Lewis Benjamin to Usher, Mary
Dec 13 1796 Or, Michael to Sheltnecht, Rosanna
Jan 30 1809 Oram, Anne to Cook, Christian
Oct 10 1783 Orem, Elizabeth to Jumper, Christian
Nov 17 1783 Orendorff, Mary to Hagar, Jonathan
Mar 17 1809 Orputt, Thomas to Prugh, Hannah
Apr 16 1808 Orr, Mary to Stem, Martin
Apr  2 1803 Orr, Thomas to Eutey, Mary
Dec  2 1797 Osborn, Daniel to Coplan, Rebecca
Mar 14 1783 Osborn, David to Bagerly, Sarah
Dec 14 1796 Osborne, Richard to Humphrey, Mary
Aug 25 1781 Ostler, Elizabeth to Penn, Samuel
May 19 1806 Ott, Elizabeth to Dern, Frederick
Apr 18 1808 Ott, Frederick to Martin, Catherine
May  9 1794 Ott, John to Shafer, Mary
Oct 27 1806 Ott, John to Ritchie, Anne
Dec 17 1805 Ott, Mary to Grimes, Elias
Apr 22 1786 Ott, Michael to Wertenbaker, Elizabeth
Sep 16 1801 Ott, Philip to Garnhart, Margaret
May 17 1806 Otto, Catherine to Grimes, Lot
Jun 13 1807 Otto, Elizabeth to Baker, Brooke
May 14 1810 Otto, John to Fleming, Ally
Mar 28 1809 Otto, Margaret to Slick, Jacob
Apr 25 1806 Ourant, Jacob to Crutzley, Dinah
Jan  7 1804 Ourant, John to Hewett, Rachel
Feb 18 1792 Ourey, Samuel to Boyer, Sarah
Jun 12 1779 Ouria, Lidia to Stevens, William
Oct 17 1807 Ovelman, Elizbeth to Loy, Jacob
Feb  1 1805 Ovelman, George to Phillips, Prudence
Nov  2 1799 Overholtz, Mary to White, David
Nov 27 1798 Overholtzer, Elizabeth to Renner, Abraham
Apr 14 1781 Overlast, Barbara to Cronie, Henry
May 27 1793 Overtosh, Mary Elizabeth to Jimeson, Samuel
May 21 1787 Owen, Hezekiah to Duvall, Elizabeth
```

```
Sep  4 1783 Owen, John to Cullom, Abigail
Jun 21 1783 Owen, Rachel to Sutfin, William
Jan  4 1785 Owen, William to Skekell, Frances
Oct  5 1797 Owens, Priscilla to Woodward, Abraham B.
Apr  1 1805 Owing, Robert to Craven, Eleanor
Sep 10 1796 Owings, Archibald to Hays, Priscilla
Dec 16 1795 Owings, Beall to Harrris, Cordelia
Sep  2 1803 Owings, Betsy to Greene, William
Apr 23 1808 Owings, Catherine to Harrison, Alexander C.
Mar 15 1799 Owings, Christopher to Worthington, Charlotte
Nov 15 1806 Owings, Cordelia to Owings, Thomas Beal
Apr  1 1800 Owings, Meranda to Evans, John
Jul 29 1807 Owings, Thomas to Sands, Bersheba
Nov 15 1806 Owings, Thomas Beal to Owings, Cordelia
Feb 13 1798 Owings, Urith to Hobbs, Thomas
Dec 13 1809 Oyler, Frederick to Willyard, Peggy
Nov  1 1799 Oyler, Mary to Fox, Peter

Nov 23 1802 Padget, Elizabeth to Davis, John
Mar 25 1778 Padgett, Benjamin to Green, Ann
Mar 27 1782 Padgett, Elizabeth to Quynn, John
Jun 14 1783 Padgett, Sarah to Perrill, William
Jan 16 1802 Padgett, Susanna to Pepper, Peter
Apr 14 1800 Padgit, William to Fiste, Barbara
Apr  6 1781 Page, Thomas to Willson, Catherine
Mar  4 1780 Pain, Michael to Cartey, Peggy
Oct 27 1798 Paine, Ann to Compton, Joseph
Mar 26 1802 Painter, William to Mitchell, Elizabeth
Sep 11 1806 Pairpoint, Samuel to Moul, Margaret
Apr 11 1805 Palmer, Henry to Sinn, Mary
Feb 20 1804 Palmer, Mary to Eaton, Leonard
Mar 11 1810 Palmer, Rachel to Jackson, James
Jan 24 1781 Pancartson, Mary to Lear, Dan'l
May 17 1803 Pancoast, Caleb to Pope, Mary
Apr 13 1796 Pancoast, Jane to Brayfield, Samuel
Sep 17 1810 Pancoast, Samuel to Metzger, Louisa
Aug 10 1784 Pantz, Maria to Berghman, Christopher
Aug 22 1809 Parason, Sarah to Bauder, Daniel
Mar  8 1805 Parish, James to Fine, Sarah
Apr 15 1790 Parker, Gilbert to Grimes, Susanna
Dec 20 1791 Parker, Hutchison to Mackbee, Sarah Price
Mar 14 1798 Parker, Mary to Harding, Vachel
Dec 15 1787 Parkes, Jane to Leggit, Samuel
Jun 27 1778 Parkinson, John to Leisle, Ann
Jul  3 1799 Parkinson, William to Beatty, Henrietta
Jul 19 1778 Parnell, Bedwell to Easton, Ruth
Apr  5 1796 Parrish, Aquilla to Condon, Eleanor
Oct 17 1800 Parrish, John to Phillips, Margaret
Oct 17 1801 Parrish, Ruth to Barnes, Dorsey
Mar 22 1807 Passey, Catharine to Sellman, John
Feb 28 1795 Patesell, John to Ramsburg, Christena
Dec  5 1808 Patrick, Catherine to Hannis, Joseph
Oct 27 1780 Patrick, Christena to Hilton, Trueman
Feb 15 1803 Patten, Anne to Mayhew, Matthew
Dec  4 1778 Patten, Jane to Rodgers, George
```

```
Sep 11 1784 Patterson, Benjamin to Price, Jemima
Jul 21 1801 Patterson, Elizabeth to Zimmerman, George
Sep  8 1810 Patterson, Jane to Ellis, Samuel
May 20 1800 Patterson, Lilly Ann to Zimmerman, Michael
Feb 17 1810 Patterson, Mary to Dean, Stewart
Dec 17 1806 Patton, George to Marker, Catharine
Jul 20 1797 Paxson, Joseph to Lusty, Mary
Dec 22 1799 Paxton, Thomas to Miller, Elizabeth
Jul 23 1802 Paxton, William to Sellman, Ruth
Dec  3 1794 Peagae, Polly to Dell, John
Jan 29 1798 Peak, John to Barber, Ann
Nov 11 1799 Pearce, Elizabeth to Hawn, Lewis
Sep 22 1801 Pearcy, Elizabeth to Sellman, Peter
Apr 13 1799 Pearl, James to Adkins, Priscilla
Dec 30 1779 Pearl, Susanna to Marshall, Alex'dr
Aug 11 1783 Pearpoint, Sarah to House, Caleb
Jan  4 1791 Pearre, Alexander to Brashears, Tabitha
Mar  1 1793 Pearrie, Eleanor to Arnold, David
Nov 15 1786 Pebble, Abraham to Waggoner, Elizabeth
Jun 15 1778 Pebble, Peter to Cepharton, Mary
Mar 26 1797 Peck, Ann to Morris, John
Oct 26 1797 Peck, Ann to Murphey, Joshua
Jan 13 1797 Peck, David to Clark, Elizabeth
Dec 27 1793 Peck, John to Negro Betty
May 11 1783 Peck, Rosanna to Thomas, George
Jul  2 1796 Peck, Thomas to Williams, Kitty
Sep 12 1796 Peck, William to Glasscock, Susanna
Apr 16 1783 Peckenbaugh, Barbara to Michael, William
Jul 19 1778 Peckenbaugh, Mary to Lowe, And'w
Jan 29 1780 Peckenpaugh, Catherine to Haring, Henry
Apr 15 1784 Peckepaugh, Margaret to Keefauver, Nicholas
Nov 10 1806 Peltz, John to Marquet, Elizabeth
Apr  5 1788 Pence, George to Gombare, Elizabeth
Dec 21 1795 Penn, Anna to Richards, George
Jan  3 1803 Penn, Benjamin to Phillips, Anna
Mar 26 1803 Penn, Benjamin to Hockley, Catharine
May 20 1793 Penn, Delilah to Clary, Zachariah
Jun 19 1802 Penn, Eleanor to Tucker, Richard
Nov  4 1796 Penn, Elizabeth to Hines, Nathaniel
Nov 23 1789 Penn, Mary to Farmer, William
Apr  9 1805 Penn, Mary to Richards, John
Apr 17 1806 Penn, Nackey to Pigman, Joshua
Jan  3 1789 Penn, Rachel to Clary, Daniel
May  7 1800 Penn, Rachel to Lenham, Robert C.
Mar 25 1801 Penn, Rebecca to Thrasher, William
Jan 26 1805 Penn, Rhody to Molen, Barton
Aug 25 1781 Penn, Samuel to Ostler, Elizabeth
Apr 21 1810 Penn, Samuel to Davis, Mary
Jan  1 1806 Penn, Sarah to Becraft, Peter
Oct 13 1787 Penn, Sarah to Conden, Wm.
Mar  1 1797 Penn, Sarah to Penn, William
Mar  1 1797 Penn, William to Penn, Sarah
Sep 24 1802 Pennybacker, Mary to Lain, John
Sep 24 1802 Pennybaker, Mary to Sain, John
Jul 25 1783 Pennybaker, Samuel to Plunck, Susannah
```

```
Nov  5 1803 Penser, Barbara to Lammerson, Richard
Jun  1 1779 Pentrin, Mary to Hargate, Abraham
Sep 13 1788 Pentz, Barbara to Brishe, David
Feb  5 1780 Pepper, Eliz'th to Collins, Patrick
Nov 22 1798 Pepper, Frederick to Gisburts, Deboro
Jan 16 1795 Pepper, Henry to Isaac, Elizabth
Jan 16 1802 Pepper, Peter to Padgett, Susanna
Oct  3 1804 Pepple, William to Linn, Modalena
Dec 21 1801 Perill, Clarissa to Barnes, John
Oct 30 1807 Perkins, Henry H. to Lyles, Margaret
Apr  3 1779 Perkinson, Mary to Hill, William
Apr  7 1789 Perknen, Christena to Ramsbergh, George
Feb 27 1802 Perril, Basil to Steel, Susanna
May 27 1791 Perrill, Alexander to Beaumont, Grace
Feb 23 1791 Perrill, Ann to Jacobs, George
Nov  3 1788 Perrill, Lucy to Darnall, Philip
Mar  5 1791 Perrill, Thomas to Calliman, Zilpha
Jun 14 1783 Perrill, William to Padgett, Sarah
May 10 1792 Perry, James to Warfield, Sarah
Oct 17 1783 Perry, Jane to Beall, Elisha
Apr 30 1793 Perry, Lyda to Giddings, Thomas
Dec 16 1787 Perry, Margaret to Fenell, Stephen
Oct  9 1790 Perry, Mary Ann to O'Bryan, Dennis
Mar 23 1799 Perry, Nancy to Arnold, Peter
Jan  2 1790 Perry, Nancy to Head, Ignatius
Dec  6 1788 Perry, Rachel to King, George
Nov 17 1780 Perry, Sarah to Bower, Philip
Apr 22 1786 Peter, John to Hollar, Catharine
Aug 23 1779 Peterson, Hannah to Laman, Jacob
Sep 28 1801 Peterson, Margaret to Sheeler, David
Aug 17 1807 Peterson, Sarah to Shealer, Samuel
Jan 13 1783 Peterson, William to Hughes, Rachel
Dec  6 1797 Petticoat, George to Dorsey, Sophia
Feb 21 1794 Peyton, Ann to Abricks, West
Oct  2 1805 Phebus, James to Rolins, Sally
Apr 12 1791 Phelps, Jemima to Woodward, Jacob
Feb 20 1808 Philips, Amelia to Coventry, John
Aug  6 1785 Philips, Amelia to Prather, John
May  6 1805 Philips, Amelia to Salmon, Frederick
Jan  9 1794 Philips, Eunice to Shelmerdine, Stephen
Apr 10 1797 Philips, Jason to Magers, Ann
Oct 24 1807 Philips, John to Hyatt, Susanna
Dec 28 1793 Philips, Margaret to Browning, Lewis
May 30 1794 Philips, Margaret to Talley, Ebenezer
Feb 12 1798 Philips, Nicholas to Wilson, Mary
Dec  1 1807 Philips, Samuel to Lyles, Rebecca
Aug 13 1808 Philips, Solomon to Maxwell, Hetty
Jun  3 1807 Philips, Wesley to Lemaster, Harriet
Jul 10 1787 Philips, William to Davis, Lucretia
Jan  3 1803 Phillips, Anna to Penn, Benjamin
Feb  3 1780 Phillips, Caleb to Darbey, Sarah
Oct  8 1791 Phillips, Eleanor to Hoffman, George
May 21 1806 Phillips, Eli to Stallings, Catherine
Feb 22 1796 Phillips, Elie to Harris, Catherine
Feb 19 1784 Phillips, Jesse to Hardy, Mary
```

```
Oct 17 1800 Phillips, Margaret to Parrish, John
Jan  7 1792 Phillips, Nackey to Holland, Samuel
Mar 15 1782 Phillips, Nancey to Davis, Rezin
Apr 25 1806 Phillips, Noah to Campbell, Ann
Feb  1 1805 Phillips, Prudence to Ovelman, George
Aug  7 1810 Phillips, Rachel to Tucker, Christopher James
Jul 23 1790 Phillips, Sophia to Knight, Joshua
Jun  4 1800 Phillips, Susanna to Baker, Henry
Dec 18 1800 Phillips, Thomas to Taylor, Rachel
Oct  6 1806 Phillpot, John to Jarboe, Ann
Jul 22 1800 Philpoott, Catherine to Hamilton, Francis
Jan 14 1799 Philpot, Charles to Gwinn, Elizabeth
Jun 22 1795 Philpot, Eleanor to Hamilton, John Alexander
Jul  4 1794 Philpott, Ann to Cramphin, Josiah
Jan 23 1804 Philpott, Barton to Gwinn, Amelia
Feb 14 1780 Philpott, Charles Thomas to Mockaboy, Elizabeth
Jan  9 1792 Philpott, Elizabeth to Boteler, Alexander
May 14 1785 Philpott, Elizabeth Warrent to Hackney, Benj'n Rhodes
Sep 15 1802 Philpott, Martha to Allen, James
Jan 18 1779 Philpott, Mary Barton to Garrett, Allen
Jan 30 1808 Philpott, Samuel to Jarboe, Henrietta
Dec  3 1781 Philpott, Zachariah to Garrott, Cassandra
Oct 29 1793 Picket, Betsy to Grimes, Basil
Apr  4 1796 Picket, Ruth to Shipley, Hezekiah
Mar  4 1808 Pickett, Charles to Condon, Frances
Jan 27 1801 Pickett, Ezekiel to Grimes, Amelia
Aug  4 1779 Pickett, John to Gannon, Ann
Feb  2 1790 Pickett, Mary to Knock, Basil
Aug 18 1801 Pickett, Rachel to Hearn, Denton
Jan 30 1810 Pickett, Sevin to Franklin, Pamelia
May 25 1783 Picking, Robert to Cost, Margaret
Feb  6 1787 Piecken, Mary to Foye, Henry
Dec 20 1792 Pierce, Anna to Higdon, Peter
Aug 19 1805 Pierce, Martha to Ingman, Ambrose
Jul  4 1808 Pierpoint, John to Clary, Henrietta
Apr 18 1783 Pierpoint, Joseph to Show, Catherine
Nov 23 1780 Piggman, Sarah to Barnett, William
Apr 17 1806 Pigman, Joshua to Penn, Nackey
Jun 25 1782 Pigott, Charles to Shipler, Lidia
Feb  3 1803 Pile, Robert to Griffith, Drucilla
May 26 1784 Piles, Richard to Lowman, Mary
Sep 19 1808 Pim, Thomas to Franklin, Elizabeth
Oct 15 1801 Pimmell, Elizabeth to Baltzell, John
Apr 25 1796 Pinkley, Catharine to Barnet, Luke
Sep 20 1800 Piper, Mary to Fout, Peter
Jul  1 1780 Piper, Philip to Huffman, Elizabeth
Jul 29 1797 Pitenger, Catherine to Eckman, Jacob
Dec 11 1809 Pitsel, Henry to Biggs, Mary Wilson
Oct  1 1800 Pitsell, Catherine to Wilhite, Frederick, Jr.
Apr 21 1800 Pittenger, Magdalen to McFarland, Arthur
Mar 26 1792 Pittinger, Elizabeth to Leagere, Geo.
Mar 28 1800 Pittinger, William to Bentzhoff, Elizabeth
Jan 27 1806 Pittinger, William to Eckman, Barbara
Oct 27 1806 Pittle, Mary to Carrolton, Thomas
Feb 10 1809 Pitts, Elizabeth to McElfresh, Charles
```

| | | | |
|---|---|---|---|
| May 30 | 1804 | Pitts, John (Rev.) to Hall, Elizabeth |
| Nov 23 | 1795 | Pixler, Jacob to Grable, Barbara |
| Sep 18 | 1780 | Plaister, Margaret to Unkles, Benjamin |
| Mar  5 | 1779 | Plank, Eliz'th to Ringer, Mathias |
| Sep 11 | 1790 | Plesinger, Margaret to Zerick, Jacob |
| Jun 27 | 1785 | Plonk, Elizabeth to Stoner, John, Jr. |
| Oct 30 | 1783 | Plonk, Mary to Shell, Charles |
| Oct  6 | 1785 | Plonk, Philipeana to Small, John |
| Jan 31 | 1781 | Plumb, George to Eater, Mary Magdalene |
| Apr  1 | 1795 | Plumley, Oliver to Myers, Phebe |
| Feb 26 | 1784 | Plummer, Abraham to Swomley, Mary |
| Sep 13 | 1796 | Plummer, Anna to Turner, John |
| Dec 12 | 1806 | Plummer, Cull to Johnson, Thomas |
| Mar 23 | 1798 | Plummer, Deborah to Miller, Joshua |
| Apr 15 | 1809 | Plummer, Eleanor to Fleming, Caleb |
| Apr 16 | 1785 | Plummer, Eleanor to Wayman, Leonard |
| May 12 | 1802 | Plummer, Finetta to Williams, John |
| Dec 10 | 1783 | Plummer, James to Cash, Dorcas |
| Dec 21 | 1789 | Plummer, Jonathan to Ward, Ann |
| May 12 | 1789 | Plummer, Joseph to Cash, Mary |
| Dec 29 | 1802 | Plummer, Joshua to Smith, Martha |
| Apr 29 | 1786 | Plummer, Mary to Bennett, John |
| Feb 20 | 1787 | Plummer, Mary Ann to Bowling, Samuel |
| Jul 24 | 1793 | Plummer, Massy to Bryan, Thomas |
| Jan 10 | 1795 | Plummer, Mesheck to Elliot, Anna |
| May 11 | 1805 | Plummer, Rachael to Jones, Allen |
| Jan  4 | 1808 | Plummer, Rachel to Slatlz, Samuel |
| Feb 28 | 1808 | Plummer, Rebeccah to Hutton, Enos |
| Nov 28 | 1791 | Plummer, Susanna to Crum, Isaac |
| Nov 27 | 1779 | Plummer, William to Jones, Margaret |
| Jan 11 | 1791 | Plummer, William to Hoggins, Linney Ann |
| Jan 19 | 1795 | Plummer, William to Hobbs, Rachel |
| Jan 15 | 1791 | Plummer, Zephaniah to Hempston, Charity |
| Jul 25 | 1783 | Plunck, Susannah to Pennybaker, Samuel |
| Dec  5 | 1780 | Plunk, Esther to Ream, John |
| Nov 10 | 1803 | Pole, Ann to Roberts, William |
| Nov 23 | 1804 | Pole, Frances to Stevenson, Edward |
| Feb 15 | 1779 | Polson, James to Durbin, Rachel |
| May 29 | 1807 | Ponder, Abraham to Dougherty, Nancy |
| May 14 | 1804 | Pool, Adam to Snyder, Elizabeth |
| Jan  9 | 1808 | Pool, Basil to Baldwin, Thomas |
| Dec 27 | 1801 | Pool, Catherine to Zimmerman, Jacob |
| Dec 16 | 1799 | Pool, Charles to Pool, Susanna |
| Dec  9 | 1806 | Pool, Frederick to Wood, Mary |
| Oct 28 | 1796 | Pool, George to Blackburn, Ann |
| Jan 11 | 1800 | Pool, Henry to Yowler, Catherine |
| Aug  1 | 1810 | Pool, Philemon to Tritt, Sarah |
| Sep 26 | 1807 | Pool, Sarah to Larned, Augustus |
| Dec 16 | 1799 | Pool, Susanna to Pool, Charles |
| Dec 12 | 1782 | Pool, William to Hall, Lilee |
| Feb  8 | 1806 | Pool, William to Hammond, Tomsey |
| Feb 28 | 1792 | Poole, Ann to Dorsey, Vachael |
| Dec 15 | 1802 | Poole, Beale to Blackburn, Sarah |
| Dec 11 | 1795 | Poole, Brice to James, Achsa |
| Jan 21 | 1807 | Poole, Charlotte to Marquam, Philip |

```
Jan 25 1794 Poole, Dennis to Gaither, Henrietta
Sep  6 1796 Poole, Elizabeth to Dorsey, Mich'l Of Jno.
May 23 1794 Poole, Elizabeth to Jones, Hanbury
Apr 25 1780 Poole, George to Raberdoe, Catherine
Feb 27 1790 Poole, Henry to James, Margaret
Dec 23 1797 Poole, Henry to Ward, Amelia
Jul 12 1778 Poole, James to Shipley, Rachel
Dec 20 1783 Poole, John to Norwood, Mary
Dec 31 1799 Poole, John to Sprigg, Prissa W.
Jun  9 1792 Poole, Joseph to Glaze, Eleanor
Sep 29 1794 Poole, Mary to Barnes, Dawson
Apr  7 1787 Poole, Samuel to Norwood, Jemima
Feb  9 1801 Poole, Samuel to Sellman, Jane
Apr 17 1786 Poole, Sarah to Hipsley, Charles
Dec 24 1779 Poole, Sophia to Nellson, Henry
Dec 10 1808 Poole, Walter to Woolf, Margaret
Aug 19 1784 Poole, William to Onion, Ann
Nov 18 1803 Poole, William S. to Rhodes, Elizabeth
Jan 23 1797 Poole, William, Jr. to Dickson, Ann
May 16 1807 Poorman, Eleanor to Ross, Frederick
May 17 1803 Pope, Mary to Pancoast, Caleb
Oct 18 1796 Porter, Isaiah to Marcus, Eleanor
Jul 26 1808 Porter, Isaiah to Bayfield, Jane
Mar  1 1810 Porter, Isaiah to Lewis, Susan
Feb 11 1807 Porter, Nicholas to Goodlin, Elizabeth
Aug 24 1778 Porter, Thomas to McDonald, Susanna
Aug 18 1801 Porters, Ruth to Manahan, Thomas
Apr 17 1802 Possamun, Christina to Baker, Thomas
Apr 18 1805 Poston, Elizabeth to Johnson, Washington
May  4 1782 Potter, Mary to Davis, John
Nov  5 1803 Potterfield, Joseph to Winpeagler, Magdalena
Nov 22 1798 Potts, Jonas to Dowlen, Martha
Dec 19 1799 Potts, Richard, Esq. to Murdoch, Eleanor
Nov  7 1782 Potts, Sarah to Ganntt, Thomas
Mar 17 1807 Potts, William, Jr. to Campbell, Susanna
Jan  2 1788 Poulson, Ann to Tolburte, James
Apr  3 1797 Poulson, Cornelius to Baxter, Rachel
Jan 28 1794 Poulson, Elizabeth to Barnes, Zadock
Jul  1 1791 Poulson, Margaret to Durbin, John
Jul 25 1795 Poulson, Mary to Tomlinson, James
Jan 24 1810 Poulton, Thomas to Silket, Eleanor
Sep  8 1788 Povey, Christian to Smeltzer, Catharine
Apr  4 1809 Powell, Delilah to Griffith, John
Jun  2 1780 Powell, Eliz'th to Jacques, Denton
Mar 24 1801 Powell, Elizabeth to Albert, Christian
May 21 1798 Powell, Hannah to Garner, Luke
Dec 24 1805 Powell, Jonathan to Yantis, Barbara
Feb  9 1805 Powell, Nancy to Jackson, Henry
Apr 11 1803 Powell, Nathan to Zimmerman, Margaret
Feb  4 1809 Powell, Nathan to Engles, Eleanor
Apr  4 1810 Powell, Nathaniel to Engles, Elein
Oct 14 1809 Powell, Susanna to Newman, George
Nov 26 1810 Powell, Thomas to Greenwood, Eleanor
Jan 11 1779 Powell, William to Edwards, Mary
Mar 18 1786 Power, Elizabeth to Kessler, Peter
```

```
May 31 1783 Powerin, Margaret to Rice, Michael
Dec  8 1807 Powers, Michael to Anderson, Anne
Jul 12 1803 Powhorn, Mary to McDaniel, Jonathan
Jun 20 1799 Powlas, Catherine to Ritter, Michael
Dec  4 1805 Powlas, Elizabeth to Routzahn, George
Dec 22 1792 Powlas, Mary to Beckibaugh, George
May  4 1805 Powlas, Nicholas to Scoff, Catherine
Mar 18 1797 Powlass, Elizabeth to Flyde, John
Oct 17 1801 Powles, Catherine to Holland, Daniel
Dec 23 1791 Powles, Mary to Young, Peter
May  7 1792 Prather, Jane to Wickery, George
Aug  6 1785 Prather, John to Philips, Amelia
Feb 22 1791 Prather, John Garrott to Sergeant, Mary Ann
Nov 14 1807 Prather, Silas to Malory, Anne
May 11 1779 Prauff, Jacob to Buckey, Ann M.
Oct 13 1787 Prengle, Elizabeth to Stoner, Henry
Sep 26 1807 Preston, Abraham to Baldwin, Susanna
Apr 18 1810 Preston, Charles to Baldwin, Nancy
Dec 18 1805 Preston, Frederick to Blackburn, Catherine
May 25 1802 Preston, John to Becraft, Sophia
Dec 22 1800 Price, Adam to Stull, Mary
Apr 28 1796 Price, Edward to Crist, Elizabeth
Feb 20 1789 Price, Elizabeth to Smith, J. T. Henry
Sep 22 1778 Price, Hanah to Ryley, Patrick
Jul 17 1801 Price, Hannah to Duvall, Mareen, H.
Sep 11 1784 Price, Jemima to Patterson, Benjamin
Feb 20 1796 Price, John to Lefaver, Elizabeth
Jan 23 1783 Price, Mary to Calmes, George
Dec 29 1796 Price, Matilda to Beall, Upton
Nov  3 1798 Price, Philip, Jr. to Sulser, Mary
Mar 22 1799 Price, Sarah to Neighbours, Nathan
Nov 10 1785 Price, Thomas, Capt. to Mackall, Susanna
Jan  3 1797 Prill, Samuel to Auman, Catherine
Aug 18 1788 Prishe, Sophia to Haas, Michael
Oct  5 1784 Prist, George to Kizer, Catherine
May  3 1779 Pritchard, Jesse to Stoner, Elizabeth
Dec 28 1796 Pritchard, Rebeckah to Rice, John
Oct 15 1796 Pritchet, Rebeckah to Whittington, John
Jan 15 1785 Pritchett, Elizabeth to Dust, John
Mar 25 1802 Proby, John to Blewer, Elizabeth
Dec 29 1804 Proctor, Abraham to Griffith, Peggy
Dec  2 1800 Protsman, Henry to Loy, Elizabeth
May 31 1803 Protsman, Mary to Winch, Jacob
Jan  4 1805 Protzman, Mary to Thomas, John
Mar 11 1809 Protzman, Sophia to Creager, Henry
Dec 21 1797 Prough, Caty to Winter, John
Aug 18 1802 Prout, Solomon to Scoggins, Charity
Nov 27 1805 Prout, William to Scoggins, Sally
Oct 21 1807 Prower, David to Gigar, Catherine
Mar 17 1809 Prugh, Hannah to Orputt, Thomas
Dec 19 1787 Prutsman, Ludwick to Rouser, Elizabeth
Oct  1 1803 Pry, George to Samsel, Elizabeth
Aug  3 1784 Prye, Christopher to Thrasher, Hannah
Jan  1 1801 Pryor, Elizabeth to Myers, Jonathan
Apr  6 1801 Pue, Jane to Yakey, Peter
```

```
Feb  7 1791 Puffinberger, Adam to Dorsey, Oner
Sep 15 1801 Pumphrey, Vachel to Maynard, Ann
Jul 28 1781 Pupp, Peter to Heffner, Catherine
Dec  9 1805 Purcell, John to Jenny, Mary
Jul 23 1785 Purdey, Ann to Howard, Henry
Dec 18 1798 Purdey, Eleanor to Richards, Joseph
Sep  5 1810 Purdin, Benjamin to Reynolds, Catherine
Nov 19 1785 Purdum, James to Browning, Elizabeth
Jun 24 1791 Purdum, Molley to Fitzgerald, Wm.
Dec 17 1802 Purdy, Amelia to Mark, John
Dec  3 1803 Purdy, Catherine to Duvall, James
Sep  7 1807 Purdy, Cynthia to Mark, George
Jun 23 1794 Purdy, Deborah to Watkins, Jeremiah
Dec 18 1792 Purdy, Edmund to Burgee, Rebecca
Apr 30 1783 Purdy, Elizabeth to Hilleary, Ogbon
Aug 17 1795 Purdy, Mary to Ramsower, Adam
Nov 19 1809 Purdy, Nancy to Richards, Mashack
Jan 12 1795 Purdy, William to Bucey, Mary
May  4 1779 Pursley, Abigail to Roads, Charles
Apr 16 1804 Pusey, George to Sellman, Sarah
Apr 26 1805 Putman, Mary to Cramer, Thomas
Mar 22 1806 Pyfer, Catherine to Buckey, Michael
Sep  5 1801 Pyles, John to Marckley, Elizabeth
Jul 11 1809 Pyott, James to Beckwith, Susanna

Jun  8 1783 Queary, Christena to Shindler, Adam
Jul 25 1778 Quinner, Mary to Little, Michael
Dec 12 1790 Quynn, Allen, Jr. to Mantz, Mary
Dec  9 1796 Quynn, Ann to Hunter, Thomas
Mar 27 1782 Quynn, John to Padgett, Elizabeth

Apr 25 1780 Raberdoe, Catherine to Poole, George
Aug 26 1798 Rabourn, Catherine to Hollar, Michael of Godfrey
Nov  5 1791 Rachel, Daniel to Myers, Catherine
Jun 18 1785 Rachob, Fred'k to Shafert, Susannah
Sep  2 1784 Rachob, Mary to Bailey, William
Apr 17 1801 Radford, Thomas to Row, Elizabeth
Dec 18 1796 Ragan, Andrew to Moule, Susanna
Apr  5 1808 Ragan, George to Smith, Susannah
Jul 16 1810 Ragan, Patty to How, James
Apr 30 1796 Ragan, Sarah to Mackey, Robert
Dec 31 1785 Rage, Elizabeth to Wertenbaker, Adam
Nov 21 1809 Rahauser, Frederick, Rev'd to Wagner, Elizabeth
Oct 31 1789 Raith, Nancy to Williamson, James H.
Apr  7 1798 Raitt, Barbara to Saylor, Daniel
Oct 30 1797 Raitt, Hammond to Norris, Eleanor
Dec 15 1800 Raitt, Mary to Norris, John
Jan 12 1799 Ramack, Rosina to Geesey, Henry
Jun  2 1796 Ramey, Lydia to Martin, Peter
Oct 11 1795 Ramsberg, Barbara to Stoner, Stephen
Dec 25 1809 Ramsberg, Casper to Bowlas, Mary
Jan 21 1808 Ramsberg, Catherine to Bost, Samuel
Jun  9 1807 Ramsberg, Catherine to Hardy, Joseph
Jun 25 1796 Ramsberg, Catherine to Niehoff, John Daniel
Apr 20 1808 Ramsberg, Christian to Snook, Mary
```

| | | | |
|---|---|---|---|
| May 10 | 1810 | Ramsberg, Christian to Sprengle, Cathe. | |
| Nov 24 | 1797 | Ramsberg, George to Culler, Caty | |
| Jan 2 | 1809 | Ramsberg, Jacob to Hardy, Susannah | |
| Apr 16 | 1796 | Ramsberg, Jacob, Junr. to Grosh, Charlotte | |
| Feb 5 | 1803 | Ramsberg, John to Morphy, Hannah | |
| Dec 31 | 1805 | Ramsberg, John to Durst, Mary | |
| Nov 15 | 1800 | Ramsberg, Sebastian to Stoner, Elizbeth | |
| Jul 9 | 1796 | Ramsberg, Stephen to Brunner, Elizabeth | |
| Dec 5 | 1807 | Ramsberg, Stephen to Eickhofe, Elizabeth | |
| Aug 18 | 1810 | Ramsberg, Susanna to Michael, Jacob | |
| May 21 | 1798 | Ramsberg, Susanna to Shafer, Jacob | |
| Mar 21 | 1795 | Ramsberg, Susanna to Stoner, John | |
| May 3 | 1800 | Ramsberg, Susannah to Stoner, Christian | |
| Apr 1 | 1786 | Ramsbergh, Cathe. to Getzendanner, Christ'n | |
| May 7 | 1787 | Ramsbergh, Catherine to Hershberger, Henry | |
| Jan 18 | 1794 | Ramsbergh, Catherine to Stickle, Valentine | |
| Jan 29 | 1793 | Ramsbergh, Charlotte to Buckey, Valentine | |
| Apr 15 | 1788 | Ramsbergh, Elizabeth to Stull, Adam | |
| Apr 7 | 1789 | Ramsbergh, George to Perknen, Christena | |
| Jan 13 | 1789 | Ramsbergh, John to Thomas, Catherine | |
| Apr 23 | 1787 | Ramsbergh, John of Adam to Miller, Elizabeth | |
| Jan 9 | 1802 | Ramsbergh, John, Junr to Stilly, Rebecca | |
| Nov 22 | 1790 | Ramsbergh, Margaret to Thomas, Henry | |
| Mar 11 | 1779 | Ramsbergh, Mary to Thomas, Gabriel | |
| Feb 28 | 1795 | Ramsburg, Christena to Patesell, John | |
| Apr 16 | 1786 | Ramsburgh, Elizabeth to Thomas, John | |
| Dec 26 | 1796 | Ramsey, John to Smith, Priscilla | |
| Nov 8 | 1779 | Ramsey, Mary to Cooper, Archb'd | |
| Nov 7 | 1784 | Ramsey, Nancey to Love, David | |
| Dec 7 | 1786 | Ramsey, Naomy to Cooper, James | |
| Aug 3 | 1793 | Ramsey, Sarah to McKiver, Dan | |
| Dec 14 | 1803 | Ramsour, Mary to Baker, Thomas, Junr | |
| Aug 17 | 1795 | Ramsower, Adam to Purdy, Mary | |
| Oct 28 | 1789 | Ramsower, Ann to Talbott, Charles | |
| Jun 18 | 1785 | Ramsower, Henry to Smith, Mary | |
| Jan 29 | 1788 | Ramsower, Margaret to Hagan, Francis | |
| Mar 22 | 1793 | Randal, Elizabeth to Russell, Wm. | |
| Jan 20 | 1798 | Randall, Doraty to Kirfman, Adam | |
| Mar 19 | 1798 | Randall, Margaret to Grimes, Frederick | |
| Mar 23 | 1809 | Randall, Marha to Rawley, Richard G. | |
| Nov 22 | 1779 | Randall, Priscilla to Sollers, Dennis | |
| Mar 28 | 1810 | Randall, Vachel, W. to Dorsey, Maria | |
| Jul 22 | 1783 | Rankins, William to Gatton, Rebeckah | |
| May 22 | 1795 | Ransdale, Stephen Chilton to Dowdle, Margaret | |
| May 16 | 1788 | Rape, Clarissa to Steiner, Frederick | |
| Mar 29 | 1802 | Rapeloch, Sally to Welck, Conrad | |
| Apr 21 | 1803 | Ratliff, Amelia to Ingman, Joshua | |
| May 25 | 1807 | Raw, John to Burk, Margaret | |
| Mar 23 | 1809 | Rawley, Richard G. to Randall, Marha | |
| Nov 21 | 1792 | Rawlings, Benja. to Gittings, Elizab Garrott | |
| Jun 15 | 1800 | Rawlings, Elizabeth to Mock, Jacob | |
| Dec 2 | 1788 | Rawlings, Sarah to Hays, Notley | |
| Aug 6 | 1781 | Rawlings, Solomon to Donaldson, Ann | |
| Jan 2 | 1809 | Ray, John to Roop, Elizabeth | |
| Sep 22 | 1778 | Ray, Mary to Dobson, William | |

```
May 20 1783 Rayling, John Ludwick to Snydern, Anne Marg't
Jun 22 1797 Raymer, Jacob to Zimmerman, Maria
Jan 22 1791 Raymer, Michael to Fultz, Susanna Margaret
Mar 14 1808 Razeler, Christena to Boone, Nicholas
May  2 1803 Razor, Elizabeth to Dixen, John Calhoun
Dec 18 1798 Razor, Margaret to Michael, William
Dec  5 1780 Ream, John to Plunk, Esther
Aug 18 1809 Ream, Sarah to Morningstar, John
Sep 20 1790 Reaser, Catharine to Scaggs, James
Mar  5 1783 Reaves, Leon'd to Boley, Juliana
Feb 25 1809 Redanor, Frederick to Shingler, Margaret
Apr 11 1805 Redburn, Elizabeth to King, Richard
May 20 1801 Redburn, Permelia to Wales, Samuel
Sep  6 1800 Redman, Ann to Murray, Joseph
Jun 13 1801 Redman, Catherine to Nugent, Henry
Oct 27 1798 Reed, Abraham to Brubecher, Elizabeth
Feb  3 1794 Reed, Alexander to Miller, Elizbeth
Jun 16 1792 Reed, Archibald to Talbot, Catharine
Dec 12 1778 Reed, Eleanor to Colbert, Simon
Mar 25 1796 Reed, Elizabeth to McDade, Charles
Aug  9 1780 Reed, Elizabeth to Trout, Jacob
Oct 15 1789 Reed, James to Gatton, Ann
Sep  1 1808 Reed, Margaret to Gilpin, William
Oct  8 1779 Reed, Margaret to Heffner, Mich'l
Aug 20 1795 Reed, Rachel to Keefer, Henry
May 29 1787 Reed, Susanna to Walling, John
Dec  2 1793 Reed, Thomas to Howard, Sarah
Aug 14 1805 Reed, Thomason to Henderson, James
Jul 27 1804 Reeder, Joseph to Russell, Elizabeth
Mar 17 1787 Reeder, Mary to McAtee, Francis, X.
Mar 29 1806 Reel, Barbara to Derr, Jacob
Mar 26 1798 Reel, Elizabeth to Gardner, Henry
Mar  7 1799 Reel, Frederick to Lucorsh, Margaret
Aug 30 1808 Reel, Frederick to Rickart, Mary
Apr 17 1810 Reel, Frederick to Simmerman, Catherine
Sep 20 1788 Reel, George to Snyder, Elizab
Dec 16 1809 Reel, Leonard T. to Lewis, Delila
Apr 29 1796 Reel, Mary to Mahoney, Barnabas
May 22 1802 Reel, Michael to Brengle, Catharine
Jun 16 1803 Reem, Elsey Catharine to Bartholow, Aaron
Aug 21 1809 Reese, Catherine to Martz, George
May  9 1808 Reese, Elizabeth to Shindler, Daniel
Nov 23 1799 Reese, John to Zachariah, Mary
May 15 1810 Reesler, Jacob to Merryman, Polly
Dec  1 1789 Reible, Catherine to Martin, David
Nov 21 1785 Reichart, Mary to Hertzterfer, John
Jul 22 1783 Reichter, Henry to Zerrick, Catherine
Aug  7 1802 Reid, Ann Lotty to Roberts, Zachariah
May 20 1807 Reid, James to Huston, Elizabeth
Nov 22 1792 Reid, John to Millan, Ann
Apr 20 1810 Reid, John to Roderick, Anna
Feb  1 1790 Reid, Matthew to Riggs, Ellender
Feb 23 1809 Reid, Patrick to Logan, Margaret
Mar  6 1796 Reid, Sarah to Crist, Jacob
Apr 17 1781 Reigh, Elizabeth to Aiter, Abraham
```

Feb 21 1785 Reighe, Catharine to Ater, Abraham
Nov 30 1810 Reily, Daniel to Mackey, Mary
Nov 25 1808 Reimer, Esther to Smith, Frederick
Apr 22 1783 de Reitzenstein, Frederick to Shenkmeyer, Catherine Eliz'th
Mar 27 1789 Remsberger, George to Sulser, Cathe.
Nov 27 1798 Renner, Abraham to Overholtzer, Elizabeth
Jan  1 1810 Renner, Adam to Kar, Rachel
Jul 30 1803 Renner, Catharine to Crumbaugh, David
Dec 27 1806 Renner, Catherine to Creager, Michael
Oct 12 1800 Renner, Elizabeth to Whitmore, Martin
Dec  7 1782 Renner, John to Wine, Mary
Aug  6 1799 Renner, Mary to Eby, Jacob
Aug 17 1799 Renner, Mary to Engle, Peter
Feb  4 1799 Renner, Mary to Young, George
Oct 16 1810 Renner, Sally to Hummer, Henry
Mar 21 1782 Renner, Wm. to Coleman, Charity
Sep  1 1804 Rep, Daniel to Roedick, Elizabeth
Oct  3 1809 Rep, Margaret to Happener, John G.
Nov  1 1799 Rep, Susannah to Lowe, Jacob
Nov  6 1799 Rep, Susannah to Lung, Jacob
Nov 10 1808 Repp, Elizabeth to Baker, Philip
Jan 23 1794 Reppert, Elizabeth to Cramier, George
Apr 12 1804 Rete, Margaret to Williams, William Roy
Apr  6 1784 Reybergh, William to Evilleng, Mary Ann
Jan 17 1805 Reynolds, Allice to Dean, William
Sep  5 1810 Reynolds, Catherine to Purdin, Benjamin
Apr 13 1804 Reynolds, Elenor to Reynolds, Samuel L.
Nov  7 1778 Reynolds, Eliz'th to Deame, Robert
Oct 13 1780 Reynolds, Heugh to Flemming, Alley
Nov 19 1805 Reynolds, Joseph to Boring, Hannah
Apr 20 1797 Reynolds, Lydia to Shank, John
Apr 13 1804 Reynolds, Samuel L. to Reynolds, Elenor
Jan 29 1789 Reynolds, Thomas to Tomlin, Elizabeth
Apr  3 1784 Rhine, Casper to Hinckle, Margaret
Aug 14 1793 Rhine, Rudy to Conner, Barbara
Oct 18 1803 Rhinehart, George to Smith, Susannah
Jun 11 1809 Rhoads, Elizabeth to Goodman, William
Feb 20 1792 Rhode, Jacob to King, Rachel
Nov 18 1803 Rhodes, Elizabeth to Poole, William S.
Oct 28 1806 Rhodes, Henry to Fine, Elizabeth
Mar 21 1801 Rhodes, John to Russell, Nancey
May 17 1791 Rhodes, Joshua to Spealman, Catharine
Jul 27 1807 Rhodes, Mary to Holland, Rezin
May  5 1785 Rice, Andrew to Need, Mary
Jan 25 1800 Rice, Ann to Miller, Jacob
Feb  4 1782 Rice, Benjamin to Hook, Purnell
Oct 30 1810 Rice, Eleanor to Keefer, Christian, Junr.
Jun 23 1783 Rice, Elizabeth to Ireland, Jonathan
Dec 20 1800 Rice, George to Toafler, Elizabeth
Jun  8 1810 Rice, Henry to Werstler, Betsey
Oct  3 1783 Rice, James to Dern, Nancy
Apr 21 1790 Rice, James to Dern, Catharine
Dec 28 1796 Rice, John to Pritchard, Rebeckah
Jan 12 1788 Rice, Joseph to Melvin, Elizabeth

```
Nov  4 1794 Rice, Joseph to Leatch, Rebeckah
Aug 23 1803 Rice, Mary to Woolf, Valentine
May 31 1783 Rice, Michael to Powerin, Margaret
Jun  7 1790 Rice, Michael to Baltzell, Elizabeth
Aug 20 1794 Rice, Perry to Duttero, Patty
Sep 27 1791 Rice, Rebeckah to Marlow, Edward
Apr  4 1786 Rice, Ruth to Roach, Micaiah
Nov 30 1802 Rice, Sarah to Scaggs, Leonard
Jan 24 1801 Rice, Thomas to Snowdagle, Susannah
Dec 17 1790 Rice, William to Hedges, Mary
Aug 27 1802 Richard, John Hart to Morris, Maria
Mar  6 1780 Richards, Ann to Candle, James
Oct 10 1794 Richards, Basil to Richards, Elizabeth
Oct 10 1796 Richards, Brice to Hart, Elizabeth
May 19 1783 Richards, Daniel to Cochran, Jane
Mar 13 1779 Richards, Edward to Roote, Jane
Mar  2 1799 Richards, Eleanor to Kennedy, Dennis
Oct 19 1778 Richards, Eliz'th to Hart, Christ'n
Oct 10 1794 Richards, Elizabeth to Richards, Basil
Dec 21 1795 Richards, George to Penn, Anna
Nov 22 1781 Richards, John to Arnold, Catharine
Feb  6 1796 Richards, John to Waters, Ann
Apr  9 1805 Richards, John to Penn, Mary
Sep  3 1806 Richards, John to Warner, Elizabeth
Dec 18 1798 Richards, Joseph to Purdey, Eleanor
Feb 11 1797 Richards, Levina to Woolfe, George
Mar  8 1793 Richards, Lidia to Weer, James
Jan 10 1809 Richards, Mary to Colbert, John
Nov 19 1809 Richards, Mashack to Purdy, Nancy
Apr 23 1791 Richards, Rachel to Stevens, John
Aug  9 1780 Richards, Richard to Nevin, Eliz'th
Aug 16 1791 Richards, Sarah to Carmack, William
Sep 11 1807 Richards, Susanna to Duvall, Thomas
Feb  4 1793 Richards, Susanna to Linton, Isaac
Jan 18 1787 Richards, William to Hyatt, Leviney
Sep 21 1807 Richardson, Elijah to Brawner, Elizabeth
Jan  7 1797 Richardson, Hannah to Henderson, Griffith
Oct 19 1778 Richardson, John to Noble, Mary
Nov  2 1787 Richardson, Mary to Griffith, Caleb
Apr 12 1800 Richardson, Richard P. to Richardson, Sarah
Apr  7 1800 Richardson, Samuel P. to Mobberley, Elizabeth
Jun  3 1799 Richardson, Sarah to Coomes, Baalis
Apr 12 1800 Richardson, Sarah to Richardson, Richard P.
Mar 25 1782 Richardson, Tabitha to Dorsey, Basil
Jan 29 1798 Richardson, Ursula to Baker, Walter
Aug 14 1784 Richardson, Ursula to Yates, Robert Elliot
Feb  9 1779 Richardson, Wm. to Davis, Nancey
Mar  2 1805 Richmond, Francis to Stottlemier, Susanna
Sep 18 1806 Richter, Catherine to Darsh, Henry
Jun  6 1807 Rickard, Elizabeth to Weddle, John
Sep  1 1797 Rickard, Mary to McGuire, John
Aug 30 1808 Rickart, Mary to Reel, Frederick
Feb  1 1779 Ricketts, Benja. to Wells, Ruth
Nov 18 1793 Ricketts, Margaret to Steward, William
Nov 30 1780 Ricketts, Rebecca to Groom, James
```

```
Sep 18 1802 Riddle, Anne to Hoover, John
Oct 31 1803 Riddle, Jane to Ringer, Solomon
Nov 21 1796 Riddle, Susanna to Taylor, Richard
Nov 29 1800 Riddlemoser, Barbara to Simpson, Thomas
Sep 23 1779 Ridenhour, Henry to Smith, Mary
May  3 1785 Ridenhour, Jacob to Haas, Susanna
Jun  9 1808 Ridenour, Adam to Miller, Elizabeth
Mar 13 1804 Ridenour, Elizabeth to Shaaf, Peter
Dec  4 1802 Ridenour, Jacob to Smith, Mary
May 31 1810 Ridge, Betsey to Hoover, Jacob
Feb  7 1783 Ridge, Cornelius to Brawner, Elizabeth
Oct 21 1780 Ridge, Edward to Creagar, Catharine
Jun 18 1810 Ridge, Rebecca to Shriver, Jacob
Nov 28 1780 Ridge, Wm. to Flemming, Barbara
Mar 31 1781 Ridge, Wm. of Benj'n to Springer, Rebecca
Dec 21 1805 Ridgely, Annie to Shahan, David
Mar 16 1808 Ridgely, Frederick to Grimes, Eleanor
Dec 28 1808 Ridgely, Frederick to Albaugh, Sarah
Nov 10 1792 Ridgely, Martha to Chun, Lancelot
Sep 24 1782 Ridgely, Richard to Templing, Rebeckah
Aug 28 1798 Ridgely, Richard to Hyme, Mary
Nov 21 1797 Ridgely, Sarah to Coale, Isaac
Feb 13 1807 Ridgely, Sarah to Harding, Lewis
Aug 24 1803 Ridgely, Sarah to Shawhan, Daniel
Feb 15 1779 Ridgely, Sarah to Winpigler, Francis
Jul  1 1791 Ridgely, Westall to Templing, Sarah
Dec 24 1799 Ridgely, Westall to Hyme, Elizabeth
Sep 12 1778 Ridgley, Drusilla to Holland, Jonathan
Nov  1 1783 Ridgley, Elizabeth to Griffith, Joshua
Mar  9 1797 Ridgley, Elizabeth to Hays, George
Feb 25 1782 Ridgley, Jane to Holland, Otho
May  7 1785 Ridgley, Mary to Fluhart, Massey
Feb 13 1779 Ridgley, Mary to Lynch, John
Dec  9 1784 Ridgley, Urith to Guiseberts, And'w
Mar 10 1789 Ridgley, Urith to Holland, Jonathan
Feb 16 1810 Ridinger, Peggy to Lemon, Jacob
Jul 31 1787 Rieston, Samuel to Deberry, Sarah
Feb  9 1810 Rife, Catherine to Ohler, John
Aug 16 1807 Rife, Jacob to Smith, Sophia
Mar 18 1795 Rigdon, Elizabeth to Norris, John
May  5 1796 Riggs, Catherine to Shivell, Adam
Aug 31 1801 Riggs, Elizabeth to Jenkins, William
Feb  1 1790 Riggs, Ellender to Reid, Matthew
Jul 28 1790 Riggs, Henrietta to McCloskey, James
Dec 12 1782 Riggs, John to Elligan, Mary
Feb  5 1785 Riggs, John to Hardy, Mary
May 21 1800 Riggs, Mary to Gates, George
Jan 14 1792 Riggs, Nancy to Hyatt, Jesse
Oct  9 1800 Riggs, Samuel to Marshall, Priscilla
Nov  6 1797 Riggs, Sarah to Tucker, Edward
Jun  7 1794 Righe, John to Stoner, Phebe
Aug 14 1789 Righter, Peter to Grove, Catherine
Mar 22 1806 Righting, Andrew to Myer, Barbara
Nov  9 1795 Rights, Ludwick to Cramer, Margaret
Mar  8 1794 Rightstine, William to Chopper, Catherine
```

```
Jun 21 1806 Rigney, John to Heisley, Sophia
Apr  2 1803 Rigney, Rebecca to Smallwood, Henry
Oct 13 1800 Riley, Edward to McGuffin, Jane
May  6 1793 Riley, Elizabeth to Crossmug, John
Jun  4 1798 Riley, Henry to Brown, Elizabeth
Feb 14 1791 Riley, John to Steel, Mary
Aug  1 1810 Riley, Mary to Maddoc, Frederick
Feb 29 1804 Rine, Elizabeth to Davis, William
Sep  3 1796 Rine, John to Wilson, Priscilla
Feb 18 1809 Rine, John to Rine, Mary
Feb 18 1809 Rine, Mary to Rine, John
Jan 26 1801 Rine, Michael to Bucey, Elizabeth
Jan 23 1795 Rine, Valentine to Clay, Mary
Jun 13 1796 Rineberger, Henry to Thomas, Sarah
Dec 21 1803 Rinehart, Hannah to Stoner, Abraham
Mar  6 1779 Rinehart, Mary Eve to Schoolmyer, John Peter
Sep 19 1795 Rinehart, Peggy to Martin, John
Mar  1 1780 Rineheart, George to Weaver, Priscilla
Apr 16 1804 Riner, Barbara to Waltz, Samuel
Oct 20 1810 Riner, George to Winebrenner, Catherine
Feb  7 1807 Ringer, Elizabeth to Sprutzman, Jacob
Mar 21 1780 Ringer, Jacob to Beamer, Ann
Dec  3 1800 Ringer, Mary to Duddero, Michael
Apr 13 1779 Ringer, Mary to Smith, Charles
Mar  5 1779 Ringer, Mathias to Plank, Eliz'th
Oct 31 1803 Ringer, Solomon to Riddle, Jane
Mar  6 1797 Ringer, Susanna to Crum, Abraham
Sep 22 1810 Ringer, Susanna to Rudy, Frederick
Oct 25 1800 Ringland, John to Hobbs, Asenath
Mar 30 1779 Risener, Eliz'th to King, Charles
Dec 14 1802 Risler, Elizabeth to Cushour, Peter
Dec 19 1785 Ritchie, Abner to Jenkins, Mary Ann
Jun 22 1801 Ritchie, Abner, Esq. to Wayne, Mary
Oct 27 1806 Ritchie, Anne to Ott, John
Dec 19 1804 Ritchie, Henry to Spoon, Mary
Feb 17 1787 Ritchie, John to Beatty, Cathe.
Apr  5 1801 Ritchie, John to Barnhold, Nancy
Dec  6 1807 Ritchie, Maria P.A.D. to Mantz, Ezra
May 16 1809 Ritchie, Robert to Cary, Maria B.
Dec 28 1794 Ritchie, Zeruiah to Hedge, Nicholas
Dec  8 1789 Ritemeyer, Conrad to Shroiner, Susanna
Oct  1 1808 Ritt, Martha to Carny, Patrick
Feb  5 1802 Ritter, Jacob to Wiest, Polly
Jun 20 1799 Ritter, Michael to Powlas, Catherine
Jul 19 1779 Ritter, Modelane to Kemp, Henry
Aug 31 1780 Ritter, Susanna to Kemp, Frederick
Dec 28 1799 Ritz, Jacob to Stull, Mary
Aug 17 1801 River, Jacob to Leonard, Catherine
Jan 31 1780 Rizeing, George to Whitehair, Dorothy
Nov 17 1783 Roach, Edward to Huff, Martha
Mar  6 1780 Roach, Mary to Carter, Thomas
Apr  4 1786 Roach, Micaiah to Rice, Ruth
Jan  6 1783 Roach, Richard to Lanham, Drusey
Mar 18 1798 Roach, Sarah to Williams, Uriah
Nov 14 1778 Road, George to Mugg, Marg't
```

```
Mar  4 1806 Road, George to Bussard, Sarah
Dec 27 1779 Road, Margaret to Gummert, Christian
Sep 16 1803 Roades, Henry to Williard, Sarah
Nov 28 1809 Roadrock, Christeana to Webster, Jacob
May  4 1779 Roads, Charles to Pursley, Abigail
May 22 1810 Roads, Elizabeth to Shoemaker, Nicholas
Dec 12 1805 Roads, George to Moch, Catherine
Feb  3 1807 Roads, Honora to Cecill, Samuel
Apr  8 1780 Roads, Jacob to Cash, Nancey
Sep 25 1809 Roads, Mary to Deever, Reuben
Nov 24 1806 Roany, Mary to Ellis, Joseph
Aug  5 1780 Roar, Catherine to Coonce, John
Oct 23 1779 Roar, Jacob to King, Catherine
Jul 30 1782 Robee, Patrick Moreland to Johnson, Rebecca
Sep 24 1787 Roberts, Archibald to Bosley, Mary Ann
Dec 21 1785 Roberts, Darcus to Coffee, John Dowden
Jan 20 1789 Roberts, Mary to Tabler, Michael
Apr  9 1788 Roberts, Mary to Woodrow, John
Dec 23 1791 Roberts, Patty to Beard, William
Jun 16 1801 Roberts, Rachel to Hammond, John
Jan  3 1798 Roberts, Thomas to Stevenson, Susannah
Oct  6 1790 Roberts, William to Hodgkiss, Sarah
Nov 10 1803 Roberts, William to Pole, Ann
Aug  7 1802 Roberts, Zachariah to Reid, Ann Lotty
Aug  9 1797 Robertson, Dan'l to Miller, Esther
Aug 16 1796 Robertson, Elizabeth to Jeffers, Joseph
Oct 23 1800 Robertson, Hannah to Maniard, Ezra
Jul 29 1802 Robertson, John to Smith, Sarah
Dec 27 1799 Robertson, Samuel to Howard, Rachel
Mar  4 1801 Robertson, William to Marshall, Mary
May 15 1786 Robertson, Zachariah to Ogbern, Mary
Sep 29 1786 Robey, Anna to Gatton, Sylvester, G.
Mar 27 1807 Robinson, Alexander to Miller, Margaret
May 30 1780 Robinson, And'w to Knave, Margaret
Nov 19 1779 Robinson, Chiles to Robinson, Elizabeth
Aug 27 1779 Robinson, Edw'd to Methard, Catherine
Nov 19 1779 Robinson, Elizabeth to Robinson, Chiles
Nov 19 1779 Robinson, Elizabeth to Robinson, Giles (or Chiles)
Nov 19 1779 Robinson, Giles (or Chiles) to Robinson, Elizabeth
Dec 13 1804 Robinson, Sarah to Cissell, Archibald
Sep 28 1809 Robison, James to Miller, Sarah
Apr 19 1788 Rochester, Nathaniel to Beatty, Sophia
Aug 15 1806 Rocker, Barbara to Geyer, Conrad
Apr 20 1810 Roderick, Anna to Reid, John
Oct  6 1807 Roderick, Jacob to Drue, Elizabeth
Mar  9 1795 Roderick, Mary to Hines, John
Sep 15 1807 Roderock, Catherine to Schelton, Samuel
Dec 25 1790 Rodes, Jonathan to Ingram, Henrietta
Jul 24 1807 Rodgers, Elizabeth to Sarjeant, William
Dec  4 1778 Rodgers, George to Patten, Jane
Oct  6 1779 Rodgers, Jno. to Tannihill, Mary
Feb  6 1782 Rodgers, John to Blair, Mary
Dec 19 1805 Rodinghiser, Elizabeth to Smelse, John
Feb 27 1810 Rodrock, John to McCleery, Elizabeth
Mar 23 1804 Rodrock, Susanna to Albaugh, William
```

Sep  1 1804 Roedick, Elizabeth to Rep, Daniel
Jun  5 1810 Roger, John to Boham, Polly
Jul 29 1793 Rogers, Ann to Kerr, John
Nov 22 1803 Rogers, Joshua to Goldsbery, Nancey
May  7 1787 Rogers, Mary to Naile, Henry
Sep 22 1810 Rohr, Catherine to Rohr, David
Sep 22 1810 Rohr, David to Rohr, Catherine
Mar 26 1807 Rohr, Jacob to Hauer, Elizabeth
Nov 26 1791 Rohr, Rudolph, Jr. to Runner, Cathe.
Nov 28 1809 Rohr, Sophia to Martin, Jacob, Junr.
Jan 29 1780 Roland, Gaidon to Dawson, Elizabeth
Aug 19 1809 Roland, George to Zimms, Frances
Oct 21 1805 Rolins, Sally to Febus, James
Oct  2 1805 Rolins, Sally to Phebus, James
Sep  8 1810 Romack, Sarah to Barrick, William
Apr 17 1799 Roof, Elizabeth to Sunafranck, George
Jan  2 1809 Roop, Elizabeth to Ray, John
Mar 29 1808 Root, Ann to Taylor, Enoch
May 14 1782 Root, Daniel to Cowell, Elizabeth
Aug 10 1779 Root, James to Umstatt, Mary
Mar 29 1808 Root, Margaret to Taylor, Joseph
Feb  7 1797 Root, Richard to Stoner, Agnes
May  5 1810 Root, Sarah to Cook, John
Mar 13 1779 Roote, Jane to Richards, Edward
Apr  2 1782 Rop, Lowery to Howe, John
May 11 1779 Ropp, Mary to Fullum, Mich'l
Dec 19 1805 Rose, Christopher to Evans, Catherine
Mar 26 1796 Rose, Frederick to Frushour, Mary
Apr 13 1807 Rose, Henry to Harding, Cassandra
Jan  7 1795 Rose, John to Lemon, Catherine
May 16 1807 Ross, Frederick to Poorman, Eleanor
Mar  4 1806 Ross, William to Johnson, Catherine W.
Mar  4 1810 Rote, Joseph to Geyer, Barbara
Dec 19 1787 Rouser, Elizabeth to Prutsman, Ludwick
Nov  6 1802 Routsawn, Benjamin to Shriver, Elizabeth
Dec 21 1803 Routshoin, George to Keller, Catharine
Apr 29 1793 Routsong, Henry to Colman, Mary Magdalena
Dec  4 1805 Routzahn, George to Powlas, Elizabeth
Mar  5 1808 Routzan, Catharine to Biser, Daniel
May  3 1804 Routzan, Catherine to Daub, John
Apr 27 1805 Routzang, Daniel to Icoff, Charlotte
Apr 26 1798 Routzawn, Elizabeth to Bowlis, Henry
Dec 26 1795 Routzawn, Jacob to Synn, Christena
Nov 16 1801 Row, Catherine to Moody, James
Apr 17 1801 Row, Elizabeth to Radford, Thomas
Apr 15 1800 Row, George to Lantz, Catharine
Oct  4 1808 Row, James to Kellison, Nancy
Sep 16 1778 Row, Margaret to Hill, Joseph, Jr.
Feb 11 1786 Row, Mary to Hart, Michael
Mar 10 1806 Row, Mary to Watt, Robert
Sep 24 1782 Rowe, Barbara to Titlow, Christian
Nov 14 1803 Rowe, Barbara to Young, John
Mar  3 1787 Rowe, Catherine to Gillion, Philip
Apr 10 1797 Rowe, Elizabeth to Fischer, Adam
Sep 16 1805 Rowe, Frederick to Wisman, Mary

```
Aug 22 1797 Rowe, Jacob to Conrod, Susanna
Apr 30 1799 Rowenzawn, Benjamin to Shriver, Pheby
Jun 21 1782 Rowser, Henry to Shitearie, Eve
Sep 19 1810 Rowzer, Daniel to Cannon, Margaret
Jun  1 1782 Rudecill, Elizabeth to Beare, William
May 31 1785 Rudecill, Elizabeth to Cover, Jacob
Sep 22 1810 Rudy, Frederick to Ringer, Susanna
Jan 27 1786 Rue, Rebeckah to Short, Richard
Feb  6 1789 Ruedecill, Jacob to Moser, Catherine
Mar  3 1789 Ruff, Catherine to Vion, John
Jul  7 1794 Runkle, Joseph to Bussard, Susanna
Jun 24 1802 Runkles, Sarah to Kemp, Jacob
Nov 26 1791 Runner, Cathe. to Rohr, Rudolph, Jr.
May 14 1794 Runner, Charlotte to Wolfe, Ludwick
Aug  8 1809 Runner, Christena to Troutman, Peter
Feb 23 1780 Runner, Christian to Thomas, Eliz'th
Mar  6 1789 Runner, Elizabeth to Show, Conrad
Jan  6 1803 Runner, Eve to Hinkle, John
Oct 17 1795 Runner, Eve to Templin, Richard
Feb 15 1804 Runner, Henry to Hoffman, Margaret
Nov  9 1808 Runner, Henry to Thomas, Elizabeth
Jan 11 1799 Runner, Michael, Jr. to Hershaberger, Eve
Nov  3 1810 Ruperd, Elizabeth to Harding, Jacob
Dec  1 1806 Rusher, Elizabeth to Handley, Dennis
Feb  1 1805 Rusher, Susanna to Kale, George
Jul 27 1804 Russell, Elizabeth to Reeder, Joseph
Oct 15 1801 Russell, John to Nichols, Nancy
Jul 24 1807 Russell, Mary to Bostian, John
Mar 21 1801 Russell, Nancey to Rhodes, John
Mar 22 1793 Russell, Wm. to Randal, Elizabeth
Aug 11 1797 Rust, John to Marshall, Elizabeth
Apr 24 1804 Ruth, Henry to Mettart, Margaret
Feb 28 1795 Rutter, Edward Hanson to McLure, Margaretta
Jan 15 1803 Ryan, Elenor to Goodill, George
Sep 27 1794 Ryan, George to Steward, Sarah
Jul 10 1778 Ryley, Eleanor to Taylor, Joseph
Jun  6 1778 Ryley, Elizabeth to Bowden, William
Oct 22 1781 Ryley, Elizabeth to Crawmer, Ludwick
May 22 1778 Ryley, Patrick to Cringland, Elizabeth
Sep 22 1778 Ryley, Patrick to Price, Hanah
Feb  8 1779 Ryne, Mich'l to Smith, Eleanor

Jul  1 1809 Sadler, Catherine to Barrick, Henry
Aug 23 1794 Sadler, John to Devilbiss, Catherine
Aug  4 1804 Saer, Israel to Taylor, Mary
Jul 11 1801 Saffell, John to Harrison, Ruth
Mar  9 1780 Saffle, Sarah to Harrison, Kens
Nov  2 1808 Saffron, Mary to McKinney, Charles
Jan 16 1780 Sage, Mary to Froud, James
Apr  1 1799 Sailer, Mary to Herring, Henry
Sep 24 1802 Sain, John to Pennybaker, Mary
Aug 26 1780 Saline, Eve to Weast, Jacob
Apr 29 1809 Salkeld, Phebe to O'Conner, Bernard
Aug 26 1809 Salkeld, Phebe to O'Conner, Bernard
Sep 25 1797 Salkil, John to Smith, Lucy
```

```
May  6 1805 Salmon, Frederick to Philips, Amelia
Nov  2 1805 Salmon, Margaret to Creger, George, Jr.
May 16 1796 Salmon, Mary to Buckey, Peter
Dec 20 1806 Salmon, Richard to Green, Charlotte
May 16 1807 Salmon, William to Davis, Sarah
Apr 23 1802 Saltkill, Mary to Fishburn, David
Mar  9 1802 Sampson, Elizabeth to Springer, John
Oct  1 1803 Samsel, Elizabeth to Pry, George
Oct 24 1793 Sanderson, Francis to Schley, Margaret
May 14 1807 Sanderson, William R. to Leatherman, Elizabeth
Oct 18 1797 Sandes, Elizabeth to Triplepp, Thomas
Oct 18 1797 Sandes, James to Sandes, Sarah
Oct 18 1797 Sandes, Sarah to Sandes, James
Jul 29 1807 Sands, Bersheba to Owings, Thomas
Oct 25 1810 Sands, Elizabeth to Murphy, William
Aug 16 1800 Sansell, Peter to Gillaspie, Mary
May  7 1806 Sappington, Harriott to Warfield, Peregrine
May 27 1789 Sappington, James to Clark, Rachel
Feb  4 1808 Sargent, Catherine to Strine, Peter
Jan  8 1805 Sargent, Elizabeth to West, William
Oct  3 1796 Sargent, George to Wells, Ann
Jul 30 1804 Sargent, Jacob to Hewitt, Ruth
Aug 11 1807 Sargent, Jacob to Finkbone, Mary
Nov 20 1787 Sargent, John to Campden, Esther
Jul 24 1807 Sarjeant, William to Rodgers, Elizabeth
Dec 15 1792 Sauffer, Mary Ann to Kennedy, John
Feb 27 1792 Sauffer, Regina to Mussetter, Christian
Sep  2 1806 Saum, Magdalena to Shrantz, Frederick
Dec 30 1806 Saum, Rachel to Cronise, John
Sep 29 1804 Saunders, Mary to Saunders, Presley
Sep 29 1804 Saunders, Presley to Saunders, Mary
Dec 20 1809 Savidge, Elizabeth to Nixon, Jonathan
Oct  7 1799 Sawyer, Margaret to Danner, Zachariah
Jul 12 1792 Sawyer, Peter to Buckey, Margaret
Jan 29 1798 Sayler, Martin to Wilson, Elizabeth
Apr  7 1798 Saylor, Daniel to Raitt, Barbara
Jan 26 1785 Scaggs, Eliz'th to Fogle, Adam
Sep 20 1790 Scaggs, James to Reaser, Catharine
Nov 30 1802 Scaggs, Leonard to Rice, Sarah
Dec 22 1795 Scaggs, Richard to Holtzman, Susanna
Dec 15 1808 Scaggs, Richard to Frutch, Catherine
Sep  5 1778 Scaggs, Sarah to Hill, Benj'n
Jan  1 1803 Schaffner, Jacob to Weaver, Phebe
Feb 24 1789 Schell, Henry to Ollex, Elizabeth
Sep 15 1807 Schelton, Samuel to Roderock, Catherine
May  6 1800 Schley, Catherine to Felius, Conrad
Apr 21 1792 Schley, John to Schriver, Polly
Oct 24 1793 Schley, Margaret to Sanderson, Francis
Apr  4 1795 Schley, Mary to Shroeder, Henry
Oct 14 1797 Schley, Matthias to Drill, Mary
Feb 22 1802 Schnerr, Charles to Danner, Catherine
Jan  8 1803 Schnertzel, George to Moler, Margaret
Apr 12 1800 Schnertzel, Susanna to Carbery, John Baptist
Dec  8 1792 Schnertzell, Cevilla (Sybilla) to Carbury, Henry
May 30 1796 Schnertzell, Christina to Hobbs, William C.
Sep 29 1792 Scholes, Mary to Barrick, William
```

```
Mar  6 1779 Schoolmyer, John Peter to Rinehart, Mary Eve
Oct 10 1799 Schriner, Elizabeth to McDonald, James
Mar 28 1807 Schriner, Rachel to Marckell, Jonathan
Apr 21 1792 Schriver, Polly to Schley, John
Dec 15 1807 Schryock, Elizabeth to Favorite, Abraham
Sep 25 1800 Schue, Solme to Brashears, Theodore
Sep 10 1803 Schultz, John to Keller, Mary
Oct 29 1785 Schwartz, Susanna to Shroder, Herman Hinrich
Jun 11 1795 Scoby, Robert to Braughan, Elizabeth
May  4 1805 Scoff, Catherine to Powlas, Nicholas
Aug 18 1802 Scoggins, Charity to Prout, Solomon
Apr 28 1800 Scoggins, Elizabeth to Briscoe, John
Jan 27 1807 Scoggins, Rachel to Gray, Joseph
Nov 27 1805 Scoggins, Sally to Prout, William
Jun 26 1809 Scott, Abey to Keesy, Henry
Jun 30 1795 Scott, Eleanor to Kennedy, George
Nov 26 1799 Scott, Elizabeth to Mitchell, Alexander
Feb  3 1796 Scott, James to Williams, Mary
Apr 10 1779 Scott, John to Strane, Mary
Oct 30 1805 Scott, John to Bruce, Elizabeth Key
Aug 22 1778 Scott, Mary Ann to Griffith, Chisholm
Dec 11 1785 Scurlock, William to Norman, Charity
Apr 18 1778 Scutchall, George to Cline, Catherine
Oct 30 1801 Seal, Mary to Cash, Isaiah
Sep 23 1778 Seaman (or Leaman), Mary to Kemp, Peter
Feb  7 1783 Seargeant, Elijah to Frasier, Margaret
Jan 18 1806 Sears, Joshua to Taylor, Elizabeth
Oct  1 1787 Sease, Paul to Birely, Magdaline
Oct 17 1778 Sechrist, Charles to Castle, Elizabeth
Sep 30 1807 Sedwick, Benjamin to White, Eleanor
Aug 28 1793 Sedwick, Elizabeth to Wilson, Joshua
Apr 10 1792 Sedwick, Joshan to Montgomery, Jno.
Apr 18 1794 Sedwith, Grace to Fox, Uriah
Jul 25 1806 Seekman, Joseph to Sweadner, Catherine
Jul 21 1794 Seesman, Elizabeth to Shriver, Frederick William
Jul 21 1797 Sefton, Charles to Campbell, Mary
Nov 23 1801 Segerfuse, Elizabeth to House, George
Mar 30 1782 Sehon, John to Burrow, Lucy
Nov  2 1779 Sehorn, Clare to Campbell, James
Oct  9 1804 Seise, Sophia to Wright, John
Feb 26 1784 Selby, Ann to Musgrove, Nathan
Dec  9 1801 Self, Mary to Veatch, Thomas
Mar  4 1783 Selfe, John to Veatch, Rebeckah
Mar  1 1800 Sellers, Hannah to Mumford, John
Jan 19 1801 Sellman, Althea to Arnold, Jonathan
Sep 16 1779 Sellman, Gassaway to Davis, Catherine
Feb  9 1801 Sellman, Jane to Poole, Samuel
Mar 22 1807 Sellman, John to Passey, Catharine
Dec 27 1803 Sellman, Margaret to Brown, Ephraim
Apr 25 1806 Sellman, Nancy to Shipley, Leven
Sep 22 1801 Sellman, Peter to Pearcy, Elizabeth
Jul 23 1802 Sellman, Ruth to Paxton, William
Apr 16 1804 Sellman, Sarah to Pusey, George
Mar  6 1810 Sellman, William to Shipley, Ruth
Sep  6 1810 Selmon, Eve to Mahagan, William
```

Feb 12 1798 Sennebaugh, Peter to Smeltzer, Mary
Sep 28 1807 Senseney, Catherine to Magee, George W.
Aug  5 1807 Senseny, Mary to Cough, Jacob
Jun 27 1786 Sensor, Elizabeth to Swedner, Henry
Apr 24 1805 Sepp, Leonard to Firmwald, Catharine
Feb 15 1803 Sergeant, Elizabeth to Thrasher, Benjamin
Feb 22 1791 Sergeant, Mary Ann to Prather, John Garrott
Jul  2 1782 Serjeant, William to Tucker, Margaret
Feb 27 1798 Sewal (Sewell), Andrew to Beale, Eleanor
Dec 17 1780 Sewalt, Jacob to Curtz, Barbara
Nov 16 1779 Sewell, Alley to Luther, Christ'n
Mar 26 1794 Sewell, Sarah to Campbell, James
Mar 13 1804 Shaaf, Peter to Ridenour, Elizabeth
Aug 28 1805 Shacklett, Elizabeth to Mitchel, John
Apr 23 1803 Shade, Elizabeth to Tice, George
Aug 14 1803 Shafer, Anne to Goslin, Ambrose
Jan 20 1798 Shafer, Barbara to Kittinger, Jacob
May  6 1799 Shafer, Barbara to Thomas, Peter
Dec  6 1790 Shafer, Catharine to Heffner, Gotlip
Jun  2 1797 Shafer, Catherine to Shroyer, David
Sep 16 1809 Shafer, Catherine to Yowler, Michael
Feb 12 1804 Shafer, Conrad to Hagan, Dorothy
Sep  6 1794 Shafer, Elizabeth to Heffner, Mich'l
Aug 27 1810 Shafer, Elizabeth to Shafer, Jacob
Jan 28 1809 Shafer, Elizabeth to Staley, Frederick
Apr 24 1797 Shafer, Elizabeth to Staley, Peter
Apr 20 1803 Shafer, Elizabeth to Wilyard, Peter
Apr 14 1807 Shafer, Elizabeth to Keppler, Peter
Dec 19 1785 Shafer, George to Stull, Catherine
May 21 1798 Shafer, Jacob to Ramsberg, Susanna
Aug 27 1810 Shafer, Jacob to Shafer, Elizabeth
May 11 1799 Shafer, John to Oat, Susannah
Dec 17 1801 Shafer, Mary to Messerly, George
May 23 1808 Shafer, Mary to Miller, George
May  9 1794 Shafer, Mary to Ott, John
May 28 1803 Shafer, Mary to Williard, John
Mar  4 1800 Shafer, Modelena to Nagle, Sebastian, Jr.
May 11 1805 Shafer, Nicholas to Fischer, Elizabeth
Oct 24 1809 Shafer, Susanna to Thomas, Henry
Oct 24 1794 Shafer, Tobias to Comfer, Catherine
Jun 18 1785 Shafert, Susannah to Rachob, Fred'k
Apr 30 1804 Shaffer, John to Ohler, Barbara
Dec 21 1805 Shahan, David to Ridgely, Annie
Apr  9 1798 Shane, Ann Maria to Falconear, John Barkley
Aug 11 1806 Shaneholtz, Catherine to Martin, John
Dec 19 1804 Shaneholtz, Margaret to Keefer, Samuel
Nov 23 1796 Shank, Catherine to Swisher, Matthias
Aug 21 1809 Shank, Elizabeth to Michael, William
Apr 20 1797 Shank, John to Reynolds, Lydia
Jan  7 1809 Shank, John to Eby, Mary
Jan 13 1803 Shank, Michael to Switzer, Catharine
Jul 24 1807 Shank, Peter to Way, Mary
Mar 16 1808 Sharm, James to Findlace, Margaret
Jun  8 1793 Sharrats, John to Crouse, Catharine
Oct 15 1808 Shauer, John to Smith, Lydia

```
Jul 13 1806 Shaugh, Jacob to Cox, Elizabeth
Aug 22 1794 Shaven, William to Essex, Elizabeth
Oct  4 1783 Shaver, John to Stull, Elizabeth
Jul 21 1783 Shaver, Tobias to Currance, Mary
Dec 17 1783 Shaw, Basil to Eck, Catherine
Oct 23 1790 Shaw, Hugh to McKay, Ann
Aug 24 1803 Shawhan, Daniel to Ridgely, Sarah
Jan 31 1803 Shawn, James to Templin, Catherine
Aug 17 1807 Shealer, Samuel to Peterson, Sarah
Sep  5 1789 Sheats, Henry to Ellis, Rachel
Mar 27 1790 Sheats, Jacob to Harple, Hannah
Nov  7 1789 Sheats, Sarah to Twomey, Daniel
Feb  7 1795 Sheckell, Elizabeth to Simpson, Rezin
Sep 16 1786 Sheckells, Susanna to Drone, Wm.
Apr 12 1785 Sheckels, John to Story, Ruth
Sep 28 1801 Sheeler, David to Peterson, Margaret
May  1 1781 Sheely, And'w to Heffner, Mary
Nov 15 1809 Sheely, Frederick to Keefer, Susanna
Sep  5 1784 Shees, Sebastian to Burckhartt, Pheby
Sep 13 1806 Sheetinghelm, Catherine to Eckhart, Anthony
Jun  5 1786 Sheets, Catherine to Hartman, John
Apr 21 1794 Sheets, Christian to Wetsell, Margaret
Dec 24 1793 Sheets, Martin to Aldridge, Sarah
Apr  8 1807 Sheffer, Adam to Tares, Barbara
Sep 14 1778 Sheffer, Mary to Bussard, Jacob
May  4 1807 Sheffer, Philip to Menser, Sarah
Jun 20 1788 Sheffey, Catherine to Brengle, Lawrence
Mar 19 1785 Sheffey, Elizabeth to Giar, John
May 29 1803 Sheffey, Mary to Giting, Abraham
Sep  9 1795 Shekel, John to Burges, Mary
Apr  3 1786 Shekells, Mary to Beall, Colmore
Mar 19 1778 Shelar, Margaret to Logan, William
Nov 30 1783 Shell, Catherine to Shull, Frederick
Oct 30 1783 Shell, Charles to Plonk, Mary
Jan  8 1795 Shell, Margaret to Brother, Valentine
May  6 1786 Shell, Molly to Holtzman, Jacob
May  8 1790 Shellhouse, Peter to Hemp, Juliana
Oct  8 1803 Shellman, Catherine to Hauer, Georgeerine
Nov  6 1779 Shellman, Eliz'th to Bair, Henry
Dec  6 1808 Shellman, Susanna to Emmit, William, Esq.
Mar 30 1778 Shellmon, Jacob to Bentz, Catherine
Jan  9 1794 Shelmerdine, Stephen to Philips, Eunice
Dec 13 1796 Sheltnecht, Rosanna to Or, Michael
Oct  1 1803 Shelton, Elizabeth to Wilson, Charles
Dec 29 1801 Shelton, John to Stockman, Mary
Mar 19 1807 Shelton, Lethe Ann to Bell, John
Sep  7 1803 Shelton, Thomas to Blackburn, Elizabeth
Oct  9 1805 Shelton, Thomas to Spurrier, Henrietta
Apr 22 1783 Shenkmeyer, Catherine Eliz'th to de Reitzenstein,
             Frederick
Sep 14 1799 Shenkmire, Susannah to Weast, Jacob
May 17 1781 Shepherd, John to Wissman, Elizabeth
Jan 16 1810 Shepperd, Mary to Houghf, John
Feb 23 1801 Sheredine, Sophia to Higgins, James L.
Aug  1 1799 Sheredine, Upton to Dorsey, Sophia
```

```
Jul 30 1801 Sherley, Samuel to Young, Mary
Sep 11 1810 Sherman, Benjamin to Harrison, Eleanor
Feb 26 1803 Sherman, Eve to Shriver, David, Jr.
Sep 25 1798 Shetinghellern, Jacob to Walter, Mary
Mar 20 1779 Shibeler, George to Everley, Elizabeth
May 18 1802 Shick, John to Wier, Catharine
Oct 15 1806 Shields, Barnet to Donovan, Susanna
Mar  7 1809 Shields, Lydia to Woakman, Joseph
Apr 22 1809 Shields, William to McKissock, Anne
Jul 18 1793 Shilling, Murray to Brown, Rebecca
Mar 27 1787 Shilling, William to Gilbert, Catharine
Dec 29 1797 Shimer, Isaac to Delashmutt, Sarah
Jun  8 1783 Shindler, Adam to Queary, Christena
May  9 1808 Shindler, Daniel to Reese, Elizabeth
Jan  8 1805 Shingle, Lawrence to Syphers, Mary
Sep  3 1794 Shingle, Mary to Shryock, Christian
Feb 25 1809 Shingler, Margaret to Redanor, Frederick
May  1 1797 Shingletaker, Jacob to Hollenberger, Catharine
Apr 10 1797 Ship, Elizabeth to Anderson, John
Jun 25 1782 Shipler, Lidia to Pigott, Charles
Jul  6 1798 Shipley, Amelia to Hearn, Mathias
Nov 11 1805 Shipley, Anne to Fringer, Stephen
Aug 18 1781 Shipley, Basil to Knox, Susanna
Mar  4 1808 Shipley, Elizabeth Owings to McElfresh, Caleb
Oct 21 1803 Shipley, Ezahiel to Cummings, Alice Ann
Apr  4 1796 Shipley, Hezekiah to Picket, Ruth
Apr 25 1806 Shipley, Leven to Sellman, Nancy
May  5 1804 Shipley, Marcella Owings to Welch, Samuel, Jr.
Jul 12 1778 Shipley, Rachel to Poole, James
Dec 15 1792 Shipley, Rebecca to Adams, Abraham
Mar  6 1810 Shipley, Ruth to Sellman, William
Oct 29 1808 Shirley, Mary to Hoffman, George
Jun 21 1782 Shitearie, Eve to Rowser, Henry
Mar 23 1781 Shitzen, Esther to Kigar, Jno.
May  5 1796 Shivell, Adam to Riggs, Catherine
Aug  8 1778 Shively, Eve to Sidle, Gudlip
Dec  7 1796 Shively, Mary to Joy, Stephen
Feb 18 1809 Shlusser, Elizabeth to Waltzheimer, John
Oct 17 1793 Shockness, Mary to Staltcop, William
Mar 29 1806 Shoe, John to Hoxie, Prudence
Jan 21 1804 Shoe, Philip, Jr. to Bone, Susanna
Oct 12 1799 Shoe, Solomon to Carn, Madelena
Oct 15 1798 Shoemaker, Abraham to Baldwin, Pheby
Feb  8 1800 Shoemaker, Anne to Everhart, Jacob
Dec 31 1800 Shoemaker, Christian to Kinzey, Annie
Aug 21 1802 Shoemaker, Christina to Smeltzer, Jacob
Jul 26 1810 Shoemaker, Daniel to Shoemaker, Elizabeth
Feb 24 1810 Shoemaker, Daniel to Hutzell, Polly
May 29 1809 Shoemaker, Elizabeth to Copeland, John
Feb 24 1806 Shoemaker, Elizabeth to Hutzee, John
Jul 26 1810 Shoemaker, Elizabeth to Shoemaker, Daniel
Jan 25 1785 Shoemaker, Hedwick to Stottlemyer, Jacob
May 22 1810 Shoemaker, Nicholas to Roads, Elizabeth
Jan 14 1809 Shoemaker, Stephen to Arthur, Margaret Ann
Dec  2 1798 Shoff, Hanner to McGuyre, John
```

| | | | |
|---|---|---|---|
| May | 7 | 1793 | Shollison, Mary to Herpster, Frederick |
| Apr | 22 | 1783 | Shonkmeyer, Catherine Eliz'th to de Reitzenstein, Frederick |
| Mar | 18 | 1782 | Shontz, Michael to Jones, Catherine |
| Dec | 14 | 1795 | Shook, Jacob to Zimmerman, Elizabeth |
| Jan | 7 | 1799 | Shook, Jacob to Clem, Catherine |
| Dec | 28 | 1806 | Shook, John to Harper, Sarah |
| Feb | 9 | 1807 | Shook, Sarah to Lane, John |
| Jul | 18 | 1795 | Shook, Walter to Miller, Ann Mary |
| Nov | 21 | 1791 | Shope, Jacob to Brengle, Elizabeth |
| Jan | 27 | 1786 | Short, Richard to Rue, Rebeckah |
| Sep | 17 | 1791 | Shots, John to Leashorn, Elizabeth |
| Oct | 5 | 1793 | Shots, Philip to Bargesser, Catherine |
| Sep | 12 | 1807 | Shott, Adam to Beard, Catherine |
| Feb | 28 | 1780 | Shotts, Clory to Marker, Henry |
| Jan | 5 | 1807 | Shoun, John to Heffner, Elizabeth |
| Feb | 2 | 1782 | Shoup, Catherine to Cross, Henry |
| Aug | 31 | 1803 | Shoup, Christian to Eller, Mary |
| Apr | 9 | 1805 | Shoup, Christian to Gaver, Elizabeth |
| Feb | 10 | 1795 | Shoup, Elizabeth to Shuck, Peter |
| Sep | 18 | 1778 | Shoup, George to Loy, Charlotte |
| Jul | 12 | 1785 | Shoup, John to Moyer, Barbara |
| Jun | 1 | 1801 | Shoup, Mary to Houck, John, Junr. |
| Oct | 20 | 1780 | Shoup, Peter to Goodman, Rebecca |
| Jan | 23 | 1793 | Shoup, Samuel to Grove, Dolley |
| Apr | 11 | 1795 | Shoup, Sophia to Friberger, George |
| Jun | 17 | 1799 | Shover, Catherine to Weller, Henry |
| Dec | 31 | 1779 | Shover, Henry to Baker, Rosanna |
| Apr | 18 | 1783 | Show, Catherine to Pierpoint, Joseph |
| Mar | 6 | 1789 | Show, Conrad to Runner, Elizabeth |
| Feb | 6 | 1787 | Showalker, Adam to Snoudagle, Barbara |
| Oct | 10 | 1786 | Showe, Eliz'th to Coleshine, Earnest |
| Apr | 25 | 1795 | Showe, Henry to Kessler, Mary |
| Aug | 26 | 1780 | Showes, Samuel to Hargishymeir, Catherine |
| Apr | 13 | 1805 | Shown, Margaret to Trout, John |
| Mar | 16 | 1804 | Shown, Peter to Wallis, Margaret |
| Feb | 20 | 1788 | Showne, Elizabeth to Harrison, Samuel |
| Jun | 11 | 1791 | Showne, Mary to Athein, Horatio |
| Sep | 5 | 1789 | Showne, Peter to Whitcroft, Sarah |
| Oct | 5 | 1784 | Shrader, Barbara to Bowsinger, Henry |
| Aug | 6 | 1803 | Shrader, Elizabeth to Oldwine, Charles |
| Dec | 30 | 1783 | Shrader, Elizabeth to Troutman, Michael |
| Sep | 18 | 1778 | Shrader, Henry to Horine, Susanna |
| Sep | 2 | 1806 | Shrantz, Frederick to Saum, Magdalena |
| Dec | 7 | 1790 | Shreaves, William to Lawrence, Elizabeth |
| Apr | 27 | 1799 | Shreup, Barbara to Hammersleigh, Charles |
| Mar | 24 | 1809 | Shreup, Catherine to Debery, John |
| Apr | 17 | 1806 | Shreup, Mary to Creager, Frederick |
| Jan | 1 | 1808 | Shreup, Modelena to Eckman, George |
| Oct | 22 | 1799 | Shrigly, Enoch to Murry, Mary |
| Jan | 29 | 1810 | Shriner, Abraham to Forney, Mary |
| Dec | 23 | 1785 | Shriner, Adam to Kisinger, Mary |
| Mar | 21 | 1799 | Shriner, George to Hollenberger, Ann |
| Apr | 11 | 1809 | Shriner, Margaret to Dudderer, William |
| Oct | 8 | 1808 | Shriner, Mary to Henry, Charles |

```
May 12 1789 Shriner, Peter to Biddle, Eve
Apr 16 1802 Shriner, Philip to Hawk, Susanna
Jan  1 1805 Shriner, Sarah Maria to Lawrence, John S.
Nov 26 1787 Shriock, Daniel to Cossell, Mary
Oct 18 1803 Shriver, Abraham to Leatherman, Margaret
Feb 26 1803 Shriver, David, Jr. to Sherman, Eve
Apr  3 1809 Shriver, Elizabeth to Brother, Jacob, Junr
Nov  6 1802 Shriver, Elizabeth to Routsawn, Benjamin
Jul 21 1794 Shriver, Frederick William to Seesman, Elizabeth
Mar 19 1779 Shriver, Henry to Walfley, Barbara
Apr 23 1803 Shriver, Henry to Houck, Catherine
Apr 22 1802 Shriver, Isaac to Leatherman, Mary
Jun 18 1810 Shriver, Jacob to Ridge, Rebecca
Apr 30 1799 Shriver, Pheby to Rowenzawn, Benjamin
Aug 15 1809 Shriver, Susan to Frey, Samuel
Oct 29 1785 Shroder, Herman Hinrich to Schwartz, Susanna
Apr  4 1795 Shroeder, Henry to Schley, Mary
Nov  9 1783 Shroiner, Eliz'th to Martz, Peter
Nov 21 1789 Shroiner, Mary to Levy, Jacob
Aug 26 1779 Shroiner, Mary Ann to Heater, Frederick
Dec  8 1789 Shroiner, Susanna to Ritemeyer, Conrad
May 16 1805 Shronk, John to Grim, Christena
Mar 30 1808 Shroyer, Catharine to Somsel, Jacob
Aug  2 1796 Shroyer, Catherine to Crown, Conrad
Nov  2 1795 Shroyer, Catherine to Smith, Philip of Phil
Jun  2 1797 Shroyer, David to Shafer, Catherine
Nov 15 1798 Shroyer, David to Fleck, Catherine
Feb 26 1808 Shroyer, Elizabeth to Dick, Levi
Apr  2 1801 Shroyer, Elizabeth to Fluke, John
Aug 17 1805 Shroyer, Elizabeth to Keans, Michael
Apr 21 1804 Shroyer, Jacob to Frushour, Susanna
Jan 14 1808 Shroyer, Jacob to O'Ferral, Catherine
Aug  2 1796 Shroyer, Mary to Haines, Joseph
Feb 13 1806 Shroyer, Mary to Herring, John
Jul 30 1796 Shroyer, Mary to Stone, John
Jun 21 1804 Shroyer, Thomas to Fry, Elizabeth
Mar 20 1797 Shryner, Michael to Worman, Ann
Jan 16 1810 Shryock, Amelia to Stephens, Septimius
Sep  3 1794 Shryock, Christian to Shingle, Mary
May 17 1794 Shryock, Elizabeth to Harmon, John
Jan 26 1801 Shryock, John to Johnson, Ann
Apr  6 1798 Shryock, Matthias to Gaugh, Elizabeth
Aug  2 1783 Shryock, Valentine to Derr, Christena
Sep 14 1790 Shttice, Ann to Smith, Matthias
Feb 10 1795 Shuck, Peter to Shoup, Elizabeth
Feb 24 1802 Shuff, Jonathan to Heller, Christena
Dec  2 1797 Shule, John to Brengle, Catherine
May 27 1797 Shull, Christian to Brunner, Elizabeth
Oct 21 1783 Shull, Elizabeth to Koontza, Frederick
Nov 30 1783 Shull, Frederick to Shell, Catherine
May 31 1783 Shull, Mary to Smith, Daniel
May 31 1779 Shultz, Alex'dr to Freeman, Eleanor
Mar 29 1782 Shultz, Catherine to Houcks, Jacob
Sep 27 1783 Shultz, David to Myers, Eve
Jun 26 1790 Shultz, Margaret to Kline, Stephen
```

| | | | |
|---|---|---|---|
|May|22|1800|Shultz, Susanna to Mason, Thomas|
|Dec|22|1787|Shuman, Jacob to Templing, Polly|
|Sep|14|1810|Shunk, Christian to Holprun, Catherine|
|Mar|15|1803|Shunk, Joseph to Wood, Aurelia|
|Sep|30|1805|Shup, Solomon to Koontz, Elizabeth|
|Aug|26|1783|Shurr, John to Akin, Elizabeth|
|Jul|29|1783|Shurte, Susanna to Zimmerman, Adam|
|Jan|7|1793|Shurtz, Uliana to Blickenstaffer, David|
|Sep|10|1790|Shutter, Susanna to Waltz, Rinehart|
|Sep|7|1790|Siars, Prethenia to Murphey, Duncan|
|Feb|22|1782|Sibert, Eliz'th to Brandenbergh, Fred'k|
|May|31|1782|Sibert, Eliz'th to Brandenbergh, Fred'k|
|Aug|3|1803|Sicafucer, John to Durham, Peggy|
|Apr|18|1786|Sickman, Mary to Noland, Michael|
|Aug|8|1778|Sidle, Gudlip to Shively, Eve|
|Jul|12|1790|Sifert, Mathias to Durff, Elizabeth|
|May|9|1793|Sigafoose, Jacob to Werner, Mary|
|Jul|11|1805|Sigler, Michael to Eller, Susanna|
|Nov|8|1785|Sigler, Phoeby to Lapp, Henry|
|Jan|24|1810|Silket, Eleanor to Poulton, Thomas|
|May|6|1798|Silman, Thomas to Harris, Ruth|
|Apr|13|1786|Silver, Anne to Butler, Peter|
|Feb|12|1791|Silver, Elizabeth Margaret to Norris, William|
|Apr|12|1783|Silver, George to Griffin, Ann|
|Apr|7|1778|Silver, John to Springer, Ann|
|Dec|4|1779|Silverin, Judy to Gay, Henry|
|Dec|13|1788|Silvia, Servant of Mr. Duvall to Smother, Thomas|
|Dec|4|1790|Sim, Anthony to Smith, Christiana|
|Apr|28|1800|Sim, Anthony to Smith, Mary|
|Feb|26|1788|Sim, Mary to Nelson, Roger|
|Nov|25|1794|Simm, Thomas to Thomas, Catherine Lewis|
|Apr|17|1810|Simmerman, Catherine to Reel, Frederick|
|Oct|21|1791|Simmerman, Elizabeth to Beckenbaugh, George|
|Apr|27|1795|Simmerman, Margaret to Fiste, Philip|
|Jun|17|1785|Simmerman, Susannah to Holtz, Nicholas|
|Aug|24|1782|Simmonds, Eleanor to Haze, Leonard|
|Dec|9|1785|Simmonds, Elizabeth to Tannehill, William|
|Aug|14|1782|Simmonds, George to White, Rebeckah|
|Aug|11|1805|Simmonds, Zachariah to Wattson, Susanna|
|Feb|13|1795|Simmons, Drusilla to Torrence, James|
|Dec|28|1793|Simmons, Elizabeth to Lucas, Thomas|
|Jul|29|1809|Simmons, Elizabeth to Myers, George|
|Oct|24|1804|Simmons, Jacob to Harding, Mary Ann|
|Oct|26|1802|Simmons, James to Simmons, Rebeckah Ford|
|Feb|24|1802|Simmons, John to Tingler, Catherine|
|Feb|4|1796|Simmons, John H. to Howard, Eleanor|
|Apr|15|1786|Simmons, Margaret to Burckhartt, Nathaniel|
|Mar|31|1809|Simmons, Marianne to Cost, Christian|
|Mar|21|1782|Simmons, Mary to Dawson, Benjamin|
|Mar|27|1807|Simmons, Peter to Jacobs, Catherine|
|Oct|26|1802|Simmons, Rebeckah Ford to Simmons, James|
|Dec|27|1808|Simmons, Ruth to Dade, Townsend T.|
|Feb|15|1791|Simmons, Samuel to Ward, Elizabeth|
|Feb|23|1778|Simmons, Thomas to Adams, Mary|
|Dec|5|1789|Simms, J. Clebborn to Beall, Mary Ann|

```
Sep 15 1798 Simon, Catherine to Fox, John
Sep 10 1808 Simon, Joseph to Bowman, Elizabeth
Sep 19 1797 Simon, Mary to Barrack, Frederick
Jun  7 1809 Simon, Polly to Brown, John
Mar 27 1804 Simpson, Ann to Williams, Curtis
Jan  5 1797 Simpson, Basil to Worthington, Henrietta
Jan  1 1785 Simpson, Benjamin to Duvall, Elizabeth
Dec 16 1809 Simpson, Betsey to Watson, John
Mar 20 1802 Simpson, Delilah to Warfield, Thomas
Jul 20 1782 Simpson, Erasmus to Willson, Lucy
May 20 1804 Simpson, John to Stoner, Sophia
Feb  3 1806 Simpson, Joshua to Burgess, Matilda
Feb  7 1795 Simpson, Rezin to Sheckell, Elizabeth
May 22 1780 Simpson, Richard, Jr. to Cumming, Catherine
Dec 19 1782 Simpson, Sarah to McCusey, John
Nov 29 1800 Simpson, Thomas to Riddlemoser, Barbara
Jan  9 1799 Simpson, Walter to Thomas, Elizabeth
Mar 11 1797 Sin, Elizabeth to Houk, John
Feb  7 1806 Singer, Catherine to Black, John
Apr 11 1800 Singer, Susannah to Eigenbrode, John
Oct 12 1792 Sinn, Catharine to Smith, William
Apr 25 1789 Sinn, Catherine to Brunner, Peter of Peter
Sep  9 1792 Sinn, Elizabeth to Sowers, Peter
Jan  2 1808 Sinn, Jacob to Black, Eve
Feb 15 1800 Sinn, Margaret to Stoner, Frederick
Apr 11 1805 Sinn, Mary to Palmer, Henry
Oct  8 1798 Sinn, Philip to Loehr, Elizabeth
Jun  6 1802 Sinn, Sally to Houkman, Philip
Dec 23 1797 Sintz, Adam to Metz, Mary
Sep 25 1778 Sipes, Eliz'th to Conner, James
Aug 29 1782 Sipes, Elizabeth to Todd, Andrew
Apr  2 1793 Sissell, Philip to Juluck, Juliet
Jul 19 1808 Skeal, Nicholas to Harding, Elizabeth
Jan 30 1787 Skekel, Ann to Leakin, Daniel
Jan  4 1785 Skekell, Frances to Owen, William
Dec  6 1796 Skinner, Henry Smith to Hilleary, Sarah
Jul 22 1797 Slagle, Elizabeth to Keller, Jacob
Nov  5 1805 Slates, Christena to Holtzman, Martin
Jan  4 1808 Slatlz, Samuel to Plummer, Rachel
Apr 19 1809 Slaymaker, Elizabeth to McAlister, William
Oct 29 1784 Sleagle, Elizabeth to Tutterow, Baltice
Mar 14 1801 Sleek, Elizabeth to Messler, William
Mar  1 1796 Slegle, Frederick to Boteler, Elizabeth
Apr 10 1798 Sleicherlan, Elizabeth to Filuse (Filius?), Joseph
Dec  6 1803 Sleighmaker, Alexander to Davis, Sarah
Mar 28 1809 Slick, Jacob to Otto, Margaret
Feb 13 1796 Slicker, Catharine to Apollo, Lewis Benjamin
Jan 14 1805 Slifer, David to Easterday, Julianna
Apr 24 1797 Slunger, John to Gross, Margaret
Jun  8 1799 Sluss, Barbara to Hockensmith, John
Jun 14 1806 Slusser, Henry to Delaughter, Catherine
Apr 14 1810 Slusser, Polly to Biser, John
Sep  9 1805 Slutman, Peter to Brugh, Esther
Apr 21 1810 Small, Ann to Murdock, William
Oct  6 1785 Small, John to Plonk, Philipeana
```

Nov 15 1794 Small, Michael to Smith, Catherine
Nov 22 1794 Smallwood, Eliz. to Hamilton, John G.
Apr  2 1803 Smallwood, Henry to Rigney, Rebecca
Mar 23 1778 Smedley, Jacob to Cline, Elizabeth
Dec 19 1805 Smelse, John to Rodinghiser, Elizabeth
Dec  8 1810 Smelser, John to Norris, Rachel
Sep  8 1788 Smeltzer, Catharine to Povey, Christian
Aug 21 1802 Smeltzer, Jacob to Shoemaker, Christina
Feb 12 1798 Smeltzer, Mary to Sennebaugh, Peter
May  1 1804 Smethen, Nicholas to Worthington, Susannah Hood
Sep  1 1798 Smith, Abraham to Lefaver, Hester
Sep 17 1791 Smith, Adam to Dodds, Sarah
Nov  7 1807 Smith, Alexander to Fox, Catherine
Jun 30 1805 Smith, Andrew to Wickham, Anna
Sep  9 1809 Smith, Ann to Ferich (?), John
Nov 25 1789 Smith, Ann to McElfresh, Charles
Jun  5 1795 Smith, Anne to Gregg, Thomas
Aug  2 1805 Smith, Anne to Kessler, Peter
Jul 29 1801 Smith, Anne to Vance, Jacob
Dec 26 1795 Smith, Balser to Caufman, Catherine
Mar 28 1809 Smith, Barbara to Creager, Casper
Jul 17 1809 Smith, Barbara to Crutchler, Vincent
May 16 1795 Smith, Benjamin to Hardy, Ann
May 11 1794 Smith, Catharine to Kensell, Jacob
Dec  6 1799 Smith, Catherine to Creger, Jacob
Apr 17 1802 Smith, Catherine to Lambright, John
Apr  7 1810 Smith, Catherine to Lighter, Jacob
Dec  7 1796 Smith, Catherine to Markle, George
Nov 15 1794 Smith, Catherine to Small, Michael
Aug  9 1788 Smith, Catherine to Bantz, Henry
Sep  6 1800 Smith, Catherine to Way, David
Apr  2 1803 Smith, Catherine Sim to Beall, Theodore
Apr 13 1779 Smith, Charles to Ringer, Mary
Dec  4 1790 Smith, Christiana to Sim, Anthony
May 31 1783 Smith, Daniel to Shull, Mary
Aug 18 1804 Smith, David to Grabell, Susan
Oct 18 1804 Smith, Dennis to Wright, Hannah
Feb 13 1792 Smith, Eleanor to Murphey, James
Feb  8 1779 Smith, Eleanor to Ryne, Mich'l
Nov 26 1778 Smith, Eleanor to Trent, John
Jan 13 1792 Smith, Elizabeth to Butler Tobias
Feb 28 1809 Smith, Elizabeth to Currens, William
May 28 1810 Smith, Elizabeth to Arthur, Charles
May 17 1802 Smith, Elizabeth to Dorsey, Allen
Dec  1 1806 Smith, Elizabeth to Delauter, David
Jun 10 1798 Smith, Elizabeth to Joy, John
Sep 14 1810 Smith, Elizabeth to Worts, Henry
Dec 17 1789 Smith, Elizabeth to Clary, Ashford Dowden
Nov 20 1787 Smith, Esther to Bevard, John
Mar  9 1805 Smith, Esther to Darr, John
Dec 13 1799 Smith, Eve to Waggoner, Jacob
Jul 17 1794 Smith, Eve to Evans, Robert
Nov 25 1808 Smith, Frederick to Reimer, Esther
Dec 21 1809 Smith, Frederick to Cover, Mary
Apr 20 1805 Smith, George to Getzendanner, Margaret

```
Mar  3 1780 Smith, Hannah to Lakin, Basil
May 21 1798 Smith, Henry to Grove, Mary
Jan  9 1802 Smith, Henry to Zimmerman, Mary
Jan 26 1784 Smith, Henry of George to Buckman, Sarah
Feb 20 1789 Smith, J. T. Henry to Price, Elizabeth
Feb 16 1779 Smith, Jacob to Koontz, Salomy
Sep 27 1783 Smith, Jacob to Iseminger, Christena
Nov 23 1798 Smith, Jacob to Norwood, Mary
Mar 26 1808 Smith, Jacob to Bussard, Eleanor
Dec 28 1809 Smith, Jacob to Vartz, Christena
Mar  4 1782 Smith, James to Tucker, Cassandra
Sep 11 1797 Smith, James to Evans, Alty
Jul  3 1803 Smith, James to Tracey, Ann
Jan 15 1784 Smith, John to Maddox, Sarah
Jan 10 1787 Smith, John to Wolfe, Margaret
Feb  4 1789 Smith, John to Highfield, Ann
Apr  4 1792 Smith, John to McElfresh, Rachel
May  9 1793 Smith, John to Beard, Margaret
Mar 27 1795 Smith, John to Fout, Mary
Oct  4 1800 Smith, John to Albaugh, Elizabeth
May 14 1804 Smith, John to Bruner, Charlotte
Sep 28 1804 Smith, John to Fralick, Elizabeth
Mar  3 1810 Smith, John to Hall, Margaret
Jan 21 1794 Smith, John Henry to Kutz, Elizabeth
Dec 15 1795 Smith, John of John to Keefer, Mary
May  2 1790 Smith, Joseph to Jameson, Teresa
Oct 21 1800 Smith, Joseph to Barton, Axions
Nov 26 1807 Smith, Joseph to Dofler, Sybilla
Jan 29 1796 Smith, Lewis to Clance, Barbara
Nov 22 1810 Smith, Lewis to Eichelberger, Elizabeth
Sep 25 1797 Smith, Lucy to Salkil, John
Oct 15 1808 Smith, Lydia to Shauer, John
May 29 1793 Smith, Marcy to Goar, Thomas
Mar 24 1804 Smith, Margaret to Cookerly, John
Feb  6 1797 Smith, Margaret to Fout, Jacob
Feb 17 1780 Smith, Margaret to Klien, Nicholas
May 12 1794 Smith, Margaret to Mount, John
Feb 18 1802 Smith, Margaret to McDermot, Hugh
Jul 17 1804 Smith, Margaret to Stover, Philip
Mar  2 1801 Smith, Maria to Hildebrand, Jacob
Dec 29 1802 Smith, Martha to Plummer, Joshua
Nov 15 1779 Smith, Mary to Bayman, Thos.
Apr 17 1801 Smith, Mary to Creager, Solomon
Jan 26 1793 Smith, Mary to Albaugh, John
Sep 14 1801 Smith, Mary to Arnsperger, John
Dec  7 1799 Smith, Mary to Davis, Jonathan
Jun 21 1785 Smith, Mary to Earnst, Jacob
Nov 17 1808 Smith, Mary to Fister, John
Apr 28 1810 Smith, Mary to Greenawalt, Christian
Nov  1 1804 Smith, Mary to Geyer, Frederick
Mar 22 1781 Smith, Mary to Holtzman, Henry
Apr 18 1801 Smith, Mary to Hoof, Henry
Nov 18 1790 Smith, Mary to Jamison, Leonard
Sep 23 1779 Smith, Mary to Ridenhour, Henry
Jun 18 1785 Smith, Mary to Ramsower, Henry
```

```
Dec  4 1802 Smith, Mary to Ridenour, Jacob
Apr 28 1800 Smith, Mary to Sim, Anthony
May 30 1789 Smith, Mary to Smith, Tetrick
Oct  5 1798 Smith, Mary to Spoont, Joseph
Sep 23 1809 Smith, Mary to You, William
Jan 23 1807 Smith, Mary Magdalene to Keever, Andrew
Mar 13 1802 Smith, Matthias to Main, Polly
Jan  7 1793 Smith, Matthias to Buckey, Mary
Sep 14 1790 Smith, Matthias to Shttice, Ann
Aug 26 1785 Smith, Middleton to Keller, Juliana
Jun  3 1808 Smith, Nancy to Williams, John B.
May 19 1801 Smith, Peggy to Keever, Andrew
Feb 21 1789 Smith, Peter to Hart, Elizabeth
Oct  4 1790 Smith, Peter to Albaugh, Elizabeth
Dec 29 1795 Smith, Peter to Gitts, Barbara
Mar 18 1799 Smith, Peter to Albaugh, Catherine
Apr  9 1802 Smith, Peter to Weaver, Catherine
Aug 24 1805 Smith, Peter to Yandis, Mary
Nov  2 1795 Smith, Philip of Phil to Shroyer, Catherine
Dec 26 1796 Smith, Priscilla to Ramsey, John
Dec  5 1806 Smith, Sarah to Munshoure, John
Jul 29 1802 Smith, Sarah to Robertson, John
Sep 11 1783 Smith, Sarah, Miss to McPherson, John, Mr.
Aug 16 1807 Smith, Sophia to Rife, Jacob
May 17 1793 Smith, Susanna to Burgher, Adam
Apr 16 1798 Smith, Susanna to Dodds, Philip
Jun 15 1801 Smith, Susanna to Woolfe, Jacob
Oct 11 1786 Smith, Susannah to Keller, Jacob
Oct 18 1803 Smith, Susannah to Rhinehart, George
Apr  5 1808 Smith, Susannah to Ragan, George
May 30 1789 Smith, Tetrick to Smith, Mary
Feb 19 1807 Smith, Thomas to White, Sarah
Feb  8 1800 Smith, Walter to Frazier, Tobitha
Jan 18 1779 Smith, William to Miller, Rachel
Dec 14 1780 Smith, William to Bodington, Pheby
Sep  2 1782 Smith, William to Brown, Mary
Oct 12 1792 Smith, William to Sinn, Catharine
May 18 1779 Smitten, Eliz'th to Gaver, Valentine
Dec 13 1788 Smother, Thomas to Silvia, Servant of Mr. Duvall
Sep 12 1796 Smouse, Marg't to Isenberger, Peter
Dec 12 1780 Smouse, Mary to Isenbergh, Nicholas
May 19 1809 Snerr, Henry to Darner, Barbara
May 25 1778 Snider, Catharine to Gedultig, Conrad
Jan 13 1803 Snider, Michael to Ingman, Delila
Oct 28 1784 Snider, Uliana to Bier, John
Mar 22 1806 Snook, Elizabeth to Gaugh, John
Dec  8 1783 Snook, John to Ambrose, Catharine
Apr 20 1808 Snook, Mary to Ramsberg, Christian
May 14 1807 Snooks, Elizabeth to Spring, Adam
Jun 16 1801 Snootz, Susanna to Spring, Jacob
Feb  6 1787 Snoudagle, Barbara to Showalker, Adam
Dec 29 1801 Snoudagle, Margaret to Bolsky, Henry
Jun 12 1782 Snow, Elizabeth to Kemp, John
Mar 22 1779 Snowdagle, Peter to Eckman, Christena
Jan 24 1801 Snowdagle, Susannah to Rice, Thomas
```

```
Sep 26 1809 Snowdigle, George to Bortle, Elizabeth
Mar 30 1780 Snuke, Peter to Mottis, Ulianna
May 10 1810 Snyder, Abraham to Nusbaum, Sally
Feb  8 1800 Snyder, Barbara to Fleck, John
Jan 15 1785 Snyder, Catherine to Feichter, George
Mar 18 1794 Snyder, Catherine to Winebrenner, Peter
Nov 14 1807 Snyder, Christena to Webster, Thomas
Sep 20 1788 Snyder, Elizab to Reel, George
May 14 1804 Snyder, Elizabeth to Pool, Adam
Apr  6 1780 Snyder, John to Waltz, Dorothy
Jun 21 1780 Snyder, John to Barrick, Charity
Aug 12 1786 Snyder, Magdalene to Brunner, Jacob
May 14 1791 Snyder, Margaret to Sueman, John
Mar 24 1804 Snyder, Mary to Kemp, George
Aug  6 1806 Snyder, Mary to Myers, Samuel
Feb 14 1799 Snyder, Mary Ann to Zimmerman, Jacob
Aug 26 1807 Snyder, Nicholas to Thompson, Margaret
Nov 21 1808 Snyder, Susanna to Nusbaum, Jacob
Aug 17 1801 Snyder, William to Dick, Susanna
May 20 1783 Snydern, Anne Marg't to Rayling, John Ludwick
Nov 22 1779 Sollers, Dennis to Randall, Priscilla
Dec 24 1806 Sollers, Sabrit to Dorsey, Mary
Oct  9 1778 Sollman, Adam to Isenbergh, Susanna
May 22 1795 Sommerkemp, Philip to Keener, Frederica
Mar 30 1808 Somsel, Jacob to Shroyer, Catharine
Jan 21 1799 Soolser, Susannah to Dutterer, Conrad
Sep 20 1804 Soper, James to Davis, Lucy
Nov 13 1798 Soper, Mercey to Buxton, John
Apr 22 1791 Soper, Priscilla to Browning, Edward
Apr  9 1793 Soper, Samuel to Kirk, Margaret
Jan 31 1795 Southerland, Alexander to Taylor, Ann
Nov 19 1802 Southgate, Samuel to Wilson, Sarah
Nov 24 1807 Sowden, Elizabeth to Storm, Leonard
Oct 19 1798 Sower, Barbara to Summers, Philip
Dec 10 1810 Sowers, Leanna to Bierly, Jacob
Aug  4 1810 Sowers, Mary to Nusbaum, Daniel
Sep  9 1792 Sowers, Peter to Sinn, Elizabeth
Aug 20 1805 Sowers, Peter to Duttero, Rosina
Aug 14 1810 Sowers, Susanna to Brown, Thomas
Jan 18 1808 Spalding, Basil to Triceks, Mary
Jan 14 1789 Spalding, Catherine to Hilton, Andrew
Jan 17 1795 Spangler, Christian to Harvey, Ann
Dec 20 1788 Spangler, John to Adams, Mary
Jul 25 1803 Spangler, John to Gillaspie, Nancy
Sep 14 1793 Speak, James to Higdon, Margaret
May 17 1791 Spealman, Catharine to Rhodes, Joshua
Mar  7 1808 Spealman, Jacob to Hoffman, Mary
Jun 14 1802 Spealman, John to Main, Elizabeth
Jan 17 1807 Specht, Conrad to Harget, Catherine
Aug  7 1798 Specht, Lewis to Cramer, Elizabeth
Dec 11 1798 Speelman, Henry to Gabler, Lotty
Jan 18 1806 Speelman, John to Bussard, Catherine
Mar 16 1796 Spencer, Edward to Wildman, Rebecca
Jun  8 1808 Spencer, Jinett to Hill, Lewis
Mar 13 1794 Spencer, Rachel to Johnson, Noah
```

```
Jun 12 1804 Spencer, William to Harris, Mary
Mar  1 1779 Spires, Zepheniah to Walker, Catherine
Jan 28 1799 Spitzenburgh, Henry to Bell, Mary Ann
Aug 25 1806 Sponcellar, John to Lambrecht, Elizabeth
Feb  7 1804 Sponsaler, Rachel to Lambrecht, George
Aug 27 1804 Spoon, Catherine to Ebbert, Valentine
Aug 18 1809 Spoon, Elias to Baltzell, Polly
Dec 19 1804 Spoon, Mary to Ritchie, Henry
Oct  5 1798 Spoont, Joseph to Smith, Mary
Mar  1 1800 Sprecher, Rachel to Emerson, Samuel
May 10 1810 Sprengle, Cathe. to Ramsberg, Christian
Oct 30 1790 Sprigg, Ann to Johnson, Robert
Dec 14 1795 Sprigg, John to Wyvil, Elizabeth
Mar 12 1803 Sprigg, John to Sprigg, Lethelia
Mar 12 1803 Sprigg, Lethelia to Sprigg, John
Jan  7 1793 Sprigg, Mary to Camden, Henry
Mar 15 1810 Sprigg, Otho to Dorsey, Ann W.
Dec 31 1799 Sprigg, Prissa W. to Poole, John
Jun 21 1783 Sprigg, Samuel to Harding, Mary
May 13 1793 Sprigg, Thomas to Dorsey, Lucy
Jul 23 1800 Sprigg, William to Moler, Margaret
May 14 1807 Spring, Adam to Snooks, Elizabeth
May  9 1804 Spring, Christina to Fawley, Henry
May  6 1802 Spring, Frederick to Kusic, Sarah
Jun 16 1801 Spring, Jacob to Snootz, Susanna
Apr  7 1778 Springer, Ann to Silver, John
Jun 20 1798 Springer, Catharine to Albaugh, George
Jun 28 1796 Springer, Catherine to Carter, Joshua
Aug 10 1787 Springer, Edward to Creager, Elizabeth
Mar  9 1802 Springer, John to Sampson, Elizabeth
Mar 31 1781 Springer, Rebecca to Ridge, Wm. of Benj'n
Mar  7 1789 Springer, Susanna to Cregar, Adam
Nov 18 1792 Springer, William to Hauer, Mary
Feb  7 1807 Sprutzman, Jacob to Ringer, Elizabeth
Dec  6 1800 Spurrier, Ann to Clary, Daniel
Apr 14 1803 Spurrier, Ann Louisa to Cumming, John
Oct 12 1803 Spurrier, Avis to Clary, William
Oct 28 1805 Spurrier, Benjamin to Harvy, Prissilla
Oct  9 1805 Spurrier, Henrietta to Shelton, Thomas
Apr  9 1789 Spurrier, Joseph to Davis, Eleanor
Mar  7 1780 Spurrier, Levin to Clarey, Eleanor
Feb 28 1801 Spurrier, Ralph to Clary, Eleanor
Oct 29 1796 Squire, Jane to Blackburn, Thomas
Jun 27 1803 Squires, Asa to Eastup, Sarah Cartwright
Nov  6 1794 Squires, Thomas to Tumblestone, Lucy
Jan 25 1802 Staley, Barbara to Hedges, Isaac
Mar 18 1802 Staley, Catharine to Wachter, Samuel
May 27 1780 Staley, Catherine to Lyder, Henry
Apr  2 1805 Staley, Catherine to Staley, George
May 10 1794 Staley, Elizabeth to Staley, Jacob
Jul 25 1800 Staley, Elizabeth to Staley, Joseph
May 30 1801 Staley, Elizabeth to Stemple, Frederick, Jr.
Jan 28 1809 Staley, Frederick to Shafer, Elizabeth
Apr  2 1805 Staley, George to Staley, Catherine
Jun 10 1780 Staley, Jacob to Castle, Ann
```

```
May 10 1794 Staley, Jacob to Staley, Elizabeth
Jan  5 1803 Staley, Jacob to Kemp, Elizabeth
Nov  5 1803 Staley, Jacob, Jr. to Wietrich, Elizabeth
May  5 1800 Staley, John to Adams, Margaret
Jul 25 1800 Staley, Joseph to Staley, Elizabeth
Nov 12 1800 Staley, Joseph to Goodman, Catherine
Nov 21 1810 Staley, Lidy to Stilly, John
Oct  2 1809 Staley, Magdalene to Kemp, Joseph
May 27 1790 Staley, Mechor to Fluke, Barbara
Aug 14 1790 Staley, Melchor to Bare, Eve Margaret
Apr 24 1797 Staley, Peter to Shafer, Elizabeth
Jan 26 1807 Staley, Solomon to Butler, Margaret
Sep 22 1788 Stallings, Benjamin to Thompson, Elizabeth
May 21 1806 Stallings, Catherine to Phillips, Eli
Feb  4 1797 Stallings, Elizabeth to Glissan, Solomon
Jan 30 1790 Stallings, Elizabeth to Keller, Conrad
May 29 1786 Stallings, Nancey to Barnett, Robert
Jan 27 1798 Stallings, Newman to Kolb, Catherine
Sep  7 1797 Stallins, William to Dern, Susanna
Oct 17 1793 Staltcop, William to Shockness, Mary
Oct 19 1808 Stanley, Elizbeth to Masoncup, George
Nov 15 1785 Stanley, Thomas to Kise, Catherine
Dec 19 1789 Stanley, Thomas to Cabler, Caroline Elizabeth
Mar  5 1802 Stansberry, Elijah to Eck, Elizabeth
Feb 21 1794 Stansbury, Abraham to Stevenson, Rebeckah
Jun 17 1803 Stansbury, Elizabeth to Stevenson, Joshua
Jun  5 1809 Stansbury, Ruth to Brown, Nicholas
Nov 18 1805 Stansbury, Sarah to Brown, Josiah
Aug  6 1803 Stansbury, William to Gwinn, Frances
Jan  4 1794 Starchberger, Polly to Apollo, Lewis Benjamin
Mar 26 1801 Starling, Rachel to Cochran, John
Nov 19 1798 Starling, Sarah to Drumon, James
May 13 1807 Starr, Jesse to Norris, Tabitha
May 26 1804 Starr, John to Ellette, Margarette
Jul  3 1805 Staub, Catherine to Grimes, Samuel
Aug 10 1805 Staub, Christian to Long, Christianna
Sep 16 1806 Stauffer, Mariah to Doyle, William
Jun 28 1800 Staup, Peter to Eller, Magdalena
Aug  4 1803 Staup, Sarah to Grim, Daniel
Feb 15 1800 Staups, Catherine to Murphy, Lawrence
Dec  1 1800 Staups, Mary to Brown, James
Feb  9 1797 Stears, Polly to Merick, John
Jan  4 1799 Steckle, Catherine to Bentz, Jacob
Nov 17 1798 Steckle, Solomon to Doll, Charlotte
Oct  7 1810 Stedman, William to Devoy, Mary Ann
Nov  6 1802 Steel, Jacob to Devilbiss, Rosanna
Mar 24 1798 Steel, James S. to Norriss, Elizabeth
Nov 27 1800 Steel, John to Umsted, Ruth
Feb 14 1791 Steel, Mary to Riley, John
Sep  6 1794 Steel, Solomon to McDonald, Mary
Feb 27 1802 Steel, Susanna to Perril, Basil
Jul 10 1803 Steere, Isaac to Greggs, Rebecca
Aug 19 1808 Stein, Reuben to Wilson, Susanna
May 10 1779 Steiner, Catherine to Heanmyer, Jacob
May  4 1805 Steiner, Elizabeth to Conradt, George I.
```

```
Jun 22 1801 Steiner, Elizabeth to Hoffman, John
May 16 1788 Steiner, Frederick to Rape, Clarissa
May 20 1806 Steiner, Henry to Murray, Rachael
Sep 21 1786 Steiner, John, Jr. to Hauer, Elizabeth
Dec 24 1787 Steiner, Marg't to Koontz, Henry
Mar 27 1790 Steiner, Mary to Faw, Abraham
Apr 16 1808 Stem, Martin to Orr, Mary
Apr 28 1809 Stembel, John to Swearingen, Eleanor
Oct 28 1797 Stemple, Catherine to Grove, Martin
Apr  6 1805 Stemple, Elizbeth to Levy, Jonathan
May 30 1801 Stemple, Frederick, Jr. to Staley, Elizabeth
Mar  9 1798 Stemple, Henry to Harman, Christiana
Mar 12 1805 Stephanus, John to Walts, Catherine
Oct  5 1793 Stephanus, Margaret to Burckhart, Joseph
May 14 1810 Stephens, Joseph to Stonebraker, Mary Catherine
Jan 16 1810 Stephens, Septimius to Shryock, Amelia
Nov 12 1803 Stephenson, Jane to Knox, Robert
Sep 25 1789 Stephenson, Nathan to Evans, Mary
Oct 10 1789 Stephenson, Richard to Wood, Usilera
Aug  2 1796 Stevens, Charles to Waltz, Margaret
May 22 1796 Stevens, Edward to Coale, Keziah
Apr 23 1791 Stevens, John to Richards, Rachel
Jun  5 1793 Stevens, John to Nailor, Jane
Apr 27 1807 Stevens, Margaret to Lease, John
Dec 11 1802 Stevens, Mary to Thomas, Benjamin, Jr.
Apr 21 1810 Stevens, Thomas H. to Crable, Elizabeth
Jun 12 1779 Stevens, William to Ouria, Lidia
Jun  4 1793 Stevenson, Ann to Brown, Henry
Nov 23 1804 Stevenson, Edward to Pole, Frances
Dec 10 1799 Stevenson, John to Hankins, Sarah
Aug 26 1809 Stevenson, John to Wagner, Nancy
Jun 17 1803 Stevenson, Joshua to Stansbury, Elizabeth
May 21 1791 Stevenson, Josiah to Wells, Margaret
Dec 30 1800 Stevenson, Margaret to Harper, Richard
Apr 18 1801 Stevenson, Mary to Brown, James
Feb 21 1794 Stevenson, Rebeckah to Stansbury, Abraham
May 15 1797 Stevenson, Ruth to Weaver, Ludwick
Jan  3 1798 Stevenson, Susannah to Roberts, Thomas
Aug  6 1806 Steward, Catherine to Nusbaum, David
Apr  8 1780 Steward, Dolly to Maddon, Jacob
Dec  8 1809 Steward, Margaret to Walker, Stephen
May 26 1806 Steward, Mary to Dicks, John
Jun  2 1806 Steward, Mary to White, John
Sep 27 1794 Steward, Sarah to Ryan, George
Feb  7 1801 Steward, Thomas to Jacobs, Ann
Nov 18 1793 Steward, William to Ricketts, Margaret
May 24 1801 Stewart, Eleanor to Coale, Vincent
Mar 24 1806 Stewart, Elizabeth to Wilson, Zadock
Sep 16 1797 Stewart, Hessey to Griffith, Henry
Feb  8 1795 Stewart, James to Dannell, Isabel
Jan 30 1799 Stewart, John to Walter, Catherine
Nov 13 1800 Stewart, Peggy to Kirk, George
Apr 30 1802 Stewart, Susanna to Worman, Henry
May 25 1807 Sticker, Elizabeth to Wickham, Andrew
Aug 27 1794 Stickle, Margaret to Boggs, James
```

```
Oct 24 1786 Stickle, Mary to Maxwell, Thomas
Jan 18 1794 Stickle, Valentine to Ramsbergh, Catherine
Nov  4 1809 Stilly, Elizabeth to Templin, Richard
Nov 21 1810 Stilly, John to Staley, Lidy
Dec 30 1802 Stilly, Mary to Fout, Baltzer
May 14 1809 Stilly, Nancy to Hagan, Peter
Jan  9 1802 Stilly, Rebecca to Ramsbergh, John, Junr
Nov  5 1809 Stimble, Barbara to Hendersor, John
Jun  7 1806 Stimmel, Abraham to Long, Mary
Dec  7 1807 Stimmel, Elizbeth to Lock, John
Mar 27 1797 Stimmell, Catherine to Cramer, John
Dec 29 1809 Stimmell, Elizabeth to Ellis, John
May 29 1794 Stimmell, Peter to Buzzard, Barbara
Mar 15 1809 Stimmell, Susanna to Clem, John
Nov 11 1809 Stimmell, Susanna to Eberts, Jacob
Oct 28 1784 Stimmell, Yost to Stoker, Magdalena
Dec 30 1806 Stine, Elizabeth to Fry, John
Aug 23 1796 Stipe, Catharine to Ury, Christian
Mar 21 1778 Stipe, James to Donn, Mary
May 28 1794 Stipe, John to Burckhartt, Barbara
Nov 16 1807 Stires, Rhoda to Dow, John
Oct 21 1800 Stockman, Ann to Hyme, David
Dec 14 1807 Stockman, Catherine to Koblentz, Daniel
Jun 21 1806 Stockman, David to Waskey, Sophia
Jan  5 1804 Stockman, George to Winpeagler, Elzabeth
Jul 27 1797 Stockman, John to Thomas, Elizabeth
Aug 16 1800 Stockman, John to Thomas, Charlotte
Dec 29 1801 Stockman, Mary to Shelton, John
Dec 27 1806 Stockman, Philip to Easterday, Elizabeth
Jun 25 1795 Stofell, Catherine to Mills, Andrew
Oct 28 1784 Stoker, Magdalena to Stimmell, Yost
Feb 12 1799 Stoker, Margaret to Baker, Philip
Jun 21 1778 Stoker, Michael to ---, Mary A.
Nov 16 1778 Stokes, Dorcas to Jacobs, Wm.
Nov  1 1779 Stoll, Mary to Boyr, Joseph
Dec  8 1792 Stone, John to Binger, Barbara
Jul 30 1796 Stone, John to Shroyer, Mary
Jan 29 1796 Stone, Mary to Frey, Isaac
Mar 27 1785 Stone, Walter Hanson to Muncaster, Ann
Sep  6 1806 Stonebraker, Anna to Dillehay, Thomas L.
May 14 1810 Stonebraker, Mary Catherine to Stephens, Joseph
Aug  9 1798 Stoneburner, Jacob to Harschell, Margaret
Dec 21 1803 Stoner, Abraham to Rinehart, Hannah
Feb  7 1797 Stoner, Agnes to Root, Richard
Apr  8 1803 Stoner, Barbara to Derr, Thomas
May 20 1800 Stoner, Benedict to Morris, Kezia
Nov 28 1795 Stoner, Catherine to Darr, John
May  3 1800 Stoner, Christian to Ramsberg, Susannah
Feb  7 1792 Stoner, Daniel to Deaghe, Mary
Oct 20 1787 Stoner, David to Fleagle, Mary
Apr 12 1797 Stoner, Elizabeth to Aiter, David
May  3 1779 Stoner, Elizabeth to Pritchard, Jesse
Nov 15 1800 Stoner, Elizbeth to Ramsberg, Sebastian
Feb 15 1800 Stoner, Frederick to Sinn, Margaret
Dec 20 1806 Stoner, Hannah to Landes, Isaac
```

```
Oct 13 1787 Stoner, Henry to Prengle, Elizabeth
Oct 11 1792 Stoner, Jacob to Bucey, Mary
Mar 21 1795 Stoner, John to Ramsberg, Susanna
Dec  4 1802 Stoner, John to Clise, Elizabeth
Jun 27 1785 Stoner, John, Jr. to Plonk, Elizabeth
Dec 20 1803 Stoner, Mary to Matthews, Edward
Jan 21 1792 Stoner, Mary to Weisenthall, Barnay
Jun  7 1794 Stoner, Phebe to Righe, John
Jan  7 1806 Stoner, Sarah to Strider, Isaac
May 20 1804 Stoner, Sophia to Simpson, John
Oct 11 1795 Stoner, Stephen to Ramsberg, Barbara
Dec  4 1800 Stophel, Catherine to Getzendanner, Jacob
Jul 21 1798 Stophel, Jacob to Eurckhartt, Elizabeth
Nov 24 1807 Storm, Leonard to Sowden, Elizabeth
May 12 1801 Storm, Margaret to Marker, George
Aug 28 1802 Storm, Margaret to Miller, Jacob
Dec 23 1795 Storm, Mary to Culler, Jacob
Apr 16 1796 Storm, Peter to Wright, Susanna
Feb 26 1793 Storms, Isaac to Wright, Sarah
Nov 29 1796 Storms, Peter to Thompson, Rebeckah
Apr 27 1804 Storng, Mary to Hicks, Joseph
Apr 12 1785 Story, Ruth to Sheckels, John
Apr 15 1808 Stottlemier, David to Castle, Jemima
Jul 27 1798 Stottlemier, John to Michael, Sarah
Dec 23 1809 Stottlemier, Magdalene to Baker, Philip
Mar  2 1805 Stottlemier, Susanna to Richmond, Francis
Nov  6 1779 Stottlemire, George to Calon, Catherine
Jan 25 1785 Stottlemyer, Jacob to Shoemaker, Hedwick
Nov 20 1797 Stoub, Adam to Freet, Ann
Aug 28 1787 Stouder, Sarah to Brown, Joseph
Aug  8 1801 Stoufer, Joseph to Cronise, Catherine
Apr  9 1803 Stouffer, Daniel Jr. to Yowler, Eleanor
Sep 10 1804 Stouffer, Hannah to Cover, Daniel
Jul 22 1799 Stouffer, Henry to Mitchell, Ann
Mar 17 1804 Stouffer, Jacob to Boak, Eliza
Dec 15 1792 Stover, John to Hauer, Margaret
Feb  4 1799 Stover, Philip to Welt, Susannah
Mar  1 1802 Stover, Philip to Koontz, Magdalena
Dec  6 1803 Stover, Philip to Mulvey, Mary
Jul 17 1804 Stover, Philip to Smith, Margaret
Nov 11 1809 Straleman, Margaret to Holtz, Michael
Apr 10 1779 Strane, Mary to Scott, John
May 13 1785 Strasberger, John to Walling, Ann
Apr  5 1800 Straver, Peggy to Wren, Bernard
Jan 26 1796 Strawsberger, John to Fundeberg, Barbara
Oct 30 1800 Streems, Eve to Griffith, Samuel
Oct  3 1786 Street, Elizabeth to Miller, John
Jan 29 1779 Street, George to Cotton, Elizabeth
Mar  7 1780 Stricker, Ann Maria to Beall, Ninian
Mar 31 1804 Strickstroke, Barbara to Hardman, George
Jun 13 1778 Strider, Ann to Howe, William Rob't
Jan  7 1806 Strider, Isaac to Stoner, Sarah
Feb  4 1808 Strine, Peter to Sargent, Catherine
Apr 28 1807 Strong, Benjamin to Hines, Elizabeth
Dec  9 1797 Strong, Caty to Barnard, Michael
```

```
Sep 28 1810 Strong, Charles to Vaughan, Telitha
Jan 21 1808 Strong, Elizabeth to Murray, Solomon
Oct 27 1797 Strong, George to Crabbs, Elizabeth
Apr 20 1794 Struble, Sophia to Mathews, Jacob
Dec 12 1808 Stuck, Catherine to Hawn, William
Apr  2 1792 Studor, Martin to Wertenbaker, Mary
Feb  7 1804 Study, Henry to Kogh, Charlotte
Apr 15 1788 Stull, Adam to Ramsbergh, Elizabeth
Oct 22 1779 Stull, Catharine to Wyer, William
Dec 19 1785 Stull, Catherine to Shafer, George
May  9 1805 Stull, Christopher to Hiner, Mary
Dec 19 1789 Stull, Daniel to Beatty, Mary
Jun 27 1795 Stull, Elizabeth to Englebright, Michael
Oct  4 1783 Stull, Elizabeth to Shaver, John
Oct 25 1783 Stull, Elizabeth to Wire, Peter
May  6 1790 Stull, John to Duttero, Margaret
Nov 21 1806 Stull, John to Hommer, Lucia
May 11 1778 Stull, Lawrence to Gassiway, Rebecca
Dec 22 1800 Stull, Mary to Price, Adam
Dec 28 1799 Stull, Mary to Ritz, Jacob
May 22 1787 Stull, Mary to Valentine, George
Jan 18 1800 Stull, Mary to Witrick, Jacob
Jun 11 1794 Stull, Phillipena to Getzendanner, Balser
Dec 19 1795 Stull, Susanna to Campbell, Matthew
Nov 11 1803 Stultz, Mary to Ogle, Peter
Mar 15 1798 Stump, Joseph to Boggess, Elizabeth
Sep 24 1791 Sturrum, Mary to Levy, David, Junr.
Dec 19 1807 Sueman, Eleanor, Jr. to Bussard, Samuel, Jr.
May 14 1791 Sueman, John to Snyder, Margaret
Jun 25 1791 Sueman, Peter to Templing, Anna
Jul 16 1806 Sulliman, Jacob to Davis, Elizabeth
Sep  7 1783 Sullivan, Hannah to Hill, Thomas
Dec 31 1802 Sullivan, Jacob to Hoffman, Elizabeth
Apr 12 1803 Sullivan, John to Brown, Lydia
Jul  5 1794 Sullivan, Mary to Fletcher, Philip
Mar 27 1789 Sulser, Cathe. to Remsberger, George
Jun  4 1796 Sulser, Margaret to Lefaver, Daniel
Nov  3 1798 Sulser, Mary to Price, Philip, Jr.
Dec 12 1807 Sulser, Peter to Brain, Sarah
Jun 24 1808 Suman, Isaac to Groft, Catherine
Aug 21 1779 Summer, Catherine to Dutterar, John
Nov 11 1800 Summer, Elizabeth to Teterly, Frederick
Mar 25 1797 Summers, Alex'r to Vinagar, Mary
Mar 20 1792 Summers, Betsey to Meek, Christiopher
Jun 19 1780 Summers, Elizabeth to Waughtell, John
Dec 28 1809 Summers, James to Wheite, Susanna
Jan  2 1783 Summers, Peter to Hefner, Christena
Oct 19 1798 Summers, Philip to Sower, Barbara
Apr 17 1799 Sunafranck, George to Roof, Elizabeth
Feb  5 1781 Sunpower, Adam to Cronise, Susanna
Jun 21 1783 Sutfin, William to Owen, Rachel
May  8 1780 Sutherland, Catherine to McDonald, George
Apr 19 1779 Swadner, Mary to Ebert, Philip
Mar 25 1797 Swaidner, Adam to Lamon, Eve
Apr  5 1799 Swaidner, Adam to Cox, Anne
```

```
May  7 1787 Swaidner, Elizabeth to Eppert, Henry
Nov 24 1800 Swails, Jacob to Vine, Catherine
May  2 1796 Swain, Jacob to Ambrose, Mary
Sep 16 1808 Swamley, Susanna to Yantz, Christopher
Feb 11 1791 Swaney, John to Berrier, Phebe
Jan  8 1781 Swawin, Anna Margaret to Albright, Henry
Dec 14 1779 Swayne, Charles to Gire, Catherine
Jun 10 1797 Sweadner, Adam to Lemmon, Eve
Jul 25 1806 Sweadner, Catherine to Seekman, Joseph
May 14 1796 Swearingen, Drusilla to Wheeler, Gilbert
Apr 28 1809 Swearingen, Eleanor to Stembel, John
Sep 12 1797 Swearingen, Elizabeth to Boteler, Arthur
Jun 21 1800 Swearingen, Joseph to Beall, Tobitha
Jun  5 1790 Swearingen, Mary to Burton, Jacob
Jun 27 1786 Swedner, Henry to Sensor, Elizabeth
Mar 25 1801 Swigart, John to Taney, Elizabeth
Aug 25 1786 Swigart, Mary to Leatherman, Peter
Jul 24 1810 Swigart, Peter to Funderberg, Elizabeth
Nov 23 1796 Swisher, Matthias to Shank, Catherine
Mar 28 1785 Swisher, Susanna to Mullindore, Jacob
Mar 30 1805 Switezer, Elizabeth to Morningstar, George
Oct 31 1797 Switser, Lawrence to Nickey, Sarah
Jan 13 1803 Switzer, Catharine to Shank, Michael
Feb 26 1784 Swomley, Mary to Plummer, Abraham
Dec 26 1795 Synn, Christena to Routzawn, Jacob
Jan  8 1805 Syphers, Mary to Shingle, Lawrence

May 21 1779 Tabler, Adam to Yesterday, Philepeana
Nov 28 1785 Tabler, Barbara to Whipp, Jacob
May 30 1789 Tabler, Catherine to Getzendanner, John
May 30 1809 Tabler, Christian to Thrasher, Sarah
Jan 21 1807 Tabler, Elizabeth to Castle, James Sampson
Jan 18 1783 Tabler, Elizabeth to Martin, Jacob
Sep 29 1805 Tabler, Lewis to Leather, Mary
Apr  7 1779 Tabler, Melchor to Berger, Philipeana
Apr 13 1783 Tabler, Michael to Coonce, Catherine
Jan 20 1789 Tabler, Michael to Roberts, Mary
Jun 16 1780 Tabler, William to Yesterday, Margaret
Dec 22 1800 Tabler, William to Jones, Elizabeth
Jun 16 1792 Talbot, Catharine to Reed, Archibald
Apr 14 1796 Talbot, Eleanor to Norris, George
Nov  3 1804 Talbott, Allen to Lawrence, Peggy
Jan 22 1797 Talbott, Ann to Boyle, John
Jul 12 1797 Talbott, Ann to Haywood, Isaac
Jul 12 1797 Talbott, Ann to Kaywood, Isac
Oct 28 1789 Talbott, Charles to Ramsower, Ann
Apr  3 1804 Talbott, Elizabeth to Cooley, Edward
Dec  5 1789 Talbott, James to Hilton, Mary
Nov 10 1807 Talbott, John to Gittings, Teresa
May  4 1800 Talbott, Joseph to Daniel, Jane
Jul 18 1807 Talbott, Rebecca to Norris, William
Jul 19 1803 Talbutt, Benjamin to Tidy, Nancy
Feb  2 1807 Talbutt, Hendley to Gittings, Juliet
Oct  1 1796 Tall, Ruth to Days, Henry
May 30 1794 Talley, Ebenezer to Philips, Margaret
```

```
Jul 12 1806 Tallhammer, Matthias to Fox, Margaret
Mar 24 1802 Tallhelm, Peter to Creager, Elizabeth
Mar 25 1801 Taney, Elizabeth to Swigart, John
Feb 22 1805 Taney, Joseph to Hughes, Harriett
Jan  6 1806 Taney, Roger Brooke to Key, Ann Phebe Charlton
Aug 29 1807 Tannehill, Harriot to Curfman, Christian
Dec  9 1785 Tannehill, William to Simmonds, Elizabeth
Dec 21 1807 Tanner, Andrew to Yost, Hannah
Feb 23 1808 Tanner, Barbara to Keller, John
Oct  6 1779 Tannihill, Mary to Rodgers, Jno.
Nov 14 1807 Tanzey, Arthur to Koontz, Anne
Apr  8 1807 Tares, Barbara to Sheffer, Adam
Jun 29 1786 Tarlton, Jeremiah to Briscoe, Mary Harbert
May 22 1806 Tarman, Aquila to Anderson, Mary
Sep 26 1804 Tavenay, Rebecca to Casey, James
Aug 15 1810 Tawney, John to Warner, Elizabeth
Jan 31 1795 Taylor, Ann to Southerland, Alexander
Mar  6 1798 Taylor, Aquilla to Knight, Rachel
Oct 31 1798 Taylor, Barbara to Zimmerman, Michael
Jul 15 1786 Taylor, Debitha to Barnes, John
Nov 10 1796 Taylor, Eleanor to Davis, Reuben
Jan 18 1806 Taylor, Elizabeth to Sears, Joshua
Oct 18 1802 Taylor, Elizbeth to Castle, John
Mar 29 1808 Taylor, Enoch to Root, Ann
Jan 17 1800 Taylor, George to Bruner, Catherine
May  3 1790 Taylor, Henry to Griffith, Ann
May 26 1784 Taylor, Jesse to Bale, Ruth
Jul 10 1778 Taylor, Joseph to Ryley, Eleanor
Mar 29 1808 Taylor, Joseph to Root, Margaret
Oct  5 1809 Taylor, Joseph to Huff, Liddy
Oct 25 1809 Taylor, Margaret to Dinsmore, Thomas
Nov 11 1806 Taylor, Mary to Bartlett, James
Aug  4 1804 Taylor, Mary to Saer, Israel
Feb  7 1786 Taylor, Polly to Meelhouse, John
Dec 18 1800 Taylor, Rachel to Phillips, Thomas
Dec  4 1788 Taylor, Richard to Johnson, Mary
Nov 21 1796 Taylor, Richard to Riddle, Susanna
Dec 26 1796 Taylor, Ruth to Zimmerman, Andrew
Jan 16 1810 Taylor, Susannah to Wynn, John
Feb 20 1781 Taylor, William to Walcore, Pugzear
Sep 29 1782 Taysor, Margaret to Green, Charles
Nov 12 1785 Teal, Henry to Nollert, Margaret
Jun  3 1802 Teaner, Adam to Hall, Susanna
Jul 24 1779 Temple, Sarah to Burn, Heugh
Jun  4 1778 Temple, Susannah to Beever, William
Mar 14 1803 Templer, Sarah to Williams, Ellis
Jan 31 1803 Templin, Catherine to Shawn, James
Oct 17 1795 Templin, Richard to Runner, Eve
Nov  4 1809 Templin, Richard to Stilly, Elizabeth
Jun 20 1793 Templin, William to Gire, Susannah
Jun 25 1791 Templing, Anna to Sueman, Peter
Dec 23 1790 Templing, Elizabeth to Yeast, Leonard
Dec 22 1787 Templing, Polly to Shuman, Jacob
Sep 24 1782 Templing, Rebeckah to Ridgely, Richard
Jul  1 1791 Templing, Sarah to Ridgely, Westall
```

```
Mar 23 1805 Tener, Adam to Leatherwood, Mary
Sep 19 1803 Tener, Catherine to Thomas, James
Apr  8 1801 Tenley, Eleanor to Bean, Benjamin
Mar 28 1810 Terry, Michael to Jackson, Bethsheba
Aug 17 1782 Tertsabaugh, Susanna to Titloe, Abraham
Jun  7 1783 Tertzbaugh, John to Keplinger, Catherine
Jul  2 1798 Teshner, Sophia to Lewis, Thomas
Mar  9 1789 Teterley, Catharine to Aubert, Martin
Nov 11 1800 Teterly, Frederick to Summer, Elizabeth
Feb 21 1799 Thomas, Mary to Karn, Jacob
Mar  3 1790 Thomas, Ann to Carter, John
Nov 14 1800 Thomas, Ann to Clary, John
Jun  2 1796 Thomas, Ann to Griffith, Richard
Feb  2 1788 Thomas, Ann to Hebb, Richard
May 12 1796 Thomas, Anna to Anderson, William
Sep 11 1797 Thomas, Aquilla to Ellis, Ruthey
Jun  2 1778 Thomas, Archibald to Trammell, Sarah
Apr 18 1810 Thomas, Barbara to Hargate, John
Aug 13 1791 Thomas, Barbara to Mathern, Philip Nich's
Sep  4 1788 Thomas, Barbary to Hilke, Christian
Dec 11 1802 Thomas, Benjamin, Jr. to Stevens, Mary
Nov 30 1799 Thomas, Casandra to Johnson, William
Dec 26 1799 Thomas, Catharine to Alexander, Ashton
Apr  1 1802 Thomas, Catharine to Myers, George Frederick
Mar 16 1787 Thomas, Catharine to Thomas, John
Dec 26 1799 Thomas, Catharine Hanson to Alexander, Ashton
Oct 14 1803 Thomas, Catherine to Dent, Aquila
Jan 13 1789 Thomas, Catherine to Ramsbergh, John
Jan 22 1783 Thomas, Catherine to Wadigdan, Christopher
Nov 25 1794 Thomas, Catherine Lewis to Simm, Thomas
Aug 16 1800 Thomas, Charlotte to Stockman, John
Aug  8 1807 Thomas, Charlotte to Thomas, George
Jan 29 1780 Thomas, Daniel to Dannelly, Peggy
Nov 24 1806 Thomas, Edward to Thomas, Elizabeth
Nov 27 1810 Thomas, Eleanor to King, William R.
Feb 23 1780 Thomas, Eliz'th to Runner, Christian
Dec 16 1790 Thomas, Eliz'th Causlet Metcalfe to Belt, Lloyd
Nov 30 1793 Thomas, Elizabeth to Good, John
Feb  1 1781 Thomas, Elizabeth to Johnson, Roger
Nov  9 1808 Thomas, Elizabeth to Runner, Henry
Jan  9 1799 Thomas, Elizabeth to Simpson, Walter
Jul 27 1797 Thomas, Elizabeth to Stockman, John
Nov 24 1806 Thomas, Elizabeth to Thomas, Edward
Mar 11 1779 Thomas, Gabriel to Ramsbergh, Mary
May 11 1783 Thomas, George to Peck, Rosanna
Aug  8 1807 Thomas, George to Thomas, Charlotte
Oct 10 1793 Thomas, Griffith to Grove, Elizabeth
Nov 22 1790 Thomas, Henry to Ramsbergh, Margaret
Oct 24 1809 Thomas, Henry to Shafer, Susanna
Nov 17 1796 Thomas, Isaac to Flack, Mary
Sep 19 1803 Thomas, James to Tener, Catherine
Apr  5 1783 Thomas, John to Wortz, Catherine
Apr 16 1786 Thomas, John to Ramsburgh, Elizabeth
Mar 16 1787 Thomas, John to Thomas, Catharine
Jun  9 1789 Thomas, John to McGill, Eleanor
```

```
Jan  4 1805 Thomas, John to Protzman, Mary
Sep 18 1805 Thomas, John to Carty, Catherine
Mar 18 1785 Thomas, Leonard to Yose, Barbara
Sep  4 1803 Thomas, Margaret to Kennedy, Francis
Jan 24 1789 Thomas, Mary to Baer, John
Mar  7 1786 Thomas, Mary to Brookover, Thomas
May  3 1787 Thomas, Mary to Crabb, Ralph
Oct 28 1805 Thomas, Mary to Demcey, Thomas
May  1 1784 Thomas, Mary to Gier, George
Jan 17 1783 Thomas, Mary to Icoff, Adolph
Nov  6 1802 Thomas, Michael to Ogle, Margaret
May 10 1782 Thomas, Nathan to Edelen, Clarissa
May  6 1799 Thomas, Peter to Shafer, Barbara
Dec 21 1797 Thomas, Philip to Lynn, Elizabeth
Jan 18 1802 Thomas, Philip to Hilleary, Rebecca
Jun 21 1800 Thomas, Rebecca to Giseberd, Guy
Nov 19 1805 Thomas, Rebecca Bellicon to Magruder, Alexander Contee
Oct 25 1796 Thomas, Samuel, Jr. to Howard, Maria
Oct 23 1790 Thomas, Sarah to Abell, John
Apr 28 1781 Thomas, Sarah to Jacobs, Wm.
Nov 24 1807 Thomas, Sarah to Norris, John
Jun 13 1796 Thomas, Sarah to Rineberger, Henry
Jun  7 1804 Thomas, Susannah to Carty, George
Mar 15 1799 Thomas, Valentine to Keller, Elizabeth
Jan 18 1805 Thomas, William to James, Esther
Apr 15 1806 Thomas, William to Houser, Catherine
Dec 10 1791 Thompson, Ambrose to Thompson, Mary Ann
Jan 30 1795 Thompson, Andrew to Lawrence, Rachel
Dec 25 1790 Thompson, Ann to Jemeson, Francis
Dec 31 1795 Thompson, Benjamin to Tripolet, Charlotte
May 18 1789 Thompson, Cassandra to Lease, Jacob
Sep  5 1796 Thompson, Elizabeth to Griffith, Abraham
Aug 30 1804 Thompson, Elizabeth to McBride, Edward
Feb  1 1792 Thompson, Elizabeth to McCrea, William
Sep 22 1788 Thompson, Elizabeth to Stallings, Benjamin
May 13 1796 Thompson, Henry to Leese, Elizabeth
Sep 20 1804 Thompson, James to Thompson, Jane
Sep 20 1804 Thompson, Jane to Thompson, James
Sep 12 1787 Thompson, John to Cross, Barbara
Feb 24 1810 Thompson, John C. to Winemiller, Margaret
Dec  6 1810 Thompson, John P. to Barnhold, Mary
Apr  1 1779 Thompson, Joseph to Brooke, Ann Elizabeth
Aug 26 1807 Thompson, Margaret to Snyder, Nicholas
May 25 1795 Thompson, Mary to Kelly, Edward
Dec 10 1791 Thompson, Mary Ann to Thompson, Ambrose
Feb  9 1793 Thompson, Prisey to McElroy, Patrick
Nov 18 1781 Thompson, Rebecca to Keller, Jacob
Nov 29 1796 Thompson, Rebeckah to Storms, Peter
Mar  2 1800 Thompson, Robert to Miller, Elizabeth
Dec  4 1798 Thompson, Samuel to Cutsail, Elizabeth
Apr 16 1806 Thompson, Samuel to Clingan, Margaret
Feb  9 1799 Thompson, Sarah to Duvall, Benjamin
Oct 23 1804 Thompson, Sarah to Davis, David
Nov 12 1798 Thompson, Susanna to Wright David
Jul 29 1784 Thompson, Thomas to Faller, Catharine
```

```
Feb 28 1807 Thomson, Mary to Graham, Jonas
Dec 25 1786 Thornberry, John to Bentley, Sarah
Apr 29 1809 Thornburgh, Ephraim to Dudderer, Margaret
Nov 18 1788 Thornbury, Thomas to Collins, Prudence
Feb 15 1803 Thrasher, Benjamin to Sergeant, Elizabeth
Oct 12 1782 Thrasher, Cassiah to Lieth, Samuel
Oct 18 1803 Thrasher, Drusilla to Lamar, William
Oct 30 1788 Thrasher, Elias to Lamar, Sarah
Oct 26 1791 Thrasher, Elie to Lamarr, Henrietta
Aug  3 1784 Thrasher, Hannah to Prye, Christopher
Sep 29 1783 Thrasher, John to Tutterer, Elizabeth
Oct 18 1803 Thrasher, Martha to Leyth, John
Nov 14 1784 Thrasher, Sarah to Hook, Stephen
May 30 1809 Thrasher, Sarah to Tabler, Christian
Mar 25 1801 Thrasher, William to Penn, Rebecca
Jan  3 1808 Thrift, Charles to Elger, Ann
Mar 12 1803 Tibbets, Jerry to Holland, Sarah
Apr 25 1795 Tice, Elizabeth to Lease, George
Apr 23 1803 Tice, George to Shade, Elizabeth
Dec 24 1806 Tice, Henry to Beckwith, Mary
Oct 19 1789 Tice, Margaret to Griffith, Richard
Nov 10 1802 Tice, Mary to Ebbert, Henry
Jul 19 1803 Tidy, James to Jones, Mary
Jul 19 1803 Tidy, Nancy to Talbutt, Benjamin
Dec 24 1801 Tidy, Sophia to Lantz, Christian
Jul 31 1806 Tierly, Sarah to Bawen, Francis
Jan  4 1809 Tillard, Eleanor to Ward, Amos
Nov 17 1792 Tilliard, Edward C. to Estep, Sarah
May 28 1809 Tilt, Margaret to Hite, I.
May 28 1809 Tilt, Margaret to Hite, J.
Sep 11 1793 Timmons, Charles to Furney, Mary
Oct 14 1802 Timmons, Lettitia to Flanigan, Malachi
Mar  3 1803 Tinderman, Elizabeth to Beall, John, Junr.
Mar  9 1803 Tinderman, Susanna to Donnavan, William
Feb 24 1802 Tingler, Catherine to Simmons, John
Apr 10 1810 Tinkens, Simon to Muse, Nancy
Dec 27 1797 Tinnely, Charles Brooke to Janes, Elizabeth
Dec  3 1803 Tinson, William to Nicholson, Margaret
Sep 22 1807 Tinterman, Elizbeth to Bell, Jacob
Dec 11 1801 Tippis, Barbara to Carty, George
Dec 19 1801 Tipple, Catherine to Curffman, Henry
Oct 29 1802 Tipple, Mary to England, Joseph
May 14 1804 Tipple, Sarah to Curfman, Michael
Dec 19 1803 Titlo, Mary to Baruger, Henry
Aug 17 1782 Titloe, Abraham to Tertsabaugh, Susanna
Sep 24 1782 Titlow, Christian to Rowe, Barbara
Oct 24 1810 Titlow, Thomas to Martin, Barbara
Mar  7 1798 Titus, Tunis to Kelly, Monarchy
Dec 20 1800 Toafler, Elizabeth to Rice, George
Jun  8 1805 Tobery, Anne to Yardley, William
Mar 28 1807 Tobery, Elizabeth to Applebee, Joseph
May  9 1798 Tobery, Mary to Dixson, John Hattin
Aug 29 1782 Todd, Andrew to Sipes, Elizabeth
Aug 29 1782 Todd, Basil to Grimes, Sarah
Apr 16 1810 Todd, Benjamin to Clary, Charlotte
```

| | | |
|---|---|---|
| Dec 17 1799 | Todd, Eleanor to Condon, Zachariah |
| Oct 29 1792 | Todd, Joshua to Hyatt, Sophia |
| Oct 12 1779 | Todd, Lucy (Free Negro) to Johnson, Benja. (Free Negro) |
| Sep 25 1788 | Tolbert, Ann to Hill, Henry Roby |
| Mar 5 1795 | Tolbert, Frances to Towner, John |
| Jan 2 1788 | Tolburte, James to Poulson, Ann |
| Mar 15 1804 | Tolle, William to Turner, Mary |
| Oct 29 1803 | Tom, George to Leather, Catherine |
| Jan 29 1789 | Tomlin, Elizabeth to Reynolds, Thomas |
| Jun 19 1790 | Tomlinson, Elizabeth to Young, Conrad |
| Jul 25 1795 | Tomlinson, James to Poulson, Mary |
| Dec 13 1808 | Toms, John to Martin, Mary |
| May 21 1791 | Toofoot, Mary to Kavanagh, William |
| Feb 1 1809 | Tool, Elizabeth to Beall, John |
| Jun 8 1782 | Tool, James to Cecill, Elizabeth |
| Oct 22 1805 | Tool, Sarah to Cecil, Aden |
| Jun 27 1804 | Toole, Martha to Cecil, Levi |
| Feb 13 1795 | Torrence, James to Simmons, Drusilla |
| Aug 27 1790 | Toughman, Frederick to Kyser, Sarah |
| Aug 8 1809 | Toup, Frederick to Fluck, Molly |
| Jun 23 1798 | Toup, Margaret to King, John |
| Aug 20 1807 | Touvell, Robert to Martin, Elizabeth |
| Dec 8 1788 | Towbridge, John to Holtzman, Mary |
| Sep 4 1810 | Towner, Catherine to Weller, Henry |
| Mar 5 1795 | Towner, John to Tolbert, Frances |
| Apr 29 1797 | Townsend, Benjamin to Coore, Christena |
| Dec 10 1800 | Townsend, Charlotte to England, Samuel |
| Jul 3 1803 | Tracey, Ann to Smith, James |
| Sep 3 1778 | Tracey, Sarah to Johnson, Basil |
| Feb 17 1801 | Trago, Aquila to Hooper, Mary |
| Jun 14 1809 | Trail, William to Hays, Abigail |
| Feb 22 1779 | Trammell, Sarah to Delashmutt, Lindsey |
| Jun 2 1778 | Trammell, Sarah to Thomas, Archibald |
| Dec 6 1804 | Traper (or Draper), Thomas to Zimmerman, Mary |
| Dec 9 1779 | Traufle, Samuel to Colebank, Mary |
| Feb 17 1781 | Trencer, Mary to Dorchester, Wm. |
| Nov 26 1778 | Trent, John to Smith, Eleanor |
| Apr 29 1789 | Trenter, Esther to Donoven, William |
| Sep 3 1782 | Trentor, Margaret to Lindsay, Thomas |
| Jan 18 1808 | Triceks, Mary to Spalding, Basil |
| Apr 3 1781 | Trinton, Thomas to Hutchcraft, Margaret |
| Oct 18 1797 | Triplepp, Thomas to Sandes, Elizabeth |
| Jul 11 1786 | Triplett, Reuben to Combs, Rebeckah |
| Dec 31 1795 | Tripolet, Charlotte to Thompson, Benjamin |
| Jul 21 1804 | Tritt, Christian to Metzger, Susanna |
| Oct 29 1803 | Tritt, Mary to Gaver, Gideon |
| Mar 25 1806 | Tritt, Paul to Lantz, Catherine |
| Nov 28 1799 | Tritt, Peter to Ceas, Esther |
| Aug 1 1810 | Tritt, Sarah to Pool, Philemon |
| Oct 6 1801 | Tromberger, Jacob to Madeira, Mary |
| Mar 11 1799 | Troshon, Catherine to Koller, John |
| Jul 13 1791 | Trott, Susanna to Fitzpatrick, Dennis |
| Aug 9 1780 | Trout, Jacob to Reed, Elizabeth |
| Dec 30 1809 | Trout, Jacob to Boogher, Charlotte |

```
Apr 13 1805 Trout, John to Shown, Margaret
Dec  8 1803 Trout, Mary to Moor, Abner
Jan 18 1806 Trout, Philpena to Deal, John
Jul 25 1794 Trout, Wendle to Kephart, Sarah
Dec 30 1783 Troutman, Michael to Shrader, Elizabeth
Aug  8 1809 Troutman, Peter to Runner, Christena
May  7 1801 Troxel, Frederick to Young, Elizabeth
Aug  2 1805 Troxel, George to Crabbs, Elizabeth
Jun  6 1793 Troxell, Elizabeth to Zimmerman, Nicholas
Mar 27 1802 Troxell, Frederick to Wilson, Catherine
Sep 15 1783 Trubey, Jacob to Isenberger, Catherine
Oct 30 1781 Trucks, John to Boyle, Catharine
Sep 26 1778 Trueman, Ann to Bucey, Henry
Oct 24 1799 Trumbo, Hannah to Wampler, John Lewis
Feb 11 1806 Trundel, James to Burn, Eleanor
Jan 18 1797 Trundle, David to Lewis, Drusilla
Nov  6 1809 Trunel, Silas to Knott, Lena
Mar  4 1782 Tucker, Cassandra to Smith, James
Aug  7 1810 Tucker, Christopher James to Phillips, Rachel
Nov  6 1797 Tucker, Edward to Riggs, Sarah
Feb 23 1796 Tucker, John to Warfield, Anna
Feb  5 1785 Tucker, Jonathan to Godman, Patsy
Dec 30 1803 Tucker, Jonathan Ross to Greenwell, Helen
Mar 21 1804 Tucker, Leah to Nicewanger, Christian
Feb  2 1786 Tucker, Littleton to Downing, Sarah
Jul  2 1762 Tucker, Margaret to Serjeant, William
Feb 25 1787 Tucker, Mary to Churchman, John Frederick
Feb 16 1795 Tucker, Mary to Downey, Alexander
Feb 18 1786 Tucker, Richard to Higgins, Rachel
Jun 19 1802 Tucker, Richard to Penn, Eleanor
Dec 28 1802 Tucker, Roger to White, Nancy
Aug 19 1778 Tucker, Sarah Ann to Jenkins, Job
Apr 28 1800 Tucker, William to Waggoner, Catharine
Mar 21 1810 Tudders, Rebecca to Burton, William
Nov  8 1806 Tull, Peter to Wertenbaker, Catherine
Nov  6 1794 Tumblestone, Lucy to Squires, Thomas
Jan 11 1798 Turner, Abraham to Brown, Eleanor
May 24 1801 Turner, Anna to Devaney, James
Sep 19 1801 Turner, Anne to Williams, John
Jan  9 1804 Turner, Elie to Ball, Teresa
Aug  9 1803 Turner, Elizabeth to Hopper, Benjamin
Sep 13 1796 Turner, John to Plummer, Anna
Dec 11 1797 Turner, Joshua to Fisher, Priscilla
Jan 16 1799 Turner, Lewis to Bradley, Sarah
Mar 13 1800 Turner, Mary to Hall, Henry
Mar 15 1804 Turner, Mary to Tolle, William
Nov 12 1806 Turner, Mary to Wine, George
May 27 1809 Turner, Richard to Wells, Mary
Dec 28 1801 Turner, Samuel to Williams, Jane
Jul 12 1792 Turner, Thomas to Harrison, Eleanor
Nov 24 1783 Turnwoolfe, Mary Eliz'th to Kreis, Christian
Sep 29 1783 Tutterer, Elizabeth to Thrasher, John
Oct 29 1784 Tutterow, Baltice to Sleagle, Elizabeth
Nov  7 1789 Twomey, Daniel to Sheats, Sarah
Nov  5 1805 Tydy, Elizabeth to Burch, Thomas
```

```
Apr 18 1787 Tyler, John, Dr. to Harrison, Catherine, Miss
Oct 19 1809 Tyler, William B. to Murdock, Harriot

Sep 11 1809 Umbaugh, Catherine to Late, Michael
Nov 10 1804 Umbaugh, George to Clem, Mary
Apr  4 1794 Umberger, Michael to Wood, Nancy
Jun  8 1805 Umford, Catherine to Crist, John
Mar  2 1804 Umstadt, David to Norris, Catharine
May 20 1780 Umstatt, Catherine to Crouse, John
Aug 10 1779 Umstatt, Mary to Root, James
Jun  1 1798 Umstead, Rachel to Hoy, Nicholas
Nov 27 1800 Umsted, Ruth to Steel, John
Mar 12 1804 Unckles, Anne to Young, John
Jan  2 1803 Underwood, William B. to Marshall, Ruth
Oct  6 1809 Ungleberger, Elizabeth to Frushour, George
Aug 11 1798 Unglebower, Katy to Grove, Peter
Jul 18 1788 Ungles, Mary to Lakins, Abraham
Apr 18 1791 Unglesby, Ann to Mullen, John W.
Sep 18 1780 Unkles, Benjamin to Plaister, Margaret
Dec 14 1797 Upcraft, Caty to Deberry, George
Apr 26 1808 Upperwood, Joshua to Linton, Joshan
Aug 23 1796 Ury, Christian to Stipe, Catharine
Jun  9 1800 Usher, Mary to Appold, Lewis Benjamin
Jun  2 1800 Usher, Mary to Oppold, Lewis Benjamin
Dec  6 1803 Usher, Susanna to Willson, Thomas
Oct 30 1797 Utt, Elizabeth to Neff, Adam

Oct 30 1809 Valentine, Elizabeth to Ogle, Joseph
May 22 1787 Valentine, George to Stull, Mary
Jan  1 1807 Valentine, George to Knouff, Elizabeth
Sep 21 1779 Valentine, Henry to Frey, Elizabeth
Jun  2 1779 Valentine, Jacob to Free, Mary
Aug  9 1797 Valkmon, Peter Adolphus to Amelung, Sophia Christine
            Dorothea
Jan  4 1810 Vallentine, Sarah to Delaplane, Jacob
Jul 29 1801 Vance, Jacob to Smith, Anne
Apr 10 1779 Vanderlin, Nicholas to Null, Mary
Jun  1 1800 Vandevander, Jane to Henry Stephen
Apr 24 1800 Vandivender, Isaac to Means, Anne
Jun 18 1791 Vanferson, Mary to Miller, John
Dec 30 1797 Vanfossen, Levi to Lease, Susannah
Oct 31 1782 Vanhorn, Dennis to Hutchinson, Sarah
Oct 15 1796 Vanhorn, Dennis to Burns, Catherine
Dec 15 1808 Vanhorn, Dennis to Merchant, Mary
Jul 15 1800 Vanmetre, Rebecca to Henry, Daniel
Jan 23 1810 Varner, John to Fread, Mary
Dec 28 1809 Vartz, Christena to Smith, Jacob
Sep 28 1810 Vaughan, Telitha to Strong, Charles
Sep 22 1807 Veach, Susanna to Harris, Jesse
May  1 1784 Veatch, Bathsheba to Wilson, Hezekiah
Oct 19 1779 Veatch, Casiah to Howard, Jac.
Feb 12 1779 Veatch, Jacob to Willson, Masters
Jul  1 1785 Veatch, Jemima to Gatton, Richard
Jun 16 1792 Veatch, John to Davis, Nancy Weaver
Mar  4 1783 Veatch, Rebeckah to Selfe, John
```

```
Aug  3 1793 Veatch, Solomon to Davis, Mary
Dec  9 1801 Veatch, Thomas to Self, Mary
Sep 29 1782 Veneble, Hesse to Gatton, Azariah
Oct 30 1799 Vennals, Richard to Miller, Ann
Feb 15 1800 Vernal, John to Jones, Susannah
May 14 1796 Vickery, Nathan to Crise, Eve
Apr 13 1787 Viers, Sarah to Jones, Hanbury
Mar 25 1797 Vinagar, Mary to Summers, Alex'r
Nov 24 1800 Vine, Catherine to Swails, Jacob
Mar  3 1789 Vion, John to Ruff, Catherine
May  9 1778 Voagh, Teney to Campbell, Mathias

Mar 28 1807 Wachter, Jacob to Widrick, Mary
May 11 1809 Wachter, Philip to Weidrict, Ann Morilles
Mar 18 1802 Wachter, Samuel to Staley, Catharine
Mar  5 1787 Waddle, Eve to Evans, Caleb
Aug 20 1785 Waddle, Mary to Brightwell, William
Jan 22 1783 Wadigan, Christopher to Thomas, Catherine
Apr 11 1801 Wadsworth, William to Barger, Susanna
Apr 28 1800 Waggoner, Catharine to Tucker, William
Apr 23 1801 Waggoner, Catherine to Warner, David
Jan 30 1798 Waggoner, Caty to Yeoder, Jacob
Aug  1 1797 Waggoner, Dorothy to Hagan, Hugh
Jun  6 1794 Waggoner, Elizabeth to Groshong, Abraham
Nov 15 1786 Waggoner, Elizabeth to Pebble, Abraham
Dec 13 1799 Waggoner, Jacob to Smith, Eve
Mar 17 1791 Waggoner, John (Pipe Creek) to Cassell, Rachael
May 17 1804 Waggoner, Mary to Yann, William
Mar 26 1800 Waggoner, Susanna to Boblon, Andrew
Oct 20 1810 Wagner, Barbara to Hale, George
Jan 25 1806 Wagner, Catherine to Lyon, Isaac
Nov 21 1809 Wagner, Elizabeth to Rahauser, Frederick, Rev'd
Sep  1 1808 Wagner, John to Albaugh, Catherine
Aug 26 1809 Wagner, Nancy to Stevenson, John
May 23 1794 Wagoner, Elizabeth to Warner, George
Feb 20 1781 Walcore, Pugzear to Taylor, William
Oct 27 1782 Waldeck, Henry to Evans, Rebecca
May 20 1801 Wales, Samuel to Redburn, Permelia
Mar 19 1779 Walfley, Barbara to Shriver, Henry
Feb  5 1802 Walker, Catharine to Bear, Michael
Mar  1 1779 Walker, Catherine to Spires, Zepheniah
Dec 19 1798 Walker, Elizabeth to Beall, William
Mar 29 1806 Walker, Elizabeth to England, Asa
Aug 20 1808 Walker, James to Haller, Catherine
Oct 12 1780 Walker, Margaret to Barnes, Caleb
Aug 27 1778 Walker, Mary to Head, Wm. Edward
Nov  2 1809 Walker, Peggy to Davis, John
Nov  3 1781 Walker, Sarah to Clarey, John
Dec  8 1809 Walker, Stephen to Steward, Margaret
Sep 27 1787 Walker, Thomas to Burnes, Elizabeth
Apr 11 1797 Wallace, Charles to Benton, Ann
Jan 16 1799 Wallace, Robert to Dwyre, Jane
Jun 15 1779 Wallace, William to Hopkins, Elizabeth
May 13 1785 Walling, Ann to Strasberger, John
May 29 1787 Walling, John to Reed, Susanna
Dec 26 1796 Walling, William to Delashmutt, Elizabeth
Mar 16 1804 Wallis, Margaret to Shown, Peter
```

```
Sep  6 1796 Walls, John to Burrier, Elizabeth
Sep  2 1800 Walls, Rachel to Davis, Samuel
Oct 18 1809 Walse, Mary to Nussbame, Solomon
Nov 20 1787 Walter, Catherine to Miller, Jacob
Jan 30 1799 Walter, Catherine to Stewart, John
Feb  5 1788 Walter, Jacob to Wintz, Mary ann
Mar 13 1805 Walter, Jacob to Luskelete, Polly
Sep 25 1798 Walter, Mary to Shetinghellern, Jacob
Feb  6 1786 Walter, Rosanna to Brandt, Christian
Jun  1 1808 Walters, Ann to Wilson, John
Jan 19 1802 Waltham, Benedict to Hays, Anne
Mar 12 1805 Walts, Catherine to Stephanus, John
Apr  6 1780 Waltz, Dorothy to Snyder, John
Oct  9 1799 Waltz, Elizabeth to Weaver, Jacob
Feb 21 1792 Waltz, Eve to Nusbaum, David
Mar 15 1793 Waltz, Frederick to Linganfelder, Mary
Jan 17 1804 Waltz, George to Nixendorff, Susanna
Sep  4 1800 Waltz, Jacob to Burrier, Mary
May 15 1800 Waltz, Margaret to Mahoney, Barnaba
Aug  2 1796 Waltz, Margaret to Stevens, Charles
Feb  1 1806 Waltz, Mary to Harriott, Peter
Mar 13 1799 Waltz, Pheby to Hurd, William
Sep 10 1790 Waltz, Rinehart to Shutter, Susanna
Apr 16 1804 Waltz, Samuel to Riner, Barbara
Feb 18 1809 Waltzheimer, John to Shlusser, Elizabeth
Mar 21 1788 Wampler, Jacob to Bare, Mary
Mar 21 1801 Wampler, John to Yingling, Elizabeth
Oct 16 1780 Wandle, Jacob to Goldie, Mary
Sep 24 1799 Wandle, Margaret to Frushour, Adam, Junr.
Aug 29 1791 Warble, Margaret to Hoppermill, John
Dec 23 1797 Ward, Amelia to Poole, Henry
Jan  4 1809 Ward, Amos to Tillard, Eleanor
Dec 21 1789 Ward, Ann to Plummer, Jonathan
Apr  9 1809 Ward, Cassandra to Winemiller, John
Aug 12 1778 Ward, Elizabeth to Hook, John Snowden
May 15 1799 Ward, Elizabeth to Kiler, Daniel
Feb 15 1791 Ward, Elizabeth to Simmons, Samuel
May  6 1794 Ward, John to Barber, Sarah
Apr 17 1806 Ward, Lydia to McClay, John
Mar 22 1803 Ward, Margaret to Calf, Martin
Mar 24 1806 Ward, Maryan to Davis, Josep
May 12 1782 Ward, Peter to Magruder, Deborah
Dec  7 1796 Warfield, Ann to Jones, Joshua
Mar  6 1780 Warfield, Ann to Lawrence, Richard
Feb 23 1796 Warfield, Anna to Tucker, John
Aug 17 1802 Warfield, Anne to Burgess, Caleb
Dec  1 1809 Warfield, Elizabeth to Burges, Samuel
Aug 24 1792 Warfield, Elizabeth to Howard, Joshua
Jun 21 1790 Warfield, Henry to Hammond, Ann
Mar  7 1804 Warfield, John to James, Fanny
Jan 29 1807 Warfield, Joshua to Welsh, Rachel
May  7 1806 Warfield, Peregrine to Sappington, Harriott
Apr  5 1803 Warfield, Rachel to Burgess, West
Jul  7 1780 Warfield, Richard to Delashmutt, Anne
Nov 26 1802 Warfield, Ruth to Dorsey, Edward
May 10 1792 Warfield, Sarah to Perry, James
Mar 20 1802 Warfield, Thomas to Simpson, Delilah
```

```
Apr 18 1785 Warner, Catharine to McComsey, Robert
Apr 23 1801 Warner, David to Waggoner, Catherine
Sep  3 1806 Warner, Elizabeth to Richards, John
Aug 15 1810 Warner, Elizabeth to Tawney, John
May 23 1794 Warner, George to Waggoner, Elizabeth
Sep 15 1808 Warner, George to Bradley, Nancy
Jan 14 1806 Warner, Jacob to Clary, Mary
Aug 28 1779 Warner, John to Henson, Biddy
Jul 21 1797 Warner, Mary to Lightner, John
Dec  5 1796 Warner, Samuel to Chamblin, Jane
May 13 1803 Warnfelts, Jacob to Measel, Mary Ann
Oct  1 1798 Warren, Mary to Greeher, Robert
Dec 23 1799 Warthan, Martin to Wilson, Hannah Ann
Apr 24 1798 Warthan, Mary to Dunn, Thomas
Jun  4 1807 Warthen, Francis to Drill, Elizabeth
Dec  6 1799 Warthen,, Wilfred to Chandler, Elizabeth
Mar  8 1794 Waskey, Nancy to Kessler, John
Jun 21 1806 Waskey, Sophia to Stockman, David
Sep 22 1784 Waters, Acena to Downing, James
Jul 23 1804 Waters, Amelia to Flanigan, John
Mar 27 1806 Waters, Ann to Frees, Jacob
Feb  6 1796 Waters, Ann to Richards, John
May 14 1805 Waters, Anne to Burgee, Thomas
Mar  7 1797 Waters, Benjamin to Baker, Elizabeth
Nov 14 1799 Waters, Catherine to Hedge, Moses
Dec  1 1797 Waters, Christena to Lucas, John
Dec 15 1803 Waters, Ignatius to Dorsey, Elizabeth
Oct 15 1800 Waters, James to Brown, Sarah
May 26 1779 Waters, Jane to Beatty, Thos.
Feb  2 1796 Waters, Josiah to Ballanger, Ann
Mar 21 1782 Waters, Mary to Ijams, John
Dec 20 1792 Waters, Mary to Janes, Thomas
May 11 1783 Waters, Nancy to Barrick, George
Nov 20 1804 Wathan, Sarah to Bolan, George
Jul 21 1787 Watkins, Ann to Noland, John
Jun 23 1794 Watkins, Jeremiah to Purdy, Deborah
Sep 15 1802 Watkins, Joseph to Norwood, Matilda
Dec 16 1809 Watson, John to Simpson, Betsey
Oct 17 1796 Watson, Walter to Earle, Jane
Mar 10 1806 Watt, Robert to Row, Mary
Aug 11 1805 Wattson, Susanna to Simmonds, Zachariah
Mar 23 1799 Wattson, Zepheniah to Jenkins, Milley
May  8 1784 Waugh, William to Whygle, Elizabeth
Jun 19 1780 Waughtell, John to Summers, Elizabeth
Nov 23 1794 Waughter, Catherine to Hoffner, Mich'l
Sep  6 1800 Way, David to Smith, Catherine
Jun 30 1804 Way, Jacob to Young, Mary
Jul 24 1807 Way, Mary to Shank, Peter
Mar 10 1809 Wayman, Amelia to Griffith, Lyde
Jul 17 1790 Wayman, John to Elliott, Margaret
Apr 16 1785 Wayman, Leonard to Plummer, Eleanor
Jun 22 1801 Wayne, Mary to Ritchie, Abner, Esq.
Dec 19 1808 Ways, Brice to Driscoll, Deborah
Feb  6 1798 Weamer, Healen to Wolf, Samuel
Mar  2 1779 Weane, Catherine to Jacobie, John
Sep 20 1808 Weary, Mary to Magers, Elias
Aug 26 1780 Weast, Jacob to Saline, Eve
```

```
Sep 14 1799 Weast, Jacob to Shenkmire, Susannah
Nov 21 1806 Weaver, Catharine to Arthur, John
Oct 30 1792 Weaver, Catherine to Davis, Benjamin
Apr  9 1802 Weaver, Catherine to Smith, Peter
Jul 10 1790 Weaver, Catherine to Wilbone, Frederick
Oct  1 1803 Weaver, Christian to Henry, Catherine
May  8 1804 Weaver, Christina to Fout, Henry
Nov 17 1806 Weaver, Daniel to McKenzie, Eleanor
Feb  7 1783 Weaver, George to Bearinger, Barbara
Oct  9 1799 Weaver, Jacob to Waltz, Elizabeth
Oct 19 1799 Weaver, John to Gorner, Mary
Jun  6 1809 Weaver, John to Bussard, Catherine
May 15 1797 Weaver, Ludwick to Stevenson, Ruth
Sep 12 1794 Weaver, Margaret to McIntire, Daniel
Mar 19 1803 Weaver, Mary to Albaugh, William
Nov 19 1808 Weaver, Mary to Dorff, George
Jan  1 1803 Weaver, Phebe to Schaffner, Jacob
Dec 23 1803 Weaver, Philip to Alexander, Mary
Mar  1 1780 Weaver, Priscilla to Rineheart, George
Jun  9 1806 Weaver, Sophia to Crumbine, John
Feb 27 1807 Webb, Susanna to Lane, George G.
Oct 11 1785 Webb, William to Meredith, Mary
May  9 1801 Webler, George Peter to Beckener, Maria
Nov 28 1809 Webster, Jacob to Roadrock, Christeana
Nov 14 1807 Webster, Thomas to Snyder, Christena
May 11 1802 Weck, Margaret to Creager, David
Dec  5 1810 Wedden, Lucy to Everhart, William
Nov 15 1803 Wedden, Ralph to Lanham, Elizabeth
Nov 27 1778 Weddin, Elizabeth to Bousom, John
Jul 25 1806 Wedding, Tabitha to House, Daniel
Aug 23 1794 Weddle, Catherine to Croft, Frederick
Sep 29 1808 Weddle, George to Bryan, Mary
Aug 12 1805 Weddle, John to Beall, Susanna
Jun  6 1807 Weddle, John to Rickard, Elizabeth
Oct  9 1779 Weddle, Margaret to Beall, Peter
Mar  8 1793 Weer, James to Richards, Lidia
May 11 1809 Weidrict, Ann Morilles to Wachter, Philip
Jan 21 1792 Weisenthall, Barney to Stoner, Mary
May 31 1790 Weisman, Conrad to Carne, Margaret
Sep 17 1803 Weiy, David to Anderson, Dorcas
Jun 20 1795 Welch, Ann to Woolf, Jacob
Dec  9 1797 Welch, James to Maynard, Mary Ann
Sep 28 1798 Welch, Ruth to Meredith, Thomas
May  5 1804 Welch, Samuel Junr. to Shipley, Marcella Owings
Mar 29 1802 Welck, Conrad to Rapeloch, Sally
Oct 27 1780 Welfley, Christian to Hildebrand, Philipeana
Nov 26 1786 Welfley,, David to Getzendanner, Magdalena
Dec 31 1808 Weller, Catherine to Lookinsland, David
Nov 17 1803 Weller, Daniel to Wilhite, Catherine
Jun 29 1807 Weller, George to Hoover, Catherine
Jun 17 1799 Weller, Henry to Shover, Catherine
Sep  4 1810 Weller, Henry to Towner, Catherine
Sep 13 1800 Weller, Jacob to Weller, Margaret
Sep 13 1800 Weller, Margaret to Weller, Jacob
Oct  3 1796 Wells, Ann to Sargent, George
Aug 29 1791 Wells, James to McHaffes, Jennet
Apr  7 1809 Wells, James to McPake, Mary
```

```
Jun 25 1781 Wells, Jane to Crusey, Rob't
May 21 1791 Wells, Margaret to Stevenson, Josiah
May 27 1809 Wells, Mary to Turner, Richard
Apr 21 1778 Wells, Richard to Coe, Edith
May  8 1793 Wells, Richard Dr. to Dyer, Elizabeth
Feb  1 1779 Wells, Ruth to Ricketts, Benja.
Dec 11 1807 Wells, Thomas to Knight, Sarah
Apr 11 1791 Welsch, Philip to Davis, Elizabeth
Oct 20 1786 Welsch, Ruth to Condon, Wm.
Mar 31 1781 Welsh, Eliz'th to Groshner, Wm.
Jan 25 1786 Welsh, Henry to Davis, Mary
Jul 11 1780 Welsh, John, Sr. to Mansfield, Susanna
Feb 28 1809 Welsh, Nicholas to Fleming, Rachel
Jan 29 1807 Welsh, Rachel to Warfield, Joshua
Mar  3 1792 Welsh, Sarah to Holland, James
Feb  4 1799 Welt, Susannah to Stover, Philip
Aug 30 1780 Welton, Magdalene to Hosselton, Edward
Feb 28 1795 Welty, Barnabas to Eichelberger, Mary
Sep 21 1785 Weltzhamer, Sarah to Clinerd, Francis
Apr  8 1797 Weltzheimer, Lewis to Meyer, Margaret
Nov 11 1793 Werner, Catherine to Gebhart, Solomon
Jul 19 1793 Werner, Mary to Messer, John
May  9 1793 Werner, Mary to Sigafoose, Jacob
Apr  9 1803 Werner, Modalena to Fogler, Henry
Nov 29 1798 Werner, William to Medcalfe, Elizabeth
Jun  8 1810 Werstler, Betsey to Rice, Henry
Dec 31 1785 Wertenbaker, Adam to Rage, Elizabeth
Nov  8 1806 Wertenbaker, Catherine to Tull, Peter
Nov  8 1806 Wertenbaker, Catherine to Zull, Peter
Apr 22 1786 Wertenbaker, Elizabeth to Ott, Michael
Apr  2 1792 Wertenbaker, Mary to Studor, Martin
Nov 12 1807 Werts, Jacob to Brawner, Lucy
Nov  6 1810 Wertz, Elizabeth to Herrin, Jacob
Nov  9 1796 West, Ann to Belt, Jeremiah
Feb  4 1808 West, Clinton to Ensey, Grace
Apr 27 1808 West, Clinton to Ensey, Grace
Nov 28 1789 West, Eleanor to McGill, Patrick
Mar 16 1793 West, Erasmus to Belt, Eleanor
Apr 12 1799 West, Harriet to Beall, Thomas Brooke
Oct 27 1786 West, Susanna to Johnson, John
Dec 30 1786 West, Thomas to McGill, Sarah
Jan  8 1805 West, William to Sargent, Elizabeth
Feb 11 1797 Westenhaver, Christian to Downey, Mary
Aug 20 1810 Wetsel, Betsy to Harton, George
Apr 21 1794 Wetsell, Margaret to Sheets, Christian
May  3 1794 Wever, Catherine to Hoover, Adam
Apr  9 1796 Wey, Elizabeth to Buckias, John, Jr.
Feb 12 1781 Weyman, Ann to Holland, Wm.
Sep 24 1808 Weymer, Elizabeth to Holtzman, Christian
Feb 19 1793 Wharton, Elizabeth to Hill, Thomas
Oct  3 1809 Wharton, James to Alexander, Isabella
Feb 19 1802 Wheatcroft, Ann to Clise, John
May 14 1796 Wheeler, Gilbert to Swearingen, Drusilla
```

```
Dec 12 1784 Wheeler, Henry to Hardy, Rebeccah
Nov  7 1782 Wheeler, Samuel to Williams, Priscilla
Jan 28 1791 Wheeler, Susanna to Hilton, Matthew
Feb 10 1790 Wheeler, Thomas to Hilton, Eleanor
Jan 27 1798 Wheeling, Mariah to Athey, Joseph
Dec 28 1809 Wheite, Susanna to Summers, James
Feb  8 1808 Whetton, John to Everhart, Mary
Sep 26 1807 Whilhite, Magdalene to Martin, Christian
Jun 18 1788 Whip, Peter to Nicholls, Elizabeth
Nov 13 1810 Whipp, George to Cost, Polly
Nov 28 1785 Whipp, Jacob to Tabler, Barbara
Jun 25 1792 Whips, Samuel to Cook, Elizabeth
Apr  7 1797 Whitacre, Sarah to Hay, Edmond
Aug 25 1792 Whitcraft, Edward to Bonham, Marey
Sep  5 1789 Whitcroft, Sarah to Showne, Peter
Dec 17 1790 White, Benjamin to Chiswell, Rebeckah
May 19 1800 White, Bewly to Davis, Ambrose
Nov  2 1799 White, David to Overholtz, Mary
Sep 30 1807 White, Eleanor to Sedwick, Benjamin
Oct 13 1810 White, Elisha to Curlin, Elizabeth
Apr 25 1806 White, Elizbeth Smith to Murphy, Joseph Aquila
Oct 27 1801 White, Esther to Glisan, James
Apr 29 1784 White, Henry to Hendrickson, Susanna
Dec 22 1809 White, James to Lankton, Elizabeth
Jun  2 1806 White, John to Steward, Mary
May 25 1805 White, Joseph to McKinnock, Letitia
Jan  6 1800 White, Letha to Bennet, William
Feb  4 1808 White, Magdalena to Winter, George
Dec 11 1794 White, Martha to Hook, Isaac
Dec 14 1807 White, Mary to Ball, James
Oct  2 1801 White, Mary to Magers, Lawrence
Dec 28 1810 White, Nancy to Clay, George
Dec 28 1802 White, Nancy to Tucker, Roger
Aug 14 1782 White, Rebeckah to Simmonds, George
Feb 19 1807 White, Sarah to Smith, Thomas
Nov  4 1778 White, Thomas to Gavin, Sarah
Jan 31 1780 Whitehair, Dorothy to Rizeing, George
Oct 23 1784 Whitehair, Mary to Hanshugh, Fred'k
Jan  1 1779 Whitehead, Sarah to Lilley, Henry
Aug 17 1795 Whitehill, John to Clemson, Mary
Jun 18 1789 Whitenacht, Elizabeth to Harley, Joshua
Jun  7 1783 Whitenack, Catherine to Bagens, John
Jun  9 1793 Whiteneck, Hannah to Albaugh, Samuel
Nov 21 1809 Whitman, Barbara to Young, George
Apr 25 1785 Whitmar, Lazarus to Eater, Wendelena
Jan 12 1780 Whitmer, Catherine to Hande, Thomas
Apr 15 1789 Whitmire, Uliana to Brayfield, John Baptist
Jul 21 1782 Whitmore, Benjamin to Hockersmith, Mary
Feb 16 1803 Whitmore, George to Kepler, Mary
Sep  1 1778 Whitmore, John to Coe, Mary
Nov 28 1803 Whitmore, John to Black, Elizabeth
Oct 12 1800 Whitmore, Martin to Renner, Elizabeth
Oct 19 1786 Whitmore, Sarah to McNeale, Archibald
Nov 29 1799 Whitmore, Susanna to Black, Henry
Jul 30 1792 Whitmyer, Eleanor to Davis, Levi
```

```
Oct 11 1797 Whittington, Dorcas to Musgrove, Gilbert
Nov 29 1806 Whittington, James to Firecoat, Elizabeth
Oct 15 1796 Whittington, John to Pritchet, Rebeckah
May  8 1784 Whygle, Elizabeth to Waugh, William
Aug 27 1807 Wickell, Barbara to Low, John
May  7 1792 Wickery, George to Prather, Jane
May 25 1807 Wickham, Andrew to Sticker, Elizabeth
Jun 30 1805 Wickham, Anna to Smith, Andrew
Dec  1 1788 Wickham, Robert to Campbell, Susanna
Nov 25 1807 Wicuff, Susanna to Brabham, William
Dec 19 1787 Widmeyer, Elizabeth to Davis, John
Mar 28 1807 Widrick, Mary to Wachter, Jacob
Mar 12 1808 Wieland, Catherine to Bechtol, Lewis
May 18 1802 Wier, Catharine to Shick, John
Feb  5 1802 Wiest, Polly to Ritter, Jacob
Nov  5 1803 Wietrich, Elizabeth to Staley, Jacob, Jr.
Sep  9 1799 Wietrick, George to Hargate, Catherine
Nov  2 1793 Wigal, Mary to Fero, Henry
Dec 22 1804 Wigle, Ann Catharine to Levy, Abraham
Nov 23 1784 Wigle, John to Myer, Barbara
Dec 24 1792 Wigle, Leonard to Harp, Susanna
Sep  4 1802 Wigle, Sarah to Beatty, Elijah
Dec 27 1797 Wigley, George to Allison, Mary
Jul 10 1790 Wilbone, Frederick to Weaver, Catharine
Jan 28 1807 Wilcoxen, William to Benson, Ruth
Nov 28 1785 Wilcoxon, Cassandra to Nicholls, John Haymond
Jan 27 1806 Wildanger, George to Long, Barbara
Mar 16 1796 Wildman, Rebecca to Spencer, Edward
Jan  4 1790 Wildman, Sarah to Binns, Simon
May  9 1808 Wile, Catharine to Brandenburg, Jacob
Sep 15 1808 Wile, George to Brandenburg, Hannah
Sep 11 1800 Wileman, Ann to Binns, Alexander
Aug  5 1782 Wiles, William to Bird, Ann
Oct  1 1792 Wilhide, Conrad to Creager, Elizabeth
Apr 15 1807 Wilhide, Elizabeth to Zellers, John
Nov 17 1803 Wilhite, Catherine to Weller, Daniel
Oct  1 1800 Wilhite, Frederick, Jr. to Pitsell, Catherine
Aug 24 1808 Wilhite, Henry to Morningstar, Catherine
Dec  1 1786 Wilkey, Ann to Hays, Thomas
Sep  5 1807 Will, George to Himes, Catharine
Apr  3 1809 Will, Kitty to Nussear, Michael R.
Sep 16 1805 Willen, Martha to Key, William
Nov 20 1783 Willett, Griffith to Grove, Mary
Jan 13 1801 Williams, Ann to Museter, John
May  6 1798 Williams, Benjamin to Harding, Elizabeth B.
Jul 20 1808 Williams, Benjamin to Maygers, Jerusha
Mar 27 1804 Williams, Curtis to Simpson, Ann
Sep  3 1790 Williams, Edward to Beall, Priscilla
Jun 14 1804 Williams, Eleanor to Harrison, James
Mar 14 1803 Williams, Ellis to Templer, Sarah
Sep 23 1802 Williams, Jacob to England, Margaret
Dec 28 1801 Williams, Jane to Turner, Samuel
Feb 19 1793 Williams, John to Hagan, Elizabeth
Feb 23 1796 Williams, John to Wood, Catherine
Feb 20 1799 Williams, John to Burns, Martha
```

```
Sep 19 1801 Williams, John to Turner, Anne
May 12 1802 Williams, John to Plummer, Finetta
Jun  3 1808 Williams, John B. to Smith, Nancy
Jul  2 1796 Williams, Kitty to Peck, Thomas
Jan  6 1810 Williams, Lucy to Nelson, Amos
Dec 20 1803 Williams, Martha to Conner, David
Apr  9 1782 Williams, Mary to Devit, Valentine
Sep 15 1810 Williams, Mary to Holter, Daniel
Feb  3 1796 Williams, Mary to Scott, James
Oct  2 1794 Williams, Pamelia to Cromes, Aden
Oct 24 1795 Williams, Priscilla to Dilworth, John
Nov  7 1782 Williams, Priscilla to Wheeler, Samuel
Dec  9 1782 Williams, Rezin to Fowler, Elizabeth
Nov  5 1803 Williams, Robert (colored) to Hannah, woman of color
Jan  6 1794 Williams, Sarah to Mahony, James H.
Mar 18 1798 Williams, Uriah to Roach, Sarah
Jan 28 1786 Williams, Walter to McGill, Ann
May 27 1786 Williams, William to Johnson, Keziah
Jun 22 1796 Williams, William to Fowler, Anna
Apr 12 1804 Williams, William Roy to Rete, Margaret
May  1 1790 Williamson, Ann to Knight, James
Mar 16 1796 Williamson, Elizabeth to Knight, Thomas
Oct 31 1789 Williamson, James H. to Raith, Nancy
Sep 24 1789 Williamson, Mary to Bonham, Malachi
Apr 21 1790 Williard, Catharine to Jacobs, Henry
Oct 11 1799 Williard, John to Kepler, Frances
May 28 1803 Williard, John to Shafer, Mary
Nov 12 1801 Williard, Mary to Ennis, George
Oct  1 1792 Williard, Peter to Honeling, Barbara
Jun 25 1796 Williard, Philip to Knouff, Catherine
Sep 16 1803 Williard, Sarah to Roades, Henry
Apr 13 1803 Williard, Susannah to Winpeagler, Jacob
Aug 10 1802 Willis, Lydia to Ogbern, Benjamin
Sep 30 1780 Wills, Henry to Coe, Jemimah
Apr  6 1781 Willson, Catherine to Page, Thomas
Nov 25 1791 Willson, Henry to Farquhar, Susan
Jan 25 1804 Willson, John to Davis, Mary
Jul 20 1782 Willson, Lucy to Simpson, Erasmus
Feb 12 1779 Willson, Masters to Veatch, Jacob
Nov 20 1782 Willson, Priscilla to Biggs, John
Jan 17 1809 Willson, Richard to Harding, Elizabeth S.
Apr 10 1779 Willson, Susannah to Cook, John
Jul 30 1782 Willson, Thomas to Fogle, Susannah
Dec  6 1803 Willson, Thomas to Usher, Susanna
Dec  5 1808 Willy, John to Fluke, Barbara
Jan  8 1808 Willyard, Daniel to Lutler, Elizabeth
Dec 13 1809 Willyard, Peggy to Oyler, Frederick
Oct  9 1806 Wilson, Ann to Cox, Samuel
Mar 27 1802 Wilson, Catherine to Troxell, Frederick
Oct  1 1803 Wilson, Charles to Shelton, Elizabeth
Jan 29 1798 Wilson, Elizabeth to Sayler, Martin
Aug 17 1809 Wilson, Greenbury to Boyer, Sally
Dec 23 1799 Wilson, Hannah Ann to Warthan, Martin
May  1 1784 Wilson, Hezekiah to Veatch, Bathsheba
Jan 24 1795 Wilson, Jacob to Hammet, Rebeckah
```

```
Jun  8 1796 Wilson, John to Chinn, Elizabeth
Jun  1 1808 Wilson, John to Walters, Ann
Aug 28 1793 Wilson, Joshua to Sedwick, Elizabeth
Jun 16 1792 Wilson, Margaret to Hilton, Luke
Oct 17 1795 Wilson, Mary to Biggs, Fred'k
Feb 12 1798 Wilson, Mary to Philips, Nicholas
Mar 24 1803 Wilson, Michael to Grimes, Orphey
Oct 10 1796 Wilson, Peggy to Green, Luke
Sep  3 1796 Wilson, Priscilla to Rine, John
Aug 11 1794 Wilson, Rebeckah to Cossen, Nicholas
Oct 29 1792 Wilson, Rebeckah to Duvall, Marsh Mareen
Nov 19 1802 Wilson, Sarah to Southgate, Samuel
May 31 1808 Wilson, Susanna to Messler, John
Aug 19 1808 Wilson, Susanna to Stein, Reuben
Apr 21 1789 Wilson, Thomas to Hoffwider, Ann
Feb 12 1808 Wilson, Thomas to Ferras, Elizabeth
Sep 13 1796 Wilson, Thomas P. to Beale, Rebeckah
Jan 16 1810 Wilson, William to Becraft, Rechel
Mar 24 1806 Wilson, Zadock to Stewart, Elizabeth
Aug 30 1806 Wilt, Susanna to Hargate, Abraham
Jun  8 1805 Wilyard, George to Kuller, Susanna
Dec 24 1799 Wilyard, Abraham to Biser, Catherine
Nov 29 1808 Wilyard, Elias to Iler, Anna
May 14 1791 Wilyard, Jacob to Grove, Eve
Jan 24 1809 Wilyard, John to McClain, Sarah
Feb  6 1802 Wilyard, Mary to Lemar, Thomas
Aug 27 1808 Wilyard, Michael to Hauver, Catherine
Apr 20 1803 Wilyard, Peter to Shafer, Elizabeth
Feb  7 1791 Wimmer, Deborah to Hays, Joseph
Sep 27 1790 Win, Magd'l to Mowerer, Adam
Nov 27 1806 Winbeagler, Richard to Harget, Elizabeth
Dec 30 1806 Winbigler, Mary to Mosburg, Henry
May 31 1803 Winch, Jacob to Protsman, Mary
Feb 17 1792 Winchester, Stephen, Esq. to Howard, Sarah
Jul 30 1801 Windsor, Nancy to Goings, Joseph
Nov 12 1806 Wine, George to Turner, Mary
Dec  7 1782 Wine, Mary to Renner, John
Oct 20 1810 Winebrenner, Catherine to Riner, George
Mar 18 1794 Winebrenner, Peter to Snyder, Catherine
Apr  9 1809 Winemiller, John to Ward, Cassandra
Feb 24 1810 Winemiller, Margaret to Thompson, John C.
Feb 24 1794 Winfield, Ann to Edwards, John
Oct  6 1795 Winhold, William to Mahony, Mary
Sep  3 1796 Winnull, Ann to Kolb, George
Mar 20 1804 Winpeagler, Catherine to Wisinger, Leonard
Jan  5 1804 Winpeagler, Elzabeth to Stockman, George
Apr 13 1803 Winpeagler, Jacob to Williard, Susannah
Nov  5 1803 Winpeagler, Magdalena to Potterfield, Joseph
Apr  2 1810 Winpigler, Elizabeth to Hughes, Hugh
Feb 15 1779 Winpigler, Francis to Ridgely, Sarah
Sep 13 1779 Winpigler, Mary to Cramer, Mich'l
May 28 1810 Winpigler, Sophia to Hymes, George
Jun  2 1808 Winpigler, Susanna to Bost, Henry
May  8 1779 Winson, William to Blackmore, Elizabeth
Feb  4 1808 Winter, George to White, Magdalena
```

```
Dec 21 1797 Winter, John to Prough, Caty
Aug  1 1810 Wintrode, John to Nelson, Betsy
Jan 25 1789 Wintz, Jacob to Fischer, Catherine
Feb  2 1787 Wintz, Margaret to Derr, Jacob
Feb  5 1788 Wintz, Mary Ann to Walter, Jacob
Oct 25 1783 Wire, Peter to Stull, Elizabeth
Dec  7 1808 Wireman, John to Campbell, Elizabeth
Feb  2 1790 Wirtz, Michael to Delauder, Catherine
Dec  7 1792 Wise, Amelia to Crum, Wm.
Jun 22 1797 Wise, Catharine to Brown, Henry
Oct 10 1807 Wisinger, George to Labe, Elizabeth
Mar 20 1804 Wisinger, Leonard to Winpeagler, Catherine
Mar 28 1799 Wisman, Jacob to Kephart, Elizabeth
Sep 16 1805 Wisman, Mary to Rowe, Frederick
Oct  3 1791 Wissinger, Elizabeth to Miller, Christian
Mar  8 1800 Wissinger, George to Kaufman, Mary
Nov 26 1808 Wissinger, Mary to Ifert, Jacob
May 17 1781 Wissman, Elizabeth to Shepherd, John
Jun 13 1797 Wistman, Ulianna to Everley, Peter
Feb 12 1800 Wistman, Valentine to Kephart, Mary
Nov  5 1801 Witherow, Jane to Cooper, Robert
Jan 18 1800 Witrick, Jacob to Stull, Mary
Jul 18 1784 Wizart, John to Miller, Mary
Mar  7 1809 Woakman, Joseph to Shields, Lydia
Sep 19 1798 Woghter, George to Beckenbaugh, Philipena
Feb  6 1798 Wolf, Samuel to Weamer, Healen
Jan 28 1809 Wolf, Tabitha to Hood, John
Oct 14 1807 Wolfe, Abraham to Glissan, Sarah
Jun  5 1804 Wolfe, Catharine to Brunner, Elias
Jan 25 1808 Wolfe, Henry H. to Hood, Rachel
May 14 1794 Wolfe, Ludwick to Runner, Charlotte
Jan 10 1787 Wolfe, Margaret to Smith, John
Mar 17 1788 Wolheim, John William to Keplar, Fredericka
Mar 15 1803 Wood, Aurelia to Shunk, Joseph
Sep 29 1798 Wood, Bennet to Hoy, Susannah
Feb 23 1796 Wood, Catherine to Williams, John
Nov  4 1784 Wood, Elizabeth to McCracken, John
Jun 23 1788 Wood, Henry to Mackelfresh, Sarah
Dec  4 1781 Wood, John to Ogle, Martha
May 24 1804 Wood, Joseph to Graybell, Anne
Apr 18 1791 Wood, Mary to Harlin, James
Dec  9 1806 Wood, Mary to Pool, Frederick
Apr  4 1794 Wood, Nancy to Umberger, Michael
Mar 15 1781 Wood, Rebecka to Bentley, Solomon
Oct  9 1778 Wood, Richard to Head, Elizabeth
Apr  6 1782 Wood, Ruth to Bentley, Abner
Jan  5 1792 Wood, Sarah to Harlin, Joshua
Oct 10 1789 Wood, Usilera to Stephenson, Richard
Aug 16 1800 Woodard, James to Asdell, Sally
Jul 19 1808 Woodman, Thomas to Hopwood, Elizabeth
Dec 21 1809 Woodman, William to Haden, Mary
Apr  9 1788 Woodrow, John to Roberts, Mary
Apr 10 1806 Woods, Elizabeth to George, John  .
Jul 27 1778 Woods, George to Loyd, Mary
Oct  5 1797 Woodward, Abraham B. to Owens, Priscilla
```

```
Apr 12 1791 Woodward, Jacob to Phelps, Jemima
May 25 1805 Woodward, Nathaniel to Culler, Mary
Aug 27 1781 Woolf, Catherine to Griffith, Elisha
May  3 1781 Woolf, Eliz'th to Drew, Mich'l
Aug 24 1807 Woolf, George to Koontz, Alice
Jun 20 1795 Woolf, Jacob to Welch, Ann
May 15 1802 Woolf, Jacob to Gittinger, Elizabeth
Dec 10 1808 Woolf, Margaret to Poole, Walter
May 30 1800 Woolf, Mary to Creager, Christian
Aug 29 1803 Woolf, Mary to Hull, John
Aug 23 1803 Woolf, Valentine to Rice, Mary
Feb 11 1797 Woolfe, George to Richards, Levina
Aug 19 1793 Woolfe, Henry to Haller, Elizabeth
Jun 15 1801 Woolfe, Jacob to Smith, Susanna
Apr 13 1782 Woolfe, John to Hyatt, Sarah
Jun 23 1780 Woolfe, Peter to Bruner, Catherine
Oct  4 1779 Woolverton, Sarah to Asque, John
Mar 20 1797 Worman, Ann to Shryner, Michael
Apr 14 1807 Worman, Barbara to Dorsey, Luke
Jun 13 1804 Worman, Elizabeth to Lookingbill, Peter
Apr 30 1803 Worman, Henry to Stewart, Susanna
Mar 12 1807 Worman, Margaret to Myers, Adam
Nov 23 1804 Worman, Modalena to Holverstot, David
Sep  4 1790 Worman, Sarah to Lookingpeel, John
Jul 27 1804 Worman, Solena to Zeagler, Christopher
Aug 27 1792 Worman, Susanna to Duttero, John
Mar 15 1799 Worthington, Charlotte to Owings, Christopher
Apr  2 1781 Worthington, Eliz'th to Dorsey, Wm.
Jan  5 1797 Worthington, Henrietta to Simpson, Basil
Jun  8 1793 Worthington, Priscilla to Hammond, Nathan
May  1 1804 Worthington, Susannah Hood to Smethen, Nicholas
Dec 21 1802 Worthington, William, Jr. to Anderson, Harriet
Sep 14 1810 Worts, Henry to Smith, Elizabeth
Apr  5 1783 Wortz, Catherine to Thomas, John
Apr  5 1800 Wren, Bernard to Straver, Peggy
Mar 10 1806 Wren, George to Duddero, Catherine
Mar 25 1796 Wrench, Susanna to Green, Sam'l
Oct 31 1780 Wright, Alexander to Gilbert, Susanna
Nov 12 1798 Wright, David to Thompson, Susanna
Dec  2 1784 Wright, Eli to Harrison, Phoebe
Jun 29 1780 Wright, Eliz'th to King, Wm.
Nov 28 1783 Wright, George to Johnson, Elizabeth
Oct 18 1804 Wright, Hannah to Smith, Dennis
Oct  9 1804 Wright, John to Seise, Sophia
Oct 24 1789 Wright, Joseph to Mumford, Mary
Apr 16 1808 Wright, Mary Ann to McMillan, Samuel
Feb 26 1793 Wright, Sarah to Storms, Isaac
Apr 16 1796 Wright, Susanna to Storm, Peter
Aug 19 1794 Wright, William to Morgan, Dorothy
Oct 22 1779 Wyer, William to Stull, Catharine
Jan 16 1810 Wynn, John to Taylor, Susannah
Dec 14 1795 Wyvil, Elizabeth to Sprigg, John

Apr  6 1801 Yakey, Peter to Pue, Jane
Oct 31 1798 Yandes, George to Moore, Mary
```

```
Oct 25 1803 Yandes, George to Heffner, Susanna
Oct 15 1806 Yandess, Barbara to Hoffman, John
Aug 24 1805 Yandis, Mary to Smith, Peter
May 17 1804 Yann, William to Waggoner, Mary
Feb 13 1804 Yantes, Catharine to Hedges, William
Nov 21 1803 Yantes, Elizabeth to Flenner, George
Dec 24 1805 Yantis, Barbara to Powell, Jonathan
Sep  9 1786 Yantz, Catharine to Balsell, Christian
Sep 16 1808 Yantz, Christopher to Swamley, Susanna
Apr  1 1786 Yantz, Eve Margaret to Heffner, George, Jr.
Mar 25 1786 Yantz, Rosanna to Brown, Michael
Jun 10 1791 Yantz, Sibylla to Hauser, Adam
Jun  8 1805 Yardley, William to Tobery, Anne
Aug  4 1783 Yates, Eliz'th to McClain, John
Jul 31 1792 Yates, Elizabeth to Filius, John
Aug 14 1784 Yates, Robert Elliot to Richardson, Ursula
Sep 15 1783 Yates, Susanna to Davis, Ludwick
Dec 23 1790 Yeast, Leonard to Templing, Elizabeth
Jun 15 1779 Yeast, Philip to Hayes, Mary
Jan 30 1798 Yeoder, Jacob to Waggoner, Caty
Apr  1 1779 Yesterday, Christian to Huff, Elizabeth
Jun 16 1780 Yesterday, Margaret to Tabler, William
Jul 22 1784 Yesterday, Michael to Gardner, Angel
May 21 1779 Yesterday, Philepeana to Tabler, Adam
Mar 21 1801 Yingling, Elizabeth to Wampler, John
Mar 26 1810 Yoncum, Barbara to Nigh, John
Dec  2 1779 Yontsey, John to Iseminger, Catherine
Apr  9 1800 Yores, Susannah to Jarrett, John
Nov 26 1793 Yorick, Michael to Greenwell, Mary
Mar 18 1785 Yose, Barbara to Thomas, Leonard
Oct 23 1781 Yost, Barbara to Johnson, Joseph
Dec 18 1786 Yost, Catherine to Keefaver, Peter
Aug  7 1792 Yost, Elizabeth to Eichenbrode, Daniel
May 11 1807 Yost, Eve to Johnson, Joseph
Dec 21 1807 Yost, Hannah to Tanner, Andrew
Dec 21 1807 Yost, Hannah to Zamer, Andrew
Aug  1 1792 Yost, John to Young, Juliana
Aug 16 1786 Yost, Ludwick to Everhart, Mary
Apr 25 1778 Yost, Mary to Keller, John
Mar 28 1798 Yost, Mary to Young, George
Dec 20 1798 Yost, Susannah to Young, Casper
Sep 23 1809 You, William to Smith, Mary
Aug  9 1800 Young, Andrew to Myers, Peggy
Oct 26 1808 Young, Andrew to Berger, Magdalena
Jun 17 1799 Young, Benjamin to Cooley, Eleanor
Dec 20 1798 Young, Casper to Yost, Susannah
Dec  3 1789 Young, Catharine to Engle, George
Jan 11 1787 Young, Cathe. to Flucke, Mathias
Jun 22 1809 Young, Charlotte to Zimmerman, George
Mar 26 1781 Young, Conrad to Leather, Margaret
Jun 19 1790 Young, Conrad to Tomlinson, Elizabeth
Mar 28 1809 Young, Elizabeth to Favorite, Frederick
May 26 1803 Young, Elizabeth to Nickam, Peter
May  7 1801 Young, Elizabeth to Troxel, Frederick
Apr 17 1779 Young, Eve to Flucke, John
```

| | | | |
|---|---|---|---|
Jun  6 1810 Young, Eve to Kephart, John
Mar 28 1798 Young, George to Yost, Mary
Feb  4 1799 Young, George to Renner, Mary
Nov 21 1809 Young, George to Whitman, Barbara
Dec  7 1802 Young, Henry to Miller, Hannah
Apr 27 1810 Young, Jacob to Leatherman, Catherine
Mar 10 1789 Young, Jane to Moore, William
Nov 14 1803 Young, John to Rowe, Barbara
Mar 12 1804 Young, John to Unckles, Anne
Mar 30 1810 Young, John to King, Mary
Aug  1 1792 Young, Juliana to Yost, John
Apr 17 1779 Young, Leonard to Crowl, Barbara
Jul 30 1801 Young, Mary to Sherley, Samuel
Jun 30 1804 Young, Mary to Way, Jacob
Feb 22 1802 Young, Molly to Kepler, John
Dec 23 1791 Young, Peter to Powles, Mary
Jun  6 1809 Young, Samuel to Koontz, Maria E.
Jan 15 1800 Young, Sarah to Cowley, John
Sep  7 1799 Young, Susannah to Engle, George
Nov 27 1796 Young, William to Hoskinson, Ann
Oct 14 1783 Younge, Peter to Coppersmith, Catherine
Apr 23 1779 Youtzell, Christian to Dickoutt, Elizabeth
Jan 11 1800 Yowler, Catherine to Pool, Henry
Apr  9 1803 Yowler, Eleanor to Stouffer, Daniel Jr.
Jan  8 1793 Yowler, Eva to Niehoof, Nicholas
Aug 30 1809 Yowler, George to Lambright, Mary
Sep 16 1809 Yowler, Michael to Shafer, Catherine
Jul 19 1785 Yustice, Elizabeth to Clancey, John

Nov 23 1799 Zachariah, Mary to Reese, John
Mar 23 1809 Zallinger, Elizabeth to Crabs, Joseph
Dec 21 1807 Zamer, Andrew to Yost, Hannah
Jul 27 1804 Zeagler, Christopher to Worman, Solena
Mar 27 1803 Zealer, Elizabeth to Brengle, John
May 21 1796 Zealer, George to Houck, Barbara
Jun 14 1794 Zealer, George to Frushour, Mary
Mar 30 1799 Zealer, Margaret to Harmon, Jacob
May 21 1807 Zealler, Adam to Levy, Rebecca
Apr 15 1807 Zellers, John to Wilhide, Elizabeth
Jan  8 1798 Zerick, Daniel to Brashear, Martha
Sep 11 1790 Zerick, Jacob to Plesinger, Margaret
Jul 22 1783 Zerrick, Catherine to Reichter, Henry
Oct 28 1806 Zies, Barbara to Huffert, Daniel
Aug  5 1806 Zigler, John to Zimmerman, Mary
Jul 29 1783 Zimmerman, Adam to Shurte, Susanna
Dec 26 1796 Zimmerman, Andrew to Taylor, Ruth
Oct  5 1808 Zimmerman, Barbara to Campbell, Richard C.
Apr  6 1798 Zimmerman, Benjamin to Eppert, Catherine
Jan 15 1791 Zimmerman, Catharine to Joss, George
Feb 19 1801 Zimmerman, Catherine to Beckenbaugh, Jacob
Mar 15 1809 Zimmerman, Catherine to Birely, Lewis
Jul 30 1803 Zimmerman, Catherine to Eichelberger, John
Jun 15 1797 Zimmerman, Christena to Allison, George
Mar 23 1803 Zimmerman, Elizabeth to Coblentz, Philip
Dec 14 1795 Zimmerman, Elizabeth to Shook, Jacob

```
Jun 22 1809 Zimmerman, George to Young, Charlotte
Jul 21 1801 Zimmerman, George to Patterson, Elizabeth
Jul 15 1797 Zimmerman, Jacob to Hedge, Mary
Feb 14 1799 Zimmerman, Jacob to Snyder, Mary Ann
Dec 27 1801 Zimmerman, Jacob to Pool, Catherine
Aug 22 1807 Zimmerman, John to Connelly, Ann
Jan 18 1799 Zimmerman, Leah to Fox, Henry
Jun 12 1783 Zimmerman, Margaret to Myers, George
Apr 11 1803 Zimmerman, Margaret to Powell, Nathan
Jun 22 1797 Zimmerman, Maria to Raymer, Jacob
Dec  6 1804 Zimmerman, Mary to Draper (or Traper), Thomas
Jan  9 1802 Zimmerman, Mary to Smith, Henry
Dec  6 1804 Zimmerman, Mary to Traper (or Draper), Thomas
Aug  5 1806 Zimmerman, Mary to Zigler, John
May 13 1780 Zimmerman, Mary Ann to Brooner, Elias
May 14 1788 Zimmerman, Michael to Cronise, Eve
Oct 31 1798 Zimmerman, Michael to Taylor, Barbara
May 20 1800 Zimmerman, Michael to Patterson, Lilly Ann
Jun  6 1793 Zimmerman, Nicholas to Troxell, Elizabeth
Aug 19 1809 Zimms, Frances to Roland, George
Apr 18 1801 Zudy, Casper to Felius, Barbara
Nov  8 1806 Zull, Peter to Wertenbaker, Catherine
```

www.ingramcontent.com/pod-product-compliance
Lightning Source LLC
Chambersburg PA
CBHW060527090426
42735CB00011B/2408